Deborah Wright graduated from Lincoln College, Oxford University, with a degree in English Literature. In 2000, she won the *Ireland on Sunday*/Poolbeg 'Write a Bestseller' competition for her first novel, *Olivia's Bliss*. Since then she has published two more bestselling novels with Time Warner Books – *The Rebel Fairy*, a modern version of *A Midsummer Night's Dream*, and *Under My Spell*, a romantic comedy about a nanny who is also a witch. She has contributed short stories to various anthologies, including *Kids' Night In* and the forthcoming collections *Ladies' Night* and *New Wave of Speculative Fiction*.

For more information please visit www.deborahwright.co.uk or email Deborah directly via deborah@deborahwright.co.uk

Also by Deborah Wright

The Rebel Fairy

Under My Spell

Love Eternally

Deborah Wright

TIME WARNER BOOKS

First published in Great Britain in 2005
by Time Warner Books
Reprinted 2005 (twice)

All characters in this publication are fictitious and any resemblance to real persons, living or dead, is purely coincidental.

'The Song of Amergin', translated by W. Reid White,
with kind permission.

A CIP catalogue record for this book is available from the British Library.

ISBN 0 7515 3704 7

Typeset by M Rules
Printed and bound in Great Britain by Clays Ltd, St Ives plc

Time Warner Books
An imprint of
Time Warner Book Group UK
Brettenham House
Lancaster Place
London WC2E 7EN

www.twbg.co.uk
www.deborahwright.co.uk

This book is

for

S.L.K.

With all my love

Acknowledgements

Thanks to my family – Mum, Dad, Lyra and my brothers. Thanks to my friends for help along the way – Lewis Walch, David W., Alex Hankey, Tristan Rogers and the other talented 'Butchers', Tom Scruton and Katy Smurthwaite, Simon Trewin, Kristian Pettersson, David Hughes, John Ashforth, Harry Pilcher, Martyn Webber, Paul Skinner, Matthew Wherry and Diana Leighton. Also to Felicity and Eric for my lovely days at Badingham before it sadly closed!

This book first began life in 1999 as a film script, so I must say thanks to the various producers (especially Paul) who took an interest and hence helped to inspire the novel.

Thanks to my fellow writer friends for their wonderful emails and sharing the highs and lows of the literary process, especially Tobias, Graham, Faith, Dylan, Jessica, Kate, Victoria, Tansy, Sean, Andrea, Dorothy, Sally, Scarlett and Tony Strong.

Big thanks to Sheila Crowley and Rob Kraitt at A.P. Watt for their enthusiasm and dedication.

A huge thank you to my editor, Jo Dickinson, who is a wonderfully nurturing, warm and intelligent editor, and who made some brilliant suggestions along the way. Also thanks to Ursula Mackenzie, Vanessa Neuling, Margaret Daly, Jenny Fry, Sheena-Margot Lavelle and all at Time Warner Books.

Big thanks to my readers for all the wonderful emails you send me, which are always greatly appreciated and very inspiring.

Most of all, thanks to S.L.K. for being my Muses.

Prologue

The moment Steve woke up, he knew that something was wrong. He rolled over in bed and ran his fingers through his hair, emitting a painful groan. Last night . . . what had he done last night? Little by little, memories seeped into his consciousness. His thirtieth birthday . . . the party . . . the pub . . . Dina, his best friend, had come . . . and he had declared his undying love for her. Told her all those feelings that had been locked up tight inside him for so long. Remembering, Steve felt a blush crawling across his cheeks like a rash and his stomach contract into a tight spiral of embarrassment. Had he really said she was the cutest girl he'd ever met? Had he really made sweeping poetic comparisons between her springy hair and, um, Curly Wurly chocolate bars?

He didn't want to dwell on it any more. Besides, his alarm clock said 5.30 a.m. If he didn't hurry, he would be late for work.

He got out of bed, his feet curling on the cold boards. His flat was a one-bedroomed studio in west London. It had the bare, lonely feel of an undomesticated bachelor. Dog-eared collections of *Nexus* and *New Scientist* towered in teetering piles, threatening to topple over his huge collection of black-and-white movies, carefully stacked in alphabetical order. A video box for *Casablanca* lay open on the table and Norah Jones smiled up at him enigmatically from her CD case as he made his way to the bathroom.

'Good God!' Steve exclaimed out loud when he saw his reflection in the mirror.

He didn't look hungover, though considering the amount he had drunk last night he ought to be. His brown hair was its usual tufty, obstinate self: creating its own peaks and furrows with the irrational wilfulness of a crop circle. His blue eyes were clear, his skin pale, his freckles light. But somehow, he looked odd. He pulled a few faces but they didn't help.

He was reminded of a fairytale he'd read as a kid. About an ugly, wizened dwarf who'd had a spell put on him so that every time he looked in the mirror a little bit of his face changed – his nose bent a few inches, or his hair developed a curl. Until one year on he woke up and found that he had been totally transformed into a dashing, handsome, winning prince.

Wishful thinking, thought Steve. He nudged the scales out from their place by the bin and stepped on to them. Every morning he never failed to be tickled by the way his goldfish, Einstein, would swish to the front of its bowl and watch with amber eyes, as though fabulously excited. Not that his weight ever varied. Steve had a fast metabolism. He could eat anything and never put on an ounce above thirteen stone. Weighing himself was simply part of his morning routine, like shaving and tooth-cleaning and cotton-budding wax from his ears.

Steve frowned and squinted at the scales. How *ridiculous*. He couldn't possibly weigh *that*. He gave a little bounce, but the red pointer didn't shift.

'I can't weigh *zero* stone!' Steve exclaimed. 'That's crazy.'

Einstein wiggled his fins indignantly.

'They must have broken. Great,' he muttered. 'I'll have a go at fixing them tonight, maybe.'

Einstein blew a few sympathetic bubbles.

If that wasn't strange enough, when he lifted the toilet seat, he found that, for some reason he had no urge to urinate. You would have thought that eight pints of beer swishing through his body over the last six hours would have left his bladder bulging and screaming for release. But – nothing. Not even one faint yellow droplet.

Steve rubbed his head thoughtfully and figured that it was going to be a very odd day.

*

Outside, he half expected the weirdness trend to continue, to discover it was raining fish or the street-lamps had come alive like Triffids and were taking over the earth. But to his relief, it was just an ordinary day. The sky was watercolour blue, dabbed with lemon, the air crisp and fresh as apples, not yet tainted by daytime fumes and smog. In the newsagent Steve bought a KitKat and a can of Coke. His usual breakfast. Mr Evans was out the back cutting loose newspapers from their blue strings so Steve left his change on the counter.

There weren't many people in the tube station. A few commuters, an old man cleaning. Steve made a promise to himself not to think about Dina, to slam a lid down on last night and seal it tight.

The hum of the old man cleaning sounded like the lament of a dying bird in the cold air. The sound filled him with poignancy. He remembered the way he and Dina had walked by the moonlit canal. How he had plucked a Coke can ring from the pavement and tried to force it on to her finger, his voice catching with tears as he explained just how much he dreamed of spending on the ring she truly deserved, and how he would save, he would slave, until at the age of seventy-eight he could finally afford to propose, and she had smiled sweetly and then shaken her head gently and talked about how she really valued him as a friend but—

Steve! he told himself. *Don't think about it. Don't think about it or it will hurt too much.*

On the tube, he opened his yellow rucksack and pulled out a book. It was a self-help book called *10 Ways to Fulfil Your Dreams*. Steve found it very embarrassing to read in public, for everyone would give him looks as if to say, 'So you've just spent £10.99 on a book written by a cheesy American in the hope you might get a girlfriend – is your life really *that* sad?' So he had removed the dust-jacket of a Booker Prize-winning novel and put it on top, and now everyone gave him respectful, fellow-intellectual glances.

Steve knew deep down that self-help books were a bit silly. But he *hated* the thought of therapists. There was something about going to a therapist that was like admitting you were really off your trolley, which he wasn't, and he knew it was a cliché but he worried they would hold up those inky blotted cards that revealed your subconscious and all he would be able to see would be breasts. Books were safe, and after all, what was wrong with trying to find more happiness in life? Because that was the point of life, surely? And happiness wasn't easy, was it? It didn't seem to be one of those things that floated about, looking for people to spill blessings on; you had to go looking for it, chase it like a butterfly and catch it in your palms. If you got clingy and squeezed too tight, you crushed it, but if you just closed your palms gently and let the butterfly breathe, it could stay fluttering there for ever. Maybe.

Life is what you make it, the book instructed, *so try to think positive thoughts before going to sleep. They will determine how your next day goes.*

Steve tried to remember his thoughts before sleep last night. He had some vague recollection of thinking he needed a pee but feeling too tired to get up. No wonder his life was going down the toilet.

By the end of the chapter, however, he still felt confused. He sometimes wondered if happiness really had anything to do with Dina, or finding a way to win the lottery, or buying that elusive holiday to a sun-soaked Hawaiian beach that the advert above his head promised would result in 'Bliss, babes and a baking tan'. Why was it that some people were born with everything and others had to spend their lives scraping and struggling to pay off the bills? Was it karma, or individual responsibility, or did God just have favourites? And could you really change your destiny by lying in bed every night and for fifteen minutes saying over and over: *Women will stop saying I am nice and cute and just want to be my friend and find me dangerous and sexy and crawl all over me like something out of a Lynx ad?* Or were you stuck in a maze for ever, scurrying about and looking for answers but trapped by the dead-ends of your own thoughts and behavioural patterns?

Then he caught himself.

'You think too much about everything, that's your problem,' Dina always used to tease him. 'You should just enjoy life, and stop worrying about it.'

He was just worrying about whether he worried too much when an old woman got into the carriage. She was wearing a filthy patchwork coat, dyed red hair trailing down her hunched back, her talon-fingers curled around a crumpled can of Bud. Steve couldn't help glancing at her and thinking: *Well, at least my life could be worse.*

Then he felt mean. But he could tell everyone in the carriage was thinking the same.

Then the woman did something extremely peculiar.

She shuffled up to Steve and *tried to sit on his lap.*

'Hey – hey—' he cried, and realising that he was about to become Flat Steve and be squashed into the furry blue-and-green-striped seat, he jumped up, only just grabbing his rucksack in time. The woman plonked herself down. Steve suppressed an urge to slap her. He felt like yelling, 'Well, just nick my seat, why don't you, and hey, if you want, you can have the shirt off my back *and* my self-help book, since you clearly need it.' But he didn't. He was always thinking one thing, saying another. Manners and shyness trammelled his anger and kept it firmly locked in his chest, and he merely grabbed a pole, dipped his nose back in his book and fumed until the tube slid into Shepherd's Bush.

Steve worked at a greasy spoon on the Uxbridge Road – specifically, the one with the smeary windows and tacky red letters that said G EASY PO N. It was the sort of place that people passed by many a time and thought: *I'd rather eat my food off the pavement than go in there.* And if they saw the things his boss did with the food, Steve thought, the pavement would indeed seem a better option.

He saw the first stream of morning commuters cross the road, swinging umbrellas, briefcases and newspapers. Funny to think that a year ago he'd been just the same: getting up and working twelve-hour days in a top city law firm, before he'd ditched it all in. He didn't envy them. He called to them silently: *OK, so you're earning ten times more than me, so I have a degree in physics and a law conversion course and now I'm mostly living off my savings, all because one day I got so sick of the rat race I decided to ditch it all on a whim. And I still don't know what I want to do with my life, but I can assure you that I love my job, every minute of it, because I get to work with Dina Harman.*

Well, I do at the moment . . .

As Steve got closer, his heart began to flutter madly. That was the trouble with declaring devotion to your best friend and the girl you worked with every day – there was no hiding the morning after, pretending they didn't exist. What would she *say*? What if – God forbid – she *resigned*? Dina was the sunshine in his day; she made life liveable: how would he survive without her nudges and jokes and deliciously wacky vacuum-sounding laugh?

He pushed open the door, his eyes flitting at once to the coat pegs above the till.

Her coat, the gorgeous grey one with the furry hood, wasn't there. He was safe. For now.

As Steve took off his anorak, he heard a noise from the kitchen down below. That would be Luigi, his delightful boss.

Steve went down the steps. Luigi was standing with his back to him. His black hair curled in a greasy mess on the back of his fat neck, a faint rash spidering across his skin. Luigi suffered from rashes frequently. Underneath his tough persona, he was probably really rather sensitive, Steve suddenly realised with a heart-skip of sympathy.

Swash! Swack! Luigi was violently sharpening a knife.

Uh-oh, thought Steve. Something was definitely up. Luigi tended to knife-sharpen at stressful moments – such as when the rents were doubled by those 'money-grabbing cock-suckers at the council', as he put it, or the health inspector visited and discovered meat in the veggie-burgers.

'Hi, Luigi,' Steve said softly.

He didn't turn round.

He must be in a really foul mood, Steve thought. He pulled an apron from the peg and tied it on. It felt grimy, although apparently they were washed on a weekly basis by Luigi's wife, a kind-hearted woman who gave Steve a Snickers bar every time she saw him, saying he was a 'growing lad'. That always made Steve laugh – he was six feet two.

'It was my birthday yesterday,' Steve added.

'Hmph,' said Luigi, or something friendly like that. Perhaps he thought Steve was hoping for a bonus.

'I had a late night, I've got such a hangover,' Steve went on, lying. He was still strangely clear-headed. He just wanted to fill the silence.

Luigi didn't reply. His shoulders were hunched, as though he was crying.

Steve was amazed. Luigi! Crying! Perhaps his marriage was falling apart. Perhaps his business was about to go bust. In a flash, Steve suddenly saw Luigi not as an evil boss who treated his employees like cattle, but as a human being, someone who could be hurt as easily as the next man.

'Luigi, are you OK?' Steve went to him, rubbed his hand gently on his boss's shoulder.

Luigi turned, suddenly. His eyes were red and glazed. Then, in an angry flash, he slashed the knife through the air.

Steve gasped. *The knife had gone right through him.*

He looked down at his stomach, waiting for the blood to belch out.

Nothing came.

And then the memories, the memories that had been whirling in the back of his head, slotted into place, formed a jigsaw. At that moment the feeling of unease that he'd been suffering all morning suddenly made sense, and he collapsed in shock.

He remembered it all.

The pub.

The party.

Dina.

Walking by the canal.

Slipping in.

The water in his lungs.

The gasping horror.

He lay on the floor, the newly washed tiles wet against his ears. In the background, Luigi was now dancing around the kitchen, leaping and waving the knife like a Samurai warrior. Rage swirled through Steve. He wanted to scream. He wanted to close his eyes, shut the world down. This couldn't be. Reaching out, he slammed his fist against the fridge door. It went straight through. Straight through two inches of steel. He wriggled his fingers in the icy refrigerated air. His hand brushed something. A jar. He pulled at it, yanked it out through the door. A jar of Branston pickle. Only yesterday he'd been spreading that on to the bottom of sandwiches, and now . . . now . . .

Smash! He threw the jar on the floor.

'Hey!' Luigi turned in bewildered shock. 'Huh! God!'

He can see me! Steve's heart leapt. *He's just pretending, playing a game.* But then Luigi turned away, picked up a dustpan and broom and started to sweep, muttering, 'Silly Luigi, knocking things over.'

'I'm here,' Steve howled. 'I'm here.'

Luigi started to whistle under his breath.

'I'm here,' Steve croaked, tears in his throat. 'I'm here.'

Luigi carried on sweeping.

A few minutes later Steve was back on the tube. Drumming his fingers insistently against a rail as annoyingly as possible, hoping for just one evil glance from a commuter. Nobody looked up.

Once off the tube, he ran all the way back to his flat.

Back home, he left his flat door swinging open, ran into the bathroom, pulled out his scales. He weighed himself again: zero. He picked up Einstein's goldfish bowl with trembling hands and put it on the scales. Five pounds.

Einstein flipped his fins and smiled up at him smugly, as if to say, 'Well, actually it seems I am bigger than you after all, so ner-ner-ner-ner.'

Zero. Five pounds. Five pounds. Zero.

Oh God, thought Steve, *it's really true. I'm a ghost.* I'm *a ghost. I'm* a ghost. For a moment he was blank with shock. And then, for no reason, the thought popped into his mind: *What on earth am I going to tell my mother?*

PART ONE

1
Dina

Dina went to work on Monday morning with no idea that she was being followed. On her way she stopped at St Simon's church. Over the last few months it had become a habit for her to slip inside for five minutes, just to gather her thoughts.

The church was small, gravestones lurching drunkenly over overgrown grass. She stopped by a gravestone and tenderly laid a sprig of flowers on it. Then she pushed open the heavy door. As usual, the church was empty, except for a plump Italian woman who was kneeling before a statue of the Madonna, praying feverishly. Dina suppressed a smile. The woman had confided in her that six years ago she had prayed to the Virgin for fertility. Now, five *bambinos* later, she was desperately asking Her for them to stop coming.

The woman got up to leave, rubbing her sore knees and tightening her black embroidered scarf over her coat. She surreptitiously watched Dina walk over to the altar and light a candle. She looked so pretty, the woman mused, with a pang of nostalgia for her youth. The girl's curly black hair was pulled into a plait and a shaggy fringe fell into her dark eyes. She was wearing a coat with a furry collar and jeans, and a pair of beige suede boots. She looked as if she belonged in a bar, laughing and drinking with friends, not entering a church every morning and squeezing her eyes shut and looking sad. The woman wondered what her story was.

*

Dina opened her eyes and looked at the row of candles left by Londoners, a long flickering line of hopes and joys and fears. She smiled. Seeing those candles – realising that there were hundreds of people sharing the same tragedies – always made her feel better, more human.

Then she checked her watch. Time for work.

God, I have to get another job, she thought for the hundredth time that week, as she unlocked the door of Luigi's Greasy Spoon. Inside, the café was ghostly grey, the upturned chairs on the tables like large warped insects. She made a cup of tea, sighing and thinking: *Dina, just what the hell are you doing working in this place?*

Dina had been born in New York and spent the first twenty-seven years of her life there. Eighteen months ago, she had moved to London. It had been a rather random decision, the result of a broken heart, a love affair that had cut her so deep she couldn't bear to be in the same country as her ex. She'd packed up all she had in a single suitcase, walked up to the airport desk and asked for a flight that would take her as far away as possible. The girl had offered her a flight to Gatwick, England, or Melbourne, Australia. Dina had tossed a coin. Heads: London. And that was the start of her new life.

There were times when she regretted that decision. Especially during her first week, when she was convinced a black cloud was following her about, it rained so much; and when she discovered just how evil London pigeons could be, and that standing beneath one wasn't a good idea unless you wanted a very unique sort of sham-pooing; and when she was disappointed to discover that none of the men looked or spoke like Hugh Grant. But, over time, she had developed a huge affection for the city. She'd grown to love the big grey watery skies in the morning, the sweet picnicky greenness of Hyde Park, and the jostling party-fun of Leicester Square on a Friday night. And it was all so different, so far off from home, that she really did feel as though she'd made a fresh start.

Working at The Greasy Spoon had been her first and only job since leaving New York. She sent postcards home telling her parents she was working in marketing and about to receive a promotion. If only. She'd been in such an emotional state when she arrived, and her CV was so abysmal, that the temping agency she'd registered with, on discovering she was interested in the catering business, had suggested she get some work experience at The Greasy Spoon first. And she'd made herself a promise: *Well, I'll just stay six weeks and move on.*

That had been well over a year ago.

Dina lit up an illicit cigarette and sighed again: the pleasure of the soothing smoke mixed with the guilt of her charred lungs. She'd managed to give up smoking, but since the stress of Steve's funeral she had started to slide again . . .

I'm stuck in a rut, she realised, *because I'm just so bloody lazy.* She kept meaning to apply for jobs, but she was always so tired at the end of work and there was always something far more interesting on television.

Oh great – she saw a filthy black Fiat pulling up outside – *Luigi was here.* She quickly stood up, stubbed out her cigarette and started unstacking chairs to look industrious.

As Luigi entered, however, she realised that he wasn't alone. He had his arm around . . . God – surely not? A girl. She was about five foot, weighed around twenty stone and had long greasy black hair that flowed over her shoulders like tar. Her figure was not enhanced by her clothes: a large black tunic with an ostentatious golden brooch pinned to her bosom, and black leggings clinging to her thighs.

She looked about fifteen years old.

'Should I be calling the police?' Dina joked cheekily, raising an eyebrow.

Luigi, wrapped up in his own excitement, thankfully didn't even seem to hear. But the girl did. She gave Dina a very frosty glance.

'Dina,' Luigi said, 'this is Fatima.'

'Hi, Fatima,' Dina forced a smile.

'She'll be working here from now on.'

Oh. Of course. Dina cringed at her mistake. Since Steve had died, Luigi had been looking for a replacement, but nobody had been stupid enough to want to work for his measly wages, so it had taken a few months to find anyone. Dina looked at Fatima sympathetically. Perhaps the poor girl was a student and was saving up for tuition fees. Luigi was probably paying her 2p an hour.

'Fatima is my niece,' Luigi added grandly.

A-ha, thought Dina. *That explains everything.*

From then on, the morning was total hell. Dina tried her best to get along with Fatima, but it was impossible. She gave her a guided tour and work instructions, but instead of paying attention, Fatima merely waved her hand and nodded grandly, as though she was a mistress approving her maid's activities. Dina was friendly and normally got on well with people, but trying to spark up a conversation with Fatima was impossible. The girl answered in withering monosyllables to Dina's chit-chat about her school, and whether she had a boyfriend. When she asked Fatima what she wanted to do when she grew up, Dina caught herself sounding patronising. Fatima, however, lit up and announced that she wanted to sing in an all-girl band.

And what will they be called, the Heffalumps? Dina wondered.

'Everyone at drama school wants to be my friend,' Fatima said gravely, 'but I keep telling them they have to learn to share.'

'How generous of you,' said Dina. 'Come on, give me a demonstration.' She bit back a smile, waiting for some dreadful whine.

She was taken aback, however, when Fatima burst into 'Hit Me Baby One More Time'. When she sang, the girl became an angel and her lumpy figure swelled with dignity and passion. Her voice was like a fine opera singer's, the bubblegum lyrics incongruous with her beautiful trills.

'Wow, that was pretty good,' Dina breathed, and then felt irked when Fatima gave a smug little smile.

By the time she sat down for her tea-break at eleven o'clock, Dina felt fed-up and exhausted. She suddenly suffered a wave of longing for her old friend and co-worker, Steve.

She recalled the day she'd started at The Greasy Spoon. She'd been feeling nervous, and when Luigi had introduced him as 'Stevie-boy', she'd felt a blush come to her cheeks and thought: *Yum!*

He was very tall – about six feet two – and he walked with slightly hunched shoulders, as though he wished he could shrink a few inches. He had silky, floppy brown hair that seemed to irritate him – he kept gathering it up in his fingers and raking it back – sweet blue-green eyes, and freckles on his turned-up nose.

He wasn't conventionally attractive. Later she noticed his faults – the fact that he was too thin and his ribs showed through his T-shirts, and that his fingers were knobbly. No, he was just *cute*. Lovable. Huggable. Like an overgrown, gangly teddy-bear. Dina felt very motherly towards him; she wanted to take him home and cook him a huge meal, fatten him up and sort him out.

Over time, she had concluded they weren't suited as lovers. Steve would have been *way* too weird to go out with. He was always reading *Nexus* magazine and he avidly watched boring programmes like *Panorama* and documentaries on conspiracy theories, while (shock horror) he'd never heard of *Friends* or *ER*. He even had a goldfish which ought to have been called something normal like Brian or James or, hell, Goldie even, but no, Steve had called it Einstein.

'Steve, I love you but you are a *total* nutter,' Dina was always telling him, ruffling his hair. Steve would just blush and give a resigned shrug.

As friends, however, they had a lot of fun. Dina felt that Steve took life way too seriously and she was always trying to get him to lighten up.

They'd had so many good times together. She had fond memories of the nights they'd gone back to his flat and played chess in the moonlight. Dina was too impatient and careless to be any good at the game, so Steve always won. Although she was better at rummy and poker, since she was good at cheating.

And oh, thought Dina, smiling fondly, *what about that time we found Luigi's flask in the back kitchen, filled with brandy instead of the so-called Colombian coffee he claimed it contained?* They'd drunk it and refilled the flask with watery tea from the machine. Then, totally smashed, Dina had forced shy Steve to get up on the tables with her; using brooms as mikes, they'd conducted their own informal karaoke duet, singing 'Something Stupid'. Luigi had unfortunately entered during their grand finale and nearly sacked them; they'd spent the rest of the evening walking on eggshells around him, red-faced, trying not to explode with giggles.

But it hadn't all been about laughs. They'd shared deeper moments together too. The nice thing about Steve was that he was such a good listener. Whenever Dina was upset, he was sensitive enough to pick up on it, sit her down and say, 'Come on – tell me everything.' He never thought she was silly or kooky; while he wasn't very good at giving worldly wisdom, he would always cheer her up with a hug or hurry off down to the shops to buy her a KitKat.

Dina sighed and came back to reality: sitting in the glum café without him. Fatima really was *no* replacement.

Dina couldn't resist reaching into her pocket and removing a very crumpled newspaper article. It had appeared in the local paper after Steve had died, and back in those black days she'd found herself reading it over and over, scratching her broken heart like a bloody scab that she refused to let heal.

Recently, she'd almost forgotten about it, but now she found herself going over the familiar words again. Tears welled up in her eyes, but at the same time she bit back a smile, for it was full of so many painful inaccuracies:

YOUTH DROWNS IN RIVER –
POLICE SUSPECT DRUGS

Local youth Steve MacFadden (16) has been found dead in the Hythe Road canal – tragically, the night of his birthday. He was last seen by Miss Dina Hardman (27), who confirmed that he had been drinking that evening. Police also believe that Mr MacFadden may have taken drugs, possibly dabbling in LSD, cocaine and heroin before taking his final fall. Local schools have responded by setting up talks on the dangers of drugs.

Well, at least they had got her age wrong by only a year, compared to the fourteen they had knocked off Steve's. Dina pursed her lips. But Steve would never have gone near drugs. He was much too responsible and sensible. The wildest thing he had ever taken was probably a peanut M&M.

Steve's death was still a mystery. Dina had been the last person to see him alive, and she would never forget walking away down that canal path, looking back at him sitting on the bench, waving goodbye to him. And then what had happened to him? Maybe he'd been attacked; maybe he'd just slipped; maybe maybe maybe.

She closed her eyes and let out a sigh. And then she felt it. That sensation again, the one she'd been experiencing now and again over the past few weeks. It had happened last night; she had forgotten it in waking but now it came back to her, hazy and dreamlike. She had woken in the velvety blue darkness with a soft warmth on her face. It had felt like breathing and its sound was curiously soothing, like the noise of the sea caressing the beach. She had fallen asleep and dreamt of night skies and stars and woken up in the dawn darkness hearing the rain gently pit-patting against the windows, feeling strangely soft and at peace.

And now it was here again. That sensation. As if something – or someone – was right behind her, looking over her shoulder, breathing down her neck. It was daytime now, and the experience was much more unnerving. She could feel all the little hairs on the back of her neck stand up on end and her spine stiffen as though icy water was being dripped down her back. She turned her head slowly, her heartbeat racing. But, of course, there was nothing there. She looked over at Fatima, who was reading *More* magazine, filling out a quiz entitled 'How sexy are you?'.

'Um, did Luigi just come over?' Dina asked.

'No.' Fatima looked at her as though she was completely loopy.

'Oh well. Fine.' Dina smiled, quickly folding up the article. 'Um, how's your quiz?' She tried to change the subject, but her voice sounded strangulated and high.

'I got top marks,' Fatima beamed.

'Come on, back to work, Dina.' Luigi came faffing back into the shop. 'I don't pay you to sit around.'

Dina was so busy, she soon forgot all about the strange sensation. Lunchtime was approaching and the café was filling up. They were the usual rabble: a couple of rowdy builders who'd been erecting scaffolding across the road; an old granny with her little Scottie dog, who, as she did every day, requested a hot chocolate without any sugar and a burger bun with nothing but butter and a bit of lettuce. And then, at noon, something rather unexpected and fantastic happened: the door swung open and a dark figure entered.

Dina's jaw dropped. She'd been filling the cappuccino jug with frothy brown liquid at the time and she nearly sploshed the whole thing down her front. She suddenly felt her gritty tiredness melting away and a big fat yellow daisy of happiness blossoming in her heart. Dear God, he was quite simply the most gorgeous, sexy, delicious and handsome man she'd ever seen set foot in the place.

Maybe it was going to be a good day after all.

She stooped down behind the counter, pretending to rearrange the burger buns, stealing surreptitious glances at him. Tall. Dark-haired. Beautiful features; cheekbones like knives. His stiff, upright posture looked English and formal, almost aristocratic, but there was a slightly wild look in his dark eyes and a strange beaded Zulu-style necklace around his neck that looked incongruous with his stylish black suit.

He had been followed into The Greasy Spoon by a rather harassed-looking mother, clutching the sticky hand of a sobbing six-year-old. Dina stood electrified as she watched him hold open the door for them. The little girl dropped her blue elephant on the floor and began to scream like a banshee. Her mother looked ready to snap.

'For God's sake, Eliza, I *told* you to leave it at home, now pick it up—' She broke off as the stranger knelt down, picked up the toy and gently returned it to her daughter with such a warm smile that the child stopped crying and blinked.

'Thanks – thank you so much.' The mother gave a flustered smile and began combing her fingers through her hair.

The stranger grinned and shrugged easily.

Oh my God, thought Dina, *this cannot be true. A sex god – with a heart of gold!*

Then she suddenly became aware that she had competition. For Fatima had stopped reading her magazine and was staring at the stranger with bright eyes and pink cheeks.

'I can serve him!' she cried eagerly. 'I need practice. What shall I do? Do I need a pad?'

'No, Fatima,' said Dina hastily, 'you're new. It's OK, I'll handle this.'

She swallowed, said a quick prayer and sidled up to him.

2

Dina

She tried not to beam like a Cheshire cat who'd got the double cream.

'Um, hi,' she said.

'Hello,' he said warmly. Oh, his grin was heartbreaking! One of those lovely wide smiles that crinkled up his dark eyes and showed off bright teeth. And his English accent was a proper one, all aristocratic, like something out of the movies.

She noticed that he gave her a quick once-over, his eyes breezing over her face and breasts and then curling down to her legs. *Stop blushing, stop blushing,* she shouted at herself, feeling her cheeks throbbing like a car heater at top blast.

'Um, what would you like?' she asked.

'What would you recommend?'

Well, nothing, Dina thought. *It would be safer to eat the napkins than the food we provide here, but . . .*

'Um, well . . . um . . . well . . . maybe a hot dog?' she suggested. 'It comes in a bun.'

'Obviously.'

'Yes, obviously,' said Dina quickly. Oh God, she sounded like a total moron.

'Well, I'd like the hot dog in the bun,' he said, but his voice was friendly, his smile teasing. 'I like your accent.'

'Um, thanks. And to drink?'

'I guess a good old-fashioned Coke would be fine,' he said.

Dina realised too late that the hot dog idea was a major mistake.

Shit, oh shit – she'd forgotten that earlier she'd spotted Luigi in the kitchen surreptitiously recycling the uneaten ones customers had left on their plates last night. Though Luigi was prone to mad economising, he wouldn't normally go this far. But this morning the delivery van had failed to turn up and he had got into a total flap, defending his recycling by crying: 'You can't have a greasy spoon without hot dogs.' Even so, Dina winced when she saw a few of them even had teeth-marks nibbling the edges. Really, it was no wonder they'd nearly been closed down last month. Finally she picked up one that didn't look too bad and lopped off the dodgy end. But when she put it in the bun, it looked stupid, like a tiny cigar-end nestling in the expanse of bread. She chucked it in the bin and finally settled on one with bite-marks, hiding them with a big splurt of tomato ketchup. There. That would do.

'Here we are.' She put it down on his table with a flourish, wishing she could somehow give him a signal that it was better not to bother actually eating it.

'Thanks,' he said, and she was just about to turn away and get his Coke when he added: 'So, d'you enjoy working here?'

'Um, yeah – it's great,' she replied, feeling flattered. He was making conversation. He was *interested* . . .

'Come on,' he cocked his head to one side, 'how much do they pay you?'

'Well,' said Dina delicately, 'let's just say it's somewhere between five quid an hour and a hundred.' They both laughed.

'You're an intelligent girl, you ought to be working somewhere a lot better,' he said, more earnestly.

'Well, thanks.' Dina flushed. 'Between you and me, I absolutely hate it here,' she said in a low voice. 'But, well – I'm actually dyslexic, you see. The school didn't realise, so I got pretty behind with my studies. It was awful actually – all the teachers thought I was thick, even retarded. But then my dad realised and I was given extra lessons by an educational psychologist. I mean – I can read and write, obviously, I'm not a moron, but, y'know, I wouldn't be much use in an office. My spelling is appalling and I don't have great English skills, so . . .' She trailed off, suddenly realising that she'd been rabbiting on and he must be terribly bored. But he merely gave her a long look of sympathy and reached out and touched her wrist. Dina felt as though someone had pressed a red-hot poker against the skin.

'God, I do feel sorry for you,' he said.

Dina gazed at him. He stared back, holding her eyes. Dina felt as though a snake was slowly uncoiling in her stomach . . .

'Oi!' One of the builders from the next table suddenly interrupted them. 'Where's my hot dog, darling? I've been waiting twenty minutes now! Can you stop chatting up your lover-boy!'

'Yes – sorry.' Dina jumped, the spell broken. She hurried back behind the counter, where Fatima had moved on to the problem pages. Silently cursing, Dina deliberately gave the irksome builder the worst specimen she could find. As she carried it over to him, she could feel the dark-haired stranger gazing at her and she burned under his gaze. Then he spoke.

'Um, my Coke . . . and maybe, erm, a napkin?'

'Oh – yes, yes, I'm sorry,' Dina stuttered. She hurried to the fridge and removed a Coke, and was reaching behind the counter for a napkin and a plastic glass when—

She felt it again.

That breath behind her neck. As if someone was right behind her.

A breath so intense it almost seemed to find shape, to form a whisper, something that sounded like . . .

No!

'Uh?' Dina spun around, her eyes flitting over the café. Everyone was engrossed in their food and conversation; her stranger was gazing at her expectantly. *I'm going mad,* she thought in a daze, the napkin fluttering from her fingers. She picked it up, walked forward like a zombie and was about to put it on his plate when she caught herself. *What am I doing? He's just seen me pick that up off the dirty floor.* Mumbling an apology, acutely aware of Luigi watching her from the kitchen door, she quickly found another napkin, folding it into a neat triangle.

'Thanks,' the stranger said.

She could feel Luigi's glare like a knuckle pressed between her shoulder-blades. She was going to lose her job at this rate. Trying to make amends, she popped open the Coke can, but she was so shaken that as she poured it into the plastic cup her hand wobbled and – *oh God!* – the liquid missed the glass by several inches and splurted all over the table.

The stranger started backwards, his chair grating. Fatima gasped and sniggered. One of the builders jeered: 'Nice one, love.' Dina started in horror at the dark puddles, popping and fizzing. An apology was stuck in her throat like a blocked cough, but before she could do anything, Luigi had rushed to the stranger's side and was flapping about like a demented peacock, cooing apologies: 'We are so sorry, we give you fifty pence reduction, she is new here . . .'

'It's fine,' he said, craning his neck past Luigi to shoot Dina a reassuring smile. 'Really, it's fine. It was just an accident, it's not her fault.'

Dina thought it was best simply to be where other people were not. She hurried into the toilet, locked herself inside, slammed down the seat and sat on it. She couldn't believe it. How could she have been such a clumsy idiot in front of such a gorgeous guy? She uncurled her clenched hands, flexing her shaking fingers, staring at the criss-cross of lines on her palm, the jagged life line spliced by a love line that forked at the end; she'd once been told by a palm-reader that it meant she'd spend her life torn between two men. Just what had happened in there? Was she hearing voices?

She waited for another ten minutes before she had the courage to emerge. To her disappointment and relief, the guy had gone. He'd hardly eaten anything. She quickly cleared away, expecting Luigi to slaughter her, but he merely gave her a glowering look and said, his lip curling in sarcasm: 'Your customer didn't leave a tip.'

After such a horrendous day, Dina could hardly wait to get home. She was sharing a flat with an Australian girl, Anita, who was kind enough to charge her a ridiculously low rent for the Shepherd's Bush area, besides letting her keep a stray dog which had once followed her home and which Dina hadn't had the heart to turn away. Then again, anyone who knew Anita well wouldn't really want to live with her.

As Dina climbed the stairs wearily, she thought: *I'm going to take Roger for a quick walk and then have an early supper. Then I'll have a long hot bath and an early night. I'm so knackered, no wonder I'm hearing voices.*

When she unlocked the front door, however, she was startled to see a half-naked man running out of the kitchen. He was carrying a tray of ice-cubes and roaring like a jungle warrior.

Seeing Dina, he started, stopped and stared. Ice dripped on to his body. He yelped; Dina winced.

Then, out of the lounge came Anita (enthusiastically chased by Roger, who clearly thought the whole thing was a riotous game). She was wearing pink stripy underwear and brandishing a fluorescent green water-pistol which she pressed with a squeal, inadvertently showering Dina.

'Uh – thanks,' said Dina, looking down at the wet patch on her blouse.

The half-naked man put his fingers to his mouth to stifle a giggle.

'Sorry,' said Anita, rather unselfconsciously. 'We thought you wouldn't be home till later.'

'Don't worry,' Dina said. 'I'll just go to my room, OK? Come on, Roger darling.'

In her bedroom, Dina found a packet of dry-roasted peanuts. She nibbled them, trying to ignore the growling in her tummy and the noises from outside. That was another reason why she had to get a proper job. She needed her own place. Anita was lovely, and good fun, but her predilection for playing Abba at top volume and inviting over her seemingly endless supply of boyfriends was not. And though Dina was vivacious, there were times when she needed her own space, when she needed to be quiet. Anita *never* needed to be quiet.

Dina had never felt she'd fit in and hadn't even unpacked properly; half her junk was still in boxes under the bed. Despite this, her room was a total tip. So messy it looked as though a tornado, a hurricane and a whirlwind had swirled into her room and had a competition to prove who could be the most colourfully destructive. Clothes carpeted the floor. Mugs hid under the bed, flushing green with embarrassment to have so much mould creeping over them. CDs glittered on her table, all out of their cases. A mauve Hello Kitty bra hung from the aerial of her little black-and-white telly.

Steve had come to visit once or twice and been horrified. When Dina had visited his flat, she had been equally disgusted. Clean surfaces, neatly folded towels, alphabetically ordered CDs. She couldn't understand people who spent all their lives being neat – how did that give them any time to live? Because once you'd got home from work and spent an hour cleaning up, spraying and stacking and dusting, you'd then have to use the towel you'd just washed or take all the CDs *out* of the cases you'd just put them in, and the whole thing was undone and you'd have to start all over again the next day. Frankly, thought Dina, it was a waste of life. And now that Steve had gone, she knew more than ever that she didn't want to waste a single precious second of her remaining years on the planet.

Another reason why she had to get a better job.

The only neat thing in Dina's room was a little row of cactus plants on her windowsill. She'd once told Steve she killed every plant she owned. So he had taken her out one Saturday to a garden centre and bought her five little knobbly greenies. 'You won't be able to kill them if you try,' he assured Dina. Sure enough, six months on, they were still thriving.

Dina shoved up the sash window – Anita hated her smoking indoors – and blew out billows of smoke into the fresh air. She thought random thoughts. Of credit cards and rent and job applications and how she *must* shave her legs before they turned into a jungle. And then:

You know, Steve, I—

She stopped herself.

I have to stop doing this, she thought. *I don't know why I do it, Steve. I know you're gone. And yet I still have imaginary chats with you. But you're the only one who I can tell the really nutty stuff in my head. I like standing by my window and looking down. I like watching the people walking through the streets. Look at them. They're all absorbed in their own little worlds. Like that woman down there, see her with the blonde hair? So wrapped up she nearly walked into that waste-bin. And that guy with the dark hair—*

Oh God, it's him!

That guy from the café.

Dina leaned out of her window, heart pounding. The guy looked up. Oh. Oops. No, it wasn't him; she was just seeing things. God, she couldn't get him out of her mind.

She was about to stub out her cigarette when it happened again. That breath, pulsing gently against the back of her neck.

OK, she told herself. *Take it slowly. S-l-o-w-l-y. Just turn around.* She dropped her cigarette with shaking hands, watching the butt fall, fall, fall, disappear. And turned.

She burst out laughing. Roger was sitting on the edge of her bed, panting.

'Oh, Roger!' She fluffed up his ears and collapsed on to the bed, laughing a little hysterically. He barked enthusiastically as she hugged him. Then she spread out like a starfish. 'I'm fine,' she giggled shakily. 'I'm not hearing breathing. I'm fine.'

I mean, Steve, she carried on that night as she stood in her holey Winnie-the-Pooh nightie, cleaning her teeth in front of the bathroom mirror, *it's not as if I'm looking for anyone right now. I know people say that and don't mean it. I've been out with my girlfriends and they toss their hair back and say airily, 'I'm really not looking for anyone right now,' whilst searching out of their corner of their eye for anything in a pair of trousers.*

But really – I'm not looking for anyone right now. Really really really. Not since America. Something happened out there I never told you about. I haven't told anyone about it. Not properly. There was this guy. His name was Jason. And he broke my heart. I never knew what that expression meant until I met him. I'd always had so-so relationships. I mean, you know, nice ones, nothing special. He was special. And when it all ended, it broke – no, that's such a lame expression – it was more like he took hold of my heart and ripped it out of my chest, and when I first got to London I felt like I was walking around with this blank space where my feelings ought to be. And I'd laugh all the time and joke around and try to fill up the space but . . .

But being friends with you changed all that. You healed me, Steve. You gave me room to open my heart without all the messiness of a romance. That's why I felt we should always stay friends. We had something precious, something that was more long-lasting than any romance I've ever had, and I didn't want to spoil that.

This guy today, he's been the first man in ages who has made me feel as if I have feelings again. Or at least seeds or rootlings. I mean, it's so rare these days to come across a guy who is good-looking AND has a brain AND is sensitive AND has a personality.

And what do I do? I throw Coke over him and act as though I belong in an asylum.

Oh well.

I guess I'll never see him again.

Night, Steve. Night.

Dina turned out the light.

All the same, the next morning, when she went into church to light a candle for Steve, she couldn't resist lighting an extra one. And praying rather sheepishly: *Look, God, I know I probably ought to be praying for Steve and world peace and an end to suffering, but all the same, d'you think you could make that guy come back and ask me out?*

3
Steve

The Greasy Spoon appeared to be empty. The shop was dark, the door locked. It was 4 a.m.; litter fluttered in torn paper ghosts up and down the pavement outside, and the street was deserted except for a man walking his dog. As they passed Steve, the poodle burst into a tantivy of barks and howls.

'Come on, Beyoncé,' the man said, yanking its lead, unaware of the splutter of laughter behind him. 'We have to get home or Mummy will be cross.'

That was a close one, thought Steve, as he walked through the door, wriggling uncomfortably and swearing under his breath. That was the trouble with being a ghost. This walking-through-doors business looked very flash, but it was easy to pick up glass and wood splinters, which throbbed in the layers of your soul and took several painful hours to tease out afterwards. Not to mention the fact that every time he passed a cat it had a cardiac arrest. Dogs were just as bad – even ones called Beyoncé. Yesterday a little Scottie had managed to sink its teeth into him, and when Steve had tried to flee, his foot had stretched out the full length of the street before the dog let go and it pinged back to him.

He went into the kitchen to make a cup of PG Tips. It was only when he'd added two spoonfuls of sugar and taken a sip that he realised: *Oh, I'm dead. This tea tastes of nothing. Everything tastes of nothing. My tastebuds seem to have dried up totally.*

It was a realisation that had kept stabbing him over the past few months: when he went to the toilet and nothing came out. Or when his phone rang at home – normally a salesperson from Barclaycard who didn't know he'd died and was trying to sell him card payment protection and couldn't hear him speaking. Or when he turned up at The Greasy Spoon and waited for Dina, even though she couldn't see him; for all he could do was watch her.

Steve went back into the café and sat down by the window. *Weird,* he thought, *this time a few months ago I was sitting in this very chair, chatting with Dina. And now look at me.* Slowly, the shock of his death was turning into indignation. After all, if you were going to die, you could at least go with a bang. Like a gangster, like Mr Orange in *Reservoir Dogs,* peppered with bullets, gasping your last breath with your hair soaked in a pool of glorious blood.

But no – his death, the wasted years of the rest of his life, had occurred all because of a mackintosh.

A mackintosh worth £3.60, bought in a sale in Oxfam.

God, thought Steve, had the strangest sense of humour.

On the day Steve had died, he'd been sitting in The Greasy Spoon with Dina. It was a Thursday. They'd had hardly any customers, Luigi was away attending a family wedding, and they'd had the place to themselves. And so Steve and Dina, rather naughtily, had put up the CLOSED sign, stolen some Cokes from the fridge and settled down for a game of chess.

It was Steve's move. But he couldn't focus. His gaze was fixed on the rutted top of his castle, but his attention was on Dina and the endearing way she was twirling curls around her finger.

It was funny – it was the little things she did that got him. Ever since Steve had set eyes on Dina, he had been madly and wildly in love with her. But he'd learned to handle it. Hide it. He'd had too many experiences of this kind in the past and he knew the pattern.

One, he'd tell his crush how gorgeous she was.

Two, a pained expression would distort her face, as though she was suffering from terrible constipation.

Three, she would mutter about not wanting a relationship right now and about just being friends.

Four, their friendship would be reduced to horrible

awkwardness, and every time he came within four feet of her she'd jump and look as though she was about to sue him for harassment.

Five, the following week he'd see some gorgeous guy picking her up in a flash car because, erm, she was suddenly ready for a relationship after all.

Steve felt his friendship with Dina was too precious to take the risk. He kept his feelings secret at work and let them run riot at home. He would play Norah Jones and lie back on his couch and picture them making love until his ears tingled with embarrassment. Or he would watch *Casablanca,* picturing Dina as Ingrid Bergman and wishing he had the cool of Humphrey Bogart.

But every so often at work Dina would just do something – some little thing like her bouncy, jiggly walk, or the way she hummed all the time in a wonderfully out-of-tune way – that would get to him. And he'd feel his emotions bubbling up his chest and a crazy urge would seize him and he'd feel the words just on the tip of his tongue: 'Dina, I think you're great. I think you're so pretty and funny and clever and I know I am nowhere near good enough for you, but if you could just give me one chance, how about we make a go of it?'

'*Steve!* Just make a bloody-fucking-get-a-move-on-move!' Dina slammed her Coke can down, bringing Steve back down to earth. 'Dear me, I wish we were playing poker, then I could cheat . . . Only joking!' she added, when Steve looked aghast. She'd won a fair number of KitKats over the last week.

'Sorry,' Steve said, hastily clearing his throat. 'I was just contemplating Scholar's Mate, though a long-term strategy involving a Knight's Defence might be a better bet.'

'Uh?' Dina looked blank. Whereas Steve always took ten minutes to make a move, Dina took ten seconds.

Steve grinned and took her queen. Dina rolled her eyes in mock disgust.

'So unfair. OK then.' She picked up her white knight, swished it about ten squares up the board and plonked it right on top of his king. 'I'm taking your king.'

'Your knight can't do that. It moves in an L shape.'

'Yeah, well mine can. It's a very clever knight, it's super-evolved and genetically engineered.'

'I take it you've had enough. Shall we call it a draw?' Steve offered, ever the gentleman. As they were folding up the board, he suddenly found the words falling out of his mouth before he could even think about them: 'Dina, I was just wondering if you're free tonight and fancied a quiet drink . . .'

Oh my God, he thought, his heart pumping like a steam train. *I've said it. Oh God. I've said it. And I didn't manage to make it sound casual. She'll have heard the 'date' vibe in my voice. And now she's looking pained . . .*

'Because,' he went on hastily, 'it's my birthday and I wanted a few quiet drinks with some friends – not just you, of course, I've got some other mates coming – and—'

'Steve, of course!' she'd cried, flinging her arms around his neck. 'I can't believe I forgot it's your birthday! Why didn't you remind me before!'

'So you're coming?'

'Definitely! So long as there are some A-list celebrities.'

'Well.' Steve looked worried for a moment. 'Er . . .'

'I'm joking.' Dina nipped his waist and he grinned in relief. 'Relax, it'll be wonderful!'

And so, that night, Steve found himself sitting at a table in a canalside pub near Wormwood Scrubs with three friends, nervously sipping a Guinness and nibbling dry-roasted peanuts. He was thoroughly regretting the whole idea. He'd planned to spend the evening watching a Bogart video alone. Instead he'd made hasty calls to his friends, and now he wasn't sure how Dina was going to take to them all. Jon, who worked in IT and weighed eighteen stone, never said much; he just grunted. Darren only ever wanted to play darts. And Martyn wouldn't talk unless he was drunk, when he started quoting Sartre, Lewis Carroll and Edward Lear and making surreal remarks about stars or potatoes. Steve felt entirely comfortable with them, for they had all been friends since studying physics at Imperial College. But Dina was probably going to find them weird, let's face it, and in turn would probably think Steve even weirder than she already did.

Finally, the pub door opened and there she was.

Steve felt his heart do a violent flip. He noticed, with a mixture of pride and jealousy, that the moment she entered, everyone looked up. She was like a blast of sunshine in the cold, dingy pub. It wasn't just her beauty. It was the sparkle in her dark eyes, the smile constantly tugging her lips, the girlish bounce of her curly black ponytail as she came over and gave him a huge hug. As always, she was wearing old jeans and his favourite sheepskin coat.

'STEVE! HAPPY BIRTHDAY!' She kissed his burning cheek. 'And here are your lovely friends. Well – aren't you going to introduce me?'

'This is Jon.'

Jon grunted.

'This is Darren.'

Darren asked Dina if she wanted to play darts; she said, 'Maybe later.'

'And this is Martyn.'

Martyn raised his pint glass and said: 'Has anyone ever told you you look like The Cat in the Hat?'

To Steve's relief, Dina howled with laughter, a laugh so loud and raucous that even Jon looked startled and blinked. Steve went up to the bar to buy her a Baileys, and by the time he returned he was relieved to find that she was chatting and laughing away with them all. That was Dina, he thought happily, she could put anyone at ease.

'So, have you had a good birthday?'

'My friends didn't get me any decent presents,' Steve moaned.

'No,' Martyn protested indignantly, 'we did get you a card.'

He pushed it over to Dina. On the outside, it had a big picture of a cartoon elephant with a goofy smile on its face, and in gold letters: 'NOW YOU ARE 3!' They had scrawled an extra zero next to the three in smeared biro.

'Well, it was all that was left in the supermarket,' Martyn shrugged. 'It was either that or "Many Happy Returns Grandma".'

'Inside is even worse,' Steve said.

Dina opened it up. There was a little rhyme for the three-year-old recipient of the card, which his three friends had modified accordingly:

Today you're a little boy full of happy cheer
May your whole day be filled with overflowing joy ('joy' had been crossed out and replaced with 'beer')
With lots and lots of presents and toys (a picture of a rubber doll and a GameBoy)
To enjoy sharing with the other girls and boys ('boys' had been crossed out heavily and a helpful tip added: 'Stick to women, Steve, life's complicated enough')

'You guys are appalling!' Dina giggled. 'That's the trouble with men, they're crap at choosing presents.'

'You ought to see what my dad bought me,' Steve said glumly.

'Oh,' said Dina, 'not another Robbie Williams . . .' She howled with laughter. Every year for the past four years, Steve's father, convinced that all young people loved Robbie Williams, had bought Steve one of his CDs for Christmas. Steve had always been polite and pretended to like them, with the result that his father, convinced he was on to a winning streak, bought him Robbie's latest for every conceivable celebration.

'You should just tell him,' Dina said.

'He can't go back now,' Martyn said, shaking his head gravely. 'He's like Macbeth: he is so far steeped in CDs that he cannot wade back, only listen, and listen, and listen again.'

'Well, anyway,' said Dina, after they had stopped giggling. 'I've bought you a decent present. Here.' She passed him an envelope.

Steve tore it open in excitement. His jaw dropped. His friends craned their necks curiously. He was holding adoption papers. For a gorilla in London Zoo called Titus.

'I just thought . . . you know . . . it would be a bit different, a lot more fun than socks and ties and Robbie Williams CDs.' Dina broke off, swallowing. 'I hope Einstein doesn't get jealous but I just thought you might like it, but no, obviously you hate it, I'll take it back—' She broke off in relief as Steve engulfed her in a hug and told her it was the best present he had ever had in the history of birthdays.

The rest of the evening had been lovely. All they did was drink, play darts and talk, but just being near to Dina was enough to make Steve happy. As the closing bell rang, he offered to escort her home, ignoring the nudges and wolf-whistles from his friends.

'Steve is a first-class gentleman,' said Dina archly, rolling her eyes at them.

Steve had pulled on his mac and they'd walked along the canal to the tube station. It had been raining and the air was moist, the trees and bushes shiny, the banks quilted with the slush of autumn leaves.

'Your friends were nuts,' said Dina. 'But what else would I expect from you?'

'Uh-huh.'

Steve could hear his heart beating like a tom-tom. Saliva crept up into his mouth and he gulped it back down. That urge was in his heart again. And now he was too drunk to lasso it with logic.

'Well, you're quiet tonight,' Dina teased him, ruffling his hair. And as she brought her hand down, he took hold of it. There, that was a start.

'Dina . . .' he said.

'Steve . . .' she mimicked playfully, but there was unease in her eyes.

'Seriously . . . I . . .' He looked down into her lovely chocolate-brown eyes and his heart just melted and he found himself pulling her into his arms, pressing her head against his chest, holding her tightly, breathing her smell, her essence, deep into his lungs. 'Oh Dina, you're so gorgeous and sweet and I think you're so wonderful and this has been one of the best nights of my life . . . and I . . .' *Say it, say it!* 'I . . . think . . .' *STEVE! GO ON! SAY IT!* 'I . . . think my gorilla is so lovely . . . and you're simply one of the cutest girls I've ever met, and your hair – it's like Curly Wurlys . . . I mean . . . I mean . . .' Looking about for inspiration, his eyes fell upon a Coke can ring, lying twirled on the ground. He picked it up, offered it to her, knowing that he was getting totally carried away, but unable to help himself; he had kept these emotions bottled up for so long, he couldn't stop them pouring out. 'I know this isn't a proper ring because I can't afford a proper one, but one day, if I saved up for years and years and years, then when I'm seventy-eight I might have a hope . . .' He laughed, trying to ease the intensity in his voice.

Then her voice, cold and pointed as a needle, punctured his bubble.

'Steve – I'm sorry . . . but . . .'

She untangled herself from his arms. The cold air rushed up between them.

She started saying she was on the rebound, wasn't ready for a relationship, was still heartbroken after Jason, her American ex, blah blah. Bullshit, he knew. Excuses. And yet he loved her all the more for trying to let him down gently, for the soft sympathy in her eyes.

'Oh, just ignore me,' Steve interrupted her. 'I've had too many beers, ha ha . . . you know me, I'm a weak drinker . . . three pints and I'm on the floor . . . I tried to pull the barmaid earlier but she told me where to go, so I thought I'd try my wicked way with you . . .'

Dina winced. Steve winced. He sat on a concrete slab which presumably had once been a bench.

'Steve, you'll get a wet butt, sitting there!' she joked. Awkward pause. She kicked a crushed Coke can his way. 'Come on, let's have a game of soccer, it'll be fun . . . No? Well, let's go on to a club. I'll buy you a drink. I'll even buy you a packet of peanuts if you're lucky . . .'

Steve shook his head slowly. His smile, stuck to his face like a label on a bottle, was peeling away.

'I, er, think I'll just hang out here for a while,' he said, staring at his hands. Out of the corner of his eye he watched her walk away. Every three steps she would look back and give him a sheepish smile and an awkward little wave and a 'See you at work . . .' and Steve felt as though his heart was breaking.

He sat there for a while, churned up inside. He looked up at the unsympathetic moon and he wanted to yell, 'Why don't women like me? Why is it that the bastards always get the nice girls? Why doesn't she want me? Why why why?'

Maybe he had bad breath.

Maybe his ears stuck out.

Maybe he was just doomed. Maybe he wasn't meant to be with anyone. Maybe he should become a monk.

He got up, shoved his hands in the pockets of his mackintosh and went to the edge of the canal, looking into its dark, murky depths. Rubbish floated about like strange, futuristic sea creatures. The moon was full, reflected three times in his inebriated vision, like a row of plates. *Go after Dina,* one last flicker of hope urged him. *Go on, just walk up and apologise. Try again. Do it properly this time.*

He let out a deep breath. *OK,* he thought, *I know this is utterly crazy and stupid and I shall probably have to leave the country afterwards, but I'm going to have another go.*

And this time I won't mince words. I won't try to be coy or clever or funny. I'll just tell her straight: Dina, I love you.

As he turned to go, his foot caught on something. A foil packet that had once contained an Indian takeaway. He skidded. His leg twisted under him. The sky turned upside down, the moon spun. And then *splash!* – he hit the canal.

His ears filled with water. Everything was muted and hazy. He opened his eyes, amazed to find himself suspended in the water, gazing down at the riverbed. The waving lichens and fronds; the junk, ghostly and beautiful: an old bicycle wheel, a shopping trolley and a pair of steel girders flung together like a cross. Then panic hit him like a sledgehammer.

His lungs felt as though they were going to explode. He gasped for air. Bubbles fluttered from his mouth. He started to flail about, but he only seemed to be sinking deeper, as though invisible hands were tugging his ankles, pulling him down. He glanced down and horror screamed through him: *His coat belt was caught, taut, on one of the steel girders.*

Get it off, get the coat off, he yelled into the water.

He struggled wildly, but his arms were heavy as lead. There was a high-pitched ringing in his ears. A pain behind his eyes until it felt as though they would pop. *Get it off, get it off!* his brain screamed.

Then he felt his body go limp. His lungs ballooning with water. For the first time he thought: *I'm going to die.*

Another panic attack gripped him. He flailed about, twisting the coat off one arm, but he couldn't move, he was gasping, his throat constricting as though someone was tying a cord around his neck, pulling tighter and tighter, his heart pumping, thumping in his ears louder and louder . . . like a brass band . . . and then there was just darkness.

He remembered hanging there in the water. Mentally he was still alive, yet he knew that his body was dead.

He thought to himself: *How strange.*

Then he remembered reading in a magazine that after death the human brain can still carry on living for three minutes.

He'd always wondered what dying people might think in those final three minutes. Now he knew.

He thought: *How odd. I'm about to die and I'm thinking of magazines.*

He kept waiting for his brain to suddenly black out, like a switch clicked off.

He looked up and saw litter, Coke and Lilt cans bobbing above him like metallic fish, and he thought: *Someone really ought to clean those up.*

Clean those up? he echoed incredulously. *Steve, you're about to die, and you're thinking about recycling.*

And yet it seemed entirely natural, just to carry on mentally musing and muttering . . .

Then there was a sudden snap.

Five minutes too late, his coat belt broke and he shot up to the surface of the canal, banging his head on a Coke can. After the thick pressure of water, the clean air felt like diamonds in his mouth. *I'm alive,* he thought, joy breaking inside him like sweet grapes, *oh thank God, I'm alive . . .*

So why am I floating?

I am dead. Oh God. I am.

People say that the soul is joined to the body by a silver cord. Steve certainly didn't see one. He slipped out of his body effortlessly, as though it was a baggy suit that was too big for him.

He was aware of standing upright, hovering on the water. Looking down at his body, face down in the water. Without thinking, he kicked it. Hard. It bobbed away, then got caught in the whirl of current and started to float towards the bridge. He watched it go, but he didn't feel sad. He felt a kind of wild freedom, a pure, unadulterated joy.

I'm free, he thought. *I'm utterly, utterly free.*

The type of joy he had felt as a child, running on beaches with the wind in his smile, or listening to the summer sweetness of birdsong in the morning, a joy he had forgotten and lost as an adult. He was no longer confined by his body and his image. He was no longer Steve: Steve who'd been brought up in a little suburban terrace, Steve who was a square; Steve who blushed bright red when he talked to girls; Steve who was always convinced people didn't like him and felt a flush of warmth when he found out that they did; Steve who was scared of taking risks, who sat on trains wishing he could talk to the strange woman opposite, who lay awake at night wondering what might have happened if he had had the courage to do zany things, to live life with a little daring. He felt as if his individuality had peeled away like a skin and revealed his true self beneath: unbounded and glorious, infinite and timeless. The words of a Celtic poem he had loved as a child came unbidden to his mind:

I have been a stag of seven tines, running
I have been a flood across a wide plain, flowing
I have been a wind over a deep lake, whispering
I have been a tear from the brilliant sun, glistening
I have been a hawk in my nest above the cliff, watching
I have been a wonder among the loveliest flowers, blooming
I have been a salmon in a clear pool, swimming
I have been a hill where poets walk, singing
I have been a boar upon the hills ruthless and red, roving
I have been a breaker from the winter sea, thundering
I have been a tide of the ocean, delivering to death and returning . . .

That is how I felt as I died, Steve thought, his heart skipping violently as the feeling rushed through him again. *At that moment, I felt universal. As though there was a divine sense of oneness and it touched me and swept through me. Later, it reminded me of how I felt when I first met Dina.*

4
Steve

Being a ghost had been fun at first. Although admittedly a little weird. For he didn't *feel* dead. More half-alive. There was still an echo of a heartbeat in his body. And he had a faint, funny, frosty sort of breath. He had discovered this when he had leaned over the little pot of snowdrops Dina had given him as a present to brighten up his flat and accidentally breathed on them. A second later, their white petals curled and fell to the earth like tears.

Well, thought Steve, *that certainly gives new meaning to the term bad breath.*

But it was amazing how quickly he had got used to his new state. And once he had accepted it, he had begun to quite enjoy himself.

'After all, Einstein,' he said, cheerfully tossing food into his bowl, 'I don't have to go to work any more. I don't have to worry about money. I don't have to pay tax. I don't have to worry about *anything.*'

He had brought Einstein's fish bowl into the living room to keep him company and they had sat down to spend the day watching TV. Trashy American soaps, and game shows, and *Richard and Judy*. Leisure telly, telly for the truly indulgent, for those without responsibilities. Steve had felt a faint rumbling in his stomach, like a memory of hunger. But when he'd tried eating a packet of crisps, they tasted like air; eating now felt more frustrating than satisfying, something to fill him up without giving him any pleasure.

That evening, he had climbed up the fire escape and on to the roof of his flat, gazing out over London: dark and chaotic and beautiful, city lights hanging like necklaces, all spread out before him like a galaxy of moving stars. And he'd felt a sense of exhilaration. *I can go anywhere!* he thought. *I can sneak on to a plane and fly to all those places I've wanted to go. America! The Amazon jungle! The Australian outback! I can meet kangaroos and talk to Aborigines about the meaning of life.* And yet he had found himself going back into his flat and waking up the next day and watching TV again. And the next, and the next.

He realised that he was afraid. Afraid of facing the world and seeing the impact his death had had on the people he loved.

He had to pluck up a good deal of courage to go to his funeral. It had been a rainy day and grey clouds skittered across the sky. Dina had read out a beautiful poem, 'Dirge Without Music', in a voice so quiet it was almost a whisper. And his father had made a well-intentioned but dreadful speech, about how Steve had liked riding tricycles and breeding snails as a boy, concluding with 'And let's say goodbye to Steve with a song he'd love.' And then, *then*, they'd played 'Angels' by Robbie Williams. *Robbie Williams!* Steve had seen Dina, who was sobbing inconsolably, stop and bite back a secret oh-my-God-Steve-would-hate-this smile, and despite the fact that she couldn't see him, he'd smiled too, as though they were sharing a private joke.

But seeing his father cry like a boy had upset him. So had watching them all go back to his parents' house for the party, nibbling self-consciously on canapés, their chatter muted and awkwardly British. His mother and Dina had sat on the sofa flicking through his photo album – pictures of him riding his first bike, playing on swings, kicking a football around, getting his university degree – and he had found himself standing behind them and crying with them.

He'd been worried about Dina and followed her home to make sure she was safe. Back in her flat, she had put 'Something Stupid' on her stereo, locked her bedroom door, lain on her bed and cried huge wrenching sobs. Steve had kept trying to talk to her and tell her he was OK. He tried pulling faces at her. But, of course, she couldn't hear or see him. She just lay there, hugging Roger the dog, until she drifted off to sleep.

Tenderly, Steve had sat and watched her sleeping. She looked beautiful when she was asleep, he thought. There was something soft and innocent about her, as though she was a princess in a fairytale waiting to be kissed awake.

He'd stood up, knowing he should go home. But he'd found himself leaning down over her. Her face was so close he could see every freckle and the flecks of gold in her eyelashes and the little chickenpox scar on her cheek. He felt her breath, warm and moist, against his nose, and he simultaneously experienced a deep sense of comfort and a deep sense of yearning. He lifted a trembling hand. He ached to touch her. To hold her tight and tell her she was fine. To stroke away her tears and say he would be around for as long as she needed him.

But he couldn't. Couldn't interfere, intervene, smash the sanity of her life apart. He had to let her be. And so he'd whispered, 'Good night,' into her ear and left her sleeping.

Over the next few months, Steve watched his family and friends slowly repair their lives. Gradually, his absence was no longer a pivot around which their emotions swung. His mother went back to work and after a while she stopped crying every time she had to answer the phone (which, considering she worked in a call centre, was very awkward). His father stopped drinking so much whisky and, instead of sleeping in a separate bedroom, went back to their double bed; at night they held each other close, sleeping nose to nose. His sister stopped dyeing her hair black and went back to college rather than bunking off and hanging round McDonald's.

And Dina. Dina. He felt almost pervy watching her, but it was beginning to become an addiction. He'd soon got bored of watching TV with only Einstein for company. TV, Steve realised, was for people who didn't really have lives. And OK – he didn't have a life – literally and metaphorically – but watching Dina was far more entertaining than any soap opera.

Steve had once read that *aura* was a Greek word meaning 'breath'. And he just loved being close to her: in her aura; close enough to feel her breath. He loved watching her in the mornings when she spent twenty minutes in front of the mirror, tongue poking out of the corner of her mouth, putting her hair up, putting it down, putting it in plaits, raking a comb through it, yelling at it to behave (Steve had never realised women's hair was so *complicated*). He loved watching her stand by her bedroom window in the evenings, looking at people in the street below. He loved watching her sit and bite her nails and listen to music; he loved watching her put little bits of cotton wool fluff between her toes and then bounce around her bedroom making rabbit noises at Roger, screaming with laughter as he chased her and she ended up in a heap on the carpet.

Of course, he'd expected Dina to move on, to find a boyfriend. Sure. She'd forget him eventually. Slowly time would bleach away his presence in her memory, until one day someone would mention his name and she'd say, 'Steve? Steve *who*?' But by then she would have found a great guy and got married and had two beautiful children. That was fair enough.

But it had all happened so suddenly. Just like that. A man had walked into The Greasy Spoon and quite clearly turned her life and emotions upside down. Steve had sensed it at once, in the blush in her cheeks, the dilation in her pupils, that frenzied, hair-quivering vibe of a woman on heat.

Steve knew it was unkind, but he'd been so pleased, so relieved when Dina had mucked up yesterday. For the first time since he'd died, he'd intervened. When she'd been serving the guy he had done everything he could to throw her. He'd stood so close to her his ephemeral body had nearly slipped into her solid one. And thank God, she'd made such a fool of herself it was pretty much a hundred per cent certain she'd never see him again. Thanks to a little nudge from Steve's elbow, she'd splashed a considerable amount of Coke all over Archie's table; it was just a shame it had missed his trousers, Steve thought acidly.

Steve jumped as he heard a key in the lock of the café door. His eyes flicked to the clock. It was now 8 a.m. – time had flown – and Dina, his darling Dina, was here.

He felt a smile spreading across his face.

'Hello, Dina,' he said.

It didn't matter that she couldn't hear him. It just made him feel better to talk to her.

She was half pulling off her coat when she saw an envelope lying on the mat and let out a little 'Oh' of surprise and intrigue.

'What?' Steve asked. He got up and went to her side, leaning gently over her shoulder.

The envelope was cream-coloured, stiff and expensive, and on the front, in spidery black writing, was one word: *DINA*.

'What the hell . . . ?' Dina muttered, tearing it open.

It was a newspaper cutting. From *The Observer*.

THE GREASY SPOON,
SHEPHERD'S BUSH HIGH STREET
Review by Archie Hamilton,
restaurant critic of the year

There was a photograph by his name. They both realised – with a simultaneous jolt – that it was Him.

'The guy who came by yesterday!' Dina cried out loud.

Steve swallowed and watched her caress Archie's photograph. It was one of those black-and-white, mean-and-moody ones, and Steve hated to admit it, but Archie did look good, the bastard.

'Archie Hamilton,' Dina repeated, savouring his name. 'Mmm.'

They read on:

Well, folks, I've been writing this restaurant column for three years now and this is my last review before I move on to pastures new (yes – my own restaurant, so all you critics can finally take revenge). So where did I go? Not the Ivy. Not a Gordon Ramsay bistro. I decided to live a little, let my hair down and go somewhere completely different.

Nobody expects a greasy spoon to earn Michelin stars. One doesn't go expecting one's taste buds to be subtly caressed; you expect your stomach to be satisfied with some good, honest, tasty British grub. And after eating out on about 346 million lamb racks over the past year, I thought it would be quite a refreshing change to enjoy a good old hamburger and a hot dog.

I was in for a shock.

'The Greasy Spoon' is an apt name for the place. Everything really is greasy – the decor more so than the food, rather as though a child with buttery fingers has smeared them over everything.

As for the food? Extraordinary was not the word.

The hot dog arrived, lovingly encased in the lips of a stale bun that looked like a ninety-year-old woman's labia. The sausage looked like a Yeti's penis. I took a tentative bite and started to chew. And I chewed and I chewed and I chewed until the cows came home, who looked at me with pity and advised I stick to grass. It was rather like eating brown Blu-Tac. In the end, all you could do was swallow and pray.

People say that chewing-gum takes seven years to go through your system. I should imagine that food from The Greasy Spoon remains in one's digestive tract for a lifetime. If I ever go into hospital for stomach pains, I shall certainly be sending Mr Luigi the bill.

Steve watched as Dina burst into hysterical laughter.

'Oh my God, Luigi will go mad!' she said under her breath.

'You might get the sack,' Steve pointed out.

Only one thing redeemed the place: the service. The waitress, to be exact. She looked utterly out of place, like a supermodel at a Butlin's holiday camp.

She glided about with an elegance of a ballerina, and despite the odd minor mishap, her manners were impeccable. I gave her a tip bigger than the bill and hoped to receive her phone number in return. Sadly, it never came.

And there, underneath, in loopy black fountain pen, Archie had written: *And since you didn't – here's my mobile: 0703 8564432. Call me if you'd like to go out sometime! Archie X*

Silence.

Then Steve said: 'You absolute bas—'

He was interrupted by Dina rushing around the café in the manner of a Zulu. She grabbed her mobile and keyed in a number. Then she stopped, and stood for a moment looking shocked, fingers curled so tight around the phone her knuckles protruded like sticks of chalk.

Steve peered over her shoulder and his heart stopped. It was *his* number she'd dialled. Without thinking. He was so touched, especially when she switched off her phone and said aloud, 'Steve, if only you were here to tell me what to do . . . I could ask your advice. D'you think I should call him?'

'Absolutely not!' said Steve. Oh God, if only she could hear him! 'Look, Dina, he is a total bastard. Really. Well, I admit I don't know that for certain, but I just have a bad feeling about him. Seriously. Forget him.' He watched her re-read the article and smile. 'Forget him.' He watched her dip into her back pocket and pull her mobile out again. 'Forget him. Please, Dina.' He watched her dial the number. He heard her breath grow shallow with nerves as she listened to it ring. Her palms were so sweaty that she had to rub them against her jeans.

'Um – hi – Archie?' she said breathlessly.

'Uh – yeah?' a peevish-sounding voice replied.

'It's – er – Dina here.'

'*Who?*'

Steve bunched up his fists and punched the air.

'Go on, Archie!' he cried. 'Just mess it all up. You don't even remember her, you stupid old git. How could anyone forget someone as gorgeous as Dina?'

'I – er – was the girl in the café who threw Coke – oh, forget that bit,' she said, her voice dropping. 'Look – I'm sorry to bother you – I've obviously woken you up—'

'What time is it?'

'Er – eight o'clock. Sorry – it *is* early, and I know—'

'No, I ought to have been up hours ago. But after several bottles of wine, my head aches rather,' he groaned. 'However, I'm feeling a lot better for hearing your lovely voice.'

'Oh, pass me the sick bag!' said Steve. 'Come on, Dina, you're not going to fall for his smoothie charm.' But Dina dipped her chin and let out a shy laugh.

'You have the most divine giggle too,' said Archie. His voice was now a pure caress.

'Thank you,' said Dina.

'So did you like my review?' he asked. Before she could reply, he added, 'My last *ever* review, don't forget – all just for you.'

'I thought it was very . . .' Dina searched for the right word. 'Astute.'

'Astute?' Archie chuckled. 'That's one way of putting it. So, are you going to let me wine and dine you?'

'Oh, I think you might have just about talked me into it,' Dina flirted back.

'Great.' The sound of yawning and stretching and bedclothes rustling. 'Let me just get my personal organiser and I can check when I'm free. Hang on a sec.'

'Sure, I'll check mine,' said Dina quickly. Scouring round, she grabbed a pile of napkins and rustled them against the phone. Despite himself, Steve laughed softly, charmed to see her so ruffled and excited.

'So – how about Friday night? Are you free?'

'Erm . . .' Dina pretended to look awfully hard at the Coca-Cola logo on the napkin. 'Yep. I do believe I'm free.'

'Cool. Pick you up at seven?'

'Sure.' Dina jumped as she heard the slam of Luigi entering The Greasy Spoon. 'Oops – I'd better go . . .'

'Well, you'd better give me your address first, OK?'

'It's Flat 16, London House, Orwell Street, Shepherd's Bush,' she said hastily, wincing as she heard Luigi call: '*Dina?*'

For the rest of the day, Dina walked around The Greasy Spoon with a smile on her face. She smiled when Luigi, having seen Archie's review (Dina didn't show him but plenty of smirking customers were more than happy to lend him a copy), tore it into shreds. She smiled when Luigi sacked her at eleven o'clock and then rehired her fifteen minutes later (no doubt realising he didn't have any more nieces and that nobody else was going to take the job). She smiled when she accidentally dropped a can of Pepsi on her foot, bruising her toe; when a customer was rude to her; and when Fatima suggested she could do with losing a few pounds. For it was clear Dina was on another planet, a planet called Archie, where she was being wined and dined for ever after.

And Steve stood in the shadows, watching her and feeling his heart slowly sink into his stomach.

5
Dina

Tails I go on the date with Archie, thought Dina, *heads I don't.*

She tossed the coin up into the air, watching it catch the sun and shimmer gold-silver until *thwack!* it came down and hit her palm.

Heads.

OK. So she wasn't going to go on her date with Archie. She was staying in.

She looked at the clock. Six p.m. He would be coming to pick her up in an hour, so she had better catch him before he left. She picked up her mobile and dialled his number. It rang once; she switched it off.

Best of three, she thought.

Half an hour later, the front door of the flat opened and Anita entered. Despite her rather late and vigorous night, she was glowing with health and vitality. Her Australian tan was still warm on her face and her sun-streaked hair was knotted into two fine, girlish plaits. A silvery fish sat in her pierced belly-button above the rim of her faded jeans and a pink mobile was tucked between her shoulder and her ear. She was talking at top speed whilst enthusiastically heaving two great handfuls of Sainsbury's shopping into the hall.

Seeing Dina's bedroom door was open, she popped her head round. Dina was sitting on the bed in a dressing gown, a cold cup of tea by her feet. Anita frowned.

'. . . yeah, well, see you later, nice talking, byeee . . .' She let the phone drop to the floor. 'Dina – why the hell are you sitting here? Have you lost your marbles? Archie – remember him? Your amazing date?'

'I'm not going,' said Dina flatly, pulling up her knees, winding her arms around them and defensively sitting her chin on the top.

'Not going?' Anita cried, dropping the bag of shopping she was still clutching. There was the ominous sound of cracking eggs and a huge melon rolled out and thumped across the floor like a bowling ball, but Anita was too agitated to care. 'Why on earth not?' she demanded, putting her hands on her hips. She was only five feet tall, but she made up for her lack of height with plenty of forceful feistiness.

'I'm a bit tired,' Dina muttered, trying to sound nasal and feigning a cough. 'I might be fluey . . . maybe . . . or something . . .' She looked down at her nails; one hand was polished in exquisite cerise ovals, the other was plain from when she'd suffered her change of heart.

'Oh bollocks!' Anita cried. 'That is absolute rot!' She marched over and sat on the bed. 'Come on. Tell me the truth.'

Dina buried her head in her lap.

'Dina, I thought you came to England to move on. I know you had some difficult times in New York, and maybe suffered a few crappy guys, but come on!'

'It's not just New York,' said Dina.

'Then what?'

A pause.

'It's Steve,' Dina admitted in a small voice.

'Steve. Oh. But Steve is dead.'

Anita did have a very blunt way of putting things.

'Well, I guess if you held a séance you could always bring him back and go on a date with him instead,' Anita agreed. Then, seeing Dina's face, she said, 'Sorry. But I didn't really think you were that keen on Steve. I mean, don't you remember how you used to ask me for advice and we'd have those long discussions about how he was your friend and you were worried he wanted more and you didn't want to ruin your friendship and it was freaking you out?'

'Well, yes,' Dina said. 'I know. I was never quite sure how I felt about him . . . I mean – we were so close, we were more like brother and sister.'

'So . . . ?'

'Well . . . it's more than that . . .'

'What, then?'

Dina didn't reply for some time. Then she said:

'I just . . . I know this sounds completely crazy . . .'

'Go on.'

'Well, I just . . . it's as though he's still around. Every day, I go to church and light a candle—'

'Do you?' Anita looked astonished.

'Yes. And this morning, something weird happened. I was at the church, looking at the message boards, and there was a KitKat lying there. Steve always used to buy me KitKats. He – and he alone – knew they're my absolute favourite.'

'Well, it might have been for Harvest Festival.'

'A KitKat?' Dina wrinkled her nose. 'You give old people tinned peaches and packets of custard, not KitKats.'

'Don't be so ageist. I once slept with a fifty-year-old who loved jelly babies and he liked to eat them off my—'

'OK, fine,' said Dina, waving her hand quickly before any more details could emerge.

'Seriously,' said Anita, 'there are two ways of reacting to grief – in fact, to anything in life. You can either let it drag you down, drown you, if you'll pardon the expression. Or you can just let it go and move on and accept that life is unpredictable. You or I could walk out of this flat tomorrow and get hit by a bus, but that's all the more reason to make the most of life and enjoy it while you've still got it. It's too late for Steve now. And look, he's probably happy in heaven.'

Dina smiled through her tears.

'I always used to joke with him that if I ever went to heaven it would be filled with KitKat trees. And he joked back that his heaven would have angels playing Norah Jones on harps, and clouds tasting of Guinness.'

'He's probably having a cloud-pint right now.'

Or he's just a skeleton in a box, Dina thought with a shiver. But then she looked up at Anita and managed another smile.

'When you're not drunk you can be very wise,' she said with gruff affection, giving her flatmate a hug.

'*Very* wise,' said Anita. 'And that's not all. Look what I found on the tube.' She rifled through her tasselled suede handbag, pulling out a dog-eared magazine. It was one of those glossy society magazines full of coiffeured stars draped on chintz sofas or leaning against fireplaces in their huge mansions with envy-me smiles plastered across their faces. Anita flicked through impatiently, finally reaching a page entitled 'Hot Gossip'. Dina winced. And then gasped. For there, there at the top of the page, was Archie.

It was a lovely photograph of him. It had clearly been taken at some sort of fancy charity do, for he was wearing black tie and it made him look terribly handsome and elegant. He had his arm loosely draped around a blonde girl in a little black dress. Dina was surprised at the spurt of acid jealousy in her stomach.

'So he's with someone.'

'No, silly!' Anita exclaimed. 'Learn to read!'

For beneath the photograph it said:

ARCHIE HAMILTON:
ELIGIBLE BACHELOR OF THE YEAR

Now that Archie has broken up with society girl Heidi Crumpington, he is young, free ('I'm certainly free for anyone ravishing,' he was quoted as saying recently) and definitely single. After the death of his entrepreneur father, Vincent Hamilton, Archie, his only son, has now inherited the trendy and exclusive 'exquisite' chain of restaurants. As well as hanging out with A-list stars, he is now also sitting on an estimated £50 million fortune. And that's not all. Archie is an Adonis with a brain. Before his father's death, he made his name as a successful journalist and columnist, including his infamously acerbic restaurant reviews for *The Observer.* He's just given up his column so he can spend more time in his restaurant (oh, not to mention hanging out on his private yacht and taking trips to the huge Scottish castle his high-flying charity-bash-organising mother owns). So come on, girls, nab him quick before Victoria Hervey makes a play . . .

'But he's famous!' Dina said. 'God – I never realised. I mean, I thought he must be pretty important if he wrote for *The Observer*, but – wow!'

'See?' said Anita. 'Now – go and get ready. You have to look fabulous.'

'But it's 6.30!' Dina panicked. 'He'll be here in half an hour!'

The next twenty minutes were absolutely frantic as Anita cast herself as Dina's Fairy Godmother. She rejected Dina's cautious suggestion of wearing jeans and a sparkly top and insisted on yanking out the little black dress that had been tucked away in the back of Dina's wardrobe, bought half-price in a sale and never worn. Then she sat Dina down on a stool and brushed her hair into a static sheen, coiled it expertly into a twirl and fastened it with two butterfly-shaped diamante pins. She smothered foundation over Dina's skin, painted her eyes with thick black eyeliner until they were two Egyptian almonds and turned her pale lips into a fuchsia pout. Finally she stopped for breath and stepped backwards, eyes sparkling, fingers aching, surveying her Pygmalion creation. She broke into a wide smile.

'You see?' she said. 'You can look utterly amazing, if you make the effort.'

But Dina pulled an uncertain face. She rubbed her bare arms, feeling cold after the fuzzy warmth of her usual thick sweaters.

'D'you think I'm a bit . . . I don't know . . . overdressed?' She turned and gave her jeans a poignant look, like a child spotting a favourite teddy bear they have been instructed to grow out of.

'Uh-uh,' said Anita, whipping them away and holding them behind her back, laughing. 'Look, I'm sure Archie is just dying to see you in a pair of jeans. I'm sure he doesn't want to see your lovely legs at all. What a way to torture him, Dina, what a way to put him off.'

'OK,' said Dina, finally managing a smile. 'I know, I know, I know. I'm just nervous.'

They were interrupted by the shrilling of the doorbell. Anita went to the window and peered out.

'Oh my God!' she exclaimed.

'What? Don't peek!' Dina hissed. 'He'll see you looking! Anita!' She burst into embarrassed, exasperated laughter. 'Anita! Come here, now!' She stamped her foot.

'Yes, but you have to come and see this.'

'No! Just tell me what. I refuse to come and peek out of the window. He'll see!'

'Well in that case, you'll have to find out for yourself,' said Anita, pushing her forward.

'*Anita!*'

'If I tell you, it will spoil the surprise.' Anita passed her her coat and bag. 'Have a great time.'

They hugged tightly. Dina felt a thump of affection for her flatmate: she might be insane, but she had the biggest of hearts.

As Anita went into the hallway to sort her shopping out, Dina picked her way down the stairs, resisting the urge to pull off her stilettos, dash upstairs and pull on her comfy boots. She paused in front of the door, wishing she wasn't quite so nervous. Then she opened it.

And there was Archie. He was wearing a sharp black suit and looking much sexier in real life than in his photo, which had failed to capture his charisma, his air of irresistible wickedness. Dina felt his eyes slide over her appreciatively and silently thanked Anita for hiding the jeans – she would have been ridiculously underdressed. The black dress was just right.

'Hi, hon,' he said, leaning in. He meant to kiss her on the cheek, but in her nervousness Dina twisted her head at the last minute. Their noses bumped awkwardly and the kiss landed on her eyelid. She laughed sheepishly and then jumped as something came thumping down the stairs and landed by her feet. A floor up, Anita called, 'Shit – sorry!'

'A melon.' Archie blinked, looking down. 'How surreal.'

'We'd better go before she starts chucking the rest of her shopping down,' said Dina, and he laughed and she laughed and some sort of ice was broken.

Dina tried not to do an obvious double-take when she saw the car. But it was hard not to genuflect. It looked like the sort of thing superheroes' alter egos drove. Long, black and as shiny as patent leather. And with a *driver,* sitting behind the wheel in a peaked cap. She slid inside, breathing in the smell of luxury, of expensive leather, of money and debauchery, and sighed. *God, I could get used to this,* she thought.

'Where are we going?' she asked Archie.

'Ah,' said Archie, 'that would be telling. That would spoil the surprise.'

And he gave her such an intense, sexy glance that she had to turn away and look out of the window. A voice in her head that sounded suspiciously like her mother kept telling her not to get too excited. But she couldn't help it; she already felt – no, *knew* – this was going to be the best date she'd been on in a long, long time.

There wasn't much opportunity for talking in the limo. Mostly because every time they were about to break the slightly self-conscious silence, Archie's mobile shrilled and he started chatting away, rolling his eyes and mouthing, 'Sorry!' – though he wasn't sorry enough to switch his phone off, Dina noted. As she started to bite her nails, he slapped her gently, and winked at her.

'Sorry, disgusting habit,' she muttered in nervous agreement.

As the limo slid through the streets, she found herself looking up, past the crowds walking by, out for clubs and dinner and theatre, past the jagged silhouette of restaurant rooftops, up to the spray of stars glittering in the sky. She remembered how Steve used to love looking up at them; he even had a telescope on the roof of his flat. He'd swivel it round and show her the Big Dipper and Lyra and Orion, and if the night was very clear, they might even see Venus, sparkling like a diamond, or the flaming orange tail of a rare comet.

She turned back to Archie, chewing her lip, watching him talking. He was telling someone off now, his face creased into a frown. Then she smiled and felt something liquid pass through her, as though she had been holding every muscle in her body tense and had now let go. *Enjoy yourself,* she echoed Anita. It was going to be a great evening.

6

Dina

After a further twenty minutes of crawling through traffic, they pulled up on a noisy street, the driver ignoring irritated toots from taxis and cars squeezing past. As they got out of the limo, Dina did a double-take. She could have sworn she'd just seen an extremely famous actress who was headlining a new production of *The Prime of Miss Jean Brodie* and had been splattered all over the *Evening Standard* just yesterday stroll past and walk into the hugely expensive restaurant in front of them.

Then she realised Archie was leading her into the very same place.

'We're going in here?' Suddenly Dina felt panicked. Look at those tiny gold letters saying *exquisite*. With a small 'e'. Restaurants with names that began with small letters cost a bomb. The starter would probably be £100. What if Archie was a modern guy and expected to go halves?

'Well, I do own it,' said Archie lightly.

'You—' Dina swallowed back several awed expletives. She remembered the article Anita had showed her. Of course. 'Wow. Great.'

He led her inside.

It was gorgeous. It positively dripped class. Waiters dressed in black glided about carrying large white plates which practically seemed to float on their fingertips, tiny cordon bleu creations crouched in the middle like modern works of art. Everywhere Dina looked, there was a celebrity. And whilst she was breaking out into a sweat of excitement, Archie was calmly calling out hellos and nodding at them.

As they made their way to the back of the restaurant, Dina felt a bit anxious. She just wasn't comfortable with this sort of scene. She was used to takeaways on her lap and watching telly on the sofa with Anita, or Pizza Hut, a place she and Steve had frequented regularly.

At least it'll just be the two of us alone now, she thought, *and we can relax and really get to know each other.*

Half an hour later, Dina could hardly believe how wonderful she felt. *Over the past few months,* she thought, taking a delicious sip of wine, *I've been spending most nights in, watching TV and feeling faintly depressed, or else getting dragged out to dodgy wine bars by Anita and being chatted up by slimeballs. And now, here I am in one of London's top restaurants, being wined and dined by one of the sexiest men I have ever met, and I can see him flicking glances at me, just little surreptitious ones when he thinks I'm not looking, as though he wants to eat me up.*

'D'you like your mushrooms?' Archie asked, smiling across at her. He had ordered for her, declaring he knew just what she would like.

'I love it, I love it,' Dina cried, and Archie laughed at her exuberance. 'No, I'm not just saying this – I really love it. I *love* food.'

'Hmm,' said Archie, sweeping his eyes over her and making her blush. 'You've very slim, considering. Still, I guess there isn't much in the way of culinary temptation at The Greasy Spoon. Have you always been a waitress?'

'Oh God – no. Only for just over a year, well, actually more like eighteen months – since I moved to England.'

'And back in the US, in . . .?'

'New York – yeah, I lived all my life there, until now.'

'Back in New York, what were you then? A model?'

'If only.' Dina smiled again, thinking that Archie was a charmer, and that flattery would get him everywhere.

'So what did you do?' Archie pressed, filling up her glass. 'Drink up, then we'll order another bottle. I want to hear everything about your life. All the jobs you've done, what your parents are like, and who your last boyfriend was.'

'OK,' Dina laughed. 'Well, y'know – I've never really known what I wanted to do, and with the dyslexia thing, I'm not all that well qualified – I didn't go to college. So I've kind of flitted from one job to another. You name it, I've tried it – I've worked in a kindergarten, with kids, I've worked in offices, pushing around paperclips and making cups of coffee, I've worked as a cleaner, um, a librarian's assistant, an artist's model – keeping my clothes on, I'd like to add. I mean, you name it, I've done it.'

'Golly. And you didn't settle on any of them? None of them grabbed you?'

'Well, you know, I have had this one dream of what I'd really love to do . . .' She trailed off, fingering a languorously dropping orchid in the vase on the table.

'Go on.'

'No – it's silly, really. I've just always had this dream that I'd like to have my own café. I'd call it Dina's and just sell the most delicious sandwiches and cakes and have this really cosy, homely place where people could just hang out.'

'Well, you should go for it,' said Archie heartily.

'Oh no, no, I mean, it'd be crazy. I don't have any experience, I'm not ready – it's just a silly fantasy.'

'Fuck that. I didn't have any experience of owning restaurants but I didn't let that stop me, I just plunged in. You should simply wake up tomorrow and buy a café.'

'Well, I don't know how long I'm going to stay in England.'

Archie's face fell.

'I mean, I mean, I was kind of planning to leave, but now I think maybe I might stay. I'm not sure.'

'I can see you enjoy making decisions.'

Dina laughed, shaking her head and gulping back more wine. Archie filled her glass again.

'I can't believe you're single!' he cried. 'Have you not met any nice British men yet?'

Dina squirmed, enjoying his flirting but wondering if she ought to tell the truth.

'To be honest,' she said, 'I haven't had so much as a kiss since arriving in England.'

Archie's jaw dropped.

'But why on earth . . . ?'

Dina swallowed and looked up at him. His face was open and she suddenly had an overwhelming desire to confide in him, to tell him all about Jason and her fear of having her heart broken again and all the lonely nights she spent in her bedroom listening to CDs and watching people and feeling like some sad old spinster.

She was thinking about how to begin telling him all this when she suddenly became aware of a group of noisy, young and rather glamorous people who had entered the restaurant and were heading towards the back. *God, I hope they don't sit next to us,* Dina prayed, fearing they would burst the bubble.

Then, to her shock, a girl with long blonde hair that was so straight it looked like it had been ironed, and wearing a tartan miniskirt and fur-lined boots, stopped beside them and flung her arms around Archie.

'Archie! Here you are! We thought you were going to be at the Groucho – we've been looking *all* over London for you!' She squealed so loudly Dina was amazed the glasses didn't break.

'Heidi!' Archie kissed her on each cheek. 'Lovely to see you.' He waved to the rest of the group and was immediately yanked into a series of hugs and kisses and slaps on the back.

Great, thought Dina, pleating her napkin and trying hard to conceal her irritation, *so much for our intimate tête-à-tête.*

Archie turned to her, and, realising that she was feeling left out, tugged her up from her seat, putting a firm arm around her and introducing her to everyone. 'Guys, this is the very wonderful Dina – whom I hope you are all going to apologise to for interrupting our dinner.'

Dina smiled, feeling slightly mollified by Archie's exuberant charm.

'Then again, maybe it's just as well you meet my friends now rather than later – you may as well get to grips with the fact that they're all *completely* bonkers. This is Jim . . .' a fat guy with a goatee grinned, 'Tina and Louise . . .' a pair of impossibly glamorous Japanese twins, who nodded unsmilingly, 'Ralph . . .' a man in a sharp suit with a sensitive face and elegant cheekbones mouthed, 'Hi', 'Brian . . .' a guy with very messy blond hair and hoary sideburns, who was wearing a dirty leather jacket and didn't appear to have washed for some time, grimaced, 'oh – and Heidi, of course.'

Heidi's lips smiled, but her eyes didn't catch up.

'D'you mind if they join us?' Archie asked Dina, stroking her cheek.

'Of course she doesn't mind!' Jim roared, clapping Dina on the back. 'Do you, Dina?'

'Well – I mean – sure.' Dina smiled uncertainly. 'Sure. That's fine.'

As they all piled into seats, Dina was more than a little taken aback to see that Heidi had stolen her chair and was now firmly plonked down next to Archie.

'Er – ahem,' Dina stood beside her, clearing her throat in a pointed fashion, arms dangling awkwardly.

'Oh, Dina doesn't have a seat!' Heidi cried, feigning innocence.

'You can sit on my lap,' Jim called out with a plump wink.

Archie saw Dina's face and opened his mouth to intervene, but Heidi had already leapt up theatrically, crying, 'Oh, poor darling – we are all being so frightfully rude leaving her standing there!'

Then, before the waiter could intervene, Heidi darted forward and grabbed a chair from a nearby coffee table, placing it between Brian and Jim. By coincidence, it also happened to put Dina as far away from Archie as possible.

Dina sat down, and was perturbed to discover that her seat, designed as it was for a coffee table, was much lower than everyone else's.

'Oh, you look so sweet down there,' Heidi giggled.

'Now I know what it feels like to be a dwarf,' Dina said, trying to jolly along. She saw Archie gazing at her with concern and she quickly smiled and mouthed, 'I'm OK.'

'Oh, this really will not do. This really will not do!' Ralph laid his manicured hands on the table and gestured for the waiter to get Dina a proper seat, apologising profusely.

'Thanks,' said Dina gratefully, wondering if she had ever met anyone as posh or as gay as Ralph.

'Ralph is *such* a gallant gentleman,' said Archie, and for some reason everyone exploded into hysterical laughter. Clearly this was a private joke, Dina thought, joining in in confusion.

'Well, since you've only had starters, we can join you for the main course,' Jim said, rubbing his enormous stomach.

They all ordered mains, Archie heavily dictating what they should have. As he became engrossed in conversation, Dina tried to strike up a friendly chat with Brian, but it was nearly impossible. For one thing, he seemed completely off his head. Secondly, he didn't look at her, so all she could see was the hooked profile of his nose and a large furry blond sideburn.

Dina felt Archie's eyes on her again. She was touched by his concern, but at the same time, a feisty, resilient part of her wanted to resist playing the damsel in distress and making him feel guilty. She wanted to prove that she was fitting in, so she nodded quickly and said, 'Really, Brian, that's fascinating.'

She was relieved, then, when Jim leaned over and whispered in her ear, 'Don't worry about Brian. He's mad, and none of us ever have a clue what he's saying. He plays bass in a rock band,' he added, as though that explained everything.

'What band is that?'

'Headbangers Inc. Nobody's ever heard of them, because every time they organise a gig, only half of them turn up, the other band members being too off their heads to bother. But they have now finally managed to get it together to release an album called *A Jagged Piece of Sleep*.'

Dina giggled.

'What do you do then?' she asked.

'I'm a film director.' He patted his fat stomach.

'Oh God, you're all so glamorous.'

'Oh, but not as glam as Ralph,' said Jim, with a grin. 'Ralph is a fashion designer.'

'Are you talking about me?' Ralph smiled.

'Yes, we are, you poofter,' Jim said affectionately. 'I was about to tell Dina how your designs are worn by half of fashionable London.'

'Oh, it's just a little hobby,' said Ralph, flushing modestly. 'And really, my designs are brought to life by the exquisiteness of the women who wear them. After all, as Marcus Aurelius once said,

"Anything in any way beautiful derives its beauty from itself and nothing beyond itself. Praise is no part of it, for nothing is made better or worse by praise—"' He broke off as Archie feigned a yawn.

'What about you, Dina?' Heidi suddenly interjected, expertly twiddling spaghetti on her fork. 'What do you do?'

'I – I'm a waitress,' Dina said.

There was a long silence.

'Dina works at The Greasy Spoon,' said Archie. 'You know, the one I wrote a review about.'

Heidi nearly choked on her spaghetti.

'Oh, how sweet . . .' She trailed off, wordless.

'Well, I want to get something more interesting,' Dina said, feeling her cheeks burn. 'But you know, I only just moved here from America, and it's a new place, and so . . .'

She was grateful to Jim when he asked her, in a kindly tone, where in the US she was from, and then started nattering on about a gangster movie he'd shot in Chicago. Relieved at the change in subject matter, Dina tried to wrap spaghetti round her fork, wishing she didn't coat her chin with a layer of sauce every time she took a mouthful.

'When I was last in the US,' Heidi said, 'I found myself standing in a bar in New York with Christy Turlington on one side of me and Salma Hayek on the other. It just made me feel so *ugly*.' She shook her head as the others murmured inevitable protests. 'No, really. I mean, I just stood there and thought, "How can I be a model? What do they see in me?"'

'Dina could be a model,' said Archie, smiling.

'Oh, I'm not sure if she's really tall enough,' said Heidi quickly, narrowing her eyes. 'But you could do small-height modelling,' she advised earnestly. 'I could put you in touch with someone.'

'Miaow,' said Jim under his breath. Dina grinned softly, relieved to have an ally.

'God, this food is just *so* delicious,' she said, tucking heartily into her salad. 'Archie must have had masses of fabulous reviews.'

'Reviews!' Ralph giggled. 'Indeed, Archie has enjoyed heaps of fabulous reviews. Except for—'

'Oh God!' Archie cried theatrically. 'No! Don't remind me!'

'What? What?' Dina asked, gazing around in confusion as everyone started laughing.

'Go on, tell her, Archie,' Jim called out.

Archie shook his head, smiling, leaving Ralph to play the storyteller.

'Once upon a time,' Ralph said, making them all giggle by putting on a Listen-with-Mother voice, 'there was a restaurant reviewer called Michael Mackman, who wasn't overly fond of Archie. Some might attribute this to Michael being jealous of Archie's success, since when Mackman tried to set up a floating restaurant in the Thames, it sank without trace – metaphorically speaking. He came in, ate a three-course meal at exquisite, on the house, told Archie he'd never had a better meal and then wrote a review declaring Archie to be a "jumped-up public schoolboy who knows nothing about food and everything about image, who is just frittering away his father's money".'

'Yes, Ralph,' Archie hissed. 'I know the review well, I don't need reminding.'

Heidi put a reassuring hand on Archie's wrist.

'Anyway,' Ralph giggled, 'a few weeks later, we're all eating in the restaurant when Mackman has the nerve to turn up, with a blonde floozy hanging off his arm, and expect to be served. So Archie writes a note, puts it on a silver tray and gets the waiter to take it over to him.'

'What did it say?' Dina cried.

'It said: "Oscar Wilde once noted in *Dorian Gray* that brains and beauty are frequently incompatible, and I feel you are simply too handsome to eat in my restaurant."' Ralph burst into laughter.

'Oh God, you should have seen the look on Mackman's face!' Jim howled. 'You never want to get on the wrong side of Archie – he's a Scorpio, with a sting in his tail!'

Dina looked over at Archie uneasily, but he winked at her playfully and she started laughing. He stared deep into her eyes, laughing too, and for one delicious moment it was as though the rest of the group had faded away and it was just the two of them, sharing their own private joke.

Then Heidi swung round and put her arm around Archie and the bubble burst.

*

They returned to their main courses, chatting and drinking and eating. Dina's friendly, affable manner enabled her to join in fairly well, but the flow of wine and good food failed to ease a certain sense of tension. She was fascinated by Archie's friends. They all had certain surface traits in common: their good looks, their charisma, their obvious wealth, their seemingly effortless success in life, their witty conversation. At the same time, they were a mixture of contrasts and oddities: Brian looked as though he ought to be manning the pumps at a petrol station, Ralph as though he'd just stepped out of the debating chamber at the Oxford Union, Heidi as though she'd been peeled off the front of a lads' magazine; and yet, unified by Archie, they made the most wonderfully colourful combination. Archie, Dina noted, controlled everything. The menu, the bills, the conversation. He was slightly less witty than Ralph, but everyone always laughed a lot harder at his jokes. His charisma was so strong that it was a little like being in a group of subjects gathered around a king.

Whilst Ralph and Jim were intermittently friendly to Dina, Tina and Louise ignored her completely and Heidi only paid her attention when she felt Archie was paying her too much. Dina longed to fit in, but she couldn't help the horrible feeling that she wasn't quite good enough for them. Then her feisty side surfaced and reminded her: *Well, who cares what they think of you?* Still she felt inadequate. They drove home the point, all too forcefully, that she had achieved nothing since arriving in England. *I mustn't go away tonight and forget this evening,* she told herself fiercely, *I must go back and make a fresh start, get my life moving, set some goals for myself. Hand in my notice to Luigi tomorrow and start applying for something more glamorous.*

'Would you like dessert?' the waiter enquired, collecting their dishes.

'I hope you have at least two chocolate-related desserts on your menu,' Dina said to Archie, 'or I think your restaurant ought to lose a Michelin star.'

Archie grinned. Heidi, who was busy working out which dessert had the fewest calories, looked vexed. Ralph remarked, rather predictably:

'Of course, the reason women love chocolate is because the pheromones are the same as a post-coital high.'

'That's why a lot of very lonely women find chocolate becomes an unhealthy addiction,' Heidi said, adding, 'I haven't eaten it for years.'

'Does eating bad chocolate feel like bad sex then?' Dina mused idly. 'You buy a cheap bar of supermarket chocolate and you have a dirty feeling in your stomach afterwards. You eat Godiva and it's so rich it has to be slow and sensual and you're in heaven for hours.'

The table burst into laughter and she nearly jumped; she hadn't even intended to be witty. Jim nudged her and whispered that she had a filthy mind. Dina felt a flash of warmth and acceptance inside. These guys were OK, she thought, with inebriated affection; underneath their pretensions they were only human.

'I'll have a fruit salad,' Heidi said, much to Dina's disgust. Dina had once known a guy who'd declared he couldn't be friends with anyone who didn't like *Captain Corelli's Mandolin.* She felt rather the same about people who ordered fruit salad. It wasn't a pudding at all. It was mostly water. It was for people who didn't understand pleasure or the point of life.

The puddings arrived. Dina ought to have enjoyed her chocolate brownie immensely. It came in a thin dark slab with a mint leaf on the top and a rich green sauce glooped around the edges, and was dusted with cocoa sugar that fluffed over her tongue and choked deliciously in her throat. But she barely tasted it, for she was too busy trying not to watch Archie, who was feeding Heidi fruit, slice by slice. As juice slithered down his fingers, her pink tongue flicked out and licked it off and Archie laughed drunkenly.

It looked as though fruit salad could be more depraved than Dina had thought.

'Naughty boy, Archie,' said Jim reprovingly.

Dina dug hard into her brownie, making herself eat every last damn mouthful. The group, having finally let her in, seemed to shut her out again. Dina felt her vivacious spirits dampen and her sparkle slipping away. It was hard to think of witty things to say when, out of the corner of her eye, she was painfully aware of Heidi leaning in to Archie and whispering private things in his ear. As time passed, it felt harder and harder to crowbar herself into the conversation.

Finally she put down her fork, feeling rather sick, and mumbled that she needed the toilet. As she got up, her napkin fell to the floor; she picked it up, aware of Archie looking up at her with unreadable eyes.

In the Ladies', she let out a deep breath. She was over-reacting, she told herself. Besides, Archie wasn't to blame. Until his posse had turned up, he had been utterly charming and sweet. Heidi was the one throwing herself at him, *and* he did know her well, *and* he was drunk. *Am I just making excuses for him?* she thought. *Am I being like one of those naïve women who marry womanisers and believe that the lipstick on their collars got there by mistake – right on our first date?* Then she told herself moodily: *Oh, I've only just met him. Stop overanalysing it. But there* was *such a strong connection between us earlier . . .*

In the toilet cubicle, she sat on the seat and put her face in her hands. *Oh God, Steve,* she said in a slurred voice, *what am I doing here? I don't belong at all.*

I wish I hadn't drunk so much. Before you died, I used to love drinking. I'd get all bubbly and fizzy and outgoing. But now when I drink it's different. I feel as if I can't escape you; I feel drawn back to you. Drawn back into the darker stuff I can ignore during the day. It seems to wash over me like liquid melancholy and I don't want to be with people. I feel distant from them, as though I've been through something none of them can understand. I just feel like I want to be on my own and sitting by my bedroom window, looking up the stars and pretending you're there with me.

She got up and flushed the toilet, checking her watch. 10.50 p.m. She hadn't called her parents yet, either. She usually rang them every night, but earlier she'd been too nervous about her date. Maybe now was a good time to make her excuses.

Back in the restaurant, she saw Heidi still whispering into Archie's ear and suddenly her temper erupted. *That's it,* she thought. *Sod him. I don't have to put up with this; I'm not going to compete against her; I'm going home.*

And she strolled right out of the restaurant, ignoring the calls and waves and Ralph's 'Is the fair lady leaving so soon?'

Outside, the night air was cool and lovely. A taxi veered past, and she was about to flag it down when Archie came storming out of the restaurant.

'I was looking for you! You ran off!'

'Well, are you surprised?' she snapped. Seeing him raise his eyebrows, she crossed her arms and turned away, saying quietly: 'I just think, you know, it's getting late . . .'

'Late! Late! What?' he cried, playfully indignant. 'The night has only just begun – we were going to go clubbing. Why, none of us are even *thinking* about going to bed before three . . . and look, it's only eleven. What happens if it gets past midnight? Don't tell me, you turn into a pumpkin. There, I've made you smile now,' he said, reassured by the tweaking of her lips. 'What's the matter, aren't you enjoying yourself? Is it Heidi?'

When Dina shrugged awkwardly, he cried:

'It is, isn't it? Look, I'm sorry about her. Sorry we were a bit . . . touchy-feely back there. I didn't mean to upset you. It's just – she's my ex, and she's madly jealous of you. She's jealous of any new girl I bring along, but she's especially jealous of you.'

'Well, I've tried to be nice to her!' Dina cried.

'Which only makes it worse. You're beautiful, that's the problem.'

Dina chewed her lip. She felt both manipulated and mollified.

'At the end of the day, it might all seem bitchy, but it's only because she's hurting like mad. She misses me, and she wants us to get back together, but it isn't going to happen, OK? Look, I'll tell her to stop being a bitch or she's not allowed to come.'

'Don't say that, she'll hate me!'

Archie responded by putting his arms around her and kissing her. It was a soft, tender kiss: one of the best she'd ever had. Dina looked up at him, at his red-laced smiling eyes, and then past him to the spray of stars stretching out across the sky, distant and lonely. She lowered her face and nodded.

'OK, I'll come.' She swallowed, and then said slightly shakily, 'But, look, I'm not going to stand around watching you flirt with other girls, OK?'

'OK,' Archie shrugged, grinning. 'I promise I'll stop being a bad boy. Just for you.'

Dina, smiling and frowning all at the same time, couldn't help feeling that Archie rather enjoyed being told off.

7
Dina

Dina returned to the restaurant and enjoyed coffee and liqueurs with the others, and by the time they headed out to Archie's car, she had drunk so much she had managed to go beyond her melancholy. Lights blurred, colours and voices swam. She was glad when she felt Archie's hand on her back, gently guiding her.

Much to Dina's relief, Heidi dropped out, declaring she had a shoot the next day and needed her 'beauty sleep'. Dina had to bite her lip to stop herself from breaking into a cheer.

After that, the night was a riotous rollercoaster of dancing, conversation and even more drinking. They went to a dimly lit private members' club where they knocked back outrageously priced cocktails and jived to 70s music. Dina, who hadn't been dancing for ages, felt herself letting go and becoming utterly exhilarated. She was spun by Archie and swirled gallantly by Ralph; she twirled between Brian and Jim, who grinned and stomped along with her. Finally, she felt accepted; finally she felt part of their crowd, and it was wonderful.

From the moment they entered the club to the moment they left, beautiful girls swarmed over Archie from all directions. Dina felt pleased and victorious when Archie behaved himself, pointedly avoiding their kisses, curling his arm around her and introducing her to them. The jealousy flashing in their mascaraed eyes and trembling in their polished handshakes was so strong Dina felt increasingly proud to have ensnared him. And then nervous. Why had he chosen her when he could have all these babes? What did she have that they didn't? Then she told herself off; she did deserve him, of course she did.

After the dancing, Dina felt exhausted and was ready to collapse into bed, but Archie insisted they all go back to Brian's hotel room; Brian had moved out of his flat because he was about to go on tour with his band.

As they entered the hotel, she noticed the manager, a small elfin man with white hair, look up from behind his desk. His glare was unmistakable, and when Archie called out a cheery, 'Evening,' it intensified. They hurried across the expanse of diamond-patterned carpet and into the lift.

'Christ, I feel like I'm back at Winchester again – a naughty schoolboy having to run past the Head,' said Archie, chuckling.

'The last time Brian stayed here,' Ralph informed Dina, 'Brian and Archie had too much to drink and trashed the hotel room.'

'We did not *trash* the hotel room,' Archie cut in, 'we merely broke the television. And that was because Brian tripped over the wire.'

Brian snorted. Dina looked from Brian to Archie and back to Brian, and laughed.

As Brian fumbled with his room key, an elderly man dressed in a red flannel dressing-gown came out of the room next door and hooked a DO NOT DISTURB sign on the handle. An elderly female voice wavered out, 'Leonard, could you call reception and ask them to bring some Horlicks up? I simply can't get to sleep.' They all exchanged glances and tried not to giggle too obviously.

They raided the mini-bar, played cards, put on music at top volume. Dina felt mildly uneasy when Brian laid out several lines of coke.

'Not for me, thanks,' said Ralph, sipping his orange juice.

'So boring,' Archie teased him, and Ralph coloured. 'But then you *are* the gallant gentleman, Ralph.'

'Come on, Dina, won't you have one?' Brian cajoled her as Archie snorted a line, his eyes glittering.

Dina felt dizzy with drink and confusion. There was something infectiously debauched about Archie; he made her feel as though she might lose all her morals and boundaries and do anything. But another half of her was pointing out primly: *Dina, this is silly. You're not a teenager, you're a grown woman. You don't have to take drugs just to please your man. You hate drugs, remember?*

To her relief, Archie sensed her doubt and told Brian to leave her alone.

Suddenly they were interrupted by a banging at the door.

'OPEN UP!' a hoarse and angry-sounding Irish voice bellowed. 'THIS IS THE MANAGER! WILL YOU OPEN THE DOOR!'

Brian tried to get up – which, given the cocktail of drugs and drinks swirling about in his system, was no easy feat. Archie pushed him back down. Strolling cockily to the door, he opened it a crack and said in a mockingly polite voice, rather like John Cleese in *Fawlty Towers*, 'What seems to be the problem?'

'The music! The people next door have complained.'

'Oh, they would,' Archie muttered. 'Next they'll be complaining that their Horlicks has curdled. God, this is boring. Come on, Dina, let's go home. You guys can stay and listen to your *quiet* music.'

Outside the hotel, Archie suddenly tensed.

'Shit, shit, shit,' he muttered under his breath. 'How the hell did they get here? I didn't even see them following us. Right, Dina. We're going to have to run.'

'What? Why—'

Suddenly a light flashed in front of Dina's eyes. A reporter seemed to come out of nowhere, yelling, 'So, Archie, is this your new girl? Heidi out, is she?'

The journalist grabbed Dina's coat and refused to let go. She panicked and thwacked him with ineffectual gentleness. Archie leaned over and hit him. The reporter yelled and fell back. Dina was in shock. Archie pulled her into his car and slammed the door. As they pulled away, he glared out of the back window, flicking V signs.

What a night, thought Dina. Feeling this was all too much for her, she leaned over and asked the driver to drop her off at her flat.

Archie slid up close and put a comforting arm around her.

'God, I'm sorry about all that. What a way to end the evening.' But as he drew back, there was a Cheshire cat's smile on his face. 'Still, at least you can say that a night out with me is *never* boring.'

Dina smiled shakily. She frowned as Archie pulled out his mobile and switched it off.

He turned to face her. She was staring at her lap. He slipped his fingers under her chin and kissed her very softly.

She pulled back, smiling shyly up at him, her stomach pure jelly. He stared down at her, unsmiling, stroking a finger down from her temple, across the angle of her cheek and along her jaw, pushing it into her mouth. She bit it lightly. Then he leaned in for another, stronger kiss.

Dina felt a sigh ripple through her.

'Are you sure you want to go back to your place?' Archie whispered in her ear, his breath warm on her neck. 'Sure you don't want to come back to mine?'

I am dying to go back to your place, Dina replied silently, but aloud she said, 'I think maybe I should just go home . . .' *Make him wait, make him wait, make him wait . . .* 'I mean, I—'

But he interrupted her with another kiss, sliding his tongue into her mouth.

They kissed the whole journey back. At first she felt self-conscious, fretting that the driver might be watching them. But Archie's caresses were secretive, playful, discreet. He trickled his fingers through her hair. Caressed the back of his knuckles down the length of her neck and across her collarbone. Under the veil of darkness, he slid his little finger just under the hem of her dress, caressing the delta of skin above her suspenders until Dina dissolved, screaming silently for him to stroke her properly, to feel his hot skin against hers. She ran her hands through his hair and down his back, feeling the strength of his shoulder blades under her palms – how she loved that muscular feeling of a man's back – and then pulled him close, seeing a tiny smile at the corner of his lips.

Suddenly she became aware of the driver coughing.

'Oh – I—' Dina leaned forwards, smoothing down her hair, dizzy and disorientated with desire. She turned back to Archie and blurted out helplessly: 'Do you want to come in?'

Archie stroked the back of her neck.

'Actually, I'd better not,' he said, smiling, but she felt that he was retaliating, playing her game back at her. 'I mean – I've got an early start tomorrow, and so have you . . . Another time. I'll call,' he called from the window, blowing her a kiss.

Dina nearly burst into tears with the delicious agony of it all. She unlocked the main door to the flats and stood in the quiet, dark hallway for a moment, her skin still tingling with the echo of his kisses. Still, she thought as she climbed the stairs, biting back a smile of frustration, it was better to wait. Better to look forward to next time.

A mug on the table. Her dresses sprayed across the bed. Make-up scattered around her table. This was her room, which she'd left in this mess just nine hours ago, but it seemed like years. As though it belonged to an old self she had sloughed off like a chrysalis.

She was about to get into bed when she suddenly realised that she hadn't called her parents. But when she rang, she heard the answerphone: her mother's voice, so wonderfully and reassuringly American after all the British accents she suffered all day. Dina ended the call. Her hand was shaking. *Don't panic,* she told herself. *They can't be in every minute of the day. Just try again.*

With every attempt, she thought she was going to break down. Her heart started to thump; her stomach clenched. Sweat broke out on her forehead. *Oh please God, please let them be OK, please don't let anything have happened to them like it did to—*

Suddenly there was a sleepy voice at the other end.

'Mum?' she cried. 'Mum, it's me!'

'Dina, you woke me up. It's eleven p.m. here. You know I've got an early start at the hospital.'

'Oh. Sorry.' Dina checked her watch. So it was. 'Sorry. I just wanted to make sure you were OK – and oh, Mom, I went out with a guy tonight and he's sexy and funny and gorgeous, and he was educated at Winchester and owns a restaurant, so you'd totally love him, but I shouldn't be calling, I was just worried, you know. Sorry. Bye. Love you,' she added quickly, but her mother had already hung up.

Dina let out a deep breath. Her parents were fine. Everyone was fine. The world was safe.

She climbed into bed, but she couldn't sleep. Her hair smelt of smoke and excitement. The Kylie Minogue song from the club kept replaying in her mind. There was a high-pitched ringing in her ears and whenever she shut her eyes she just kept replaying every detail of the evening.

Oh Steve, she thought with a burst of confused and sleepy happiness, *this has to have been one of the most exhilarating nights of my life. But I really don't know about Archie. What do you think? He's mad, bad and dangerous to know, but I've never met anyone quite like him. And God, all those girls running around after him! It made me wonder what good things I've done in my past life to get him. Though that awful Heidi would surely love to have him back. Oh, and we had so much fun, all that lovely dancing and . . .* She yawned, sliding off into sleep *. . . he makes me full of* joie de vivre *again and . . . night, Steve . . . night . . .*

8
Steve

Normally Steve loved the rain. He knew that the majority of Brits were sun-worshippers, stripping off the moment a little watery yellow leaked out of the gloom, gazing poignantly at the sky as though they wished they could catch hold of a ray and yank the sun out from behind the clouds. But Steve didn't suit the sun; he was pale and just suffered freckles and headaches. When he was a kid and his parents had been arguing, or Rachel had been playing death metal at top volume, or he'd been bullied at school, he liked to escape by taking a walk in the rain. He liked the way the world wrapped itself away indoors with cosy yellow lights and fires, giving the streets a sense of space and freedom. He liked the way the ugliness of East Acton became romantic, mystical under the blur of water. He loved the beautiful danger of the brooding sky overhead, the energy of lightning tearing the sky apart, the caress of water on his hair, washing over his face like a baptism. As he walked, his jumbled-up thoughts would fall into place like a jigsaw and by the time he was home, he would feel if not at peace, then at least reconciled to life, to his lot, his situation.

Tonight it was raining but Steve felt he could not be reconciled to life or to death; to anything.

He wanted to tear down the sky, topple buildings, split open the earth. He hated the world. Hated the people carrying on with their smug, happy lives; hated the wind whistling through his body; hated the rain falling on him, each drop like acid poison.

Steve had never been one of those people who was happy with

the status quo. He couldn't understand people who just sailed through life wrapped up in their own little cotton-wool realities without caring about what a dire state the world was in. That was why he shunned religion; he felt it was truly the opium of the people, a way of avoiding the truth, along the lines of: *What does it matter if people are dropping bombs if I'm in church making my pact with God to seal a place in heaven?* Steve devoured books by Michael Moore and John Pilger and went on peace marches. He always felt simultaneously uplifted and saddened afterwards; glad he had made a contribution, but aware of how small that contribution was, a raindrop in the ocean of life. And at night he often lay and worried that he ought to be doing more, and if so what, and why he had to do it in the first place. *What's the point?* he mused. *Why do I have a nice life with decent food and water and luxuries whilst thousands of people thousands of miles away would give anything to have a bowl of rice? And why, though I have a nice life, aren't I grateful for it?*

That feeling of sheer pointlessness was nothing compared to how he felt now. He was just a waste of space, only he wasn't even that because he didn't take up any space. He walked through things. He was a human cloud. He had no presence, no use, nothing, and now Dina had been on a date with Archie and they'd kissed and it looked as though she was falling for him big-time.

Unable to bear the very thought, he began to run. Faster and faster down the streets, the rain tearing through him.

Suddenly he stopped.

Something had caught his eye: the red-brick building across the road. Shepherd's Bush library. He'd used to visit it once a week. And he knew the old lady with the pink rinse who was now locking the doors, for he was always ordering obscure science books, and she'd give him a sweet smile and say, 'Golly, you must be a clever young boy to read books like that!' Steve had always wished she was his granny (yes, he did have a real one, but she farted and drank a bottle of gin a day).

He crashed through the door and stormed down the aisles, rain leaking out of his soul and leaving a dark, spidery trail behind him. Past the pastel blue and pink covers of Mills & Boon. Past the black covers of crime novels. Past the kids' picture books. *Here*, he thought. The 'Supernatural' section. Books on crystals and telepathy and astrology and all that stuff he had once dismissed as bull, for the closest he had ever come to believing in religion was science as an absolute; his gods were Einstein, Hawking and Penrose.

But Hawking couldn't help him now. *The Bumper Book of Ghosts, The Mysteries of the Supernatural, The Guide to Ghosts of the World.* He stacked them up on the desk in front of him and sat down. As he faced the pile, he suddenly thought of Dina. Was she in bed with Archie right now?

He quickly flipped open a book and started to read.

Freud, it said, *believed that ghosts were the visions of people who were afraid of death; a reflection of their subconscious mind.*

Steve snapped the book shut and let out a breath of despair. Freud was another one of Steve's heroes. He picked up the next book and tried again.

Over the next half an hour, he read every theory on ghosts going. He read that Jung thought that ghosts were a symptom of the collective unconscious. He read that one in ten people was able to have contact with ghosts, but rarely saw them; it was mostly through 'touch, sound, smell, sensations and electrical disturbances such as flying toasters'. (*Toasters,* thought Steve wryly. Why did weird supernatural happenings always involve the cruel desecration of *toasters*?). He read that children were more likely to see ghosts, and so were women – great. Then he read that the higher your IQ, the less likely you were to see them – and his heart sank. Dina was a bright girl. Then again, maybe it was cynicism that prevented intellectuals from tuning in. Dina was more intuitive than that. *But what the fuck did it matter?* he thought sadly, since she was with Archie, and would soon forget who the hell Steve was.

He read about famous ghosts, about the ghosts of Anne Boleyn and The Brown Lady of Raynham Hall and Lady Howard, England's most famous ghost, who drove a phantom coach made from the bones of her four husbands. Ghosts who had stuck to haunting the same place for hundreds of years.

Imagine, thought Steve, *if I'm still hanging about in four hundred years. It's OK for Catherine Howard to wander about Hampton Court; she's famous and it makes sense for famous ghosts to linger, to let the world remember them in all their glory. But who am I? A nobody. If I'm still around in four hundred years, people will be driving spaceships. And I'll just be walking around Shepherd's Bush like some sad old git.*

The thought was so awful he shoved the book away, jumping as he sent his pile tumbling to the floor.

'Sod it,' he muttered, tears in his eyes. He turned and walked out.

Outside, the rain had stopped. He suddenly became aware of a man across the street. He was sitting Buddha-style in a doorway, staring at Steve with penetrating eyes, as though he could see him. Steve shivered and walked away, deciding to pay his parents a visit.

They were watching *Who Wants to be a Millionaire?* with their next-door neighbour, Mr Harris. He was ninety, and rather senile, but Steve's mum was always making him cakes and letting him in because he had no family left, and she fretted that he was lonely.

'What was the name of Henry the Eighth's first wife?' Chris Tarrant asked.

'Anne Boleyn,' said Steve's mum.

'No, it was Catherine Howard,' said Steve's dad.

'Greta Garbo,' said Mr Harris.

'Catherine of Aragon,' Tarrant concluded.

'Close,' said Mr Harris.

Steve watched his mum roll her eyes at his dad and hide a snort, and he smiled affectionately. He looked at them, sitting on the sofa with a tartan blanket wrapped over their knees, fingers laced together, and felt a lump in his throat. That was one good thing that had come out of his death. Death reminded people of how precious love was: not a thing to be neglected or thrown away. It was as though they had realised what a priceless jewel their marriage was and rubbed it clean.

Steve took a wander off upstairs, peering into his bedroom. He was touched to see that it was preserved just as it had been: brown carpet, fresh sheets smelling of washing powder, a poster of his old teen idol, Michael Hutchence, on the wall. He sat on the bed and couldn't help thinking sadly about how infrequently he had come to visit his parents in the year before he died. Of course, like all parents, they'd forget that he was almost thirty and treated him as though he was about twelve. They'd kept dropping nervous hints about girlfriends. His mum had told him off for not putting his mug on a mat and making a drink ring on the coffee table. Steve had reacted with irritation and then got even *more* irritated because he knew he in turn was acting like a sulky twelve-year-old.

Now he wished he could just turn back the clock and say a few words to them. Say hi, look guys, you're not perfect and my childhood wasn't perfect. You bought me clothes from M&S and crappy trainers which meant I was bullied for years. You didn't let me get my ear pierced and had the barber cut my hair in an awful crewcut. But hey, I know you loved me, and there are so many parents out there, plastered across newspapers, who can't even seem to summon a droplet of liking for their kids, let alone love, and I do appreciate that. I do.

After *Who Wants to be a Millionaire?* had finished, Steve went back downstairs and noticed with curiosity that his mother was showing Mr Harris a small oblong metal object.

'The vicar's wife recommended it to me,' she said in a low voice. 'It helps create good vibes. You know – just in case he decides to pay us a visit. Steve.'

Steve looked closer, frowning. He didn't know whether to laugh or cry. It was an ioniser.

After Mr Harris had gone home, Steve's parents didn't make Horlicks and trundle off to bed. He watched in surprise as they put on coats and went outside. He followed them at a distance, shaken when they slipped into their local church. Steve had always been a bit cynical about his parents' faith, convinced it was based mainly on routine and fear of not getting an entry ticket to heaven.

They sat in a pew at the front of the church. Candles flickered, lighting up the dirty faces of figurines, throwing shadowy tongues across the stained-glass windows.

Steve watched his mother break down in tears. His father pulled her to him and clutched her tightly, rocking her in his arms.

'My only son,' she said through her sobs. 'I'll never have another. He was my favourite . . .'

Your favourite, Mum? Steve wanted to say. *But I always thought you loved my sis Rachel the most, because she's a girl.*

'It's all right love, he's at peace. We're going to be all right.' He kissed her on the lips and held her tightly. 'We've got each other. I love you.'

'I love you too.' She rubbed her nose against his.

Steve was so touched, he couldn't help it. Without thinking, he drew closer to her. And then he stopped. She'd felt him. She drew in her breath quickly, laying a thin hand over her chest, and Steve was horrified to suddenly realise how frail, how mortal she was. He paled away into the shadows, watching her shake and clutch his father. *God*, thought Steve, *all I can do is inspire terror in the people I love.* It reminded him of the time he'd put on a black skeleton costume for Halloween when he was eight years old. He'd got tired of scaring people, but the costume had become stuck and he'd started crying because he was afraid it would never come off and he'd be a freak for ever after. Finally, his mum had had to cut it away with a pair of scissors. That was how he felt now: as though he was wearing a scary costume sewn over the top of him, and there was nobody to help him cut it away.

He watched his parents walk away down the aisle and realised he couldn't follow them. He had to leave them, just as he had to leave Dina, and let them be. Which meant he could only ever be alone.

He ended up getting very drunk and going to London Zoo.

Ghosts weren't really supposed to drink, Steve realised that, but he didn't care. He crept into an Oddbins and stole a bottle of whisky. He'd never liked the taste of alcohol all that much, and now it was worse than ever, burning through his frail membranes like acid.

At the zoo, he went searching for the gorilla cage. There – just as Dina had promised on the night of his birthday – was a plaque that said: TITUS IS ADOPTED AND SUPPORTED BY STEVE MACFADDEN.

Steve eyed up the gorilla. It seemed to be looking at him.

'Hi,' he said in a slurred voice, 'I'm Steve. I'm your sponsor. I was reading that animals can see ghosts, so I thought maybe you'd like to be my friend.'

The rain which had previously softened now began to patter down harshly, and dark clouds gathered together. Steve's memory of what happened next was hazy. He remembered leaving the gorilla cage and running through the streets, throwing down his empty whisky bottle, seeing it fall to the pavement with a satisfying smash. His loneliness and anger and frustration burned inside him, propelling him on, until he found himself walking on the top of a block of flats in Shepherd's Bush.

Despair ate through his soul.

'It's all too late!' he yelled out at the sky. The stars hung, winking obliviously. The traffic purred below. People hurried through the rain, hiding from him under their umbrellas. Nobody cared. His life was over. 'I'm going to jump, I am!'

Up above, the sky raged. Down below, a trio of teenage girls linked arms and started to skip, trilling, *'We're singing in the rain . . .'*

'God,' Steve yelled up at the sky in a slurred voice, 'I really am going to jump. I mean it. I know you don't exist anyway, but I am going to jump.'

No reply. Lightning tore through the sky, highlighting an aeroplane jostling through the clouds.

'I mean, if you can just show me a point to me, if you can give me a reason to stay, I'll stay. But . . .'

The rain softened a little. A taxi tooted.

'And as for you lot down there!' Steve ranted, 'don't think it's going to be easy for you, either. Do you think you have any answers?'

As he stepped forward, he lost his balance. He cried out in shock. The air tore up through him, clawing tears from his eyes, whistling bullets through his ears. Windows, offices flashed past in a metallic grey blur. *Oh God, I didn't mean to jump didn't mean to jump please don't let me go to hell didn't mean to jump just wanted a second chance* . . . He saw the cars and ground coming up towards him and let out a piercing howl . . .

9
Dina

Why hadn't he called?

Why hadn't he called?

Why hadn't he called?

Dina checked her mobile for the fifth time that morning before slotting it back into her pocket, picking up her knife again and carrying on chopping lettuce to fill the sandwiches. It was Luigi's new initiative at The Greasy Spoon, his baby, his lightbulb flash of genius – 'Burger Express down the road have gone all healthy. We need to keep up. Let's offer SANDWICHES!' he'd cried, as though sandwiches were some wondrously nutritious invention of the twenty-first century. Dina had started to get a number of creative ideas involving lushly filled ciabattas, and naming them after tube stations – yes, maybe it was nuts, but fun too, she thought. She'd been disappointed when Luigi had gone back to his old tricks: 'And what's more, we'll offer *two* flavours – cheese and tomato, *and* egg and tomato! But only use quarter of an egg per sandwich. And only two *very* thin slivers of tomato.' Now Dina sighed and smeared margarine across two slices of stale white Mother's Pride bread as her mobile winked its disappointing green flash from her pocket.

What made it all the more frustrating was that she just wasn't the sort of girl who worried about men who didn't call.

It wasn't her style. She wasn't a needy type, and as much as she liked the heady fun of a relationship, she was happy being single and independent. She liked life; she liked herself. Normally, in fact, she enjoyed having a few days' breathing space after a first date to digest things, shake her feelings out and see if she wanted a second helping.

Then again, Archie was like no guy she'd ever dated. She felt as though he had picked her up like a genie on a flying carpet, and, like something out of *Arabian Nights,* shown her a dazzling array of wonders, spells and magical enchantments, then deposited her down and left her waiting for more. She still felt dizzy with passion from their kiss; any doubts about him had been swept away. Oh God, if he didn't call, she thought with melodramatic passion, she would spend the rest of her life being miserable.

Suddenly her mobile shrilled.

'Hello?'

'Dina! You were home *very* late last night. Roger was getting quite worried, and I said you were on a date and then he got jealous and said if you were going to go off with Archie, he was going to have a fling with a poodle.'

'Anita!' Dina laughed breathlessly.

'You hoped it was him calling, didn't you?'

'No.'

'Oh yes you did. Now, tell me all the details.'

Dina was torn between wanting to indulge deliciously in recounting and reliving every detail, and worrying that Archie might, given sod's law, call just when she was on the phone.

'I don't know where to begin. It was so different from anything I've ever experienced before—'

'Shit—' Anita suddenly cut her off. 'My stupid boss is back. Sorry, I *have* to go, he'll sack me if he finds out I'm making a personal call!'

Dina put her phone back in her pocket and sighed.

The morning dragged by. Dina found herself staring up at the clock only to discover a mere thirty seconds had gone by; the hands seemed to be cloaked in wet cement. Normally she found her job merely boring, but today the dullness of it all seemed to take on a new level of irritating grittiness. When she was doing the washing-up, she felt like chucking plates on the floor.

'Go take your lunch break.' Luigi waved her off.

Outside, the air was briskly cold and Dina pulled her denim jacket tight around herself. She knew her discontent had been acutely heightened because of last night. She felt as though she had been sleepwalking through life for the past year and meeting Archie and his friends had slapped her violently awake. Here were people who fizzed as though permanently on a champagne high, who lived life in seventh gear. The type of life she had dreamed of in New York. The type of life she could have if she just got off her butt and found a decent job.

She checked her mobile reception. It was fine.

She guessed she ought to get something to eat, though she was hardly hungry. She had no money so she stopped at a cashpoint.

She pushed in her bank card, and keyed in her pin. The machine whirred for a moment and Dina said a prayer. But God was clearly busy sorting out more important things, for the horrible, smug, irritating machine came back with SORRY, YOUR LENDER HAS REFUSED YOUR REQUEST.

Returning to The Greasy Spoon with a grumbling stomach, she pondered her money problems miserably. When he had been alive, Steve had frequently berated her gently over her lax attitude to her finances. He had always known exactly how much money he had in his account, down to the nearest penny, *and* he had a pension, *and* a savings account – one of those insanely tortuous ones where you put money in and didn't take it out until a year later. Dina never had any idea how much was in her account. She worked on a philosophy that involved writing cheques and realising her account was empty when they bounced, and if she really needed something, stick it on a credit card. But this philosophy couldn't go on for ever. At the end of her first few months in England, she'd been £200 in debt. Now it was more like £2000. Every time she thought about it she felt panicky, told herself, *I will deal with it soon, somehow*, brushed it into a cupboard at the back of her mind and slammed the door.

Worse, she still wasn't having any success in finding a better job. Writing job applications wasn't easy with her dyslexia, and she always got nervy in interviews and tended to bottle up her usually vivacious personality. With every rejection, she felt her confidence slide down another notch.

If the morning had been unbearable, the afternoon was sheer torture. Her mobile rang again – but it was only Anita, telling her that her boss, rather than sacking her, had asked her on a date!

An hour passed.

And then another.

And another.

Her mobile rang. A name lit up on the screen. Oh my God, it was Him.

'Hi, it's me.'

'Archie! Hi.'

'Uh-huh. How are you? Oh God, did you see the papers? We're in the *Mirror*! Coming out of the hotel. It's such a pain, really, but don't worry, they don't bug me that often, just when they've run out of gossip.'

'Oh my God!' For a moment Dina felt a thrill zip through her: *I'm famous!* Then she cried without thinking, 'I always look bad in photos! Do I look terrible?' *Whoops, now I sound totally vain*, she thought.

'Don't be ridiculous. Listen to what it says underneath: "Archie seems to have ditched society girl Heidi for good and has found a gorgeous new mystery girl."'

Dina giggled, hugging herself.

'So how is Heidi taking that?' she asked casually. The moment she said it, she could have kicked herself. Damn – so obvious. So jealous. So clingy. Bound to put Archie right off her.

'Heidi is fine,' said Archie in a faintly amused voice. 'Look, there's nothing going on between me and her any more, OK?'

'Oh? Oh really?' Dina said, as though amazed he should be volunteering such *utterly* irrelevant information.

'Yes. Really. We dated for a year, on and off . . .'

'Well, it did look like she wants you back,' said Dina.

A silence. Damn. She'd crossed the line again.

'I think you're right,' Archie admitted. 'We are friends, but friendships between men and women are never really friendships, are they? Let's face it. They're an illusion. Someone always wants a little more than friendship, but the other doesn't. Most of the time male–female friendships are just a nice cover-up for unrequited love.'

Dina fell silent, thinking of Steve.

'But,' Archie said firmly 'Heidi and me have been there, done that. We're only friends because – well, we hang around with the same group of people. Look, next time I promise there'll be no Heidi. I swear. It'll be just me and you, OK, sweetie?'

Sweetie. How – sweet. Dina felt a glow of warmth inside her.

'That sounds lovely,' she said. 'And sorry – sorry to be so . . . you know . . .'

'Not at all.' Archie was suddenly brisk again. 'Anyhow. How about coming over to my flat, since you missed it last night? I'd like to cook you dinner . . .'

Life is so *wonderful*, Dina thought, after they'd finished speaking. *I love Luigi. I love sandwiches!* When a new customer came in and ordered a cup of tea, she resisted the urge to kiss them.

She was just leaving work when she realised that she'd been so Archie-engrossed she had completely forgotten her appointment.

She half considered ringing Mrs MacFadden and calling the whole thing off, but then again, she was intrigued. It was an odd thing to do, not the sort of thing Dina would ever normally have got involved in. But she had to find out; she had to know for sure.

10
Steve

Vroom! Vroom! Vroom!

Wheels whizzed past. Exhaust fumes wafted over his face. Steve lay in the middle of the road. The same place he'd landed last night.

He hadn't died, of course. He had known that a dead ghost was an oxymoron, but all the same he'd half hoped that the shock of dying a second time might suddenly knock some sense into his soul, kick off some automated mechanism that would send him flying towards heaven or hell. It hadn't happened. He hadn't even been hurt. He'd just hit the road, sunk into the sticky tarmac and then, with great difficulty, hauled himself out to find his soul encrusted with little black bits of tar. Now he was lying in the road, watching the sky change shape above him, from clear to cloud-blurred, sunny to overcast. He knew he was behaving like a sulky teenager who'd locked himself away in his bedroom and was refusing to face the world, but he didn't care. *There's no point in getting up,* he told himself. *Nothing for me to do. If God or anyone would like to show me a point to my existence, then maybe I'll reconsider. But until then, I'm going to lie here. OK, God?*

'Ouch!' Steve rubbed his nose as a speeding taxi whizzed right through his head.

On the street, commuters strolled past. A pretty girl wearing a denim jacket, the wind tugging her ponytail like a naughty schoolboy – *Dina.*

Dina!

Steve found himself leaping to his feet.

She was talking into her mobile, and his heart sank when he heard her words, the joy bubbling in her voice: 'Anita, he actually called – yeah! I know, I know, I played it cool, at least I'm trying to play it cool. Yeah, I'm going over next week . . . Nah, I won't be in tonight. I'm going to the gym.'

Steve thought he might as well follow her.

To his surprise, she passed by the turning to the gym and carried on walking. Why had she told Anita she was going there? What the hell was going on?

And then Steve realised that the road Dina was turning into was terribly familiar. Harth's Crescent. His parents' road. And sure enough, she was walking up to number 39. He watched her stand on the step, adjusting her cuffs, clearing her throat, indecision scrawled all over her face. Then, with a nervous gulp, she pinged the doorbell and waited for Steve's mother to let her in.

Steve could not believe it.

This was completely insane.

At first he simply hadn't been able to work out what was going on. As well as Dina, his mum had also invited over Mrs Dickens. Mrs Dickens was the local vicar's wife. The vicar, with his predilection for giving raucous sermons, was obnoxious enough, but Mrs Dickens seemed determined to outdo him. She was very stout, with salt-and-pepper hair, and wore clashing pink and red tweeds. She sang all the hymns in a painfully loud, out-of-tune baritone. She gossiped wildly after the services about all the parishioners' lives, happily embellishing if the truth wasn't readily available, or juicy enough, and Steve had often heard his mum saying to his father after the service, 'Honestly, she's enough to make me want to go to that Buddhist centre and start taking up yoga' – which, to Steve's mother, was on a par with becoming a Satanist.

So it came as something of a surprise to Steve to find his mum welcoming Mrs Dickens in with a warm hug and then introducing her to Dina, who she described as 'a very spiritual person'.

And then things got even weirder. His mum led them into the living room, where the rose-patterned curtains had been drawn tightly shut, and all the lights turned off. She had covered the coffee table with a black cloth that belonged in Rachel's room, taken down her best white china plate and placed a candle in the middle of it. The flame was eerie, casting more shadows than light, and flickering in the skeletal nooks and crannies of their faces, the worried orbs of their dilated pupils.

She offered Dina and Mrs Dickens PG Tips (Mrs Dickens asked instead for herbal tea, declaring that ordinary tea interfered with her aura) and returned with a tray and a plate of custard creams. They all sat and sipped awkwardly. Dina, as she always did, broke her custard cream apart and nibbled at the pale icing. Steve could tell she was nervous.

'Did you see *EastEnders* on Monday?' Steve's mum asked, clinging to the safety of the trivial.

'Oh God, yes,' said Dina, with relief. 'God, I couldn't believe it when they got together!'

'And him becoming a gangster behind her back.'

'And her being married to his ex-wife's brother.'

Silence.

Mrs Dickens put her herbal tea down on the floor and suddenly took Dina's hands in hers. Dina jumped.

'Calm down, I just wanted us to get a little closer. It's important that all our energies mingle for this to work. Now, tell me again what happened, what prompted you to call Mrs MacFadden?'

'Well – it all started a few days ago. I could feel him breathing, a cold sort of breath on the back of my neck. It was as though he was there. Especially when I was going to sleep at night. And once or twice, I swear, I've heard him say something. Just simple things.'

'And what does his voice sound like?' Seeing Dina hesitate, she clasped her hands more tightly. 'Be open. Nobody thinks you're silly.'

'It sounds just like Steve. Though he sounds clearer when I hear him in my dreams. I have this dream about him and I keep dreaming it over and over.'

'Tell us about your dream, Dina,' said Mrs Dickens.

'Well . . .' Dina lowered her eyes and looked at the floral pattern on the rim of her cup. 'I dream that it's that night – the night he died. I'm back at the canal with him, talking.'

'You were talking about work, weren't you?' said Steve's mum, who had written down every detail, every snippet Dina had ever told her.

'Yes,' said Dina, flushing at the torture of having to lie. 'We were talking about work. Then I said I was tired and I had to go. I asked him to come too, but he wanted to stay. And in my dream I walk away, down the canal, down the street and to the tube station. In my dream I know something's wrong, and the urge is so strong that I turn back – in fact, I start to run. I run back and I'm there, walking back past the water, and I'm looking for him, but he's gone. He's gone and it's dark and cold and the wind is howling and I can't find him. I jump into the canal and I'm in the water, and when I look under the water, I see bodies – bodies of strangers, floating, some of them ghostly, their faces blurry, some of them waving to me, all skullish and spooky. They want to draw me down, they want me to die too and keep them company, and I feel like the easiest thing would be to sink down. But I don't.' Dina swallowed. 'I get out and I'm standing there, alone, and I feel so lonely, as though everyone in the world is dead and it's all my fault – there's this sickening feeling that I've done something terrible. And then – he's there.'

She looked up. Her audience – human and otherwise – was transfixed.

'He's there and he comes up to me and holds me. It feels like a light shining into my soul and I don't feel sick any more. He holds me tight and he says he loves me and he says I mustn't worry, because he's watching me and keeping me safe. He says everything will always be all right.'

Steve's mum's eyes were shiny with tears. Mrs Dickens put a hand to her throat.

'Well, Dina, I think that's very significant.'

Steve stared, stunned, when Mrs Dickens suggested they hold hands and form a circle.

I can't believe it, he thought. *They're holding a seance. For me. And Dina hates seances. I remember she told me she hates anything to do with the occult because it totally freaks her out.*

'Just sit still and allow yourself to feel the atmosphere,' Mrs Dickens said.

Steve stood and watched Dina close her eyes, biting her bottom lip with worry and concentration. Half of him wanted to burst into laughter, and the other half was so deeply touched he wanted to gather her and his mum into his arms, hug them tightly and tell them how much he loved them for doing this.

But that would be unfair. Steve could see exactly what would happen if he so much as said *hello.* Just one word would be fatal. They'd be holding seances for breakfast, lunch and supper. His mum would fill the house with ionisers and nutcases and women in purple shawls stinking of incense all claiming to be Steve's best spiritual friend. His father would go mad; Dina would fall apart. They'd never rebuild their lives, heal their hearts, move on.

And yet . . .

'Steve Brian Nigel MacFadden,' said Mrs Dickens grandly, and Steve smiled, for it reminded him of being back at school, 'please let us know if you wish to speak to us.'

Steve, a fierce voice in his head said sharply, *don't say a word. It might be tempting, but don't.*

But, a tiny voice inside him objected, *I'm so lonely.*

Don't be selfish.

But I want to be selfish. I haven't spoken to anyone in days. Days. Yesterday I even phoned up the speaking clock and chatted to it for an hour. The only living thing I can talk to is my goldfish. The only conversation I get back is bubbles. I watch kids' TV and I'm thirty. I'm so, so alone.

'Steve, can you hear us?' Dina whispered.

Steve swallowed and opened his mouth. Words hovered on his tongue. Tears filled his eyes. His chest was burning. Voices screamed in his head.

Let it alone, Steve, his voice of reason and responsibility warned him. *Just turn around and walk out of the house. Let them go. Let them get on with their lives.*

But if Dina's definition of getting on with her life is to get off with Archie, then what good is that?

And then, from nowhere, a voice suddenly said:

'I can hear you. It's Steve.'

Huh?

Steve spun round.

'I heard him,' Dina suddenly cried, her eyes opening.

'I didn't hear anything,' Steve's mum wailed, pulling her hand away.

'Nor did I,' said Mrs Dickens, grabbing it back. 'Don't break the circle. Dina may be imagining the voice if I can't hear it, but it may also be a sign that Steve is coming closer. Yes, I can feel him entering the room. Steve, can you hear us?'

'I can hear you guys all right,' the voice went on. It was loud, confident, cheeky. 'And I think you, Dina, are one foxy chick.'

Just what the hell is going on? Steve cried silently.

Dina blinked, scratching her neck where an embarrassed blush was slowly crawling up to meet her jawline.

'It doesn't sound like Steve,' she whispered shakily.

'You may just be imagining it,' said Mrs Dickens airily, a frown indenting her forehead. 'Just focus.'

'So how about it, you gorgeous sexy babe?'

'Well,' said Dina. 'I . . . er . . . I can't quite, er, make out what he's saying . . .'

The voice appeared to be coming from the corner of the room. Steve strolled over and flailed about in the darkness, grabbed something. It turned out to be a cold arm. In the gloom a face appeared: slitty black eyes, teeth gleaming in a leering smile. Steve felt fear building in his chest – who or what was this *thing*? But his curiosity that it might be similar to him overrode his fear and he tugged it out into the centre of the room.

'Hey,' the thing hissed. 'Who the hell are you?'

'I'm Dina,' said Dina in a bewildered voice, glancing round. The flame pirouetted on the plate; the room seemed to be filled with energy and moving air, but all she could see was darkness.

'What's he saying?' Mrs Dickens hissed.

'He's asking who we are,' Dina whispered.

'He's asking who we are,' Mrs Dickens announced loudly, squeezing Steve's mum's hand.

'Just what the fuck do you think you're doing?' the thing asked Steve.

'He just said, "What the fuck do you think you're doing?",' Dina repeated.

'That is *not* my Steve,' said Steve's mum indignantly, dropping her hand. 'Steve *never* swore. I can't remember him ever using language like that. Well, only when he was fifteen and accidentally shaved his eyebrow off. This is simply silly, and you're scaring Dina.' She got up and tore open the curtains, spilling the sun into the room and lighting up the mysterious stranger.

For the first time since he'd died, Steve forgot about Dina. He failed to notice her bursting into confused sobs, and his mum sitting down beside her and crying too, and the pair of them hugging and clutching each other and speculating as to whether he'd really been there whilst Mrs Dickens awkwardly removed the custard creams.

Steve was simply fascinated by this stranger; every fibre of his being quivered with anticipation. He was six feet tall and human-looking. Alive, he had been a young Chinese guy. His olive skin was smooth and his dark fringe flopped over his forehead. He wore black jeans and a black T-shirt and an earring in his left ear. The bright sunlight streamed right through him and lay in splashes on the carpet, highlighting his outline with a shimmering gold aura. Steve was reminded of those gaudy Catholic cards you see in tourist shops in Europe: tilt it one way and you see a lurid Virgin Mary; tilt it another and a garish Christ appears. From one angle the stranger was a ghost, but shift your gaze an inch and he blurred into distorted shadow, merged into the background like a chameleon. Steve realised with a sense of troubled awe: *That's how I must look, to humans who can see ghosts.*

'Hi,' the stranger said. 'I'm Harrison. Pleased to meet you.'

'He just spoke again!' Dina was on the verge of hysteria. 'I heard him, he said his name was Harrison!'

Steve's mum held her tightly, shushing her. As Mrs Dickens put on a spiritual face and moved in closer, holding out her hand, Steve's mum gave her a terrifying look.

'Go into the kitchen and get the paracetamol and a cup of hot tea,' she hissed.

'Yes, of course, sorry,' Mrs Dickens muttered sheepishly, running off.

Harrison opened his mouth again, but before he could speak, Steve grabbed him and yanked him straight through the front window and on to the lawn outside.

'Hey, get off me! Give me my arm back!'

'Sorry. I just had to stop you. Didn't you see how much pain you were causing her?'

'Yeah, but you have to admit, it was funny.' Seeing the look on Steve's face, he shrugged. 'Sorry, didn't realise it was personal. She your wife?'

Steve breathed out slowly.

'She's someone I care about a lot.'

'But you know, going to seances can be a real laugh if you've nothing better to do. Yesterday I gatecrashed this group of women who were trying to contact some old geezer, and boy, I had a laugh telling them I'd secretly wanted to shag them all . . .' Harrison laughed. Steve reckoned he must have turned a lot of heads with that laugh when he'd been alive.

'So you're – a ghost?' Steve asked quietly.

'I might be.' Harrison suddenly looked cagey and stuffed his hands in his pockets. 'Who are you?'

'I'm Steve. Steve—'

'Steve Brian Nigel MacFadden,' Harrison echoed, grinning cheekily. 'Yeah, I'm a ghost. I'm actually a pretty special ghost. You know the Angel Gabriel? He's a *very* close friend of mine. We're like *that.*' Harrison held up crossed fingers. 'I get to decide who goes to heaven. That's why I busted your seance. Your time's up.'

'It is?' Steve was amazed at the relief he felt, washing through his veins like honey.

'Why are you smiling? What makes you think you're heaven fodder?' Seeing Steve's face, he nudged him. 'Hey, I'm just joking. I fooled you there, didn't I?'

'Yeah,' Steve muttered.

'Nah, I'm just a regular guy. But hey, it's good to meet you. There aren't many ghosts around here that are worth talking to—' He broke off, seeing that Steve was staring at him intensely. 'What?'

'Nothing,' said Steve. He couldn't even put it into words: the wild joy at finding out that there were others like him, that he was not alone.

Before they left, Steve checked that Dina was all right. She seemed to be recovering, shakily. Harrison suggested they take a trip to

Leicester Square. On the way, Steve began to appreciate what a truly mischievous ghost Harrison was. They took the tube, where Harrison kept obstructing the doors so they kept sliding open and shut and delaying the train, and unzipping businessmen's flies. When they got off at Leicester Square, he insisted on running up the escalators the wrong way and then sliding down them, crying: 'WHOOPEEEEEEEEEEEEEE!'

Steve joined in, and though he behaved as though it was immature, he secretly enjoyed such laddish fun. *Whoosh!* he slid down the escalator, passing by a line of bored faces, and something in his heart split open and a butterfly danced out and fluttered around his chest. He realised that for the first time in a long time he was happy. Having fun. With a friend.

It was still twilight, but Leicester Square was already beginning to froth with Friday-night crowds. People of all colours and cultures poured in and out of the tube, the cinemas, the Hippodrome, the cafés, and the square buzzed with colour and noise and the scent of vanilla and roasting chestnuts. A group of Africans were playing tom-tom drums, the beat pulsating gloriously through the pavements and tickling the undersides of Steve's feet; and there was a performance artist, painted entirely gold, standing frozen whilst the crowd surveyed him in awe.

'I mean – he doesn't even blink,' one American woman whispered to her friend in a hushed voice.

Then Harrison prodded him and he collapsed in a heap. The crowd sighed in disappointment. Harrison burst into wild laughter.

'Harrison, stop it!' said Steve, laughing too.

'Sorry,' said Harrison, sitting down on a bench. 'I am a bastard, I admit, but it's the boredom. You find it gets to you after a while, and then you get pissed off that all these people are alive and you're not, and you want to wind them up.'

'You don't feel that maybe the point of being a ghost is to be a guardian angel, to look after the people you love?' Steve asked, his voice red with embarrassment.

Harrison gave him a long, strange look.

'Fuck off. Who are you, Mother Teresa?'

Steve swallowed. 'I can't believe I've found another ghost. I mean – I mean . . .' and suddenly all the questions that had been dancing in his head for weeks came pouring out like lava. 'Why are we here? Are we waiting to go to heaven? Or hell? Are we cursed, or do we have a purpose? Are we stuck here for good? Or maybe – I mean, I know this sounds crazy, but I've had a lot of time to think about this – I was thinking about that saying about whether we're all a dream in the mind of a butterfly, you know the one I mean, and maybe, maybe this is all a dream, an illusion. Maybe we think we're still alive because we're attached to life on earth and none of this is really real—'

'Whoah, whoa,' Harrison interrupted him, laughing. 'D'you think if I knew all the answers I'd be sitting here? I'm as fucked as you.'

Steve kicked his feet against the bench.

'But doesn't it drive you mad?' he asked desperately. 'I mean, how long ago did you die? *How* did you die?'

'A year ago.'

'*A year?*'

'Yup. I died saving someone's life. There was this little old lady, and she was being mugged, and I chased after the robber and grabbed her bag back and he knifed me and . . . oh fuck it, I may as well tell you the truth.'

'That was a lie?'

'Yeah, well, it sounded good, didn't it? I just feel it sounds cooler if you die with a purpose. But the truth is, I – and my family: my mum, my dad, my brother, my aunt – died in a car crash last year.' Harrison noted that Steve looked as though he was going to cry; God, he was a sensitive soul. 'Don't worry,' he said, patting his shoulder. 'It was better that way; we all went together. It'd be worse to have left my mum or dad behind.'

Steve winced. 'But are they around?' he asked. Hey, they might even adopt him. They could be a ghost family. They could have cosy meals and read to each other and live in their own haunted house and brave this out together.

'No,' said Harrison. 'I'm the only one still left in this lifetime.'

'How come?'

'My family are all Chinese Buddhists. My parents came over to live here in England thirty years ago. We all believed in reincarnation, but in order to move on, a body must be cremated and the proper funeral rites conducted by the monks in our local temple. My uncle organised the ceremonies, and for some reason, he's always disliked me. He's very strict, and not impressed by my wild living. I had to stand and watch the funeral rites. All my family were released and went away – I know they've gone to their next lives – but I'm stuck here.'

'So is that the answer?' Steve asked in wonder. 'Reincarnation?' He nearly added that he'd always thought that reincarnation was the biggest load of shit, the sort of thing mad hippies believed in, but he stopped himself in time.

Harrison shrugged.

'I reckon that whatever you believe in determines what happens to you in the end.'

'Well, I don't believe in God. I don't believe in heaven. I'm a scientist and an atheist. I believe that we just end,' said Steve. 'We die, and that's it. So what's gone wrong for me? Does that mean I'm stuck here for ever?'

'Chill out,' said Harrison. 'You think too much and you worry too much.'

'That's what Dina always used to say to me,' said Steve sadly.

'You're going to have to tell me more about this Dina,' said Harrison. 'Come and see my place; we can talk there . . .'

Dina dried her raw eyes and then closed them for a moment, drawing in a deep breath and blowing it out. When she opened them, she saw Mrs MacFadden sitting on the sofa, smiling at her, and her heart cleaved open in compassion. It was hard to imagine what Steve's mother was going through, day after day.

Now that the seance was over, Mrs Dickens had left, declaring that she had a roast in the oven, and begging them not to tell the vicar: 'I went to see Britney in concert and he almost left me, so you can imagine what would happen if he found out about this.'

After she'd gone, Dina and Mrs MacFadden had had a bit of a snigger. The more they discussed the seance, the more they concluded it was silly and convinced each other that any voices had been the result of hysteria and imagination, but the whole thing had, at least, been a useful way of relieving some pain and getting something out of their systems.

Before Dina left, Mrs MacFadden gave her two things. The first was an envelope.

'There's just a few photos in it, and some photocopies of newspaper articles about Steve – like when he passed his Eleven Plus and they covered it in the *Shepherd's Bush Advertiser* . . . Sorry, I do know it's silly . . .'

'No, no, it's lovely,' Dina protested quickly. Her eyes filled with tears when Mrs MacFadden pressed a goldfish bowl into her hands. 'Oh, I can't. I can't take Einstein.'

'We've only just cleaned out his flat – for the last few months I haven't even been able to face going in there. I think one of his neighbours must have been feeding the goldfish because it's still alive. I'd like you to have him.'

'Thanks,' said Dina, clasping her awkwardly into a tight hug as Einstein flipped between them. 'Thanks so much.'

Back home, she carried the bowl into the living room, shooing away Roger, who sniffed about curiously. She placed it on the table and the sunset pouring through the window lit up Einstein's fins in a fire of red and gold. It was funny, thought Dina, because Einstein did remind her of Steve; he had the same innocent look on his face, the same slightly wide-eyed amazement that the world was so nutty and unfair.

Dina didn't dip into the envelope. She felt that some wounds had healed during the seance and she didn't want to reopen them with more memories. So she put it at the bottom of the wardrobe and then started checking out outfits to wear for her date with Archie, humming brightly with fresh anticipation.

11

Dina

One week later, Dina found herself standing outside Archie's flat. She felt like a teenager. There was a bowling ball in her stomach and her breath hovered in her throat like a fluttering bird. She was terrified that Archie would see her raw nerves and she kept telling her body to keep calm.

She rang the bell.

'Dina!'

Archie was looking gorgeous. His dark hair, newly washed, flopped over his forehead. He was wearing corduroys and an open-necked shirt and an apron. The apron had a picture of a yellow plastic duck on the front, and the childish softness of it was a sexy contrast.

He gripped her shoulders as though to pull her in for a kiss, then held her away from him thoughtfully.

'You look lovely,' he said, looking her up and down.

Dina smiled, relieved that all the effort (three hours' shopping, £300 on her Barclaycard, two hours' getting ready) had been worth it. Then, as he engulfed her in a warm hug and a sensuous kiss, she felt as though her whole body was melting. She had never understood the expression 'weak at the knees' before, and as he pulled away and took her coat she was frightened he would see her hands shaking.

'It's lovely to see you too,' she said, aware that her voice was sounding high, and in an effort to collect herself she pretended to look out at the view.

Archie came up behind her, looking over her shoulder. It was a genuinely great view. But all Dina was aware of was the closeness of his body. She had never felt such raw desire for someone.

'I'll get on with dinner,' he said.

'You've cooked for me!' Dina was delighted.

'Of course,' said Archie. 'What did you think we were having, a takeaway?'

Dina hid a smile. There was something endearingly boyish about the way he couldn't be straightforwardly nice and had to cover it up with offhand sarcasm.

Dina asked him where the bathroom was; she didn't really need it, but she wanted to have a quick snoop around Archie's flat. It was very plush and she suspected it had cost a lot of money. His tastes were very minimalist. The walls and carpets were mostly white; the sofas in the living room were large and black and squashy. He was freakishly neat. The only publications lying on his coffee table were a copy of today's *Times* and an art collector's monthly. Dina was convinced that this all had to be a show. Under his bed, she told herself, would be a ton of junk he'd hastily stuffed there at the last minute. On her way to the bathroom she passed his bedroom and couldn't resist taking a quick peek in. To her surprise, it was just as clean and neat as the rest of the flat. White carpet. Mirrors. A large modern art piece, a sprawl of garish red and blue oils splashed across a canvas. A huge double bed. She snuck a quick look behind her – the coast was clear – and bent down. There was nothing, *nothing* under the bed except for a pair of black velvet slippers trimmed with gold.

As she entered the bathroom, Dina couldn't help making mental comparisons with the bathroom in her and Anita's flat, which was crammed with various bottles of shampoo, conditioner, moisturiser, body scrub, foot cream and whatnot, most of them with green foam congealed in patches down the sides, most of them half empty or empty, which they couldn't be bothered to throw away. Their bin was always overflowing with discarded lipstick-marked tissues and cotton buds and the floor was generally littered with the chewed-up toilet rolls that Roger loved to play with. Their shower curtain was mint-green and fraying and half of it was coming away from its metal bar, and their shower was covered with limescale and only agreed to spurt out hot water with a good deal of violent encouragement.

Archie's bathroom, on the other hand, had five thin metallic bottles lined up neatly on a shelf. It had a holder for toilet rolls, and spotless white towels. There were photographs on the walls: moody black-and-white shots of a naked girl in various poses. When Dina looked closely, she was infuriated to discover they were photos of Heidi.

Sitting down on the toilet, she felt confusion cloud her mind. Why hadn't Archie taken those photos down? Maybe he liked to have them up there in a laddish sort of way, a trophy commemorating his previous conquest. Or maybe he was still carrying a flame . . .

The door suddenly opened a few inches and she cursed herself – she and Anita never bothered to shut the toilet door. She was about to call out in an embarrassed voice, 'Excuse me, I'm—' when she realised that it wasn't Archie. It was a cat.

A very beautiful cat. Its eyes were green and almond-shaped and its sinewy muscles rippled beneath its short black coat, shiny as patent leather. It rubbed its head against Dina's ankles, purring, and she giggled and tickled its chin.

As she made her way back to the kitchen, the cat followed her.

'Ah,' said Archie, 'this is Jupiter, by the way.'

'I hadn't put you down as a cat person.'

'I'm not, really,' said Archie. 'Heidi bought him for me. She said' – Archie rolled his eyes as he turned to take down a packet from a cupboard – 'that it would be good for me and help bring out my feminine side. Well, I threw a fit at first because we're not really supposed to have cats in these flats. Luckily, the doorman has a soft spot for me and allowed me to be an exception. I only planned to have him a month and then pass him on to my mum, but I found myself getting attached to him.' Archie picked him up, rubbing his cheek in his fur. 'You're my bachelor pal, aren't you, Jupe boy?'

Dina was enchanted. Archie put Jupiter down and the cat ran to its bowl, purring. Dina noticed that Jupiter didn't get plain old Whiskas; there was some rather expensive-looking white fish in the shiny bowl. *Archie utterly pampers him,* she thought with affectionate delight.

'I've got a dog called Roger,' she said. 'He's gorgeous too, you'd love him.'

'Hmm, I'm not really a dog person. They smell,' Archie said disdainfully.

'Oh,' said Dina, slightly deflated. 'So what are we having?' She changed the subject as Archie opened up the oven and a bouquet of delicious smells floated out.

'Oh, nothing fancy. Smoked salmon for starters, lamb and vegetables for the main,' said Archie. 'Apricot mousse for dessert.'

Dina was touched. After the mayhem of their last date, she'd been left feeling unsure as to what Archie wanted from her – a one-night stand, a fling, a relationship? And in truth, she wasn't sure what she wanted herself. The fact that he had made so much effort to tidy his flat *and* cook her such a splendid feast was more than promising.

She realised then that she wanted more than a fling too.

They sat down to eat at Archie's kitchen table. He turned the lights down low and Dina breathed in the food blissfully.

'What was the last thing you had to eat?' Archie asked.

'Oh,' said Dina. 'Urgh. Yuk. It was this lunchtime and I was a bit rushed because Luigi had to have his ingrowing toenail taken out and I was the only one serving. So I had a Mars bar in batter. It was foul. But I ate it. What?' She shivered; Archie was looking at her with incredulous eyes.

He leaned across and put a hand on her forehead. For a moment his expression was so solemn she felt genuinely unnerved.

'And you're still alive?' he whispered.

Dina, remembering his review, shrieked with laughter.

'Dina,' he took her hand in his, 'you must promise me never, *never* to eat anything out of that place again. I'm serious.'

Dina could not have been more flattered.

'How did you come to set up your own restaurant?' she asked.

'Well – if you want my CV, it goes something like this,' said Archie. 'I went to Cambridge and managed to get a third. I guess the three years of non-stop partying didn't help. Then I spent a year travelling and meeting people, and when I got back I got into journalism. The fact that my father had a restaurant chain meant I got to do some of the reviews. Then because Dad was ill and wanted to retire, he suggested he train me up to take over exquisite.'

'Wow,' said Dina. 'I mean, that's so amazing.'

Archie shrugged.

'It's all relative,' he said nonchalantly. 'I meet people all the time who are worth much more than me. As soon as you succeed at something, or get what you want, it becomes boring. So you go for something harder that's just out of reach, and so on.'

Dina was intrigued to hear Archie talking seriously and from the heart. She wondered idly if his philosophy also applied to women.

'So what's the secret of your success?' she asked.

'I never give up,' said Archie, looking her straight in the eye. 'When I want something, I put every inch of myself into having it, and I carry on and on until I get it.' He took a sip of wine and let out a faint sigh. 'That said, I hardly think my restaurant chain *is* a great success story at the moment . . .'

'What d'you mean?' Dina cried. 'I thought things were going really well for you.'

'They are, and they aren't. I'm having trouble with . . . Oh, sod it, you didn't come to dinner to hear about my work stuff.'

'No, tell me,' Dina persisted. 'I'd really like to know.'

'My chef,' Archie said at last. 'He is just a fucking pain in the backside. We keep agreeing on menus, and then the next week he decides he wants to change it, and add some utterly ridiculous thing like, I don't know, caviar on toast with peanut and champagne dressing – a slight exaggeration, but you get the gist. And he is *so* pig-headed. He is always convinced that he's right and I'm wrong, when the truth is that I am always right and he is always wrong.' Archie let out a breath.

'You know,' said Dina, 'when I was in New York I once worked with a really difficult woman, and I remember my dad telling me a story about heaven and hell that I found useful.'

'Uh-huh.'

Archie sounded slightly wary, and there was a faint frown on his forehead. Dina felt paranoid that he was secretly thinking: *Er, hello, I do run a chain of restaurants, and you are just a waitress, and what could you possibly say that's any use to me?*

She decided to plunge in and tell it anyway.

'It's just a story,' she said hurriedly, 'about a man who asked an angel to show him, briefly, heaven and hell. So the angel takes him up to a beautiful place, where people are sitting by a table piled high with sumptuous food. "This must be heaven," he thinks, but he can't work out why everyone is looking miserable and nobody is eating. Then he sees the spoons they have to eat with – they're so long that every time they scoop up some food, they can't bring it back to their mouths to eat. So they're all starving.

'Then the angel takes him to a second place. It looks exactly the same: beautiful scenery, tables piled high with food, but here everyone is happy and smiling. They're all using the spoons, but they're using them to feed each other.'

'Right,' said Archie, raising an eyebrow. 'And the moral of the story is . . .'

'Look,' said Dina, laughing and blushing slightly, 'I'm not patronising you – God, I don't know how in the world I'd handle a difficult chef, except that maybe if you just try and work with each other, and maybe listen and consider that the other person might be right, then, well, it might work out better . . .'

'Or I could take the short cut.'

'What's that?'

'Fire him.'

Dina burst into laughter and Archie grinned, topping up her glass.

'No,' said Archie, seriously. 'As a matter of fact, you're right.'

Dina could see it took him a little effort to admit such a thing and she gently hid a smile.

'No – you are,' said Archie. 'Before my father died, he said pretty much the same thing. I am a good businessman, but I admit sometimes I can get impatient with people. I guess I just have a very clear vision of how I want things done, and it gets me when people can't see that. But you're right. Dad said, "Remember, Archie, you have to give a little in order to get a little."'

'That's very sweet,' said Dina.

Archie paused, coming out of his train of thought, and stared at her with such intensity that the food in her mouth suddenly melted with nervous saliva.

'Yes, it is,' he said, a teasing note in his voice, his pupils dilating. Then he pulled away and picked up the bottle of Chardonnay. 'Have some more wine.'

By the end of dinner, Dina was blissfully full. Archie went off to make coffee and she had picked up her handbag and was diving inside for her mobile when he suddenly came up behind her, running a fingertip along the back of her neck.

'Come and sit down,' he said.

Dina picked up her bag and followed him into the living room.

It was dark, but he didn't turn on the lights. He went to get the coffee. Dina was so excited, she couldn't sit still. There was a grand piano by the window and she opened the dark polished lid, remembering her unfulfilled childhood desire to learn. She gently touched a key, listened to the note quaver across the dark room, and then fade poignantly.

Hearing the chink of cups on the coffee table, she jumped. Suddenly she couldn't look at Archie. She bent her head and pressed another key.

She heard his footsteps padding across the carpet. His breath on the back of her neck. His hands stroking her hair.

He gathered her hair into one dark sheaf, twisted it and lifted it up into a knot, then kissed the back of her neck. Dina closed her eyes and breathed out a shaky sigh. Then a troubling thought rippled across her consciousness and she found herself stepping away, banging her elbow against the keys in a painfully clashing chord.

'I'm sorry,' she said, aware of the confused irritation on Archie's face. 'I need to ring my parents.'

Archie stood by the window, hands in his pockets, staring at the view. His expression was cold. Dina berated herself but she couldn't help it. She sat on the sofa and rang them on her mobile. She kept getting the answerphone. She tried several times. It was no good.

She sat very still and tried to push away the fear enveloping her. Archie turned away from the window.

'I can't get through to them,' she said in a small voice.

'I can call you a taxi home if you like,' he said coolly.

Dina saw in a panic that Archie thought she was making excuses to avoid going to bed with him.

'No – I'm fine . . .'

Archie heard something in her voice. Frowning, he came and sat beside her on the sofa.

'Are you OK?'

'I'm sorry,' said Dina. She was horrified to find her voice choked with tears.

'Dina, tell me what's wrong.' Archie threaded his fingers through hers. 'Are your parents ill? What?'

'No, they're fine. I just like to call them every night. I – they – they think I call for a chat, and I do. But I just like to know they're safe.' She stared down at the contrast of Archie's large, blunt fingers against her pale, slender ones.

Archie waited patiently, his eyes suddenly soft.

'I just – I lost someone I loved recently – well, a few months ago, and it was a shock,' said Dina. 'I know this is really silly, but last week we even had a seance to see if we could contact him. Afterwards, I realised it was nuts, even though I thought I heard him. I won't do that again.' She glanced up with liquid eyes and saw that Archie looked unbelievably touched. He realised she had told him something very personal. He held her even more tightly to him, as though he wanted to protect her from the world, and gently kissed her temple.

'Well I hope that during your seance you said hi to Elvis from me,' he said, and smiled when she laughed. She flicked her tears away with a finger, and as soon as her hand fell, Archie took it in his.

'It's just the fear. Up until Steve died, I was innocent. I just went through life thinking we all live until we're seventy or whatever. I thought that I was in control of my life and that if anything went wrong – well, that I was strong and I could handle it. But I fell apart when he died, for a bit, and it changed my attitude to everything. It drove home to me that life isn't like that. It's unpredictable, and fate isn't a kind thing. It can do anything it wants at any point.'

'Steve – that's his name?' Archie asked carefully.

'Yes.' Dina read his thoughts. 'We were just friends. He was only thirty.'

'Well, if this helps, I went through the same with my father. He died two years ago.'

'I'm sorry,' said Dina, apologising in part for failing to pick this up in their conversation earlier. She chewed her lower lip. 'So you understand what I mean.'

'Yes, I do. But I also felt, in a way, strengthened by his death.'

Dina was surprised. She had always assumed the emotions she had felt to be universal.

'Well, it was a different situation. My father was old and in a lot of pain. It was his time to go. I felt a sense of peace, a sense of responsibility, a new sense of wanting to get my teeth into life, as though I was carrying on, the next generation. His death made me grow up a bit. I wish you'd met him,' he said a little sadly, and Dina felt happiness wash over her. 'He was very wise.'

'He sounds it.'

'Every so often, you know, I just miss being able to go and ask him what to do. I mean, my mother's remarried,' Archie went on, 'and I don't want to sound like bloody Hamlet, and I admit their marriage wasn't exactly perfect . . . but it all feels too soon. She's pretty formidable, my mother. She didn't even cry at the funeral, and people thought she was being cold, but I knew she was in agony inside. She just has a steel veneer, and she thought she had to pick herself up and get on with things, and marrying again was part of that.'

'What's your stepfather like?'

'Urgh – stepfather. I hate the word. I don't even use it. I just refer to him as Ian. He's OK. But tell me more about Steve. What was he like?'

'He was . . . he was . . .' Dina closed her eyes and pictured Steve, and suddenly it was as though he was with her again, his breath gentle on her face. She felt tears sliding down her cheeks and tried to brush them away, feeling embarrassed, but they kept on coming. She opened her eyes, blinking thickly, gazing up at Archie. 'I'm sorry,' she said shakily. Suddenly all her feelings poured out in a naked rush: 'It's just – I miss him, so much. I miss just being able to call him up – he was my best friend. I feel so lonely now he's gone . . . I feel so alone . . .'

Oh God, she thought, catching herself and hastily gulping back a fresh torrent of tears, *now I sound completely sad, as though I have no friends.*

But to her amazement, Archie didn't look pitying at all. His eyes were tender with sympathy.

'Don't be lonely,' he whispered softly. He removed a handkerchief from his pocket and wiped her tears away. Then he leaned down and kissed her, as though he wanted to kiss all her hurt away, draw it up inside him and help her share the pain. Dina kissed him back just as softly, overwhelmed by his tenderness.

Slowly, the ache in her heart faded away. His kisses became warmer and firmer. Desire flared up through her stomach, fluttering in her throat. Previously, her desire for him had been motivated by sheer lust for his looks and charisma. Now it was emotional and blossomed from a deeper place inside her. She wanted to go to bed with him and shower pleasure on him, to kiss and caress him, to make him burn for her. She wanted to feel his hands on her body and see delight on his face when he made her moan. Afterwards, she wanted to lie in his arms and tell him more about all those intimate things she felt she couldn't discuss with anyone else.

Archie pushed her down on to the sofa. Dina felt his kisses run down her neck and she dug her fingers into his dark hair. She smiled up at the ceiling, as though thanking fate for the sweetness of the moment, and then closed her eyes again and let desire wash over her, taking her away on its tide . . .

Suddenly there was a loud banging on the door.

'Ignore it,' said Archie in a muffled voice, his mouth still hot on hers.

A few gasping seconds passed. The knock came again; and magnified into a pounding. The letterbox banged and a voice wailed through, shrill as a banshee.

Dina shuddered and Archie jumped up in shock.

'What's going on?' Dina cried. 'What on earth—'

Archie straightened his shirt and went to the door.

Dina remained where she was, as though trying to pretend this nightmare interruption hadn't happened.

The moment the door opened and she saw a flash of blonde hair, her heart twisted into a hot, sharp ball. Despite the fact that she was being firmly propped by Ralph's arm, the girl managed to half fall into the room, forcing Archie to lean forwards and catch her.

'Heidi – what on earth . . .'

Heidi looked hideous. Her face was a spider's web of mascara tears, her eyes like pulped tomatoes. Archie led her to the sofa and she collapsed in a hysterical heap. Dina felt a certain satisfaction that Heidi looked so dreadful, and then felt mean.

'I'm sorry,' said Ralph. There was a black Sobranie twitching between his lips as though it had been there for some time. Archie drew out a lighter and the flare lit the cigarette with an orange glow. Ralph breathed out smoke in relief. 'It's all Brian's fault. Brian, I loathe to say it, is a cad.'

Archie pocketed the lighter and ran his hands through his hair.

'Jesus.'

'But I think we know what Heidi's motivations are. As Havelock Ellis said, "Jealousy, that dragon which slays love under the pretence of keeping it alive",' Ralph quoted.

'Jesus.'

'For, in the words of Helen Rowland, "Falling in love consists merely in uncorking the imagination and bottling the common sense".'

'Stop sounding like you've swallowed the bloody dictionary of quotations and make some coffee, for Christ's sake.'

'Sorry,' said Ralph meekly.

Archie sat down next to Heidi and enveloped her in a tentative hug. She clung to him like a bruised kitten. He gave Dina an apologetic glance.

Ralph returned with some coffee. Heidi took a sip and then spat it out in a fresh explosion of grief.

'Can we talk in private?' she begged Archie.

'OK,' Archie agreed.

Dina tried to appear relaxed as they disappeared into Archie's bedroom and the door closed behind them. But her fingers slipped to the cushion on her lap, twisting its gold tassels tightly around their tips.

'I'm so terribly sorry about all this,' said Ralph. 'I really am so sorry.'

'Well, maybe you could stop saying sorry and tell me what the bloody hell Heidi is doing in there with my boyfriend—' Dina caught herself, wondering if Ralph might raise an eyebrow at the word 'boyfriend' but to her relief, he didn't react.

'Ah. That's quite a story. I shall need my knitting while I tell you.'

And to Dina's amazement, he reached into his pocket, drew out a piece of blue knitting and began to beaver away with a pair of long, thin grey needles.

'I find it helps relieve stress,' he explained. 'Well. Heidi, as you know, is a little upset at losing Archie, and Heidi, as you might not know, doesn't like to be without a man.'

Dina snorted, but Ralph's pale eyes were full of sympathy.

'She's a good girl,' he defended her, 'she's just a little insecure. Anyhow, there was Heidi – a fluttering, vulnerable butterfly, seeking a flower to comfort her. And there was Brian – now, if Brian were a flower, what would he be?' Ralph mused. 'Well, certainly not a rose. Something spiky and thorny. Anyway, there was something terribly wrong with Heidi's antennae, for Heidi landed, and now her wings are damaged.'

'So you're saying Heidi slept with Brian to make Archie jealous?'

'Yes.' Ralph reverted to plain-speak. 'And he threw her out of his flat and his life just a little too quickly. Tonight we all went to the Groucho and Heidi had too much to drink and saw Brian with another blonde, then flung herself at him and . . . and so on. But look. Look. I was chatting with Archie yesterday and he was saying how much he likes you. How funny and sweet you are, and rather special.'

'Really?' Dina asked, trying not to sound too breathless.

'Really. Archie's a bit laddish, you know. He's not very good at showing his emotions. Remember that in the future,' said Ralph.

Dina was about to express her gratitude when the doorbell rang again. Seeing that Ralph was tangled up in his knitting, she went to answer it, her heart heavy.

It was Jim.

'Hey, Dina,' he said, with a troubled grin. 'Ralph! Is Heidi here?' When Ralph nodded and tilted his head at the bedroom door, he said, 'Shit! What a night!'

Dina experienced a terrible sense of déjà vu. The evening, had, as before, started off with just her and Archie. Now there were five of them. Perhaps by the end of the evening the entire flat would be filled with nosy friends, all wanting a piece of the action.

'Would you like some coffee?' she asked Jim. She tried to sound polite but her tone was snappish.

'Yes please.' Jim looked nervously at Ralph, who raised an eyebrow and quickly shook his head, as if to say: *Don't upset her.*

Dina went to put the kettle on. She drummed her fingers, staring out through the window at the patch of night sky. Chatter buzzed in the background, irritating as wasps. Despite the presence of Jim and Ralph, she suddenly felt terribly lonely.

A few minutes ago, when Archie had been holding her, she had felt something extraordinary happening inside her. She closed her eyes and relived the sensation, struggling to define and understand it. She thought then of Steve's funeral, of how she had cried afterwards in her bedroom, releasing a torrent of grief. But since then she hadn't cried once, and yet her grief had not fully healed. It was as though the deepest part, the grief that was beyond tears, was lodged in the core of her heart like a splinter. But tonight Archie had changed that. She felt herself turning liquid inside, thawing, opening up to him. It had been frightening and thrilling all at once. And there had been a desperate sense of relief too, for he had made her feel human again; she had sensed her own capacity to love, to feel warmth, to enjoy life again.

Now she felt opened up, vulnerable, confused. She ached to be back in his arms again, to see what other magical alchemy he might perform on her emotions. Then, hearing Heidi emit a high-pitched wail, she realised with resignation that she was going to have to wait until next time.

12
Steve

'Why?' Steve said out loud. 'Why?' He held his head in his hands and hissed through his fingers: '*Why why why?*' His voice faded to a limp whisper: 'Why?'

Harrison, who was sitting on a lamppost next to Steve, gave him a manly, consolatory clap on the back that nearly sent him flying off. Up above, a couple of blackbirds perched on a telegraph wire eyed them suspiciously.

'I know, Steve. It's not fair. That's life. Women are complicated. I mean – I've had hundreds of girlfriends but I still don't get 'em.'

'Archie's just such a total git. WHY is she with him?'

'But women don't always want nice, Steve. Otherwise, where did the expression "treat 'em mean, keep 'em keen" come from? Sometimes they're masochistic, and they like men to lash them with emotional whips.'

Steve pondered then disagreed, saying, 'No. Dina's not a masochist.'

'Well, there is another alternative.'

'Yes?' Steve asked brightly.

'Well, she must be falling in love. Because when love gets into the heart, it poisons the head. Think of Shakespeare!' Harrison threw open his arms, getting into his stride – he could be surprisingly eloquent when he forgot to be crude. 'He compared love to a disease. Plato said it was like a grave mental illness. Love sends logic flying out of the window. Dina probably doesn't see Archie for who he is – love blurs the judgement and turns reality into fantasy. Love is blinding her to his faults, love is turning them into endearing little traits. To try to make sense of it is hopeless.'

'Great, Harrison. Thanks for making me feel so much better.'

'Ah well, life's a bitch.' Harrison wandered off on to another tangent and Steve wandered back into his thoughts. Was Harrison right? Oh God, why did he have to be so horribly honest?

That was the trouble with Harrison: he was the most wildly fascinating person Steve had ever met, but he was also the most deeply irritating, and both elements were intertwined parts of his personality, two sides of the same coin.

All the same, Steve was extremely grateful to have found a friend. In many ways, Harrison was his saviour. The night they had met, he had taken Steve to his base: a large, luxurious empty house in Hammersmith which was selling for such an exorbitant price that it had been on the market for a year. Steve, in turn, had taken Harrison to see his flat – only to discover that his parents were shoving boxes of the last of his stuff into the back of their green Mini. Steve and Harrison had followed them and salvaged Steve's movie collection, as well as a few books, creeping off with the box while everyone was asleep.

Harrison had suggested that Steve might like to come and live with him. After all, his house did have ten bedrooms.

And so for the past fortnight, Steve and Harrison had spent the majority of their time hanging out together. Harrison was certainly good for Steve because he refused to let Steve slip into a sluggish routine of staying indoors in front of the TV, shut up alone in his room, replaying his old black-and-white movies in a melancholy blur. He made Steve come out with him at night and play rather pointless games of footie in Hyde Park or the beautiful gardens of Buckingham Palace. He dragged him out to the cinema, where they watched blockbusters and got bored with the same recycled plots and tossed popcorn at unsuspecting viewers. Most of the time, they would sit on the roof of a building and talk. Or, rather, Harrison talked. The phrase 'verbal diarrhoea' could have been invented for him. One minute he would be putting the world to rights, the next he'd be boasting about all the girls he'd dated when he was alive, recounting colourful tales of supermodels who had left their celebrity boyfriends just for him, bowled over by his charm and bedtime abilities, all of which Steve found vaguely entertaining but suspiciously like something he might have read in the *News of the World*.

The more Harrison talked, the more Steve missed Dina. Dina was a talker too, but she never let Steve play the listener all the time. She encouraged him to come out of his shell and open up.

'The thing is,' Steve finally managed to get a word in edgeways, 'what really gets me is . . .' He flushed, realising he was on the verge of something he hadn't told anyone before and suddenly feeling self-conscious. Then he thought: *What the heck, I'm dead, I ought to be beyond embarrassment.* 'What gets me is that I've always been so slow at everything. I mean, d'you remember that story you used to hear when you were a kid, about the race between the tortoise and the hare? Well, I'm the tortoise. When I was at school, I always used to begin my classes being bottom of every one, and then I'd rise to the top. It just seems to be a pattern in my life – it takes me a while to get the hang of things, to suss things out. It means I always end up getting overlooked or people underestimate me. And I just think if I'd been around long enough, I would have got Dina in the end. Maybe it would have taken a year, or five years, or whatever, to woo her, but I would have done it.'

'Well it's too late now,' said Harrison bluntly. Then he added in a playful voice, 'I can think of something to cheer you up.'

'What?' Steve asked warily. Harrison seemed in a bit of a hyper mood tonight. What was he about to suggest? Visiting a ghost brothel?

'People-watching!' Harrison cried. 'I mean, it really is the best way to see how women tick, Steve. When I'm bored, I do it a lot. I watch women being chatted up by men, I listen to them talking to their girlfriends, I watch them being wined and dined, and Good Lord, Steve, you wouldn't believe how many interesting things you learn!'

'I don't know, Harrison,' Steve said. 'I think I'd feel a bit funny. I mean, these are people's private lives. I wouldn't like to be watched if I was still alive. It makes me feel like some sleazy tabloid hack spying on someone.'

'So what d'you want to do instead?' Harrison exploded. 'Sit here and play Trivial Pursuit with the blackbirds?'

'Well . . . it's an idea.'

Harrison started to rant. 'Steve, listen to me. We're *not* normal people any more. We're not tabloid hacks. Because those people have lives, and they have innumerable possibilities to still do useful things with those lives, to make better choices. They have families and jobs, children, friends. People who need them, who depend on them. What have we got? Nothing. We're dead. Gone. Useless. And just you wait. You might be getting all high-and-mighty now but wait until you've been a ghost for a year. You think you can run away from the loneliness? Travel and see the world?'

'I . . .' Steve had to admit it had been floating on the surface of his mind over the last few days.

'Well, I've been there and done it. It was one of the first things I did when I became a ghost. I've seen it all, the Seven Wonders of the World. I've been in the desert and watched tribes make offerings to their gods to bring them water. I've seen flamingos running across the sand, and I tell you, Steve, it was the most beautiful sight, like pink flames flaring against the blue of a sunrise. I've swum on the backs of dolphins round Hawaii, I've sat beneath the Niagara Falls, the water cascading over me like a curtain of crystals, I've clung on to a plane and swooped right through the Northern Lights, through the green and pink layers of cloud, and it felt like I was flying through a gate to a celestial realm. But none of it brought the joy I'd expected. Because what does any of it matter when you don't have anyone real to share it with?'

Steve stood very still, letting Harrison's words seep into his soul.

'You're the first ghost I've met,' said Harrison gruffly, 'who I feel could be a good mate, who I could share stuff with. And I tell you, the odd bit of female-watching *is* the answer to keep lost souls like us going,' he continued, as if his recent burst of eloquent profundity was such a shock to his system that he had to quickly go back to being crude again. 'Come on, Steve, I tell you, we're going to see some awesome stuff!'

Steve wasn't convinced that it was an awesome evening, but he had to admit, it was fascinating. Harrison kept up a running commentary the whole way through.

'Wow, isn't that girl in the restaurant so sweet, what on earth is she doing with a greaseball like him, I mean, he can't even hold a knife and fork, and oh whoops, I just appear to have knocked his fork out of his hand . . . I'm not spoiling their romance, Steve, there is no romance, oh, OK, let's move on . . . Hey, look at these flats and why is she looking so ill, oh God, so PMT isn't just an excuse they make up to win an argument – it's real. Poor thing, I wish I could console her . . . And oh look, nice bedroom, he's asleep and she's – a-ha! – awake, and what's that she's texting to her friend? *It was awful. He's never heard of 4play!* God, this isn't the first time I've heard this, Steve – I mean, would you believe it but I really do think women actually *like* foreplay. I mean, I used to think it was just a joke, something women's mags made up in order to look sensitive – but they do! Oh look, now he's woken up, maybe he's going to have another try, oh well, this should be a laugh . . .'

'Harrison, we are getting out of here. *Now,*' Steve said, the tips of his ears burning red. To his relief, Harrison looked a bit red too and for all his laddish bravado also seemed keen to make a speedy exit.

'Maybe we should get back,' said Steve, out in the cool night air.

'But Steve, the night is still young! Come on, it's your turn to pick a place.'

And then inspiration struck.

'Hey – let's go in here,' Steve suddenly cried. They were standing outside a large, plush block of flats framed with fairytale gates. 'Follow me.'

They strolled in past the doorman, who was sitting slumped in a booth, reading the *Daily Mail* and looking thoroughly bored. He didn't blink when the lift doors swished open and closed and the lift, seemingly empty, tunnelled upwards to the third floor.

'Here,' said Steve. He had stopped outside a door with the number 21 picked out in gold italics.

They slipped inside. It was just as Steve had pictured it: swimming in luxury and expensive things. There was a tell-tale mess of clothing on the floor. A discarded pinstriped shirt and a rumpled pair of trousers. Bra straps looped around a skirt. Hastily shed stockings, still clipped to a suspender belt, curled on the floor like a black snake.

Harrison wolf-whistled, thinking Steve had the right idea after all.

Steve wasn't so sure. Doubtful excitement fluttered in his stomach. And as they approached the bedroom, something in him, something decent and moral, made him catch hold of Harrison's elbow.

'Don't,' said Steve. He smiled weakly. 'We mustn't. It's – it's Dina, you see. It's *her*. This is Archie's flat.'

Watching Dina by himself was one thing. Alone, he could persuade himself that he was her guardian angel, looking after her, rather than some sad stalker. But there was something sick and voyeuristic about bringing Harrison along for the ride.

'But if you watch them making love, then you can see *exactly* what Dina likes, stupid,' Harrison insisted.

He pushed past Steve and went into the bedroom. Steve shoved his hands in his pockets, holding back, biting his lip, knotted in agony. He had to admit that the thought of seeing them together – the girl he loved, the man he loathed – provoked a sharp jab of desire in his groin. And Harrison was right. He was curious to discover what Dina liked. How she liked to kiss. God, he had whiled away hours wondering if she liked hard or soft kisses, quick or lingering ones, restrained or passionate.

Then he shook himself. No, this wasn't right. He absolutely could not watch her. And neither could Harrison. He rushed into the bedroom, determined to drag Harrison out.

The bedroom was incredibly plush. A white carpet, soft as a cat's coat. Wall-to-wall mirrors. And an enormous double bed.

There were a couple making love on the bed, and the sounds of their lovemaking were so intimate that they made Steve blush. Archie was on top of her, mouth pressed down on hers; then they rolled over and she was on top, showering his face with kisses, her hair snaking over his neck.

Steve opened his mouth to yell at Harrison, and then gaped. *Hang on*, he thought, *something isn't right here . . .*

At first he thought he was seeing things. Then a car passed by in the street below, spraying a hose of amber light into the room, highlighting them: Archie's good looks, the sweat on his forehead, his dark eyebrows; her sinewy limbs, her slender face, her *waterfall of blonde hair.* And Archie groaned: 'Oh God . . . Heidi . . . Heidi . . . oh God . . .'

'Wow – has Dina dyed her hair blonde?' Harrison said.

'No, she hasn't,' said Steve. He giggled and let out a deep breath. 'She hasn't. Dina, I mean. It isn't her.' Suddenly he felt wildly happy. *Ha*, he thought savagely. *Ha ha ha. I told you, Archie, I told you you weren't good enough for her. And now I've been proved right. And Dina is going to find out all about this, oh yes she is. I'll see to it that she does.*

13
Dina

The note lay tucked in Dina's pocket all morning. It was neatly folded, its point peeking like a swan's wing from her pocket as she walked to work. It nearly fell out when she bumped into an elderly gentleman but an unseen hand quickly shoved it back into place.

She didn't notice the note as she unloaded chairs from the tables of The Greasy Spoon and pinged open the till to put in some change. She was too engrossed in thinking about Archie. He was all she ever seemed to think about these days. She found that the conversations in her head with Steve had been replaced by interactions with Archie. She wanted to confide in Archie but she hadn't yet felt ready to completely open up to him, so mostly she found herself thinking up witty, exaggerated anecdotes about her life in the US, refining and sculpting them anxiously like a comedian who knows he will face a tough and demanding audience. She was very conscious of the fact that Archie was like a child who got bored easily; she must make sure she stayed interesting. No, more than interesting – *fascinating.*

Archie had taken her on one more date since their last Heidi-tainted fiasco dinner at his flat. It had been delightful. They'd had dinner at The Ivy. Nobody had interrupted them. They'd laughed, chatted and bonded intimately. But at eleven o'clock, his mobile had rung and he'd been called away on a business crisis. Yet again, all they'd done was kiss. A very deep, sensual kiss in the back of a taxi – but still, no more than a kiss. It was ironic, Dina thought: normally it was the other way round – men were desperate to get women into bed. She half wondered if Archie was just teasing, playing a game, but he was such a curious mixture of sensitivity and cynicism, his actions such a blend of sincerity and manipulation, that it was hard to tell.

It was only in her lunch hour, when she was standing in a newsagent's, rooting in her jacket for 42p for her KitKat, that she found it.

Dina's pockets – like her handbag – were always full of crap. She pulled out a tangle of tissues and sweet wrappers, studded with the sticky, stale crumbs of a half-eaten cereal bar. And there was the note. At first she assumed it was just a flyer she had pocketed: junk mail. Then she unfolded it, saw the writing and shivered.

'Here's your change,' the shopkeeper repeated irritably.

'Sorry – thanks.' Dina took the coins, but her hands were shaking and she dropped them amongst the chocolate bars and took a few minutes to retrieve them.

She thought about it all day. Who on earth could have put it there? Who would want to? What did it mean? Was it a sick joke, or a helpful truth? The Greasy Spoon was frantic because Fatima was auditioning for a record company and Luigi was terribly slow, moaning and groaning about his ingrowing toenail as though he'd had a major operation. And yet whatever Dina did, it was there, beating like an anxious pulse at the back of her mind, until by the end of the day she felt she couldn't bear it any longer. She went into the toilet and balanced a coin on her fingers.

Heads I go, tails I don't, she told herself, tossing it. She caught it in her palm with a thwack. Tails. *Oh God,* she fretted, *but if I don't go, I'll be left wondering.* She longed to call up Anita, but she was away for two weeks, visiting her folks in Melbourne, which meant Dina had nobody to help her untangle her indecision.

She stared down at the coin. *OK,* she decided, *best of three.*

Well, here she was.

Dina checked her watch, and let out a deep breath. Then she knocked.

No reply. A cool breeze shivered over her.

She knocked again. No reply. *I'm just being silly,* she told herself, turning to go. *I mean, what am I going to say to him anyway? Oh, hi, Archie, by the way, I got a weird note about you in my pocket this morning and maybe you know something about it?*

Then the door opened a crack. Archie was wearing old boxer shorts and a rumpled blue-and-white pinstriped shirt. It was splattered with what looked tomato ketchup and covered with a sort of white dust. His hair was greasy, stubble flecked his chin and his eyes were shadowed with violet. Despite all this, he was still wonderfully, horribly, shy-makingly gorgeous. *Who cares about a stupid note?* Dina thought weakly. *I just want him, I want to eat him all up. Oh God, I like him so much.*

When he saw her, he almost visibly jumped.

'Hi.' He didn't look or sound terribly thrilled to see her.

'Hi.' Dina felt pain in her stomach. This was all a big mistake. 'Er – I was just passing and I'd thought I'd drop by, but you're obviously really busy. I'm sorry.'

Something in his eyes suggested he didn't believe a word of it.

'Well,' he said, 'I'm actually just, er, experimenting with a recipe.'

If any of Dina's friends had been experimenting with a recipe, it would normally have been something simple like chocolate cake, and they would have immediately invited her in to try a slice. But the look on Archie's face was dreamy, intense, as though he was still deep in a river of concentration and hadn't quite come up to the surface.

'Well, I love cooking!' Dina said exuberantly. Then she caught herself. *I love cooking.* She sounded like a kid in *The Sound of Music.* Calm down, she told herself. Play it cool. 'So what are you making?'

'Mango cream tart with elderflower and passionfruit sauce.'

'Well, you seem pretty, ah, busy, so I think I should leave you to it.'

Archie hesitated just a fraction too long.

'No . . .'

'No, really, it's fine.' She turned and saw that the lift doors were open and dived into it, on the verge of tears.

Archie – still only in his boxers – dived after her. She had just pressed the button for the ground floor and the doors were sliding shut when Archie prised them open and forced his way in. The door slid shut behind him; the lift began to descend.

'Look – forgive me – when I'm cooking something I lose myself in it,' Archie explained.

Then he closed in and kissed her.

'I've been thinking about doing that all week,' he whispered, and Dina smiled in relief.

'So have I,' she said.

They were still kissing when the lift doors opened on the ground floor and a small boy entered, clutching his mother's hand. He was wearing school uniform – dinky grey shorts which showed off his knobbly knees. His mother was wearing a lilac suit and she patted her coiffeured hair and pursed her crimped lips when she saw Archie's bare legs and Dina's dishevelled curls.

Archie pressed the button for the third floor.

The woman pressed the button for the second floor.

Archie and Dina glanced at each other and bit back smiles.

'Hey, you're wearing shorts too,' the boy said to Archie.

'Uh-huh, this is my school uniform,' said Archie in a deadpan voice. The boy laughed as though unsure whether to believe him.

'Don't talk to strangers, Bartholomew,' said his mother in a stern voice, clutching his hand and staring straight ahead of her.

After they had left, Dina and Archie burst into laughter. Then, as the lift doors closed again, he pushed her up against the mirror, put his knee between hers and looked deep into her eyes before kissing her again.

'Oh God, I bet she thought we were having sex in the lift,' Dina mumbled as Archie buried his lips in her hair.

'We are having sex in a lift,' said Archie, pushing up hard against her and making her gasp.

But what about the note? a small voice asked.

For goodness' sake, she shouted back, *just forget about the silly note, I mean, God, this guy is the best kisser in the world, just give in, just—*

Dina broke off. It was no good. Though it was the sort of thing she'd fantasised about many a time during her dull hours at The Greasy Spoon, this was reality, not fantasy; and it wasn't just about sex. She couldn't quite give herself up to him; a part of her held back, resentful, still confused, mistrusting. She thought with a wistful pang of that night she'd cried in his arms, the way he had kissed and caressed her with such loving tenderness.

And so, as he began to slide his fingers up her ribcage, she stopped him. The lift halted smoothly at the third floor and the doors pinged open.

'So let me see your tart,' she said. 'I want a taste.'

Archie stepped back, his eyes glazed. Then he leaned in and kissed her neck. 'You taste much nicer,' he assured her, biting her skin gently.

Dina giggled and pushed him away, her smile coy and conciliatory. Archie let out a frustrated sigh and then grabbed her hand, drawing her into the flat.

Dina was delighted to see that the kitchen was a complete mess. While fastidious neatness of the rest of his flat was a bit spooky, here was glorious chaos. Flour on the floor; orangey gloops of egg yolk trailing like snail's goo across the worktop; exhausted lemons with their juice squeezed out; balls of pastry, cups full of creamy liquid, and three experimental jugs of sauce, one deep scarlet, one cerise, one pale and rose-coloured, and there, in the centre of it all, was the tart: a large creamy circle, flat and hard as a cheese, wrapped up in soft, frilly pastry, with ribbons of sauce slashed across its top. It glistened as though aware of its own deliciousness, as though its own mouth was watering.

'Wow, it looks yummy.' Dina suddenly realised how hungry she was.

'You're not allowed to have any,' said Archie. 'Absolutely not. It's just an early version and it's not quite right. I'm like a painter,' he explained defensively, 'who does a few sketches for a picture. He doesn't show them to anyone, he doesn't let anyone have a look until the final painting is totally finished.'

'Oh go on, just let me have a bite.'

'No,' said Archie. 'The balance isn't right. It's too sharp, but I don't want to just dump a load of sugar in and ruin it.'

'I know what you mean. I'm the same when I bake brownies. I think there's a real yin and yang to it,' she said. 'You want to get just the right balance of sharp and sweet, teetering in the middle so it teases you as to whether it's one or the other.'

'I like that,' said Archie, looking impressed. 'You understand food. But you still can't have any.'

'Please?' Dina asked in a girlish voice. 'Please please *please*?'

'No. It's going in the bin.'

'You're kidding me.'

'No. We can have some tea, though.'

As Archie turned away to remove some cups from the cupboard, Dina found herself suddenly overcome with a terribly naughty urge. She couldn't resist. She reached out her forefinger and dipped it right into the centre of the tart; it made a delicious squidgy, sucking noise. Then she pulled it out and licked off a large, buttery chunk.

'Wow,' she breathed as the flavours flowed over her tongue. 'It is delicious.'

Archie spun round. He nearly dropped the cups. He looked so mad that for a moment Dina was genuinely terrified.

'You ate my tart,' he said in a quiet, intense voice. 'When I told you not to.'

'So I did,' Dina said, sounding a lot more brave and bolshie than she felt. She reached out and dipped her finger again. 'God, it tastes so nice.'

'You do that once more and there will be big trouble.'

Dina paused. His eyes, dark as elderberries, were deadly. *Is he really mad with me?* she asked herself, squirming uneasily. *Or is he just playing? And aren't I meant to be confronting him? But that can wait. Here and now is just too exciting.*

She couldn't resist. In slow motion, she reached out, dunked her finger in the tart again and licked it with ostentatious defiance.

'I can't believe you just did that.' Archie put the cups down. Slowly, as though approaching his opponent in a duel, he began to walk towards her.

'Right,' he said. 'Take off your top.'

'I'm sorry?' Dina spluttered, a squiggle of excitement curling up her spine.

'I said, take your top off.'

Dina blinked. Archie was standing a foot away from her now, arms folded, eyes playful but definitely threatening, and though his command was scary, it made it all the more sexy.

She pulled up her navy T-shirt and dropped it to the floor. Suddenly she felt more naked than if she'd stripped off completely.

Archie didn't look at her body. He held her gaze.

'Take off your jeans,' he said.

Her hands were shaking so much she fumbled with the button and the zip. Then they dropped to the floor and she stepped out of them, her toes curling.

Archie stepped forward until they were so close they were very nearly touching, the cotton of his shirt just breezing the bare skin of her belly so that all the little hairs stood up on end. He reached across and dipped his finger in the pie, and as he brushed against her she felt herself shiver. Archie noticed, and smiled. He put his finger in her mouth and she sucked it. The taste of his skin was stronger than the pie.

He cupped her face in his hands and leaned in to kiss her, but drew away at the last minute. Dina let out a light gasp of frustration, and a smile curled at his lips. He pressed a finger into the hollow of her collarbone and slowly trailed it down her body, in between her breasts, over the arch of her ribcage, the soft, sweet swell of her belly, skirting the lace edge of her knickers; at the same time, he ran a teasing line of kisses along her jaw, so faint they were more like impressions, thoughts of kisses than kisses themselves. His fingers fluttered at the lace; he was so close she could feel his breath mingling with hers, taste the scent of the tart in it.

'You're so sexy,' he whispered.

'You're so sexy,' she whispered back, deliriously, the note completely forgotten now in the fire of her passion. Then his resolve broke and he leaned in and kissed her, his fingers delving into the lace . . .

Archie played with her for hours, and then they took a shower together. Dina thought it was terribly touching when Archie dried her off, taking care to remove every drop of water from her body, even behind her ears and between each toe. Then, as they returned to his bedroom, he wrapped his stripy duvet around her and told her she looked cute.

'I think we need some tea, don't we?' he said. 'I mean, I've got a sneaky sort of feeling that we're about to have one of those so-what's-going-on-between-us chats. Whenever I'm going into a heavy situation, I need a good old British cup of tea in my stomach.'

'I feel the same about Oreos,' Dina joked, for the moment he'd mentioned a chat, butterflies had woken up in her stomach.

'Well, I'm afraid I don't have any Oreos.'

'You could always make me another tart while you're in the kitchen.'

'You' – Archie kissed her forehead – 'are very cheeky.'

Dina smiled and wriggled. After he'd gone, she crept into the bathroom. She eyed up her reflection uneasily, running her fingers through her damp hair, fretting about this *chat.*

Here, she thought, was the moment to confront him about the note. But how could she say it? It all sounded so mysterious and weird . . .

Back in bed, they sat with pillows behind them, sipping tea.

'Now I feel as though we're Morecambe and Wise,' said Archie.

Dina asked Archie if he was referring to his solicitors. She couldn't understand it when he exploded into laughter, before finally enlightening her.

'Oh God, you're really missing out, not having Morecambe and Wise,' he sighed. 'You Americans are so deprived. Still, I guess you have culture too. You have, um, Jerry Springer.'

Dina gave him an evil look and Archie grinned wickedly. Then he stopped grinning and the silence grew thick with expectation.

'Archie,' Dina said. 'Look, I – I have something to ask you. A friend of mine – who I can't name, I promised I wouldn't – he – he was at a party and he, erm, heard, from someone, that you're – you're seeing someone else.'

'What!' Archie cried, looking tense. 'Look, Dina, people gossip about me all the time. The bloody press are always trying to claim I'm going out with the latest member of the latest all-girl band, and it's not true!'

'Right,' said Dina, chewing her lip and suddenly feeling guilty about her accusation. 'Well. Good. So . . . what was it you wanted to say?'

'Well,' Archie blew out his breath, 'the thing is, when it comes to relationships I . . .'

Oh my God. Dina took a gulp of tea and nearly took a layer off her tongue. *Relationships?*

'. . . I – well, I've no intention of settling down, much to my mother's disappointment. I mean – don't get me wrong, I do love women, I love having a girlfriend and the sex and spoiling her and all that, but you know . . . Then there's the other side of my life, that pulls me the other way – my work, and so on – and then I always feel mean, feel I'm being neglectful, and I *hate* that, I don't want to be some horrible bastard. So I think it's better not to get heavy to begin with, and then I don't cause disappointment.' He leaned over and kissed her shoulder. 'I just thought I should say all this so you don't get the wrong idea from the start.'

Oh. Well hang on a minute, thought Dina hotly. *Aren't you being just a tiny bit arrogant? Assuming that I'd be so desperate to rush into a heavy relationship with you?*

'Well, I'm not big on commitment either,' she lied, determined to have the upper hand.

'You're not?'

'You look surprised.'

'Well, you just seem . . . quite romantic.'

Dina snorted. 'Me? Romantic? Give me a bunch of flowers and I'd chuck them in the bin.' She was really getting into her stride now. 'I like things casual too. I'm sick of going out with guys who want to tie me down. There's no way I'm having screaming babies or getting locked in with mother-in-laws, God, no. So it's cool. I'd like to keep it casual too.'

'Well, good. But . . .'

'But . . .' Dina frowned.

'I kind of think . . . look, here's the truth. When I first met you, you know, you're a waitress, and obviously we lead very different lives, and I just thought I'd love to have a fling with you and maybe see how things went—'

'What!' Dina cried in outrage. 'Oh, so I'm bloody Eliza Doolittle, am I? Jesus, I told you I'm only a waitress because I really want to go into catering—'

'I know, I know!' Archie interrupted. She began to poke him indignantly in the stomach and ribs, and he fought her off, laughing and catching her wrists.

But Dina wasn't laughing. She suddenly felt tears hot behind her eyes. *I should never have fallen for him,* she thought. *This is just like Jason all over again. How can it have happened? I ought to have protected my heart. Well, bugger him. I'm walking out—*

'Look, I'm just being blunt, OK?' he went on. 'I am who I am and you can take me or leave me. So, I thought we'd just have a fling, and leave it at that, but now I feel . . .'

Dina lowered her head, fiercely threading the sheet between her fingers.

'. . . now I feel . . .' Archie took a big gulp of tea. 'Differently.'

'Differently? Archie, just tell me what you mean!' Dina cried, her voice so savage he blinked in surprise.

'I really like you,' he blurted out, all in a big rush. 'You make me laugh and I think you're great and the reason I haven't yanked you into bed before now is because I thought you were worth waiting for. And then today you turned up at my door looking so sexy and I just couldn't resist. And it scares me a bit, because . . .'

'Because?' Dina asked, biting back a smile.

'. . . because I just have this – this self-destructive streak, this tendency to screw relationships up. I don't know why I do it, but I do. It's funny, really. When it comes to business, I'm all there. But relationships – they're like violins, all tricky notes and scores and fiddly strokes . . . so I just . . . don't want you to get too close to me, either, because I don't want to hurt you. But then maybe if you're a bit nervous of commitment too, then we're OK, right?' He smiled boyishly, nervously.

'I won't get hurt,' Dina said. Suddenly she felt like laughing. Archie thought she was special. She wasn't just another one-night stand.

'So is that all agreed then?' Archie said. He took her hand and squeezed it, his face full of affection.

Dina wasn't sure what had been agreed: one minute he was dangling her at arm's length, the next he was implying he wanted to cup his hands around her heart and keep it safe. *But that's OK*, she thought, *I can heal him. He's scared of relationships so we can take it slowly. I won't push him or pressurise him. Things will unfold and Archie won't screw up, I won't let him, we're going to have such a good time together that he'll never want to let me go.*

Before she could muse any more, Archie took her mug away and said he felt that they ought to complete their chat with a celebration of their new arrangement.

*

This time, Archie went to straight asleep afterwards.

'Poor love, I've exhausted you,' she whispered, kissing his shoulder and getting up to go to the bathroom again. She was feeling chilly, so she picked up her cardigan on the way. In the bathroom, she pulled the note out and read it once more.

Dear Dina,
This is a note from someone who loves you very much. I don't want to cause you any harm or hurt, and it breaks my heart to tell you this, but A. is cheating on you. Please go and confront him, and then walk away. Please do this for your own good.
I love you.

Dina sighed angrily, her forehead knitted into a frown. Then she folded the note neatly, tore it into shreds and flushed it down Archie's toilet. The note was silly and childish. Someone was just playing games with her; probably Heidi. Well, she wasn't going to play along. Smiling, she strolled out and got into bed, relishing the warmth of Archie's naked body.

Steve watched in choked agony as Dina went back into Archie's bedroom. He'd waited for ages outside the flat, hoping to see her storm out, but it hadn't happened. Now he watched as Archie lifted up his arm sleepily and Dina slipped under the covers. Archie's jaw slackened in sleep, and Dina lay awake, gazing at his face with horrible fondness. Then, taking care not to disturb his arm, which he'd sleepily slung over her, and wake him, she gently rolled over to face him, buried her face in his chest and closed her heavy lids.

Steve lay down on the bed, facing Dina's back. He gazed into the dark swirl of her curls and whispered, 'Oh Dina, I love you. I love you so much.'

She sighed restlessly in her sleep. Steve lay by her for some time, watching the sky sparkle with stars that gradually faded as heavy clouds covered the night.

14
Steve

'I'm bored,' Harrison announced in a loud whisper. Roger was sitting on the window ledge, his tail splayed out like a silky, red fern leaf. Harrison couldn't resist flicking it.

'Ssh!' Steve whispered furiously as Roger burst into a tantivy of barking. 'It's just getting interesting.'

Anita and Dina broke off from their conversation. They were sitting on the sofa, drinking tea out of large mugs. Now Dina patted the sofa.

'Come on, Roger! What's the matter, honey?'

'He's probably spotted a cat,' Anita giggled.

'Roger? Not likely. He's a complete coward! You know the ginger tom in the flat downstairs? Well Roger is completely terrified of it. It only has to flick its tail and Roger practically wets himself.'

Roger, growling piteously at these two unwanted tail-flicking strangers in his mistress's living room, bounded up on to the sofa and curled up next to Dina, his tail thumping protectively against her thighs.

Dina and Anita returned to their conversation. Anita had just got back from Australia, and Dina had been telling her about sex with Archie. Listening to her account, Steve had spotted a few embellishments: Dina had claimed that Archie had been really pleased to see her the moment she turned up at his door, which was definitely a white lie. Or maybe just a rose-tinted lie, a love-blurred untruth. He had watched Dina throughout the morning; whether she was doing her washing or cleaning her teeth, sunshine would pass across her face and she'd suddenly bite back a little smile and flush, her skin glowing as though ecstasy throbbed beneath her skin. It was as if each time she remembered Archie, she painted a layer over the top, until her memory of the evening was the perfect picture she wanted it to be.

'So – that's kind of it,' she said now, blushing.

'Wow, it's amazing,' said Anita. 'And so how big was his—'

She broke off, giggling, as Dina shoved her and yelped, '*Anita!*'

'So are you going to see him again?'

Dina was silent for a moment.

'There's one last thing,' she said slowly, as though uncertain whether to reveal it; which, of course, made Anita sit up and *demand* that Dina tell her.

'Well, afterwards we had this chat. He suggested that because neither of us is all that great at relationships, and neither of us wants something heavy, we should just keep things quite casual, because he can sometimes get a bit funny about commitment, even though he really cares about me.' She broke off, seeing Anita's face darken. 'What? I mean, I want to keep things casual too. It suits me fine.'

'Really?' Anita asked incredulously. 'It just – it just sounds a bit rich to me, Dina. Like he wants to have his cake and eat it. Are you sure he's not just messing you around?'

'No – *no* – listen to the other bit of the story, there's more. At the end, we were lying in bed together, and I thought he was asleep, and then he whispered, "I love you."'

'No!' Anita was wide-eyed.

'Yes! And it wasn't one of those corny, getting-you-into-bed I-love-yous – after all, he'd already got me into bed. It was so tender. I could feel the love in his voice, hear it in the very syllables.'

Over by the window, the clouds broke open and shafts of sunlight slanted through the window and straight through Steve's soul. They failed to warm the feeling of ice in his stomach.

'God,' said Anita, 'I don't know if that's worse than him wanting to shag around. I mean, God – men. These days they're the ones who are romantic and seem to want to get heavy and have babies and all that. And we're left getting freaked out when they say "I love you".'

'I kind of wasn't freaked out. I kind of thought it was romantic.'

'Oh my God!' Anita cried theatrically. 'You're in love now! I'm away for two weeks and you go and fall in love.'

'No, no, no, *no*, NO!' Dina kept crying as Anita threw amorous accusations at her like Cupid with his arrows.

Harrison rolled his eyes.

'If we have to sit here listening to this girly chat for one more minute, I am going to die of fucking boredom,' he hissed quietly. 'Come on, Steve, can we please just go and have some fun now? Seriously, I've found something that is going to take your mind off Dina. Trust me . . .'

As Steve and Harrison made their way down Shepherd's Bush High Street, Harrison chatted non-stop. But Steve's mind was on other matters. He was feeling deeply disturbed by the conversation they had just observed. It wasn't merely his disappointment that his note had failed so abysmally. He had known it was a long shot, and certainly not the best way to say it – but what else could he do, given his limitations? Paint a message in the sky with clouds? All the same, it had been a cruel twist of fate that his note hadn't made Dina see reality, but only helped her jump into bed with the stupid bastard, *and*, worse, made her think that he loved her. As if Archie had the slightest clue what love was! He probably had only ever said it to his bathroom mirror, thought Steve bitterly.

No, it was more than that. Archie had brought out a side to Dina that shocked Steve. Steve had thought he knew Dina well, and he loved the way she was so together, so inherently happy, anchored by her sunny disposition and her optimistic outlook, like the roots of an oak tree.

But since meeting Archie, she had become a different Dina. She was giggly and indecisive and clingy and confused. Her judgement, which was normally sound, seemed utterly skewed. Her vulnerability touched Steve, but also made him feel terribly afraid for her. He wasn't just motivated by jealousy; he genuinely believed that Archie was going to take her apart, piece by piece.

'Nearly there,' said Harrison, leading Steve across Tesco's car park, where families were packing shopping into cars and trying to fend off bawling kids demanding their sweets right away.

What does she see in him? The thought kept circling in his mind. OK – aside from the fact that he was rich. And good-looking. And had his own restaurant chain. And had achieved an insane amount at a young age. But those were all *surface* things. Even if Dina really thought Archie loved her, *I love you* was just words. Actions were what counted; showing *I love you,* not saying it. And since when had Archie shown her any love? He'd got off with Heidi behind her back and then been displeased to see Dina when she turned up on his doorstep . . . until he'd realised it was a great chance for a shag. Surely Dina didn't think this was *romantic*? Surely she knew it didn't add up to *I love you*; it was like trying to add one and two and make five. Then he remembered Harrison's claim that love was a form of madness . . .

'Here we go,' said Harrison in a bright voice.

Steve blinked. Harrison had led him past a bundle of stranded trolleys and stinky bins. The ground was flecked with beige cigarette ends from workers taking their fag breaks. Harrison brushed them aside, kicked up a lump of turf and, to Steve's amazement, revealed an iron ring. He pulled it up. Steve peered down. The smell of wet earth and insects wafted up.

'You have a secret club under the Shepherd's Bush Tesco?' Steve asked in amazement.

'More than just a club,' said Harrison. 'Just you wait, Steve!'

He climbed down a short ladder. Steve, feeling rather like Alice going down the rabbit-hole, followed.

They found themselves in a corridor. The floor was covered with dirty lino and the earthy walls were illuminated by flickering neon bulbs. It was full of doors. As Harrison led the way, Steve caught glimpses of ghostly debauchery: a pub full of ghosts drinking from dark glasses, a massage parlour, and an entrance covered by a dirty beaded curtain which looked as though it might lead to the ghoulish equivalent of a red-light district. Finally they came to a door with a sign on it that said:

WELCOME TO THE SHEPHERD'S BUSH GHOST DATING AGENCY!
Feeling a little lonely? Missing your loved ones?
Never fear – find yourself a ghostly friend!

'What the hell is this?' Steve grumbled.

'I came across it my first week as a ghost,' said Harrison. 'Don't worry, it's really cool.'

He tried to take Steve by the arm, but Steve shook him off violently.

'What?'

'I can't go in there,' said Steve. Suddenly his stomach was full of butterflies. Years of disastrous relationships flashed before him as though he was dying all over again: a miserable kaleidoscope of school discos and fake phone numbers and failed crushes.

'Stop whingeing,' said Harrison, 'and bloody get in there, Steve. What you need to take your mind off Dina is some damn fine ghostly pussy!'

Inside, Steve was surprised to find it looked very much like a human dating agency would. White walls, a bulletin board advertising forthcoming events (*Vampire Morgue Trip!* and *Celebrity Ghost Karaoke Evening – Star Guests include Anne Boleyn and the Headless Lady of Black Hall*), a thin beige carpet and a reception desk where a young woman was talking on the phone. She kept them waiting a minute before slamming it down and smiling up at them – though, Steve noted, her smile was a tad frosty.

'Can I help you?'

'Hi,' said Harrison, and Steve noticed how his easy manner softened the girl's expression a little. 'I'm Harrison and I'm already on your books, but my mate Steve wants to join too.'

'Well, if Steve would just like to sit down, I can take his details.'

Once again, Steve felt an anxious desire to bolt for the door, but Harrison forced him down on to the swivel chair.

Steve let his hands dangle in his lap and eyed up the girl. Her fingernails were painted purple and her hair was coaxed into a henna quiff.

'Name?'

'Steve. Steve MacFadden.'

'Reason for death?'

'I, er, was saving a woman from being mugged and the mugger shot me,' Steve found himself saying, ignoring Harrison's rude nudge.

'What's your ideal woman?'

'Um . . . God . . . that's a hard question.' Steve stared down at his palms, for the girl's hawkish stare was putting him off. 'Well, I have to admit, I've got quite high ideals when it comes to love. Basically, I think it should be about making the other person happy, about being happy together.' He thought of Dina again, his words tumbling out with passion. 'It should be about knowing each other inside out. And being able to be yourself with the person you love. You ought to be best friends, you ought to be able to completely and utterly trust each other—' He broke off, realising that she was looking bored and trying to interrupt him.

'All I need to know at this stage is what eye colour you'd prefer.'

'Oh. *Oh.* Oh right. Er . . . well, any colour is fine. I mean, green . . . green is nice,' Steve said, flushing madly.

'Any preference over size . . . and I don't mean eye size.'

'Oh. Oh, right. Er – well, I don't mind. I mean . . . er . . . as small as 32A is fine, but I don't mind big ones—'

'I mean, size of body. Do you mind if you date someone who's large-sized?'

'Oh. Er, er . . .' Steve eyed up her plump form, noticing her frown deepening. 'No – no, any size, colour, whatever, is totally one hundred per cent fine.'

Beside him, Harrison was nearly biting off his lip trying not to laugh. *Oh God, I hate interviews,* Steve moaned inwardly. How much longer was this awful interrogation going to drag on for?

'Height?'

'Anything is fine,' said Steve, waving her on.

'Minimum number of limbs?'

'Well – four?'

'A lot of people at our agency were killed in unusual ways. We try to discourage discrimination and ask our customers to avoid being limbist.'

'Oh – of course, of course – well, anything is fine,' said Steve hurriedly.

'As a matter of fact, Steve has a fetish for women with wooden legs,' Harrison chipped in, ignoring Steve's furious glance.

'Right, I'll just make a special note of that,' said the woman.

Steve thought: *Harrison, the moment this interview finishes, I am going to hit you.*

'Well, that's all fine, that just about wraps it up,' she said.

'So when can we meet all these girls?' Harrison demanded. 'Hey – look!' he cried, spotting a jazzy poster pinned to the noticeboard. '"Dating Dinner Swap Special". That's tonight! Can you squeeze us in?' He ignored Steve's ferocious 'no!' signals.

The girl frowned. 'It's pretty much chockablock. We've just had a team of vampires arrive from Birmingham. Let me check . . .' She clicked her mouse, flick-flacking through spreadsheets. 'Ah – as a matter of fact, we've had a last-minute cancellation. Two fairies, Charlie and Puck, who've cancelled to go to a goblin party instead – I mean, I appreciate that DJ GreenSnot is playing, but even so, these fairies are *so* unreliable. We could fit you in.'

'Cool!' Harrison clapped his hands together. 'Don't look so worried, Steve – it'll be great. I did one of these nights last year. We'll be on a double date.'

Later, as they went back down the earthy corridor and stopped for a drink in a bar, Harrison tipped back his Slug Vodka™ and said, 'I don't think she liked me very much, do you? Did I say something to offend her, or d'you think it was just PMT?'

'Er, this may be just a guess, but I think it might be the former,' said Steve glumly.

'Cheer up!' said Harrison, raising his glass. 'I promise you, Steve, tonight all your troubles will be over! I guarantee that by the end of the night you'll have forgotten who the hell Dina is!'

Dina stood by the window in her bedroom, looking over the green heads of her cactus plants into the street below. The sunshine had pushed through the clouds and was splashing in yellow puddles on the pavements, arrowing off the windows of the office buildings opposite.

I didn't really tell Anita the truth, Steve, she confided to him in her heart. *I don't want a casual relationship with Archie. I can't forget that moment when I was lying in his arms and he told me he loved me. Nobody's ever told me that before. And as I lay there, I drifted off into sleep and yet I was constantly aware of him. I felt totally protected and at peace; I felt as though I'd come home. Ever since I moved to London, I've felt at a loose end, wondering all the time if I made the right decision to come here, if this is where I'm meant to be. But lying with Archie, it all seemed to make sense. All my restlessness faded away and I felt content.*

I wondered if I'd found the one.

Mind you, I thought my last boyfriend, Jason, was the one, and look what happened there.

But now what? Dina frowned, running her fingers over the spiky nobbles of the little green plant, a fancy Latin name swirling across its thin white tag. There were other details that she hadn't told Anita, that she'd been too proud and sheepish to disclose. She hadn't mentioned, for instance, that since then Archie had changed tack.

A fortnight had passed since they'd slept together and he'd only called her once. She'd called him three times. He'd been as funny and sweet as ever, updating her on the artistic and culinary development of the mango cream tart with elderflower and passionfruit sauce ('You simply have to come over and try it!'), but each time they tried to arrange a date, he'd say, 'I'll ring you next week and confirm,' and then the next week he'd be busy and say, 'I'll ring you soon.' It was as though she was something to be squashed into a gap in his schedule, Dina thought; and a hot flush of irritation prickled over her as she acknowledged that, like it or not, he had gone cold on her. Just as he had warned her, he was screwing up.

Perhaps the very act of confessing his love had embarrassed him. Perhaps it was the first time he'd ever said it. Or perhaps it was just his plain old fear of commitment.

She felt her heart contract. She remembered the pain she had suffered from her last love affair with Jason. She didn't want to go through that all over again. She didn't want to suffer any more hurt. She needed to protect her heart.

Her mobile rang and she picked it up despondently. Then she saw Archie Hamilton displayed on the blue screen, and her whole body started to shake. Her thumb hovered on the little green button. She swallowed. The ringtone cut off. She let out a shaky breath and put the mobile down on the bed.

Then, slowly, an uncertain smile trembled across her lips. *Serve him right,* she thought. *Maybe I'm not going to be in the next time he calls, either. Maybe he's going to have to chase me a little bit. I might be out with another guy right this very minute.*

Dina wasn't the type who normally played games. She was warm-hearted and generous in her affections. For her, the whole point of a relationship was simple: to be happy. To bring happiness to the person you were with, and to be made happier by them in return. To be able to call them up at any time and tell them any silly thing on your mind. To be able to trust them, utterly and completely.

But Jason, and now Archie, had convinced her that life wasn't that simple. When she was a teenager, she'd believed in princes and fairytales and being swept off her feet. In her early twenties, she'd believed in the possibility of an imperfect but ultimately warm and loving relationship. That was before Jason. Now, having suffered a broken heart once, she wasn't sure what she believed in. All she knew was that love wasn't fair or democratic as the Hollywood movies promised. Love in real life was uneven, unfair, unbalanced. In any relationship, one person always loved a little more, one person was loved a little more. One took, the other gave. She and Archie were at the tender, uncertain moment in their affair where it was balanced like a see-saw, ready to tip either way. And she could see that Archie was used to being the beloved, that he had probably been spoilt as a child, and later as an adult by an endless stream of women fawning over his looks. That was why he was so selfish. And that was part of his charm too: the way he simply assumed that you were going to adore him and give everything up for him.

And I do adore him, Dina admitted to herself, *but I'm not going to show it. I want to be different from all the other girls buzzing around him like flies.*

I'm going to make him work for me. I'm going to make him *chase* me. *I'm going to make him give to me. It's the only way I can keep him, the only way I can hold his interest, the only way I can get past his commitment-phobia.*

She looked at her reflection in the wardrobe mirror and suddenly a wave of shame passed over her. She stepped back from herself and thought: *What the hell am I doing, playing games? Isn't that just the type of relationship I want to avoid? One of those relationships where you can't be yourself, you've always got to be thinking up the next move, the long-term strategy, like a bloody game of chess?*

She started pulling old hair, meshed into a dark fluff, out of her hairbrush, her forehead knitted into a frown. She thought back to that moment when he had said those three glorious little words, and told herself that the games were worth it. Archie wasn't a straightforward guy; he was complex, and required complex courtship tactics.

The question was, would her strategy work? What if it backfired? What if she ignored him and he in turn just ignored her?

She let out a shaky breath and prayed that he would take the bait.

15
Steve

There was another reason why Steve didn't like Robbie Williams, aside from the fact that he'd been played at his funeral. Steve always associated songs with moods and people and events. They were filed in his mind according to their colour of memory. Whilst 'Something Stupid' (the Sinatra version, of course) would always remind him of Dina, Take That's 'Promises' would always send him straight back to a dark, shadowy school hall. Being sixteen years old. Swigging from a lemonade bottle filled with wine, siphoned off from his parents' supply. There was a row of plastic seats along the side of the hall, and sitting at the end of the row was a gorgeous girl with dark hair. Her combination of shyness and sweetness and grace had reminded Steve of Audrey Hepburn.

Steve had kept glancing at her, and she'd kept glancing at him. He'd kept telling himself to go and ask her to dance. Wham, 'Come On Eileen' and the Pet Shop Boys had crackled out through the speaker system before he had finally walked up to her and, his face burning beneath the strobe lights, asked her to dance. She'd said no. As the slow dances had come on and 'Promises' had crooned across the dance floor, the school heartthrob had walked up and asked her to dance. She'd said yes. Steve had sat on the plastic chairs, watching them sway across the floor, his heart breaking. Back home, he'd cried all night, berating himself for being such a baby, but convinced he'd been dealt a marked card, that girls would never fancy him. He had acne; he was too tall; his arms were too long and gangly; everything was wrong with him. He was a freak.

It was strange, thought Steve, how the first time you did something seemed to set the pattern. Like a domino that fell and dictated where all the subsequent events would fall too. Take chess, for example. When Steve had played his first game of chess at fifteen, he had managed to beat Luke Wilson, the sixth-form champion. Ever since then, he'd loved playing. It had taken him quite a while to realise he'd only beaten Luke by fluke and that he was winning on confidence, not skill. He wasn't really all that great a player. But because he believed he was a winner, his actions met his expectations.

With love, it was the reverse.

That first school disco had kicked his confidence right in the balls. After that, he'd been doomed to spend his teenage years alone. The closest he got to hot babes was watching *Baywatch,* and even then the fact that they were all made of plastic put him off: Steve liked wholesome, earthy girls. His last girlfriend, before he'd met Dina, had been an accountant called Eileen, who was attractive in an understated sort of way, with brown hair and specs. As they'd gone up to her flat for sex, she'd asked him if he was a virgin.

'Jesus, I'm twenty-eight years old!' Steve had cried. 'Do I seem like a virgin?'

'No, no, no,' she said hastily. 'You just seem shy, that's all, and kind of goofy. Steve, don't be upset. You're cute. All my friends at work think you're cute too.'

Steve had been deeply offended for two reasons.

Firstly, he was a bit embarrassed by the fact that Eileen was only the second girl he'd slept with. He'd lost his virginity at Imperial College, thanks to a drunken freshers' week, and a voracious PhD student who'd ravished him and then, to Steve's relief and delight, used and abused him on and off for the next three years; she was in love with a married professor and she affectionately called Steve her 'bit of stuff'. Sexually speaking, his twenties had been a bit of a barren patch. He'd had a few crushes and they'd led to some dates, but he had always, always found himself mucking up before the bed stage. Besides, he wasn't keen on the idea of one-night stands even when, in the dreary, sweaty midnight hours of winding-down nightclubs or closing time at pubs, they'd been offered to him.

Secondly, he hated being called cute. Cute was obviously

femalespeak for nice, and boring. He wanted to be like Archie, he thought now. Mad, bad and dangerous to know.

Steve didn't really believe that the ghost dating dinner would cure him of his love for Dina. But hey, Harrison was right: he needed to get out. It would help him to polish his dating skills. He might even meet someone who fancied him, and that, at least, would be good for his ego.

The ghost dating dinner was being held on the third floor of an abandoned multi-storey car park in Shepherd's Bush. It was due to be pulled down for a private housing development, but for now it was perfect for a bit of ghoulish fun.

Steve had to admit they'd made a nice job of it. The dull grey floors were carpeted, the walls spangly with glitter and tinsel. Before they went in, Harrison dragged him into the rather makeshift loos so that he could do his hair.

Earlier that afternoon, Steve had told Harrison he needed a nap. In reality, he'd dipped into his dating self-help book, reminding himself to think positive, think positive, think positive. As a teenager, he'd always felt that his lack of success at that dance was due to fate. But as he had matured, Steve had gradually become aware that he was creating his own failures. When he went out to dinner with a girl, even before he left the house, he looked in the mirror and saw himself saying embarrassing things and spilling food down his shirt. He saw the girl wincing at his jokes. He saw himself walking home on a dark street, hands in his pockets, surrounded by an aura of loneliness.

But look at Harrison. He wasn't worrying about inner conflicts and outer pain. He wasn't even thinking. He was just being; being Harrison. He was slicking water through his hair until it lay in a flat sheen, smooth and shiny as patent leather. Steve just stood in a urinal, hands tight in pockets, occasionally making a few half-hearted attempts to sculpt – or, rather, *subdue* – his hair, but it only ended up looking worse.

'I'm hungry,' he complained, rubbing his stomach and swallowing. Though he knew the empty feeling in his stomach was due to a lot more than hunger.

*

The moment they entered the 'restaurant', the noise hit them: the roar of conversation, the clash of knives and forks, the yells of waiters giving orders to the kitchen, all underlaid with tinkly piano music. Steve noticed a vampire sitting behind a grand piano, his forehead furrowed and fangs protruding in mournful concentration as he hammered out Beethoven.

Harrison checked the seating plan.

'We're on Table Forty-Eight,' he said excitedly.

They wove their way through the teeming restaurant. Faces flicked past: tense frowns, high laughter, mouths frozen in smiles. Everyone trying desperately to be relaxed.

At Table 48, they found two empty seats and two girls waiting for them.

'Well, hel-*lo*, ladies,' Harrison said in a caddish voice.

Steve cringed at such a pathetic attempt at being smooth. Did Harrison want to put the girls off within thirty seconds of meeting them? But then, to Steve's surprise, the girls laughed.

'So nice to meet you gor-ge-ous babes,' Steve added.

The girls stopped laughing. And exchanged glances as if to say: *Who is this slimeball?*

Harrison shot him a look and Steve felt his stomach clench. *What?* he thought. *What did I do wrong? I just meant to be—*

They sat down.

'I'm Harrison,' said Harrison, shaking their hands. 'I'm a ghost.'

'And I'm—' Steve began in a whisper, but Harrison was already adding loudly:

'And this is my good friend, Steve.'

'I'm Nancy,' said the first girl. She tossed back a waterfall of dark curls. She had a pierced nose but an air of class, Steve thought. She reminded him of a film star. Dina would have been able to tell him who, but Steve's knowledge of celebs was too vague to pin her down.

'I'm Beth,' the other girl said, staring down at her plate. She was small and elfin, with very wispy brown hair that brushed her shoulders.

The girls passed the menus. Steve winced uneasily at the suggested list of specials.

Starter
Earwig soup *or* crushed spiders on toast

Main course
Spider ravioli

Dessert
Try our fun sundae, Knickerbockerghouly
with whipped scream on the side

See the board for other deserts

'Don't worry,' Harrison whispered to Steve. 'It's not *real* earwigs. It's just part of the ghoul jokes, the tradition – the whole thing is meant to be a send-up.'

'Well, good,' said Steve, who, oddly enough, had never really fancied finding out what insects tasted like.

'Ready to order, ladies?' Harrison asked, and they giggled and nodded and Harrison beckoned a waiter.

He creaked up to their table, dragging his wooden leg behind him, and swept his dark, soulless eyes across them.

'Killed by a shark,' he announced in a coarse Australian voice, as though Steve and Harrison were personally responsible. 'Surfing off the Gold Coast, '86. They slit the fucker up. Now, whaddaya want?'

'I'd like the crushed spiders and the ravioli,' Harrison said.

The others duly ordered, and the waiter scratched their choices down on his pad, pressing so hard the pencil nearly went through the paper. Halfway through, a customer from the adjoining table interrupted him: 'There were meant to be extra flies in my soup but I don't see any . . .'

'All right, all right, I'll see what I can do,' he snapped. 'Right. Food'll be ready soon. Stay put. Don't die in the mean time.' When none of them laughed, he grimaced and dragged himself off, nearly sending another waiter, who was carrying a plate piled high with hors d'oeuvres, flying across the tables.

They all looked at each other and repressed smiles.

A slightly awkward silence fell over the table. Steve tried to think of an ice-breaker. Maybe he should ask, 'So what did you used to do?' Oh

God, he was never very good at socialising in crowds, at superficial chit-chat, nor was his ego strong enough for entertaining people with wonderfully witty anecdotes; he preferred the sincere intimacy of one-on-one.

'So,' Harrison said, 'how did you die? Let's get that out of the way first. I mean, it's the big cliché at these things, isn't it?'

The girls laughed.

'Well, being a total dumbass, I started smoking at the age of fourteen, like forty Marlboros a day. By the age of twenty-eight I had lung cancer; by the age of thirty-four, I was dead,' Nancy said. Every time Steve looked at her, he appreciated a little more of her beauty.

'You poor, poor thing – what a waste,' said Harrison. He then proceeded to tell the story of his car crash and cruel, scheming uncle with great aplomb, evoking sympathetic *oohs* and *aahs* from the girls. Then he turned to Steve.

'I – was saving an old lady from being mugged and then the guy started to chase me and—' Steve began.

'Oh, Steve is about to spin his usual bollocks for the ladies. He is such a smoothie,' Harrison said. 'But basically, it's all bullshit because actually he fell into a canal when he slipped on a curry packet and his mac got caught on, like, a Coke ring or something, and he drowned.'

Steve felt fury hot in his chest. *You bastard,* he burned, *you absolute bastard.* But then Harrison nudged him, and he realised he was just teasing, and he quickly joined in the laughter, though he felt his cheeks might crack.

'How did you die?' Harrison asked Beth.

'A piano fell on my head,' she said numbly.

Steve started to laugh, but Beth stared at her plate. Nancy gave him a 'God, you men can be *so* insensitive' glare.

'Nice one, Steve,' Harrison whispered out of the corner of his mouth. 'Just keep putting your foot in it.'

Fortunately, they were interrupted by their scary waiter, who unceremoniously dumped their plates on the table, splashing them with earwig soup.

'Er – actually, I ordered the crushed spiders on—' Harrison began, but the waiter glared so violently that even Harrison was silenced. They waited patiently until he was gone, then passed the plates round so they all had the right orders.

Steve started to tuck into his soup. He had to admit, it tasted good. And eating at least gave him something to do; shut him up from making any more faux pas.

Harrison, meanwhile, started telling bad jokes.

Steve had to hand it to him. Harrison only knew crap jokes; being with him was like being with a walking Christmas cracker. But tonight he cleverly dressed up the jokes in ironic wrapping, declaring he'd once had a girlfriend who'd told terrible jokes, such as 'What's white and black and blue all over? A ghost who can't walk through walls!' or 'What happens when ghosts live in theatres? The actors get stage fright!', giving them all a licence to laugh.

Steve started laughing too, but he felt the strain of his shyness. Five minutes passed – he kept following the arc of his watch-hand under the table – and the girls hadn't looked at him once. After the main courses arrived, he started to feel like stabbing himself with a fork. *I've got to say something,* he kept telling himself desperately, *I'm behaving like a total lemon.*

OK – what shall I say? I could tell them about my life. About working in a greasy spoon.

Maybe not.

'Where do baby ghosts go during the day?' said Harrison. 'A dayscare centre!'

Or . . . about . . . things I like . . . like physics . . . and astronomy . . . and . . .

And he ended up not saying anything at all. He wished Dina were there. She always put him at ease. She was so sparky that her charisma rubbed off on Steve; around her he glittered, he could make jokes, he could shine. But put in an awkward social situation where he had to compete, grab a spotlight, he could only wilt.

'STEVE!'

Steve suddenly became aware of fingers snapping in front of his eyes.

'He's miles away!' Nancy chuckled.

Steve saw that the waiter was back.

'We're ordering desserts,' Harrison explained, as though Steve was five. 'That means you have to look at the board, scan down the list of exciting choices and pick which looks the most appetising.' He rolled his eyes at Nancy and she rolled her eyes at Beth.

Steve hastily ordered a bowl of ice cream in three flavours: batwing, grub and dust.

When the desserts arrived, they bore no relation to their choices. Nancy hailed their waiter.

'Erm – I can't eat this. I have a woodlouse allergy.'

'Well, why did you order it then?' the waiter demanded crossly, rolling his eyes and taking it away, then plopping it, rather randomly, on someone else's table.

'Here,' said Steve generously, 'have my dessert.'

'No – I couldn't – you won't have one . . .'

'No, really.'

'OK.' She took a mouthful; a look of orgasmic pleasure sighed over her face. 'I really shouldn't be eating this, I'm meant to be on a diet.'

'Yep, you definitely look as though you need to be,' Steve tried to tease her, Harrison-style. He winked and smiled to let her know it was a joke, but she looked red and huffy.

'Well, I think I can let my diet go for just one night.'

'I didn't mean – it was just a . . .'

'I did attend WeightWatchers whilst I was alive, and as a matter of fact, I lost a stone, which was over my target.'

'. . . joke,' Steve finished flatly.

Silence. Nancy took small, angry bites out of her sundae glass. Steve longed for the floor to swallow him up. Harrison winced. Steve turned his attention to Beth, who was munching her snail syllabub. But he couldn't think of a single thing to say. He just felt totally limp. He was out of synch; the stars, the universe were grinding against him. This just wasn't his night.

As Harrison whispered something intimate into Nancy's ear, she suddenly screamed with laughter.

'I always hate these things, don't you?' Beth said quietly. 'I get so nervous before, I'm convinced nobody will ever fancy me. Then afterwards I spend the whole night thinking, "I wish I'd said this" or "I wish I'd said that".'

Steve smiled in sympathetic relief. They started talking. It was an awkward, shy, stumbling conversation, but it was a conversation nonetheless. He became aware at one point of Nancy looking over and he felt a gleam of pleasure at her surprise.

'I'm just really lonely,' said Beth, on an honesty roll now. 'Sometimes when I come to these things I make up a story about a guy I was going out with just before I died.' She gave a hollow laugh. 'The truth is, there was no guy. I was single for two years before I died. I worked in an office with a boss who didn't even get my name right after five years of loyal service. I had a cat. I was an old spinster with a cat at the age of twenty-two. And I feel even more lonely now.' She flicked up her gaze shyly, and a blush mounted in her cheeks.

Well, at least someone fancies me, thought Steve, cheering up a little.

'I find these things so hard. Everyone is putting on an act, nobody feels they can just be themselves. I don't want a guy who's flashy and a would-be stand-up comic. I just want someone who's nice,' Beth continued. And then she reached out and gently put her hand on Steve's wrist. A direct invitation.

Steve smiled and wondered why he felt relief when she drew her hand away. Then he realised that his feelings towards Beth simply weren't sexual. They were a mixture of sympathy and recognition; both feelings motivated by the fact that she was too much like him.

Beth was the female equivalent of himself. He could see that she came to these things with just the same dread, with the aim of surviving them rather than enjoying them, of dragging herself through the night with minimal humiliation. She probably didn't really fancy Steve. She just thought that she couldn't do any better.

Steve and Harrison took a break and went to the gents'.

'Maybe we should go home,' Steve said uneasily.

'Are you kidding?' Harrison was really quite drunk now, the whites of his eyes laced with red. He gave Steve a manly clap on the back. 'Come on, can't you see we're totally in there with those babes? Beth's wild about you, and Nancy's just told me she's not wearing any knickers, the wicked vixen!'

Sadly, Harrison's night of wild passion with Nancy was simply not meant to be. For, after they returned to their table, Harrison managed to get himself into a fight. It was all quite unfortunate.

Harrison, having had one too many Slug Vodkas™, had a collision with a waiter who had just come spinning out of the kitchen doors carrying a tray of Caterpillar Cocktails. The cocktails went flying over a table of Dutch ghosts; the waiter screamed at Harrison, *Why don't you look where you're going?* and Harrison screamed back, *Why don't you look where you're going?* and in the ensuing fracas, he was picked up by a pair of burly bouncers and deposited outside on the pavement. Steve followed him, flicking a frantic, apologetic wave at their table.

Outside, Harrison moaned and groaned about how that bastard waiter had ruined his chances with the gorgeous Nancy. Steve tried to sound sympathetic, but frankly, he was just relieved to be out of there.

He looked up at the stars and a deep yearning for Dina trembled in the pit of his stomach. If only he could see her again. Just one glance would soothe him, wash the night away, fulfil his fix.

'Harrison, we need to go check on Dina,' he said, ignoring Harrison's whingeing about how was he supposed to go anywhere with a bruised arm and a broken leg (broken in the sense of being able to walk on it with an exaggerated limp, as far as Steve could see).

At Dina's flat, they found Anita sitting up late, watching TV. Harrison slumped on the sofa beside her; Steve crept into Dina's bedroom.

It took a while for his eyes to adjust to the gloom. A shaft of moonlight slanted through the curtains, and all he could see was Dina lying on her side, fast asleep, her eyelashes fluttering as she snored gently. Steve felt his heart cleave open. He wondered how he could ever have imagined Beth might be worth going for; how could he ever have considered second best? He couldn't bear it; he had to touch her. *Just once,* he promised himself. *I won't wake her. I'll just stroke her cheek. Just once. Just to feel the softness of her skin.*

And then he realised Dina wasn't the only one in the bed. He breathed in, caught a whiff of a distinctly masculine smell. A figure suddenly groaned, rolled over and planted a kiss on Dina's head, slinging an arm over her. Dina smiled dreamily in her sleep.

Steve frowned. He waited, and watched.

At first he thought Archie was having trouble sleeping. He was staring at Dina, wide-eyed. Steve went to the curtains and drew them back a cautious inch, letting in a trickle more moonlight, highlighting Archie's face.

It was as though the Archie of the daytime, the Archie who wheeled and dealed and sneered at his rivals and charmed his friends had been stripped away, leaving his expression naked, almost boyish. And he was gazing at Dina with such tenderness that Steve felt sick.

What about Heidi? Steve wanted to scream. *No, Archie, this isn't you. You're meant to be a two-timing bastard.*

He suddenly became aware of Harrison slipping through the door.

Harrison took one look at Dina and Archie and realised that what Steve needed right now was a good friend to stop him from going completely over the edge. He grabbed Steve's arm, yanking him out.

Outside, Steve threw up. His ghostly sick was a thin, yellowy vapour. It lay across the pavement like a glinting, dying seahorse and then rapidly vaporised until the concrete was bare again. *Oh God,* he moaned inside, *Archie can't feel for her what I feel. He's not capable. He doesn't have the heart.*

And yet the worst thing was, deep down, Steve understood. Dina was so wonderful, she had made Archie change; she had brought out another, more tender side to him.

'I know just where we can go to cheer ourselves up!' Harrison cried, as overly enthusiastic as a *Blue Peter* presenter. 'Debenhams! Yeah, Steve!'

Debenhams was locked up for the night, the shop floor dark and still. Despite their subtle presence, the alarms picked them up, beeping briefly as they slid through the windows. Harrison swept up a mannequin in his arms and began to dance around the shop. Steve felt like being sick again but, realising how hard Harrison was trying, he joined in and scooped up a doll. They danced about, ricocheting between racks of designer clothes, posh party dresses and tweed suits. At first Steve even managed to laugh. Then, as Harrison warbled 'Unchained Melody', he stared at the blank face of his synthetic-haired doll and felt like crying. Beth or Nancy or a doll – what was the difference? His shyness, his social stumbling, his inability to show the real Steve, to free it from the blur and blunder of his nerves: things were no different as a ghost than they had been on earth. Life was repeating itself with the same pattern.

Tonight had made him realise an awful truth. Even if he was able to rewind time, to go back and not take that walk along the canal, to be alive at this point and dishing out burgers in The Greasy Spoon – even then, would life be any different?

No, thought Steve. *Dina would still have met Archie.*

He thought back to that night on the canal. When she had said to him, 'I'm really not ready for a relationship right now.' And despite the fact that he knew it was a well-worn line, a part of him had believed her that night, and continued to believe her. He'd treasured the fantasy that if he'd been alive something *might* have blossomed. But no. She'd never been interested in him. That night on the canal had been complete bullshit.

What if I'd still been alive today and Archie had walked into The Greasy Spoon? Like Beth, or Nancy, or any girl for that matter, she would have chosen Archie over me: his good looks over my ordinary ones; his money over my poverty; his smoothness over my shyness. I'd still be aching in every corner of my soul for her. Archie is the guy who always gets the girl. I'm the one who just stands on the side and watches the beautiful couple ride off into the sunset. Dead or alive, it makes no difference: Archie would have won.

I'm never going to have Dina.

Ever.

And I can't live without her, or die without her, or whatever I am without her – whatever it is, I just can't bear it.

PART TWO

16

Dina

The moment Dina pushed open the door of The Greasy Spoon, a loud voice accosted her.

'DINA – DO YOU KNOW HOW LATE YOU ARE?'

'Sorry.' She was normally good at buttering Luigi up. But this morning, no matter how hard she tried to inject sincerity into her voice, it failed to show. Perhaps it had something to do with only having had one hour's sleep and feeling as though she was made of cotton wool.

'I SAID, DO YOU KNOW HOW LATE YOU ARE?'

'Er, no,' said Dina, chewing her lip.

Behind Luigi, Fatima smiled a smug smile.

'Fifty-five minutes. And that is not all. Yesterday, thirty minutes. The day before, fifteen. And the day before – twenty again.'

'That's not fair – I was only ten minutes late on Tuesday and that was because – because – I had to go to the dentist. And the day before that, my goldfish died,' she lied, feeling like a kid in high school faking an excuse note.

'You think Luigi is stupid, huh?' he demanded. 'I know what this is all about. You have a boyfriend! Yes! I've seen him dropping you off every morning.'

Dina made a mental note that from now on Archie must drop her off round the corner.

'I've seen you in the car, kissing, I know why you are late, Dina, and it is not due to goldfish, or dentists – unless you call *that* dental work.'

Dina cringed. The thought of slimy old Luigi peering out of his dirty windows and eyeing up her precious, passionate goodbye clinches with Archie made her feel rather ill.

Then she thought of the credit card statement she'd received in the post this morning.

'I'm sorry,' she said meekly. 'I promise I'll be on time in future.'

'Well, good,' Luigi huffed. 'Otherwise, I dock your pay, and I mean it, Dina.'

It didn't take long for Dina's irritation to fade away. For she didn't really care, not deep down. She was on a high. Floating in clouds like a lovesick teenager.

Everything was going wonderfully with Archie. In fact, so wonderfully that Dina was almost unnerved. She kept wondering if she was about to wake up from a dream, if this glorious iridescent bubble was about to burst.

Her playing-hard-to-get plan had worked. It had worked so well even Dina had been astonished.

Over the past eight weeks, they'd barely spent a day apart. It was as though Archie had suddenly decided, just like that, with a snap of his fingers, that he wanted them to date and that was that.

With most men, Dina would have found such a breathless intensity of pace much too suffocating or, worse, tedious. With Archie, it was utterly exhilarating. He was like a drug, and when she took him the world was bright and magical and roared with noise and colour. And the more she took him, the more she wanted him.

Archie wasn't one of those guys who wanted to stay in in front of the TV with a takeaway. He loved nothing better than surprising her, telling her to dress up and then whisking her off somewhere wonderful. One night he took her to a restaurant overlooking the South Bank. There, he told her his philosophy on life.

'As far as I'm concerned, life is an adventure, not a fucking cross to carry on one's back. I want to *enjoy* it. More than that – I want to squeeze as much fun and entertainment and happiness out of it as I possibly can. I want good food, money, success and beauty.' His whole face was aglow with *joie de vivre*; his eyes sparkling with intensity. 'What about you?'

'I just want to be happy,' she agreed. 'And I'm happy tonight.'

Archie had smiled at her – a sweet, gruff smile – and proposed a toast to hedonism.

He still seemed to struggle with his commitment-phobia, for she never heard him say 'I love you' again. If anything, he was prone to being a tad critical. He had just given up smoking, so he insisted she give up too (and yet when she objected to his occasional drug use, he told her off for being a square). He told her that biting her nails was vulgar and managed to stop her habit by slapping her hand every time her fingers crept up to her mouth. He also found her indecisiveness weird, and was greatly amused by her habit of making choices by tossing a coin. Dina argued back that she liked letting fate decide. Archie declared that he didn't believe in fate; individuals made their own luck, controlled and shaped their own lives. But for all his criticism, he had become increasingly affectionate. He held her hand in public. He bought her flowers. He told her she was beautiful. She felt utterly exhilarated and alive in his presence.

As she fell back in love with life, she found her fear of death diminishing. Days would go by and she'd realise she hadn't called her mother; she was so busy having fun she barely had time for more than a ten-minute gabbled chat. Her mother, however, seemed delighted that Dina seemed on the up.

Dina had recognised early on in their relationship that in order to date Archie, she needed to adapt to his life, his routine, his friends, rather than vice versa. Which was fair enough – his life was so much more exciting than hers. His friends had been the hardest part, but gradually her warmth and sense of fun had endeared her to them until she truly felt one of the gang. Brian was always asking her to listen to CDs of his band's latest single (their titles were along the lines of 'Fish in My Underpants' or 'Last Exit to La-La-Land' and they normally sounded like Roger playing with cutlery, but Dina managed to smile and say, 'Wow, that's really . . . *interesting*'). Jim regularly invited her over to dinner and gave her tickets for film premieres. Once, she even got to meet Tom Cruise. Well, stand close to him, anyway. And Ralph, the sweetie, had adopted her as his 'kid sister' and regularly sent her silly, eccentric text messages; he'd even knitted her a pair of pink socks.

The only member of the gang who didn't like her still was Heidi.

No surprises there. But Heidi had stopped hanging round with them and, to Dina's relief, seemed to have admitted defeat. The final nail in Heidi's coffin came when gossip columns from *The Times* to the *Tatler* declared that Dina was now Archie's definite new girl. Dina couldn't help feeling thrilled at her fifteen minutes of fame; she rushed into the newsagent's and flipped through the magazines, resisting the urge to cry at strangers, 'Look, that's me! I'm with Archie Hamilton, and look, on page fifty-six, he's voted the fifth sexiest guy in London!' At moments like this, none of his bad behaviour seemed to matter. After all, she was the envy of practically every female in London, so surely a bit of moodiness was worth putting up with?

Archie's friends, though, all seemed like pastels compared to the rich vibrancy of Archie's personality. After three weeks, Dina felt as though she knew him much better, and at the same time as though he was a stranger with endless layers to unpeel (it seemed no coincidence that Archie's favourite food was onion). He was impossible to pin down, and as soon as she felt she'd got to grips with the quiddity of his character, around the corner was sure to be lurking some surprise, some quirk, some act of unexpected tenderness, some flash of temper. All the same, she loved the process of discovering him. Finding out one morning that his favourite tea was Earl Grey and he couldn't survive without it. That he couldn't drink coffee because the caffeine made him hyper. That he was allergic to nuts. That he loved beautiful clothes and sighed over them as though he was a girl. That he was terribly vain and always looking in the mirror; that he sculpted his hair, cleaned his teeth an obsessive four times a day and even wore eyeliner. And then there was the morning that she heard a wail from the shower and discovered he was scared of spiders and had to gigglingly remove it for him while he waited, shivering, in the hallway.

'Did you kill it?' he demanded, coming back nervously into the bathroom.

'Of course not!' cried Dina. 'You can't kill spiders, it's bad luck. Anyway, it's mean. I couldn't kill anything.'

'You're a real softie,' said Archie, giving her a grateful kiss and then pulling her into the shower with him.

But he still refused to show any interest in Roger, which hurt Dina more than she would show, for she feared he'd think her silly and sentimental. He was frighteningly dynamic and he only needed five hours' sleep (Dina needed nine minimum). He thought lie-ins were boring and she often woke to find him sitting up in bed, hammering away at his laptop. If anything, he seemed to relish pressure and deadlines and worries and rebellious chefs and all those other things that would send most people into hospital with a stomach ulcer or a cardiac arrest. If things were going well, he seemed bored and restless. In fact, even when he had challenges, that restlessness was still there; life never seemed to be exciting enough for him, like a little boy who wants every day to be Christmas.

Maybe it was his restlessness that made him so fond of arguing. Dina's parents had never, ever rowed. But Archie's, apparently, had enjoyed throwing crockery and Archie seemed to have learnt from them. Sometimes he just seemed to pick fights. One night, he took her to an expensive seafood restaurant, knowing she hated seafood, and then, on the way back, had a go at her for not eating her meal.

'I must have wasted at least a hundred pounds on you. I mean, don't you think you could have at least *tried* to eat it?' he said, staring at her with a dark, goading expression. Then he ran his eyes over her and for a minute she wasn't sure if he was going to kiss her or hit her.

He's getting off on this, Dina realised with alarm. *He actually wants me to yell at him.*

So she did. It felt both satisfying and strange. Satisfying because she could give him a damn good telling-off, but strange because in all honesty, she didn't really like yelling at people. And yet she had to admit that the making-up, the crazy, furious, sweaty lovemaking, certainly took on a frisson she'd never had with anyone else before. She'd also never had such a varied sex life; Archie loved experimenting and playing games. Sometimes, though, she wondered if he just suggested things to see the shock on her face, to goad her. 'It's good to push people's boundaries,' he was always saying, 'it's good for the soul.' He liked nothing more than going out to a party with her or taking her to dinner, and then, in the middle of the meal, leaning across and whispering into her ear what he was going to do to her when they got home, just for the pleasure of making her blush.

The trouble with the rowing-before-sex was that the next morning she'd remember with horror her awful insults and feel utterly mean.

'Sorry I said you were a spoilt, arrogant, pig-headed bastard,' she'd apologise sheepishly.

'What?' Archie shrugged cheerfully. 'Forget it. I called you a dirty vixen, didn't I? Or was that . . . Anyway, forget it. I have already.'

He was about to walk out, when he saw her face; he quickly backtracked and pulled her into a tight hug, kissing her softly.

'Sorry,' he said, rubbing his nose against hers. 'I can be such a miserable bastard sometimes. I don't want to hurt you. Next time you can just slap me – really, I deserve it. Just forget what I said.'

'I already have,' Dina smiled, kissing him back.

But she hadn't forgotten. She was too sensitive. His insults prickled into her subconscious like splinters and stayed there, throbbing uncomfortably. Sometimes hurt and exasperation got the better of her; sometimes she felt close to throwing up her hands and walking out, even if he was the bloody fifth sexiest man in London. Then she would punish him by ignoring his calls for a day, which drove Archie wild. Realising he'd gone too far, he'd do something wildly fabulous, like buy her a pair of earrings from Tiffany, or whisk her off to Paris for a weekend, or, like Richard Gere in *Pretty Woman*, take her to Oxford Street and buy her thirty gorgeous outfits. He seemed to derive great pleasure from ordering all the assistants around, and shaping Dina's new look. Afterwards he took her home and made wild, triumphant love to her, then told her to throw away everything else in her wardrobe, declaring it was 'only fit for Oxfam'.

The trouble was that even though all this was genuinely wonderful, in every other respect Dina's life was going down the toilet. She was supposed to be getting a new, glamorous job and sorting out her horrendous debts. But now she had neither the time nor the energy. Archie wasn't helping. Over the past few weeks he'd persuaded her to take four sickies. Nor had he any qualms about dropping her off late for work.

Dina felt utterly exhausted. As the hours passed, her body felt as though a cocoon was slowly being woven around it, adding layer upon layer of heaviness. By midday, she was ready to sink down on to the dirty tiles and collapse. She kept getting orders wrong and Luigi kept tut-tutting and she kept wanting to flick him a V-sign, until she remembered just how much she'd built up on her credit cards.

In her lunch hour, Anita rang. Dina looked at her mobile but didn't dare answer it. Later, in the toilet, she listened to Anita's slightly terse message: 'Dina, I hope you're coming home tonight. I haven't seen you for seven days! Roger's starting to wonder if he's an abandoned doggie orphan. By the way, your bank also left a message about you being overdrawn. Anyway, maybe tonight we could have a chat. Bye.' *Oh God.* The moment Dina got home she just wanted to sink into a warm bath. Like a man in the desert plagued by mirages of water, she saw visions of her lovely, delicious bed with its plump quilt and huge floral-patterned pillows. She couldn't face a chat. Yet she knew Anita had good reason to be huffy with her. Dina had been out so much that Anita had been forced into the position of Roger's surrogate dog-walker, and she did feel guilty that she was neglecting him – but being around Archie was like being sucked into a whirlwind.

Archie . . . She sighed dreamily and thought of his dark eyes. She thought of the way they'd glinted in the darkness as he'd pushed her back on to the bed, and then leaned in and kissed her, flicking his snakish tongue into her mouth—

'Dina, stop hiding away!' Luigi shouted. 'The dishwasher needs emptying.'

Dina picked up a damp fistful of knives, forks and spoons and returned to the main café. She went up to the little table which held napkins and packets of salt and pepper and three empty red plastic pots labelled, *FORKS, KNIFES* (Luigi's spelling) and *SPOONS*. As usual, she couldn't be bothered to sort them out but let them all drop into one crammed pot. As she did so, she jumped so violently that the pot overturned and she dropped the whole lot in a clatter of curves and prongs and sharp edges.

'Dina, Dina,' Luigi chided her angrily. 'For goodness' sake. Just pick them up and put them back in the pot; a few germs are good for the immune system anyway.'

Dina followed his instructions distractedly. She couldn't believe it. For there, wedged behind the *SPOONS* pot was a KitKat. It looked as though someone had hidden it there just so that Dina would find it.

Dina pulled it out, fingering its red-and-white wrapper uneasily. *This isn't the first time this has happened either,* she acknowledged. *Didn't I find one the other day, left on my bedside cabinet?* She'd just assumed that Anita had left it there, as a nice present. But really, now she thought about it, it didn't really add up: Anita was pissed off with her, and why would she sneak into Dina's room anyway?

Oh, and then there was the one I found in the bathroom, balanced on my shampoo bottle. She'd assumed she'd just left it there herself – she did like lying in the bath, reading and nibbling on chocolate. But surely she would have eaten it, not left it there . . .

Just what is going on? Where are all these KitKats coming from? It's utterly bizarre. I mean, there's only one person I know who likes eating KitKats, and he—

'Dina!'

God, would Luigi just let up for one minute?

'Customers!'

The KitKats were instantly forgotten. It never rained but it poured, Dina mused. Typical – The Greasy Spoon had been quiet all day and now there were *six* of them shunting through the door. There was a trio of builders, who nodded politely at Dina. Ever since a sexual harassment case at their work, they'd stopped wolf-whistling and making obscene remarks every time she picked up a pepper pot. Now they politely addressed her as 'ma'am', which Dina thought was hysterically funny. They were followed by the old lady who always liked her bit of lettuce in a bun – she was late today – and two young men wearing pinstriped suits who looked as though they belonged in a wine bar and glanced about the place with ill-concealed distaste.

Dina took an order for three mugs of tea from the builders, who looked as though their eyes might pop out from the strain of not staring at her breasts. She spelt it as 'tee' on her pad; in her tiredness, her dyslexia was rearing its ugly head. Then she turned to the pinstriped boys, a wave of dizzy muzziness sweeping over her.

'Didn't Archie Hamilton do a review on this place?' one of them was saying.

'Yeah, he totally hammered it but said there was at least some good totty,' said the other. 'Personally, I can't see any.'

Charming, thought Dina.

'Do you serve espressos?' one of them asked.

'No. Sorry. We have what's on the menu.' She didn't mean to sound facetious, but being polite required more energy than she had. 'But we do serve coffee,' she added, dredging up every last drop of energy to inject a note of enthusiasm and apology into her voice.

'That'll have to do,' Pinstripes 2 said, drumming his fingers on the table. 'Can you hurry? We have to be at an important meeting in half an hour. We're only here because the restaurant down the road is closed.'

Dina forced a smile and hurried to the kitchen. It was easy to quash her irritation. As she poured out the teas, she only had to draw her mind back to last night; to sitting with Archie during dinner whilst he forked a lump of *foie gras,* insisting she try it, and slid it into her mouth.

She picked up the lettuce-in-a-bun for their regular old lady and then took two mugs over to the yuppies. Then it was back to the kitchen to get the . . . to get the . . .

'Excuse me!' Pinstripes 1 called her back. 'Hi – this doesn't really taste like coffee.'

'It tastes like tea,' Pinstripes 2 said.

'Sorry.' Dina became horribly aware of Luigi's eyes bulging with fury. 'No – the tea was for the builders. You wanted the lettuce in the – I mean, coffee.'

'Yes, we'd like coffee without lettuce, thanks.'

She picked up the mugs of tea and without thinking, took them over to the builders. Then she thought: *Dina, what are you doing? The Pinstripes have drunk out of those.* She whipped them back and hurried to the kitchen, pouring two coffees. Her tiredness had been sitting in her head like a grey fog; now, irritated by such concentration, it began to take shape, to form something throbbing and black and close to a headache.

She dashed back out with the coffees.

'Excuse me, there was no lettuce in my bun,' the old lady said.

'Oh, really? I must have forgotten – I'm so, so sorry.'

In a panic now, she set the mugs of coffee down on the table. One of them keeled over, spewing hot drink everywhere.

'Oh my God, I am *so* sorry – I'm just having a nightmare day—'

'Well, you'd better clean it up, hadn't you?'

'OK, *OK*,' Dina gasped. She was horribly aware of Luigi watching incredulously from behind the counter. Fatima had also arrived for her shift – great, just in time to see Dina make an utter fool of herself. Dina threw a napkin on to the mess with her right hand; it immediately soaked up the beige puddle. With her other hand, she reached backwards for the cloth she'd left on the table earlier. Grabbing it, she began to mop.

The yuppies began to chuckle.

Fatima went white. Luigi went scarlet.

Dina heard a shrill, quavering voice behind her say, 'There seems to be a terrible wind blowing through here . . . did someone open the door, and if they did, could they please shut it?'

Dina looked down at her hand. In horror she realised that she had grabbed the wig from the old lady's head. She dropped it as though it was a dead animal. She was so shocked she was completely wrapped up in her own thought processes, oblivious to the looks of horror she was receiving from all around her, the delirium spreading through the café. The old lady was still gazing dolefully at her bun, lamenting the lack of lettuce, and though her shoulders were hunched in theatrical defiance of the cold, she hadn't seemed to notice the absence of her wig. Dina picked it up and, ignoring Fatima's frantic hand signals, attempted to put it back on the old lady's head.

Big mistake.

'What happened? Hey, my wig, my wig! Someone tried to steal my wig!' As the old lady clutched at it, rivulets of cold coffee streamed down her face.

Luigi stepped forward.

'I am so sorry – we have a leak.' He pointed up at the ceiling. 'All my customers sitting in that seat have been getting wet this morning. Now, Mrs . . . ah, um, my dear niece Fatima will take you into the back to help you dry it.'

As Fatima drew the stuttering old lady away, Luigi turned on Dina. Behind them, the Pinstripes were nearly on the floor with hysterics.

Dina gulped. Her mouth felt dry. She wanted to apologise, but a tidal wave of tiredness hit her, so strong she sank down on to a chair.

Unfortunately, Luigi interpreted this as a sign of her utter laziness; it was the straw that broke the camel's back.

'You're fired!' he screamed.

Dina stood up, shocked. Luigi couldn't fire her. It simply wasn't possible.

'But – but—'

'No buts. You're fired. You can have last week's pay.' Luigi pulled a thin sheaf of notes from the till and shoved them into her hand. Then, while she stood dumbstruck for a few seconds, he removed one of the notes and passed her three pound coins instead. 'I'm docking two pounds for damage.'

Dina blinked. She looked round at the customers, who quickly pretended to return to their mugs and supposed conversations.

'Fine, I resign,' she said quickly, desperate to maintain one last shred of dignity. 'I resign.'

Luigi laughed incredulously.

'You're not resigning, you're fired!' He slammed his fist down on the counter, making the till shudder, and the cash tray slid out with a nervous ping. He slammed it shut emphatically. 'You are fired.'

'No, I'm resigning, I've been meaning to for ages,' Dina said, but as she said it, it sounded unconvincing, and she could see from the increasingly smug smirk on Luigi's face that he didn't believe her. She looked at Fatima, who was staring goggle-eyed. Anger boiled in her chest. She longed to fling the money back in Luigi's face, but – fuck – she needed it. She turned to face the silent café, her cheeks burning. And then she made a very rapid exit.

Fatima dashed after her, catching her just outside the door. To Dina's amazement, she cried:

'Dina, I'm really sorry you're going. I mean, I have an uncle uncle who needs a cleaner in his curry house, maybe I could put a word in . . .'

Dina was incensed. Had her life come to this? To being pitied by a seventeen-year-old for being fired from a greasy spoon?

'It's fine,' she said hastily, forcing a smile. 'I was planning to go back to the US anyway, really. Thanks.' She felt a flicker of genuine affection for Fatima and leaned in and gave her a hug goodbye.

Dina walked down the street, trying to fight back tears of despair and humiliation. Diving into her handbag, she spotted the KitKat and tore off the wrapper, cramming the chocolate down her throat, hoping it would make her feel better.

It didn't.

In the end, to Dina's complete amazement, it was Archie who came to the rescue.

Emergencies always brought out the best in Archie's character. When Dina phoned to tell him the news, he cried that they'd bloody well sue Luigi for compensation.

'Go back to my flat,' he ordered her, 'and wait for me. Don't worry, we'll sort it all out.'

When Archie turned up half an hour later with a huge bunch of flowers and a large box of Godiva chocolates, Dina found herself bursting into tears.

'Now, why are you crying?' Archie asked, stroking her hair. 'Don't be silly. Come on, I'll run you a bath and then we'll have a nice takeaway, and we can talk it all through, OK?'

As Dina lay in the hot, strawberry-scented bubbles, Archie's legs curled around her waist while he lightly massaged her shoulders, she felt some of the tension slip out of her body. Archie gently stroked the back of her neck, declaring it was the part of her body he loved the most, that smooth swan's curve of white skin.

'You mustn't, mustn't worry about your job,' he said. 'You don't need to work any more, anyway. I've decided' – he let out a deep breath – 'that you absolutely have to move in with me.'

Dina spun round, splashing him. Archie laughed, wiping bubbles off his face.

'Oh my God. Are you serious? No – no – I mean – I don't want you to feel pressurised, I mean I know I've got fired, but I really don't want you to do this if you just feel you ought to.'

'Since when have I ever done anything because I *ought* to do it?' Archie laughed. 'I only ever do things I want to do, and only if I *really* want to do them.' He paused, brushing his nose against hers in an Eskimo kiss. 'And I really want you to move in with me.'

Dina felt so overwhelmed with elation that she had to turn away from him, pretending to pop bubbles, so Archie wouldn't see just how wide and giddy and inane the smile was that stretched across her face. She resisted the urge to whoop and yell and run around dancing and punching the air and tearfully thanking God.

Then a worry struck her and she turned back.

'I'll get another job,' she assured him hastily.

He stared deep into her eyes and whispered smilingly, 'You don't need to. Come on, I'm hardly going to charge you rent.'

Dina smiled back and let him kiss her. But she felt fear rise up in her chest and broke off.

'Archie – I do actually need a job, because . . .'

'What?' Archie's beautiful face creased with consternation.

'Well . . .' She stared down into the bubbles, watching several pop on the sharp edge of Archie's elbow as he sat up in the bath, frowning. *Oh God, please don't let him be mad with me, please don't let this ruin it all,* she begged. For a moment she thought about lying. Then she shook herself. She had to tell him. 'I have some credit card debts,' she said. 'The thing is, you know what it's like, I got one, and then it kind of filled up and there was a zero per cent offer, and I got another, and then—' She broke off as Archie burst out laughing, looking up at him in amazement.

'Is that all? Jesus, you had me worried there. I thought you were going to say you'd robbed a bank or something. Don't worry, I'll clear them for you. What's the damage?'

'No – you don't understand.' Dina swallowed. 'Archie – I owe *five thousand* on my cards, so—'

'Is that all?' Archie laughed again.

'Is that all?' Dina repeated. She looked up and saw that he was serious, that five thousand really was just a drop in the ocean of his wealth. Then she burst into laughter too, wondrous with relief. 'But – but—'

'But what?' Archie spread his hands theatrically.

'Archie, I can't,' she sighed regretfully. 'I mean, I would just feel too guilty.'

'Well, how about we turn it into a loan?' said Archie. 'Come on, those cards charge ridiculous interest rates. I'll pay them off and you pay me back with no interest, whenever you like.'

‘I don’t know. I mean, if I was going to get a loan, I could go to my parents, though it would just make me cringe to ask them.’

‘Well then.’

‘But I don’t have a job and—’

‘Well, you’ll get one eventually. And there’s no rush. It would be nice just to have you around for a while. There’s no pressure.’ Seeing her bite her nails savagely, he slapped her hands and took them in his. ‘Seriously, Dina, it’s cool. Everything’s fine.’ He brushed his lips against hers in a loving, tender kiss, stroking his finger along her collarbone. ‘Besides,’ he added, flicking his tongue between her lips, ‘I can think of plenty of ways that you can pay me back . . .’

Dina laughed and kissed him with all her heart and might.

The next morning Dina woke to see Archie standing above her, fully dressed, putting on a very smart stripy blue tie. Remembering last night, she felt a wave of happiness gush through her. Archie had solved everything; she didn’t need to worry about anything any more.

‘Hi sweetheart.’ He leaned down and kissed her on the nose. ‘Get up for a midnight snack? I think you’ve found every chocolate bar in the flat.’

‘Sorry?’ Dina blinked.

Archie nodded at her bedside table. ‘Chocolate, hmm? Well, don’t eat too many, Ralph and Heidi want to take us out to dinner tonight, OK? Bye, darling.’ He kissed her again and then left, waving cheerily.

Dina sat up, blinking away the sleep from her eyes. Then she froze in disbelief.

There, on her bedside table, were no fewer than seven KitKats, sitting in a red-and-white pyramid, glistening with deliciousness and mystery.

17
Steve

It had been Harrison's idea that Steve should go and see Jether. Since the dating agency night, Steve and Harrison seemed to be on opposite ends of a see-saw, Harrison hitting a high whilst Steve sank to an all-time low.

Harrison was wildly happy because, despite his appalling behaviour at the dinner, Nancy had got in touch.

Steve, sinking into a depression, had snuggled up in an old blue sleeping bag in front of the telly and barely moved from it for a week, shutting out thoughts of Dina by immersing himself in old black-and-white movies. That was when Harrison, who was becoming seriously worried about his friend, had suggested that he ought to go and see Jether.

'Who the hell is Jether?' Steve asked morosely, staring at the screen.

'Every ghost goes to see Jether at some point in their early days,' said Harrison. 'He does help. Kind of. Well, in my opinion, he spins a lot of bullshit, but it's very soothing bullshit, and I think you need it.'

So now, at nearly nine o'clock on a Friday evening, Steve was wandering around Piccadilly, his eyes burning from neon lights, his ears from screechy traffic and the rowdy noises spilling out of pubs. He'd walked round the Haymarket and found himself returning to the same huge Lilt ad three times. Harrison's directions were useless. He drew in a deep breath, resisting the urge to scream. He felt hot and prickly with despair; normally he would have just shrugged and gone home, but over the last few days he had gradually built Jether into a ray of light at the end of his tunnel, and now he felt as though the whole world was conspiring to block him, to keep him in a dark, miserable place.

He was just about to give up when he spotted two young female ghosts drifting from an alleyway. He asked them for directions and finally found the door he was looking for, realising he'd walked straight past it three times earlier on. It just wasn't what he'd expected; he'd envisaged a hippy-style entrance, all beads and Indian scarves, but this was a solid black door that looked as though it led to a private members' club. He slid through and found himself in a dimly lit hallway. He could hear a voice – Jether's voice – wafting from a room next door. It was beautiful to listen to. It was so serene it made him want to fall asleep, but it also had a vibrancy that made him tingle with alert pleasure. Instantly, the irritation of his journey melted away. He was so entranced he nearly failed to notice the small Chinese girl in front of him, who was sporting a name-tag on her black rollneck jumper that said 'Alice', and glaring at him in a very unfriendly fashion.

'You're late,' she snapped. 'Jether's talk began at eight thirty. It's now finishing. You have to stay and listen here.'

'Can I see him afterwards?' Steve asked.

'Sorry,' said Alice doubtfully. 'Everyone wants to see Jether. Go home. Come back another day.'

Steve stood and listened for a few more minutes as Jether finished telling the story of the life of Buddha. Then the ghosts who had been at the talk filed out and Alice shooed him away. He turned and walked a few paces. And then he felt another wave of misery swim over him. Go home, Alice had said. Well, he didn't have a home. Not a real one any more.

He turned, his chest squirming with emotions. He felt a need to unload his problems, a need so great he was like a child on the verge of tears, aching for the comfort of a parent.

He stood by the wall for a moment, then took a deep breath and walked right through it, straight into Jether's chamber.

As he entered the room, he created a breeze that set the candle in the lamp flickering. Alice had just entered, carrying a shawl to drape around Jether's shoulders; she turned; Steve froze. And then the golden light vanished and the room was full of darkness and confused voices.

Then Alice lit the lamp again and Steve stared, transfixed. Later on, when he savoured the moment, he thought that Jether reminded him of the caterpillar in *Alice in Wonderland,* sitting on his mushroom. He was short and squat and bald, but there was something beautiful about him. It wasn't just the silky yellow robes he wore, or the exotic haze of incense shimmering around his head like a halo, but the glow behind his leathery face. It was an exquisite face: round and dimple-cheeked, a face that was both old and young; there was a kind of boyish playfulness in his dark eyes, combined with an elderly wisdom, as though he'd been alive for seven hundred years and seen all that there was to see, known all that there was to know.

Then Alice noticed Steve and began to squeal at him.

'You! Again!'

'Let him stay,' said Jether.

'What – I – oh. OK.' Alice bowed meekly, gave Steve a poisonous look that Steve was sure wasn't very Buddhist, and left.

Steve felt suddenly self-conscious. A calm smiling was floating on Jether's face, but his peaceful state only seemed to highlight and exacerbate Steve's awkward one. Steve waited for Jether to tell him to sit down, but Jether seemed to be waiting for him. So Steve sat down on a wicker chair. Jether was sitting cross-legged, so Steve crossed his too, though they immediately felt uncomfortable, pain shooting through his shins.

'So, what's the problem?' Jether asked. He seemed to know what Steve was here for, which was also unnerving, for Steve wasn't sure himself.

'I'm not happy,' said Steve. It was a relief to admit this to someone. He didn't feel he had to prove himself to Jether, or put on an act like he did with Harrison. He could just speak the truth.

'Why not?'

'It's a long story.'

'The night is only just beginning.'

'OK.' Steve smiled and uncrossed his legs, feeling better. 'Well – there's this girl Dina . . .' And so he told the whole story, from start to finish. At the end Jether said:

'And what else?'

'Well – there isn't much else, really. Well, I guess there is other stuff. Like all the stuff that happened before Dina. I mean – it's just – I don't feel I had much of a life, dying at the age of thirty. I went to school, I went to uni, I worked in a law firm, I worked in a greasy spoon. End of story. I'm hardly going to go down in the history books, am I?'

'Why d'you feel so unsatisfied?' Jether asked.

'I don't know.' Steve thought for some time and finally said: 'I guess there's just this pressure on everyone to feel they've died achieving something. And – it's just our culture. Every time I used to go to work at The Greasy Spoon, I'd go into the newsagent to get my Coke and my KitKat, and there'd be all these magazines on display, all with front covers sporting a photo of some celebrity sitting in some mansion with about three cars. And you know it's an illusion, you know they don't have much talent and most of their relationships are just for publicity purposes, and they're probably addicted to coke and are going to die with only one nostril.

'I mean, I had a friend who went backpacking to Japan and he said there's an emphasis there on a sense of community. They don't have as many celebs over there, because they're more fixed on the idea of doing something for society rather than doing something for yourself. Celebrities are the ultimate sign of a selfish culture. But hell, it's the one I live in. I'm stuck in that mentality. And after I'd seen these magazines, I'd walk into work and just look at my crappy bank balance and my boring love life and think, 'Why can't my life be like that? Why do they get that and not me?' I used to do the lottery every week hoping I might win and my whole life would change.

'I just wish I'd achieved more. I mean, I think that's why I gave up my law firm job – apart from the boredom, I wanted to do something with meaning, make a mark on the world, only I never quite got round to it. God, I wish I'd made a movie, written a best-selling novel. You know, I used to think it was really sad that, say, a genius like Blake was never appreciated during his lifetime. I mean – what a waste. To have all those gifts and just be thought of as a madman. Imagine if Blake's ghost was walking about now, thinking, "Well hey, it's about time people did appreciate me."'

'But in the end we all go. You won't be a ghost for ever, Steve. And whatever books you've written or songs you've sung will, in time, be forgotten. Everything dies in the end. It all means nothing, in the end.'

'You say that, but I don't know how to get out of this trap I'm in.' Steve heard the frustration in his own voice. 'I mean, maybe I'm here to help Dina. D'you think that's it? I keep thinking I'm her guardian angel. Like a sort of celestial version of Lassie.' He laughed in a high voice.

Jether smiled.

'It has nothing to do with Dina, why you're here.'

'What?'

'You're just using her as an excuse.'

'What then?'

'*You*' – Jether pointed the end of his pipe at Steve's chest – 'you have to find peace. You have to find fulfilment. It's your very frustration that's keeping you here. You're attached to the world and all the things you haven't done. You're attached to your idea of your body; you can't really believe it's gone. You have to find peace; you have to let go, and then you'll move on. You're still here at the moment because you *want* to be here.'

Steve paused, stunned, realising the awful truth in Jether's words.

'I guess,' he admitted weakly, 'I am attached. I just can't let her go, you know. Because . . . even more than all the money and fame I never got, I just feel . . . I feel stupid admitting this, but . . .'

'Go on.'

'If I could really pick one thing to have achieved before I died, it would have been to know love,' said Steve. 'To have had a really deep, proper love affair. Not a crush or a fling or one of those crappy relationships that peter out after a year when you find out what the other person is really like. But something truly intimate, something as romantic as big love stories. My favourite film is *Casablanca*. And I know it ends unhappily, but that doesn't matter. I really believe it's better to have loved and lost than never to have loved at all.'

Steve realised he was speaking straight from his heart and suddenly felt self-conscious. A pink flush crept up his cheeks and he laughed slightly. But Jether didn't laugh. He was looking at Steve with compassionate eyes. Steve, feeling compassion was just one step away from pity, suddenly felt riled.

'But fuck it. It's too late now.' He shrugged.

'Next time, maybe,' said Jether.

But I don't want to wait for next time, Steve thought. *God, I don't want to wait for rebirth. Fuck – I don't even* believe *in rebirth. I want Dina* now.

And I feel so alone, so alone for never having experienced that love. As if my heart is a hollow waiting to be filled, but just moss and old things live there now.

'You know,' said Jether, going over to the window, 'look up at the stars. See how huge the sky is?'

Steve looked up at the infinite sweep of sky, but instead of feeling better, he only felt more alone. The stars seemed cold, the moon distant, as though the universe was far too grand to be interested in him.

'It helps to remember how small we are. When we're caught up in our little desires, tiny little problems, they seem so big, so vast, like oceans that threaten to drown us. But they're nothing, in reality. All our worries are useless, a waste of time.'

Steve smiled and said good night to Jether.

'Thanks, I do feel a bit better,' he said in a cheerful voice. 'You've helped me put things in perspective.'

He walked away with a false spring in his step, and though he felt a little lighter and he knew there was truth and wisdom in Jether's words, there was still an ache in his heart, an ache that thumped day and night to the rhythm of Dina.

Without thinking, he found himself walking over to Dina's flat; outside, he paused, the night air cool on his face. He slipped his hand into his pocket, fingering the wrapper of the KitKat inside. Jether's talk had sobered him up, and now he felt slightly silly about the KitKats. He wasn't even sure what sort of game he was playing by leaving them about. All he knew was that he'd been frightened over the last few weeks, seeing Dina and Archie grow closer. It was as though for the first time she was beginning to forget him, and that was something that scared him more than anything.

He thought back to yesterday morning. She had been slightly freaked out by the pile of KitKats, as he'd feared. But then, with typical Dina merriness, she'd sat down and munched her way through them, happily flipping through a magazine as she did so. He had stood by her, watching with fond delight. And then, *then,* just as she had reached out for her third KitKat, muttering at herself for being such a pig, he could have sworn that she turned and did a double-take. It was almost as if she'd *seen* him – or, at least, a glimpse of him. Which was impossible, of course, because Dina might have the ability to hear ghosts, but she certainly couldn't see them. And yet . . . and yet . . .

Sod Jether, Steve thought. His heart trembling with frightened excitement, he slowly slid up the stairs to Dina's flat.

Dina wiped away a tear, sniffed noisily and carried on packing. She wished she wasn't such a hoarder; her cupboards were full of letters, postcards and mementoes she couldn't bear to throw away. Worse, her head felt foggy and she could barely concentrate. She was feeling utterly miserable because only a few hours ago she'd said goodbye to Roger.

For the first week after Archie had asked her to move in, Dina had been ecstatic. Suddenly her moving to England, which had seemed random and crazy, made sense; she had been fated to come, to meet Archie, to find the love of her life, to move in with him and live happily ever after.

And then the subject of Roger had come up.

'You don't mind if he comes along, do you?' Dina had asked. 'I assure you he makes a very wonderful hot-water bottle.' And Roger had barked in proud agreement, as though warming feet was something he deserved medals for.

Unfortunately, Archie wasn't impressed.

Dina had been horrified when he'd said that Roger couldn't possibly come and live in his flat. They'd had a terrible row, which had ended in Dina bursting into tears and telling him that she wasn't sure she wanted to move in either, and Archie storming out in a huff.

For Dina was terribly attached to Roger. She knew it sounded dumb, but when she'd first moved to England, she'd felt closer to Roger than to many of the Brits. Roger hadn't ever told her off for walking on the wrong side of the escalators or smirked when she pronounced tomato the wrong way or asked for jello in the supermarket. With his total devotion and lack of judgement, he had seemed like her only real friend.

In the end, it was Anita who came to the rescue. She said she had some Australian friends, a couple called Melissa and Sean, who'd moved to London a year ago from Perth. They'd had a German Shepherd pup who'd died just a few months after they'd bought him, in a road accident. She'd given them a ring and they'd said they'd love to look after Roger for a short time – anything up to six months. And Dina would still be free, of course, to come and visit him and take him for walks and so on.

But Dina still couldn't get that frightful journey out of her mind. She'd sat in their white van, Roger on her lap, swivelling his head left, right, left, right, in that way he always did, trying to take in the whole bustling, busy world at once. She could almost sense the frantic exuberance of his doggie thoughts – look at that lady pushing a pram, look at that punk and his silly poodle, look at that couple snogging! And every so often he would look up at Dina as if to say: *Dina, you're looking too, aren't you? Make sure you don't miss anything.* He'd sniffed around his new home with doggie enthusiasm at first, but when Dina had said goodbye, he'd howled in bewilderment, and she had felt as though her heart was breaking.

Archie had since apologised and been very sweet about the whole thing. And, in all honesty, she knew he was right – Roger and Archie's cat, Jupiter, would have been an impossible combination. But even so, she still felt down. And, she admitted it to herself, rather nervous about moving. Tomorrow Archie was going to roll up in his car and her new life would begin.

She gazed at her reflection in the mirror, smiling tiredly. As she turned away, she was sure she saw something flit past, a shadow curl into the wardrobe, and she jumped, doing a double-take.

But – nothing there. Just a plain old wardrobe with her denim skirt hanging on the door. That was the second time that week it had happened. Clearly, she needed a trip to the optician.

She was just emptying out the bottom of the wardrobe when she discovered, beneath a pair of boots she'd bought in a sale and never worn, a fat brown envelope. She let out a gasp. Oh God. She'd completely forgotten. This was the package Steve's mother had passed on to her way back when they'd had that crazy seance. She'd put it aside and now weeks had passed and she hadn't even *looked* at it . . .

She frowned, musing that this morning there had been yet another KitKat lying on her bedside table. She still couldn't work out what the hell was going on; she just kept eating them and trying to laugh the whole thing off. It had to be Archie, she thought, playing a joke, and no doubt Anita was in on the whole thing. Maybe this morning's offering had just been Archie's way of saying sorry.

Lying back on her bed, trying not to miss the feel of Roger curled by her feet, she lit a cigarette, drawing the nicotine out. She hadn't smoked in months but she felt so upset over Roger all her resolve had collapsed.

Finally she opened the envelope. There were lots of photographs, some newspaper cuttings and a dog-eared notebook.

Dina looked at the newspaper cutting first. It was from a local newspaper, describing how seventeen-year-old Steve MacFadden had won the county chess championship. He had a frightful crewcut, which had no doubt been his mother's idea, and had obviously been told to say 'cheese' by the photographer. Next she examined the photos: Steve, aged three, being carried on his dad's shoulders; Steve, aged eight, riding his first bike; Steve, aged fifteen, playing with a Gameboy and grinning with the new shyness of adolescence. Her heart opened up, and all the love she had felt for him, which had been squashed away and forgotten over the last few months, flowed out again, and tears welled up in her eyes.

At last she looked at the notebook. It was thin and yellow, with narrow lines. She'd often seen Steve fiddling about with it in The Greasy Spoon; she'd teased him that it must be full of secrets because he'd never let her look in it. Once she'd stolen it from under his nose and Steve had laughingly chased her through the café before finally wrestling it from her.

She stubbed her cigarette out and flicked through randomly. There were lots of scribbly, incomprehensible equations – Steve had always been keen on physics. Then, at the bottom of the page, she saw some writing that had been scrawled backwards. She quickly held it up to the mirror and read: *D. came in early again today. She was wearing the red jumper. Looked beautiful. Every night I dream of her and she seems like . . .*

Dina felt her heart cave in. She shoved everything back into the envelope, grabbed her bag and keys and ran out of the flat, ignoring Anita's cry as to whether she was OK, whether she was still upset over Roger.

She went back to St Simon's church and sat in a pew at the front. Her mind was in turmoil. At last she got up and went to light a candle. *This is symbolic*, she whispered, *symbolic of a new stage in my life. I'm saying goodbye to my first phase in London, to The Greasy Spoon, to living with Anita, to my time with Steve; tomorrow I'll be with Archie and it will mark a new era in my life.* But, as though fate was frowning on her, a draught gushed in through the doors and the candle was blown out, a thin tendril of smoke spiralling up from the wick. Suddenly she thought of the KitKats she kept finding. What if they weren't a joke? What if she really had heard Steve's voice at the seance and he was trying to get in touch? What if he was trying to tell her something, tell her . . . *Oh God*, she panicked, *have I got it right? When I remember Steve, I remember how sweet his love was, how sincere, how open his heart. Archie's love seems so complex, so riddled with ups and downs, so conditional on compromises, in comparison. Am I making the right decision? But I can't change my mind now, can I?*

She blew out a deep breath, and gently resolved the crisis inside her. Her panic had arisen from her usual indecisiveness. She had to move on. She couldn't go back to the past. Things might not be perfect with Archie – but when was life ever perfect? When was love ever simple?

She lit another candle, and this time it glowed. There. That was better.

Outside, she went to Steve's grave. The daffodils in the jam jar were fresh, placed there by Steve's doting mother. She sat beside the grave, ready to cry out the very last of her grief, to say her final goodbyes. But, perversely, the tears wouldn't come. The more she tried to drag them up from her heart, the more obstinately they stayed locked inside. Her eyes remained cold and dry. She sat there for some time as the wind gently blew pink blossom from the trees and the air became chilly and crisp, and the sky darkened to a smoky blue, and she rose and slowly walked home.

18
Dina

During the first three weeks after Dina moved in with Archie, Steve watched her closely, curious to see if he made her happy.

She seemed to enjoy the intimacy of being with Archie. She cuddled up close to him in the mornings, trying to keep him in bed for as long as she could before work. Steve saw her eyes brighten and linger at the novelty of her presence in Archie's flat. Her toothbrush in his bathroom cup, her bendy bristles kissing his clean white ones. Her long line of shampoos and face creams next to his stylish collection of expensive aftershaves. Her rainbow dresses lined up next to his charcoal suits.

When she was with Archie, she seemed happy. Sometimes she got fed up with the nights he spent working, either locked away in his study at home, or away in the restaurants. But he always did his best to make up for it by using his spare evenings to take her out so that her social life was a ritzy kaleidoscope of cocktail parties, restaurant openings, romantic dinners and film premieres. Dina and Archie looked sickeningly beautiful together, like some sort of celebrity couple, always laughing and kissing and surrounded by swirls of glamorous friends.

But in the daytime, Steve saw a different Dina. In Archie's company, her life had purpose and meaning. But when he was absent, she seemed slightly lost. When they had worked at The Greasy Spoon together, Steve had always sensed a restlessness in Dina. Her dyslexia had knocked her confidence that she would ever have a brilliant career, but she was an intelligent and energetic girl. Before she started dating Archie, she'd been bubbly and cheerful. Now she was jobless, she seemed confused. Archie kept telling her she didn't need to worry about money, she could pay back her loan any time, but twice, Steve had found her going through Monday's *Guardian* jobs section, eyeing up adverts and chewing on her nails uneasily.

Archie had given Dina a credit card and told her to buy whatever she needed – so long as she kept within the thousand-pound limit every month. Dina said no at first; she felt the loan was enough. But Archie kept insisting and Dina caved in and learnt to enjoy being spoilt by him. At first it was fun. She spent hours in shops and came out laden with glossy bags. She went to massage parlours and beauty salons. She had her thick eyebrows plucked into slender arches. She had her toenails shaped and her feet massaged with an expensive mint-scented lotion. She bought about twenty handbags and an insane number of shoes, and regularly called up her mother or Anita to cry, 'Oh – guess what I bought today!' Her mother was always pleased for her. But Anita, sensing their lives were becoming very different, and rather fed up with only being able to afford bargains from New Look on her tiny salary, become more and more distant.

Then, after just a week, the shopping trips began to dry up. Dina started to get up later every morning, sometimes not until midday. She'd go to Starbucks for lunch, flipping restlessly through magazines, skimming facile articles about boob jobs and celebrity diets. Sometimes she went to the library and wandered restlessly through the aisles as though a book might, by magic, fall from the shelves and tell her just what she needed to do with her life. Once she visited the Tate, but Steve sensed her loneliness as she slid past rows of pictures. Dina was so bright and vivacious that she wasn't the sort of person who liked doing things alone; she needed someone to share things with, to laugh with, and tease.

The only constant part of her routine was Roger. She went to visit him every afternoon and took him for a long walk, but the agony on her face, and Roger's howls every time she left him, led Steve to conclude the outings brought her more pain than pleasure.

During those first three weeks of living together, Dina and Archie had several rows. Steve watched them all, trying to be detached, but suffering as though Dina was his Siamese twin and he felt her emotions as deeply as though they were his own.

And then came the row to end all rows.

That night – the night the simmering tensions erupted – Dina sat curled up on the sofa, reading *Birdsong.* Yesterday the moving trench scenes had made her cry, but this evening she couldn't quite concentrate. She kept feeling as though someone was reading over her shoulder, but whenever she turned to look there was nothing but wallpaper.

Or maybe she was just too aware that it was a Friday night and Archie was locked up in his study, working. As usual. Why couldn't he just be domestic for once, Dina had asked him, and come and snuggle up on the sofa and share ice cream or crisps and watch a video?

Sighing, she gave up on her book and picked up the TV remote, flicking despondently from sitcoms to soaps. A minute later, the door of Archie's study banged. A menacing silhouette appeared in the doorway.

'Dina.' Archie ran his hands through his hair. 'Can you please turn the volume down? Look, the walls in this bloody flat are too thin, and I'm up to my eyeballs in work, OK?'

Dina turned and pressed the remote so that the line of little green squares indicating volume shortened considerably. She swallowed, opened her mouth, closed it. Should she risk the stress of a row? Then, as Archie let out a huffy sigh, as though she was some inconvenient *lodger,* for crying out loud, she turned and called after him:

'Is the work situation really bad? I was thinking if it isn't that urgent, you could leave it until Monday. I mean, it is the weekend.'

Archie turned back slowly. There was a pulse flickering in his jaw like a snake.

'Jesus, Dina, I'm *busy,* OK? And we went out last night.'

'I know, Archie, but I don't always like going out – I mean, the restaurant was lovely,' she added, guiltily remembering the expense of the meal. 'But when we do spend time together, we always go out, we always party. I just think it would be nice to stay in – y'know, just chill out, talk, play chess . . . whatever . . .'

'Play chess? Talk?' Archie said, as though Dina had just

suggested they go to a Women's Institute meeting and make jam together. 'Well, my chef is about to be lured away to Gordon Ramsay's restaurant, if that's interesting enough conversation for you. So please turn down the TV, thanks. Look, we can do the video thing later, OK?'

'OK.' Dina saw Archie turn to go and chewed off her thumbnail. 'How much later?'

'Sorry?'

'I mean – is it going to be three a.m., or a more reasonable time, like eleven?'

'Jesus, Dina, what are you, my boss?'

'OK, OK, look, I'm sorry. I know you're busy . . . but I'm freaking out too because I have to call my mom and I haven't called her for three days and she's worrying, so . . .' That was the problem with Archie having the phone in his study. He ought to damn well get a cordless.

'Can't you use your mobile? I'm expecting an important call.'

'It'll cost a bomb, calling America.'

Archie paused. 'Well, look, you'll just have to call her tomorrow, OK?' And with that, he strolled off and slammed the door behind him.

OK, Dina echoed sulkily. She went back to the TV, lowering the volume a few more nervous notches. She felt cross, more with herself than him. Cross because she knew that tomorrow she would wake up and feel like packing her things. And then Archie would cajole her and kiss her gently and she would find herself melting into forgiveness. Uneasily, she thought of Ralph and how he had warned her once at a party, 'Archie always manages to get away with doing things nobody else does. Because he's Archie.' And Dina, despite her anger, found herself smiling affectionately: Archie *was* Archie, and though when he was in a bad mood he was the biggest bastard on the planet, when he was in a good one he balanced it out by becoming the sexiest, sweetest, most charming Adonis that had ever existed.

She painted her toenails pink; in the past she'd always considered toenail-painting to be overly girly and rather pointless, since the British weather hardly ever permitted sandals. Still, it was something to do. Now what? Nine p.m. *Maybe,* she thought, *I could go and do something really exciting like making a cup of tea.*

She headed for the kitchen, half limping because one foot was still wet and she knew if she got any glittery pink nail polish on the spotless white carpet, she'd die a long, slow, painful death. Passing Archie's study, she suddenly heard a deep chuckle. Hello? What was so hysterically funny about Archie's important call and his major work crisis? Dina pressed her ear against the door. She heard Archie chuckle again and then say in a low, conspiratorial voice: 'Heidi, you are *such* a minx, I can't believe you just said that!'

Dina promptly forgot the tea. She went back into the living room and walked about in figures of eight. She stopped and stared numbly at the glitter of her polished toes. She went back to the study. She had been hearing things, surely? But no: Archie was still laughing. She caught the name 'Heidi' again. She raised a hand to knock on the door, but her arm went limp. She went back to pacing. Her heart trembled in her chest. She slumped on the sofa and, as her hurt turned to anger, she took the remote and flicked up the volume until it was nearly maximum.

Archie's study door banged open. She waited for him to begin the row and give her an opening. But he merely said cheerfully:

'Going deaf, are we, honey? I was just going to take a break – you're right, I am working too hard.' He came up behind her and took the remote, switching the volume off, then massaged her shoulders. 'D'you want a cup of tea? I was just going to get one.'

'Earl Grey would be great,' Dina heard herself say. And then: 'Had a nice chat with Heidi, did you?'

She turned and saw his expression flicker with surprise, and then rapidly smooth back to normal.

'Yeah. She sends her love. Now, I'll get the tea.'

Dina sat, mouthing in outrage. She jumped up, steeling herself for further confrontation, but as she headed towards the kitchen, the phone rang and the answerphone clicked on. She heard her mother's voice ringing out.

'You'd better answer that,' Archie called from the kitchen, 'or you might not catch her later. I've still got more calls to come.'

Oh, I'm sure you do, Dina seethed, picking up. She found herself gossiping on autopilot. Her mother had finally received a photo of

Archie in the post and was gushing on about how lovely he looked and how lucky Dina was. Dina closed her eyes in pain at the irony of it all.

'I'm so glad you're settling in now,' her mother said. 'To tell you the truth, Dina honey, I've been really worrying about you. I felt you weren't happy, and you kept calling all the time. Every night. Now you never call at all.'

'I'm sorry, Mom,' said Dina. 'I will call more, I promise. I'm just – you know' – she put on a happy voice – 'too busy being happy. Well, bye now. Love you.'

As she put down the phone, a wave of homesickness suddenly assailed her. Archie's flat suddenly felt small and claustrophobic, the corners reverberating with secrets and lies. She strolled into the kitchen and said, 'Archie, I want you to tell me straight – are you seeing Heidi again?'

'How's your mother?' Archie banged a cupboard.

'I asked you a question!'

'Jesus, Dina!' Archie filled up the kettle, flipping on the switch. 'I mean, what is it with you? You know I like being friends with women, you know I like being friends with my exes, and yes, Heidi is an ex, and she is a friend. And if you have difficulty with that, well, I'm sorry, but that's your problem.'

Dina folded her arms. She sensed Archie was only being so outrageously rude because she'd caught him off guard and he was on the defensive.

'Oh,' he added, filling the mugs with hot water, 'and by the way, when you moved in here, we made a pact that you were going to keep things tidy, but you keep leaving the fucking empty toilet roll in the holder. I mean, would it be too much trouble just to pull it out and throw it in the bin and put a new roll in? And I found a hair in the bath this morning. It was disgusting.'

'What!' Dina shook her head, taken aback by his wily ability to suddenly turn a fight around and send the arrows of accusation flying back at her. 'Look, Archie, you're trying to change the subject, we're talking about Heidi—'

'No, we're not, and I'm not changing the subject, and that long, slimy, filthy hair is *still* in the bath.'

'Well, what d'you want me to do with it?' Dina's voice shook with savage sarcasm. 'Arrange to have it arrested? Burned at the stake?'

'I want you to go and get rid of it. And I want you to do it now. This minute. Go on.'

'Archie, you are being completely anal,' Dina cried, losing her temper. 'I know I can be messy, but this whole cleanliness thing you have is just completely obsessive, and a sign of you being way too perfectionist about everything, and maybe if you could be a bit more perfectionist about relationships, we might have something approaching a normal relationship rather than . . . than . . .'

'Than what?' Archie's face was ugly now, his eyes slits.

'Than you lying to me and calling up Heidi—'

'Will you just give it a rest over Heidi!' Archie slammed the sugar bowl down on the table, spraying granules across the surface. 'Jesus, Dina, I'm in a really stressful situation with work and yes, I called Heidi, because I wanted a fun chat to cheer me up, which is more than you can do, and if you don't like it, then you can go! I mean it – just go, OK?'

'Go?' Dina asked in a small, shocked voice.

'Yes – go! I mean, what's the point? I don't need this shit. Just go!'

He stormed past her into the bedroom and she followed him with wide eyes, watching him throw her case on to the bed. He slid open the wardrobe, removed all of her dresses in one swoop and tossed them into the case. Next he went to the drawer and grabbed handfuls of her knickers and bras and socks and threw them on top, all higgledy-piggledy. He zipped up the case.

'There!'

Dina suddenly realised that this row wasn't like their other rows, when insults would ping back and forth between them like a ball, until Archie would storm over and burst into laughter and then kiss her furiously. This was different. Archie had lost it. Every vein in his face was a violent beetroot colour and his eyes were bulging like some cartoon psycho.

'Archie – we can talk about this,' said Dina, swallowing tears. 'I mean, I really care about you, I know I'm annoyed about Heidi, but can you blame me—'

'No. I've had enough! Just get out. I need my space, I want my own—' He broke off, as though his words had crushed together in a pile-up of anger. He let out a deep breath, holding his temples and blinking, trying once again to get a grip on himself. 'I just need my space. You have to go. Take your suitcase and go.'

'But—'

'*Dina.*'

His voice was absolute.

'OK, fine! You don't bloody deserve me! I'm going!' She picked up her case and lingered for one miserable moment, but he just carried on staring out of the window, jaw set, eyes cold and bleak. She felt as though he was surrounded not only by a wall but by a bloody electric fence; as she walked towards him to say goodbye, he bristled so visibly that she stepped backwards, half stumbling. Everything seemed blurry through her tears. Sounds were muted as though she was underwater. After a moment, she turned and walked out.

Outside the flat, she stood in the hallway, wiping her cheeks with her sleeves. She waited. She swung back and stared at the door. He didn't come.

She couldn't face the lift and the merry-go-round of people going out for Friday-night fun. She dragged her case down the stairs, letting it bang after her. Halfway down, she stopped and had another crying fit: shoulders shaking, stomach wrenching. She pushed out through the swing doors blindly, the cold air slapping her face, clawing cheeks that were already sore with tears.

Outside, it was freezing; spring seemed to have forgotten itself and reverted to winter. She stood on the stone steps with her case, shivering violently. A few people were walking down the street, chatting and laughing. A taxi with a brightly lit FOR HIRE sign trawled past and she knew she ought to flag it down, but the energy required even to raise her hand seemed beyond her. She found herself slumping on to the steps. Then she burst into loud tears.

Several onlookers turned and shared embarrassed glances, hurrying by. Dina was beyond caring. She sat and let tears and snot stream down her face. She felt gripped by a whirlwind of emotional thoughts that flung her about from one feeling to the next until she was thoroughly bruised and battered. Archie was a bastard; the most evil bastard she had ever dated. She loved him; she hated him. The whole relationship was a farce, a mistake. Should she go back and try one last time? There was no hope. She didn't understand him. He had never understood her. How had her life unravelled and come to this mess? A rational voice told her she ought to go and find somewhere to stay and begin organising herself, but a childish, furious part retaliated and screamed that it was all too unfair, she was going to damn well sit here on the steps and cry her heart out.

Suddenly she felt a cool breeze, like a breath, pour over her and she shivered. Then the breath, which at first had merely seemed like a movement of air, appeared to become more of a presence, a sense of heat. *What the hell is that?* she thought.

She felt fear in her chest, but she forced the emotion back with mounting curiosity, fearing that she might somehow push the presence away. She had felt this before, this soft breath, but this time it was acute; it could not be mistaken or brushed off as imagination, and in her fragile, sensitive state she felt her heart begin to skip and all the hairs on her skin quiver to their very points. The warmth seemed to touch her. It laid hands on her hair and face. It brushed and breathed across her neck. Her fear melted away. She felt as consoled as a screaming baby picked up by its mother; as though a hand had reached inside her heart and pulled out her suffering. Her tears dried on her face and she looked out at the arch of lamppost-tinted sky above her and the dark serenity of the park across the road, and the emotions that had overwhelmed her only minutes before seemed distant. She closed her eyes, willing the presence to stay, luxuriating in it. She said in her heart: *Who are you?* And she felt it brush the hairs away from her ear and whisper, 'Dina, it's me.'

I know that voice.

Her eyes flicked open.

'Steve?' she whispered.

She heard footsteps behind her, and yet in front of her something seemed to be taking shape, as though someone was gently sketching a black outline around it.

'Steve?' She turned.

It was Archie. He opened up his arms and pulled her into them. He buried his face in her shoulder.

'I'm so sorry,' he whispered. 'I don't know what gets into me. I'm so sorry.'

*

At first Archie couldn't understand why Dina wouldn't stop crying. He guided her back up the steps, carrying her case for her, apologising and shushing her relentlessly. But then her behaviour became most peculiar. She slumped on the sofa, crying, 'Are you there? Are you there?' She kept looking around, staring up over Archie's head at the blank wall, out of the window. Archie, fearing she was seriously hysterical, went into the kitchen to make her some hot, sweet tea. He watched the steam puff from the kettle, creating grey aeroplane trails. He'd never had a girlfriend who'd overreacted quite this badly. When he came back in, she jumped as though she'd seen a ghost.

'Are you OK?' he asked, relieved to see that she seemed to have calmed down.

She nodded, sniffing, gratefully accepting the tissue that Archie passed her.

'I – it's just – something happened to me out there, Archie – he was so close. I – felt him—'

'Who was so close?' Archie became irritable again. 'What the hell are you talking about?' He sat down next to her on the sofa. 'Dina,' he said gently, 'you're spouting absolute gibberish. Now, why don't you drink your tea and then we can talk about us. OK, darling?' He stroked her hair back from her face.

She stared at him, eyes wide and glassy, and for one strange moment he feared she was in some sort of hypnotic state and had completely lost touch with reality. Then, as though a switch had clicked inside her, she seemed to flip back to normalcy. She tucked her hair behind her ears. She nodded and blew her nose. She drank her tea and stopped crying, though she still seemed broody and preoccupied ten minutes later when she put down the empty mug. An awkward silence arose.

'Let's go into the bedroom,' said Archie.

They lay down on the bed, face to face, holding hands.

'Look,' said Archie, all in a rush, 'I know I'm crap at relationships. When it comes to business, I know exactly what I'm doing. But when it comes to relationships – I mean real relationships, not just flings or romance or all the wining-and-dining stuff – I just feel as though I'm floundering. Which is probably why you're the first girl I've ever lived with, and why I'm not making a great job of it.' He pressed his hand into hers and squeezed it. 'I'm finding it hard . . . y'know, sharing my space, sharing my life with someone. I'm so used to just doing my own thing whenever I want and having things my own way. I know I need to be less selfish . . . but you also need to be more tidy . . . and . . .'

'And?'

'I guess . . .' Archie stared up at the ceiling, suddenly unable to look her in the eye. 'I loved my father, I loved him very much. But when I was six years old, I walked into his bedroom and found him in bed with another woman.'

'What!'

'Uh-huh. He gave me double pocket money so I wouldn't tell my mother. But then it turned out she knew about that woman, and all the others too. Once, when I was a teenager, I asked her why she put up with it, and she said that it was just his nature. She dealt with reality by pretending it wasn't happening. She was a Catholic, you see, and didn't believe in divorce, and she used to snap, "Your generation gives up on marriage too quickly." I think it's partly why she became so tough, to cover up her pain.

'I still admire him.' Archie's voice cracked. 'And we all find out at some point that our parents aren't perfect. But I guess – I guess it's why I have this phobia about relationships . . . I guess I haven't exactly grown up with a great source of inspiration . . .'

'Oh God. I'm sorry.' Suddenly it all made sense – his commitment-phobia, his swings between deep affection and then pushing her sharply away.

Dina knew that she still ought to confront him about Heidi, but suddenly she didn't have the heart or the emotional energy. She was still numb from the shock of hearing Steve's voice; she couldn't quite focus on the present, bring herself back to reality. In addition to all this, Archie's confession had thrown her; she needed time to digest it.

So she forgot about Heidi and laid her cheek against his chest in a gesture of reconciliation. Archie let out a soft groan and curled his arm around her, and they lay like that for some time, letting forgiveness flow between them . . .

*

Later that night, Dina lay in bed watching Archie sleep. They'd gone out for a meal and then made love, but it had felt awkward, as though they couldn't quite give themselves up to each other. Dina had found herself faking an orgasm, looking forward to the good bit, when they would cuddle and talk. But Archie fell straight to sleep.

I guess I knew the honeymoon part would eventually end, Dina thought. It had to; that was life. She remembered her mother once telling her that you couldn't really tell if a relationship was real until it hit its first bad patch. The bad patch was a test, to see if you could ride the stormy waves together, and then, when everything was calm and sunny and sparkling again, you came out so much stronger. *We'll be all right,* she told herself. *We had to reach this point, we had to have this row. At least now I have a little more understanding about why Archie is how he is.*

She gazed towards the window. A white gloss of frost had already formed on the glass; by the morning, it would be pure ice. Suddenly fear gripped her like a chill. She had shut out what had happened after the row; she hadn't wanted to think about it, unravel it, analyse it, had just pretended it didn't exist. But there, on the window, the letters, written by a ghostly finger, slowly formed:

DON'T WORRY, BE HAPPY

19
Dina

Dina looked into the mirror as Henrique, the top stylist at Jasmine's, threaded a chunk of her hair through his slender, bony fingers, and then – *snip!* – sliced away a good three inches. Her hair fell to the floor in a dark, feathery cloud. In the mirror, Dina watched Archie pacing about, chatting on his mobile, doing business. As usual. She glanced down at the copy of *Marie Claire* in her lap and decided it was best not to look up again until Henrique had finished.

It had been Archie's idea to drag Dina to the hairdresser's, declaring that Henrique was the best in the business and one of his oldest friends. Dina knew that it was his way of saying sorry, and she was touched by the gesture. They had spent the weekend both making a huge effort to repair things and be nice to each other. But the row had still left wounds that hadn't healed. Every time Dina repeated his words in her head, it was like sprinkling salt into the cuts in her heart.

As Henrique began to twist her hair up into little foil packets, Dina resisted the restlessness prickling over her. She realised, with a vague sense of surprise, that she was bored, and uneasy. She also realised that if Archie had brought her here three months ago, she would have been utterly enthralled by the excitement of being pampered. *Maybe I'm getting spoilt,* she told herself, *maybe I'm forgetting how lucky I am. I mean, how many other girls get taken out on a Sunday afternoon for an expensive haircut?* Catching Archie's eye in the mirror, she smiled, and he gave her a thumbs-up and blew her a kiss. *It's going to be all right,* she told herself again. *The row's forgotten, it's going to be all right.*

Henrique left her for a while to give her highlights a chance to take, but she found it hard to concentrate on her magazine. She glanced up into the mirror again and suddenly, impulsively, found herself blowing hard on the glass. *Oh God, why did I do that?* she wondered. Her heart began to beat hard as she stared at the misty circle, waiting for more words to appear.

As the mist slowly faded away, she felt a sense of deep disappointment wash over her. *What if he never comes back?* she thought.

Henrique reappeared and untwisted her hair, combing and drying it.

'Da–da!' he cried eventually. Archie came up behind him, admiring Dina's new look. Her hair was all shades of golden and brown and buttercup, falling about her face in a sleek, choppy cut.

'It's lovely,' Dina exclaimed, but she couldn't help feeling odd. 'I look so . . . different . . .'

'You look sophisticated,' said Archie. 'Those curls were so messy.'

The weekend passed. On Sunday night they talked again. Dina promised to make more of an effort to be tidy, and Archie in turn promised to be less anal and more comprising. Then they made love, and this time it felt almost like their old lovemaking again, passionate but tender.

On Monday morning Archie went off to work and Dina tried to drop off again but she couldn't. She felt fluttery and jumpy. It was the first time in forty-eight hours that she had been alone.

She found herself showering and dressing and putting on make-up. She had a couple of late-morning appointments – a manicure, and a facial, which Archie had also booked as treats for her. She phoned up and cancelled them. She made herself a bagel with cream cheese for breakfast, then sat on the sofa. She flipped through a magazine. Chewed her nails. Tied her hair back in a scrunchy, irritated by the tendrils which kept falling about her face. She told herself that it was a waste of time and it was silly. But still she waited.

By the time eleven o'clock came, all she'd done was read a copy of *Harpers,* check her email twice to discover she had nothing but junk mail and watched a bit of daytime telly. She felt stupid for wasting a morning, for nurturing such absurd notions. She decided to go out to Starbucks for a coffee.

Then she felt it. Just as she had felt it before.

A change in the atmosphere. As though the wind was turning in on itself to blow in a fresh direction. The curtains swirled. Jupiter jumped down from the windowsill and clawed the rug, yeowling. Dina saw faint impressions, like pools of water that instantly evaporated, appearing on the hall carpet. Her earlier anticipation melted into fear. She picked up her bag, searched wildly for her keys. She found them on the coffee table, sending magazines spinning to the floor. She left them there and began to hurry down the hallway to the door. Jupiter followed her.

'Dina?'

Steve's voice, from behind, stopped her. She paused, rigid with fear.

'It's only me.'

When she turned, she had a shock. She could *see* him. Just about.

He was a little like the charcoal pictures she used to do as a girl: a shadowy outline, blurred at the edges.

She stood very still. He stood still too, staring at her. She felt panic, like the first whirl of a hurricane, beginning to rise up her stomach. She squeezed her eyes shut and told herself, *It's all right, Dina. It's just an hallucination. A trick of the light. You've been tired recently; you haven't been sleeping all that well at night. Now. Just count backwards from five. Open your eyes and you'll be fine.*

Five . . . four . . . three . . . two . . .

In her nerves, Dina cheated and flicked them open early.

Oh my God.

Oh my God. Oh my God. Oh my God.

Fear screamed through her. She turned blindly, grabbing the front door, the latch, ready to run, to crash down the stairs, fling herself outside. But then she heard him say, in a friendly voice:

'Dina – don't go. It's *me.* I'm not going to hurt you.'

Dina swallowed. She turned round slowly, letting out a deep

shaky breath. He took a step forward; she immediately took a step backward. She pressed herself up against the door. He stopped, flinching and looking hurt.

Minutes passed. Dina found she couldn't look at him for very long. She kept letting out deep breaths, staring down at the floor, or her hands, and the straps of her handbag curled so tight around them that blushing furrows formed in her skin; then she would flick her eyes up at him, drink him in, and look away again incredulously. All the while, her mind kept scurrying this way and that, torn between logic and superstition, reason and reality. She kept remembering articles she had read where this really happened to people, and then thinking, *But God, this can't be happening to me, it can't*, and then, *But surely this isn't happening, surely it's just a product of my grief, surely he isn't real?*

Steve watched the emotions flitting across her face and he waited patiently, listening as her ragged breathing gradually slowed and softened. He ached to run forward and hold her but he forced himself to remain still, as though he had discovered some rare and beautiful animal out in the wild and could only wait until it learnt to trust him.

Dina uncurled her handbag from her fingers and gently let it drop to the floor. Then, one step at a time, she slowly walked up to him.

As she came closer she could see his face, and though his eyes were pale and transparent, she saw the emotion in them; if anything, it was more naked than ever. She saw that he was scared too and realised how much courage it had taken for him to come. She stopped feeling afraid.

She walked a little closer to him and let out a laugh. Yes – this was Steve. He still had freckles and a snub nose and his habit of hunching his shoulders and balling his fists in his pockets. She felt love pour through her. She leaned forward to engulf him in a hug . . .

. . . and found herself lying on the carpet, a sharp pain throbbing at her temple, and something warm and sticky running down her cheek.

'Dina?' She felt his hand on her temple. She blinked, forgetting her pain, for as he pulled his hand away she saw a splash of her blood, strikingly bright, on his greyish fingers. 'Are you OK? You fell.'

'I was trying to hug you,' Dina giggled, slightly hysterical.

'Well, there isn't much of me to hug.'

'Did I fall straight through you?'

'Yes, and then you hit that . . .' Steve pointed to Archie's small hall table.

Dina went into the bathroom and grabbed a box of plasters. As she washed the cut on her temple, she stared at herself in the mirror and thought incredulously: *What is this? What are you doing, chatting to a ghost?* But she slapped the plaster on, and hurried out to the living room. Her fear had passed now and had been replaced by an overwhelming curiosity.

Steve was gently flicking his fingers in Einstein's bowl. They didn't create waves as a normal human's would, just tender little currents. Einstein shot up to the surface, fins wagging as if to cry: *Is it feeding time already?* Steve yelped as Einstein nibbled his finger.

Dina sat down and giggled. Then her laughter faded away, and she swallowed.

'Well, how are you?' she asked, instantly cursing herself. Stupid, stupid question.

'Erm, OK. Ish.' Steve laughed self-consciously. 'Really, I'm OK. Don't worry about me, I'm fine.'

Dina stared at her nails. She was aware of Steve looking her over and she fluffed her fingers through her new haircut.

'Your hair looks great,' Steve said.

'Thanks.'

There was another long silence.

'Look,' said Steve heatedly, moving in front of her, 'I do realise this all seems crazy, but I'm still the same old Steve. Really. I still play chess. I still read *Nexus.* I still like physics and star-gazing.'

'Do you still worry too much?'

'Yep.' Steve smiled.

'I'll never forget that day we were sitting in The Greasy Spoon and you said "Where do all the radiators go after we've finished with them?" Only you – and I mean this in the nicest possible way – could ever come out with that.'

'Well,' Steve gave a small shrug, flushing like mad, 'it's because

I'm a deep person,' he said ironically. 'By the way, I saw Luigi the other day and he's selling *vegetarian* sausages, but I spotted him in the back kitchen surreptitiously stuffing old bits of burger into them!'

'You're kidding!' Dina thumped her cushion. Then her expression changed; he kept seeing fear rippling across her face and then receding, and his last statement was like dropping a stone into water. 'So you can watch people. I mean, do you ever – ever . . . ever . . . watch me?'

'Yeah,' Steve admitted. 'I mean, I just like to make sure you're OK . . .'

'Like my guardian angel?'

'Yes,' he said fondly.

'So, how often d'you watch me, then?' Her voice changed note.

'Now and again.'

'That's kind of freaky,' Dina said. 'I mean . . . have you ever . . .'

'What?'

'Never mind.'

'I've never watched you and Archie, if that's what you're saying,' Steve burst out.

'No, I didn't mean that!' Dina cried, flushing. She fiddled with her watch strap. 'Well. OK. Maybe I did. I'm sorry. It's just all a bit . . . strange . . .'

'You keep saying that,' said Steve in a flat voice.

There was an awkward silence.

'So what have you been doing?' Dina asked hastily. 'I mean, where've you been living?'

'Hammersmith. I haunt a deserted mansion.'

Dina felt an odd twist of disappointment. She realised she'd wanted to show her flat off to Steve, her new life, to show that she had moved on since The Greasy Spoon and made a fresh start. But Steve, with his ghostly advantages, had beaten her to it.

'And if anyone comes in, you rattle your chains and put a white sheet over your head?' she joked lightly.

'Yeah, and we throw ectoplasm at them made out of flour and water. Actually,' Steve said, 'I don't really know why there's this big myth about ghosts wanting to haunt people. I mean, most of them want to be left in peace. Harrison – he's a friend of mine, another ghost – and I might have to move soon because the house is on the market . . . it's a bit of a nomadic existence.'

'So you're ghost gypsies.' It was as though she could only cope with the situation by joking about it. 'But . . . why aren't you . . . you know . . . in heaven?'

'They threw me out,' Steve said.

'Are you kidding?'

'Yeah. I got drunk one night and stole an angel's harp, then fell through a few clouds, hit Gabriel and knocked him out . . . OK, I'm kidding. I'm kidding. To be honest, I'm not quite sure why I'm not in heaven. I – I don't know. I don't know how to get there. I mean, you're a Christian, aren't you, so if you have any bright ideas, then let me know.'

Dina swallowed, looking anxious. Despite Steve's flip manner, she suddenly sensed how lost he was. Her heart ached with pity for him. She opened her mouth to suggest that maybe he should pray, or go to church, and then realised how silly and patronising she might sound, and quickly snapped it shut again.

There was another awkward silence.

'Well, I guess I should get going,' said Steve at last.

'No, you don't have to go . . .' she said, uncertainly. She bit her lip, aware that it seemed outwardly as though she was being rude and cold. *I don't mean to come across like that,* she wanted to say. *I just . . . I just . . . I just need time to digest this. Absorb it. I don't want you to go but I need to be on my own for a while, I think.*

Steve, who had been lingering in the hope that she might ask him to stay, swallowed and forced cheerfulness into his voice. 'It's fine. By the way, shall we swap mobile numbers?'

Dina's jaw dropped and then quivered to fight laughter as she saw Steve pull a thin, transparent, silvery mobile from his jacket pocket. She bit her lip hard as Steve told her his number, and in return she reminded him of hers. *This has to be one of the most surreal moments of my life,* she thought. *Exchanging mobile numbers with a ghost.*

'Well, bye,' said Steve. He looked doleful and suddenly she stopped laughing and felt wrenched with guilt, aware that she hadn't been welcoming enough. She waved a sheepish goodbye. Steve moved away into the shadows and for a moment there was a chaos of dark shapes and she couldn't tell if he was gone. Then, suddenly, he was back, stepping into the room, carrying a book. A fat book which he'd left lying in the hallway when he came in.

'It's just a present for you,' said Steve. 'I thought it might help cheer you up.'

Seven p.m. A key turned in the front door. Archie, who just got home from work and was delving in the fridge for a pot of raspberry yoghurt, turned to see Dina entering. Her collar was flicked up, her face flushed. She gave him a hello kiss and said she'd just been out for a walk.

'You OK?' Archie licked yoghurt from the lid, his pink tongue flashing.

'Fine,' said Dina. She turned away from him quickly and went to the sink, filling a glass with water, downing it thirstily. Something moved behind her reflection in the window, and she jumped, then realised it was just the wind playing with the trees. She ached to tell Archie what she'd been through today. Up until this point in their relationship, they'd told each other everything. But what could she say? *Hey, Archie, this morning I met a ghost who used to be an old friend of mine and he gave me his mobile number? And then afterwards I took a walk to his grave, feeling awkward and embarrassed that he might be following me. But I seemed to be alone, and I sat on his grave, and all the grief that was knotted up before came pouring out. I cried my heart out for hours. I kept thinking:* This is crazy, I've found out he's still with me, why am I crying? *I couldn't quite understand it. I still don't. Maybe seeing him again simply triggered a memory of what he was, and what he might have been. Now he just seems half himself, a shadow of the old Steve. Unreal, incomplete, a little frightening.*

And worse, I'm afraid he's going to come back. And I don't want to tell him to go. And then what?

'Well, I made a special effort to get my work out of the way, so d'you fancy going out for a meal?' said Archie. 'I mean, we could stay at home, I guess, but that might be boring . . .'

Dina nodded eagerly and said, 'Sure. I'd really like to get out. Let me just grab my bag.'

Anything was better than being home. Alone. Waiting to see if he might come back.

She came back into the kitchen to find Archie brandishing a fat book. On the front it said *COOKING FOR FUN!* in big bright red letters.

'Where did this come from?' Archie asked. 'It's not as though we don't have enough cookbooks in the house.'

'Oh, it, er, kind of turned up,' said Dina, checking in her bag for her keys even though she'd only just put them in there. 'I mean – Anita dropped by and left it for me. Anyway, shall we go?'

'You haven't seen Anita for ages, have you? All the same, it's a bit of a crap present,' said Archie, flipping through. 'I mean, the author's hardly a big name. Look at this – recipe for chocolate cup cakes. How twee.'

'Well, it's the thought that counts, isn't it?' Dina said, suddenly feeling strangely protective towards Steve. 'Come on, let's get going.'

'Archie, can I ask you a question?' Dina asked, twisting her napkin in her lap.

Archie glanced up from his menu, looking nervous.

'Do you . . . I don't know how to put this without sounding crazy, but here goes . . . I was wondering – do you believe in the supernatural? In ghosts, that sort of thing? D'you think they really exist?'

Archie put down his menu.

'I knew I shouldn't have cooked you those mushrooms for breakfast. There was obviously something in them.' He grinned as Dina burst into exasperated laughter. 'Seriously, Dina – I think ghosts are a coping mechanism. When people go, we like to feel they're still with us, and thinking they're still around is a psychological crutch.' He broke off as a couple entered the restaurant, suddenly jumping to his feet. 'Marvin and Melanie Plockington-Smith! Excuse me for a minute, darling, but I haven't seen them for ages!' He kissed Dina on the cheek and then glided over to their table.

Dina nibbled self-consciously on an olive. She'd been hoping for an intimate dinner, a deep discussion which might somehow help her to sort out these nutty things that were happening in her life. But no, Archie was too busy table-hopping.

Suddenly she heard a beep from her mobile and its green light flashed to red. She drew it out of her bag.

It was a text message from Steve.

Hi. What r u doing? I am at a ghost rock concert, listening to Boyz'n'Spooks.

Dina suppressed a snort of laughter. How utterly zany.

She found herself texting back:

Hi. I am in a restaurant. About to eat.

She paused, trying to think of something witty and interesting. Looking up, she caught sight of Archie and found herself adding: *Archie is flirting with three women. Yawn!*

She pressed SEND and quickly dropped her mobile into her lap as Archie returned.

'Sorry – I just wanted to congratulate Melanie on her new boutique,' said Archie, picking up the menu. Instantly, a waiter came scampering up. 'Yes, we'll both have the rack of lamb for the main course – extra potatoes for me, thanks – and no dessert.'

As Archie finished giving the order, Dina's mobile beeped again. She picked it up and read: *Well, why don't you try shagging the waiter? That might get his attention, the bastard.* She couldn't help emitting a squeal of laughter.

'Who's that from?' Archie asked casually.

'Oh – just Anita. Girls' stuff.' Dina was itching to reply but she slipped her mobile back into her handbag.

She didn't mention the subject of ghosts again.

When they got back at midnight, Dina went into the living room and let out a cry.

Einstein wasn't in his bowl.

He was lying on the floor, Jupiter's black paw soft on his belly. Dina yanked Jupiter away; Jupiter retreated, yeowling.

'What?' Archie stood in the doorway.

'Look.' Dina picked Einstein up from the floor. He felt so fragile, like an aqueous butterfly. She put him back into his bowl, her heart beating violently – what on earth would she say to Steve if . . . ? To her relief, Einstein picked up his fins and started to swim in circles, though he gazed out anxiously as though fearing another attack.

Jupiter, sitting by Archie's feet, began to purr.

'He's just playing.' Archie shrugged. 'No big deal.' He mimicked Jupiter's purr, reaching out and stroking Dina's hair. His eyes were bloodshot from the wine and she could feel the desire in his fingertips, but she found herself pushing him sulkily away.

'For God's sake, Dina!' Archie spat out. 'It's just a bloody goldfish – are you nuts? OK, fine. You're nuts, without a doubt.' Shaking his head in disbelief, he picked up Jupiter and walked out, an angry black tail swirling behind him.

Dina remained silent for some time, staring into the bowl and watching Einstein's tiny bubbles of life rise and pop on the surface of the water.

20
Dina

Dina tipped eight grams of flour on to the scales and felt an unexpected flash of happiness dart through her. She turned back to her *COOKING FOR FUN!* recipe book, running her finger down the list of ingredients and seeing that she needed four ounces of light brown sugar. She twisted the radio knob round to Capital and started to hum along to the song that was playing. She was amazed at how much she was enjoying herself, when all she was doing was following a simple recipe for chocolate cake.

She'd got the idea this morning. She'd woken up early, at nine o'clock, and had been looking for something to wear, flipping through the skirts hanging up in her wardrobe. They were all short and filmy and made of layers of lace or net. They looked gorgeous – Archie had chosen them – but they were all a pain to wear. She wanted to take Roger for a walk and she could just picture herself staggering about in Regent's Park, yanking down the hem whilst trying to hold on to his lead.

And then, at the back of the wardrobe, she spotted her jeans. Blue and faded and battered, white tendrils of denim hanging from the seams. They were one of the few items of clothing Archie hadn't been able to persuade her to throw away. She dragged them out and pulled them on. They were like old friends. She sighed at their comfort and dragged out her favourite old navy T-shirt. Then she gathered her choppy hair up in a ponytail, went into the kitchen and decided to try a recipe from the book Steve had picked out for her.

She had just about recovered from the shock of seeing him. It hadn't been easy. Last night, whilst Archie had been asleep, she had stayed up until one in the morning, typing GHOSTS into Google and visiting various websites, trying to glean information from the tangle of fact and fiction. She'd scribbled down the names of a few mediums, but, waking the next morning, had vigorously crossed them out. She recalled the seance she'd shared with that frightful Mrs Dickens and thought it better not to go down that road.

No. She wanted to keep Steve her private secret from the world. She didn't want grief counselling, or people telling her she was mad; she couldn't even tell her mother, who would no doubt try to get her put straight on to medication. She wasn't sure how or why it had happened, but it had. These things – angels, ghosts, UFOs, whatever – were a part of life, and nobody could really explain them or understand them, no matter how many clever theories the men in white coats came up with. She realised that if she tried to analyse Steve's presence, she'd only tangle her mind into knots and drive herself mad and then *really* be in need of medication. It was easiest just to accept it, just to be innocent about it.

And, in truth, a part of her was deliriously blissful that it had happened. Seeing Steve again had reminded her just how much she had missed him. When he'd been alive, he had always made her feel comforted, as though no matter what happened to her or what she did, he would always be there for her. It reminded her a little of being a kid and playing in the back garden, knowing that her mother was just a few yards away in the house, treasuring that cradled feeling of safety as much as she was enjoying her game.

A sense of comfort was something she'd been craving lately. Although she adored Archie, life with him was like an emotional roller-coaster; every morning she woke up not knowing whether he was going to make love to her, make her laugh, or make her cry. Being with Steve was like putting the brakes on and just enjoying the view for a while.

She realised that whilst she'd been mulling over things, half an hour had gone by; the cake had to be ready! She had just pulled it out of the oven, breathing in its delicious chocolate and vanilla-scented fumes, when she felt the wind stir and her heart flip-flopped. She emptied the cake on to a wire rack, pulling off her oven gloves.

Then she felt someone tug her ponytail and she squealed.

'Steve!'

'Yup, it's me!'

'How are you? Have you been haunting anyone fun?' Dina teased him. She couldn't believe how happy she was to see him. This time she didn't feel so freaked out by his ephemeral presence; slowly but surely she was getting used to it.

'Sure,' said Steve. 'I just paid Tony Blair a visit in Parliament.'

'Glad to hear it,' Dina laughed. 'Look at my cake. Are you impressed?' When Steve beamed, she sighed and said, 'If only it wasn't so hot, we could have a slice.'

'Maybe later,' said Steve. 'I actually had a fun idea. I mean . . .' He looked shy again. 'I was wondering if you're free today.'

'Well, I have a *really* hectic schedule,' said Dina. Then, seeing his face fall, 'I mean – I have to walk Roger, watch *Neighbours* and cut my nails.'

'Well if you could just squeeze me in,' said Steve, his expression lifting, 'let's go to the zoo. London Zoo! We can pay a visit to my gorilla.' When Dina didn't reply, he went on, 'You know – the one you bought me for my birthday.'

'Steve,' Dina let out a deep breath, wondering how to avoid offending him. She pulled off a chunk from the corner of her cake, nibbling nervously. 'It's a lovely idea, but . . . but . . .'

'But?'

'Well, it's not exactly practical, is it? I mean, I can hardly have a conversation with you. People will think I'm talking to myself and I'll get carted off to the loony bin.' She looked at Steve with big, worried eyes, concerned that he would be upset. But to her surprise, he refused to back down.

'So? Haven't you ever heard of whispering?' he cried, all a-sparkle with the craziness of the idea. 'Besides, I took a walk through the zoo this morning and it's practically empty. It was half-term last week so all the kids are back to school, and it's a bit of a crappy day' – he pointed through the window to the blustery, depressed sky – 'so there aren't many people about. Come on, get a move on.'

Dina burst out laughing. Shaking her head, she found herself running into her bedroom and pulling on a jumper and her denim jacket.

Steve was right. The British summer was being typically erratic, and despite the fact that it was May, the weather was exceptionally cold and the zoo was virtually empty. The queue for tickets consisted of a pair of American tourists dragging round their obese son. He didn't seem very impressed by the zoo; as they passed across their credit card, he beat his fists on the wet ground, screaming that he wanted to go to Alton Towers and go on *rides*, not see bloody boring animals. Steve and Dina rolled their eyes and exchanged smiles.

'Americans, eh?' Steve whispered in her ear.

'Er, two adults, please,' said Dina, elbowing through Steve.

'Two? For today, is that?' The assistant peered past her, seeing nothing but a patch of damp concrete.

'I mean one,' said Dina hastily. 'One for me, and I guess my invisible friend gets to go, erm, free.'

The assistant gave her a quick look and Dina picked up her ticket hastily, flushing and trying not to laugh as Steve cried 'Oh, so I'm your invisible friend, am I?'

Dina tried to kick him, which, of course, didn't work. Her boot went straight through his leg and she nearly fell to the ground. The assistant shook her head, blinking, as though Dina was some sort of head case. Steve was nearly crying with laughter.

'I can see you need practice dealing with ghosts, my dear,' he said, looping his arm through hers. 'Come on, let's go see the animals.'

Half an hour later, Steve was delighted at how much Dina seemed to be enjoying herself. Over the past few weeks, her face had appeared shadowed and slightly pinched. Now she looked like the old Dina again, her eyes sparkling, cheeks flushed, and she sighed and smiled and oohed and ahed over pandas, giraffes, lions and penguins. She didn't possess an ounce of squeamishness and got just as excited about the reptile section, the snakes and spiders, as over the more cuddly and fashionable animals.

'Oh, I always wanted a tarantula when I was a kid,' she sighed. 'I loved animals. For a while I even fancied being a vet. Only you know – the dyslexia thing got in the way. All that science and all those Latin words – I couldn't even cope with English ones. After that, I just never really knew what I wanted to do for a career. Except I kind of thought recently . . . I kind of thought . . . oh, it doesn't matter. Nothing.'

Steve felt a profound sympathy for her. With a sudden flash of ghostly insight, he saw in her what he had sensed when they'd worked in The Greasy Spoon: Dina, like Steve himself, was a little disappointed by life, by what it had offered her. She had more *joie de vivre* than him and managed to shrug off upsets more easily, but there was a restlessness in her, a sense that there ought to be more to come, which might, over time, solidify into cynicism if her dreams were left unfulfilled.

'Come on, let's go and see our gorilla,' he said hastily, keen to cheer her up.

Their gorilla was sitting in his cage, munching grass. Dina was chuffed to see that the adoption plaque was still up.

'I want a plaque!' The American boy came waddling up, seeing Dina pointing to it. He turned back to his parents, who were straggling on the path behind, carrying the remains of his half-eaten orange lolly and looking thoroughly exhausted.

'Did you know,' Steve whispered, 'that since I became a ghost, I've discovered that I can talk to animals?'

'You can?' Dina whispered, conscious of the American trio coming up behind. 'Tell me what he's saying!' She watched in fascination as Steve closed his eyes, his forehead furrowing, and appeared to be listening intently to the gorilla. The gorilla carried on eating grass, looking entirely oblivious.

'He says,' says Steve, 'that he really likes you. He thinks you have a special aura about you. Oh, and he says you're very beautiful. In fact, he says he wishes he was a human—'

'Oh – what bullshit!' Dina cried. 'You had me fooled, you bastard!' Then she turned and realised with a hot flush of embarrassment that the Americans were gazing at her in astonishment. They quickly took hold of their son and began to hurry him away.

'But Mom, that mad woman was talking to herself!' he cried in glee.

Dina felt mortified. Steve suddenly looked awkward and began to whistle. He was almost relieved when the sky, which had been shifting to an increasingly threatening shade of grey, suddenly burst open, drenching them with hailstones. They ran for cover and waited for a good ten minutes, hoping it would ease off. It didn't.

'I guess we should go home,' said Dina. 'God, British summers are just a joke!'

'Uh-huh,' said Steve sadly.

As they hurried out on to the street, Dina pulling her collar up tightly, Steve became convinced that she couldn't wait to get away from him. No doubt she had found the whole afternoon completely weird and ridiculous and was fed up of people thinking she was a nutcase who liked talking to the voices in her head.

Then, in the middle of the pavement, she suddenly stopped and looked up at him. Steve looked down at her. Dina looked down at her feet. Then she looked up at him again.

'We're getting awfully wet,' said Steve.

'I was just, erm, thinking . . .' Dina suddenly felt self-conscious. 'Why don't we go see a movie? I mean, I can't take Roger out for a walk in this weather, and it might be fun. And I mean – I just – I don't really fancy spending the rest of the afternoon alone, you know – watching TV and . . . and . . . all that.'

'Sounds great!' Steve felt an electric thrill of happiness zip through him.

Unfortunately, the nearest cinema was a good twenty minutes away. The rain began to beat down furiously, so they had to make a run for it, laughing and whooping as they became thoroughly soaked. As they blundered through the double doors, the usherette looked up in surprise to see Dina entering, absolutely drenched, droplets of water sliding down her beaming face.

'Two – I mean – one ticket, please,' she said. 'For whatever film's on right now.'

'Well, *L'Amour* started five minutes ago. I'm afraid that's all I can do.'

'Oh, not a boring, poncy French film!' Steve whispered.

Dina ignored him and said that would be lovely.

'Hang on,' said Steve, as Dina walked past the food stands. 'Can't we get some grub? I'm starving.'

'Can I have a box of popcorn, please?' Dina asked. Then, as Steve gave her a nudge, 'Make that two. And, er, two Cokes, and a big tub of ice cream – three scoops, please.'

'Look at her face,' said Steve, as the young girl tried to hide her bemusement and politely scooped popcorn into the cardboard box. 'She thinks you're having a mad binge! Go on, get some Maltesers while you're at it!'

Dina bit her lip and only just managed not to giggle.

To her relief, the cinema was empty apart from a gangly, goatee-bearded youth who was sitting at the back, chatting on his mobile. He left about ten minutes later, and Dina and Steve had the place to themselves. They kept having to whisper to work out what the film was about, and soon they had drifted away from it and started chatting.

'You know – when I was baking the cake this morning, I felt so happy,' Dina said, munching on a salty nugget of popcorn. 'And it made me realise what a boring, flat life I've been living. I've turned into a real couch potato. It's no wonder I've started putting on weight. I mean – baking that cake was the first time in a long time I've actually *done* something!'

'Well, I think you should do more things,' Steve teased her gently.

'I should,' said Dina. 'I . . .' She trailed off, and Steve suddenly sensed there was something on her mind.

'Go on,' he said, touching her wrist. 'Tell me, tell me, tell me. This is Steve, remember?'

Dina looked up and smiled, remembering that this was indeed Steve, Steve to whom she could tell anything.

'It's just – for a while now, I've been thinking that I'd like to open a café. I admit I've been even more inspired recently by seeing Archie and his success with his restaurants. I mean, it's one of those things – unlike being a vet – that doesn't involve having to be the world's greatest speller. I mean, I know it helps, but, you know, it's also about the business side of things, and organising people, and having a passion for food, and knowing how to treat people. I mean, Archie says he hasn't used his degree one bit for his business. And I think I'd make a good job of it.'

'So do I,' said Steve. 'I think you'd be brilliant. I think you have to do it. And you have to do it *now*. Don't put it off, Dina, don't waste your life like I did. Do it. I'll be so proud of you.'

He suddenly realised that he was saying too much, and that Dina was staring down at his hand. The beat had changed between them, from the innocence of friendship, to the awkwardness of what's-going-on-between-us-here? Dina blew out her breath and stared at the screen, gazing unseeingly at the subtitles.

'I – er – should probably get back soon, and, you know, see Archie.'

'Me too. I have to get back. I actually have a girlfriend,' Steve blurted out.

'You have a girlfriend?' Dina nearly choked on her popcorn. She couldn't help a giggle escaping her lips. Then she saw Steve's haughty profile and flushed. 'I'm really sorry, I just . . .'

'I have had girlfriends before, you know,' said Steve. 'I had one at uni, and then there was Eileen, this accountant—'

'No, no, it's not that,' said Dina quickly. 'I mean, I know you've had girlfriends, Steve, of course you've had girlfriends, you're really cute.' She bit back a smile as a faint blush softened Steve's face. 'But – I mean – this girl, she's a ghost, right?'

'Yes,' said Steve. 'Her name's Beth. She's really pretty and young and loves yoga. So you don't have to go around thinking that just because I want to help you with your café, I'm going to keep coming on to you, because I won't.'

'I didn't think that!' Dina flushed, for she knew quite well she had. 'Steve, you can be so embarrassing! Anyway,' she poked out her tongue at him, enjoying their banter, 'I don't find you remotely attractive.'

'Well, good, because I only fancy ghosts.'

'Well, good, because I only fancy humans.'

'Besides,' Steve went on, smiling, 'your new haircut looks shit.'

Dina looked shocked, and Steve was about to apologise, feeling he'd gone too far, when she burst into laughter.

'You're right,' she admitted. 'It is dreadful, isn't it?'

'You want to know why?'

'Because I look like a peroxide scarecrow? That's what I thought when I looked in the mirror this morning.'

'No, because it makes you look like Heidi.'

Dina looked horrified for a minute, and then she burst into laughter again. 'Oh God, you're right!' she said. 'I do! Oh God . . . you're so right . . .'

Feeling their tickets had been a total waste of money, they tried to sit and focus on the last thirty minutes of the film. Steve felt relieved that they were at ease again, though he felt a little ashamed to have lied to Dina. The truth was he hadn't seen Beth since the dating agency dinner, despite her numerous invitations to ghost yoga classes. But what else could he say? He didn't want to rush or force things. He could hardly believe that they'd come this far, that they were sitting in a cinema together. This, for now, was paradise.

When they came out of the cinema, the rain had stopped and the sun was sparkling through the clouds, lighting up raindrops like diamonds.

'Why don't we go to The Greasy Spoon!' Dina suddenly cried. She didn't want the day to end.

'We won't be able to talk there,' Steve reminded her, though he didn't want to let her go either and in truth would have happily followed her to Neptune if she'd suggested it.

'I know, but it'll be so funny. Luigi will have to serve me with a smile. And I can be all snooty and send my food back for not being up to scratch.'

But their trip to The Greasy Spoon never quite happened. For, as they turned into Uxbridge Road, Steve suddenly pointed to the place at the end of the road. It had once been a rather run-down sandwich bar. Now the windows were boarded up and someone had stuck a load of blue posters over the top advertising a rave.

'So?' Dina hissed quietly, aware now of passers-by drifting past.

'It's for sale,' said Steve. 'Your café. It's perfect.'

'I . . . I . . . yes, but I couldn't really,' she said, weakly. 'I mean . . .'

'Why not!' Steve exclaimed. 'What's the point of having a dream if you don't go through with it?'

'But Archie . . .' she whispered, without thinking.

'What? You're saying that Archie wouldn't like it?'

'Well . . .' Dina knew full well that Archie damn well wouldn't like it. A few nights ago she'd suggested getting a job, and he'd suggested she work in his restaurant as a waitress. Dina wasn't entirely convinced that he'd been joking.

'I mean, what are you, his *slave*? Are you saying you're not allowed a life outside his? Why can't you both be successful in your own right?'

Suddenly Dina felt a flare of optimism and determination in her stomach.

'Maybe you're right,' she whispered. 'I could think about it.'

But soon she found she couldn't stop thinking about it. For they could talk of nothing else all the way home. The idea had put down roots in both their minds and they bounced ideas back and forth excitedly.

'Well,' said Steve, as they reached Dina's door, 'I guess we should talk more about this another time.'

'Great,' said Dina, grinning. 'That would be good.' As Steve turned to go, she reached up on tiptoe and gently placed a kiss on his cheek. 'And – and – thanks. Thanks for such a lovely day – I – I'm just really glad you're back.'

'I'm glad I'm back too,' said Steve, smiling down at her. She smiled back at him and for a moment they stared at each other. Then Dina quickly turned away and twisted her key in the lock, calling out another soft, 'Bye then!'

Steve walked away, an enormous smile singing across his lips.

Dina let herself into the flat, grinning just as broadly, to find Archie was back home. He was sitting on the sofa, tucking into a large slice of her cake.

'Hi, honey,' he said with his mouth full.

She shook herself; after such a strange and whimsical day, it felt jarring to come back to real life.

'D'you like the cake?' she asked him anxiously.

Archie chewed thoughtfully, licking his lips and frowning as though he was an expert wine-taster who'd just taken a gulp of something rather unusual.

'Well, put it this way, you could be on *Masterchef*!'

Dina knew this wasn't a compliment. Archie loathed *Masterchef* and all those other cooking programmes, which he regarded as deeply amateur.

'You bastard!' she cried, attacking him with cushions. Archie roared with laughter and winked at her, but she still couldn't quite work out if he was joking.

She felt mollified, however, when he went into the kitchen to get a second helping.

'God, this really is so disgusting,' he carried on, chewing voraciously. Having finished the slice, he paused for a moment, licking his lips, then got up and headed for the kitchen again.

'So you're not going for a third slice, are you, Archie?' Dina called.

'Wouldn't dream of it,' Archie called back.

Dina rolled her eyes and hugged a cushion to her chest, grinning smugly.

21
Steve

It was a Monday morning. Dina and Steve were sitting on the sofa, flicking through the *Guardian,* when they saw the ad.

RESTAURANT MANAGER
At exquisite

'Oh my God – look at that. I – I could—' Dina broke off, swallowing uncertainly. Steve looked up at her sharply, and in that moment he saw, quite acutely, the series of images flicking through Dina's mind: restaurant manager, big success, branching out, her own café. Then he blinked in surprise as she snapped the paper shut, stretched like a cat, casually fingered her ponytail and said, 'Fancy a cup of tea?'

'We don't have time for a cup of tea,' Steve said.

'Sorry? What?' Dina turned to him eagerly. She wondered if Steve had planned another zany outing out, and with a burst of delight, she thought for the hundredth time: *It's so good to have him back.*

'You,' Steve said passionately, turning quite pink, 'have to phone up Archie and tell him that he has to give you that job.'

'Oh, don't be silly, Steve.'

'What, so you're saying that you don't want that job?'

'No, I—'

'Come on, give me an honest, black-or-white answer. If right now, someone could wave a magic wand and say, "Dina, you can have that job at the restaurant," or, "Dina, you can sit around here all day without a job," what would you choose?' Steve saw the look on her face and nodded fiercely. 'Right.' He picked up the phone and handed it to her.

Dina held it in her hands. She knew Steve was right, but now, when it came to the crunch, she could only see her fears flapping around her like black bats. What if Archie thought she was crazy? Worse, what if he gave her the job and she couldn't cope? What if he was so disappointed in her that it ruined their relationship?

She was about to punch in the number when suddenly the phone rang. Dina let out a sigh of relief – fate had saved her from making a fool of herself.

'Hello?' she said. For a moment, she heard soft breathing. Then the caller hung up. 'Funny. That's the second time that's happened this week.'

'Dina!' Steve exclaimed. 'So it was just a wrong number. Stop making excuses! *Call!*'

Dina put down the phone and reached into her pocket.

'Maybe I should just toss a coin.'

'Dina!' Steve stood up, struggling to find the right words, to speak the sweet truth without offending her. 'Look, Dina – you – it's – look. One of the things I've learnt since I died is that you can't spend your life living in a fantasy world. Because people do, Dina. They do it all the time. That's why people are stupid enough to believe in religion rather than science. That's why we have books and films and paintings and video games and celebrities. They're all fantasies, but they make reality survivable. You know what it was like when we were in The Greasy Spoon. I mean, I remember single mothers coming in desperately doing their lottery tickets, praying they'd win and their lives would turn around. I'd listen to builders saying they were going to break out on their own soon, and get their lives together. I'd hear office workers saying that sure, they hated their jobs, but something would turn up. Life is crap, and we deal with it all the time by thinking up better alternatives that are never going to happen. I mean, God . . . I admit . . . I was just as bad. You know how I told you I gave up my law job to work in The Greasy Spoon whilst I decided what I wanted to do? Well, I never did, did I? I just kept drifting through the days. It's so much easier for you to sit there having this vague, rosy fantasy of this café that you might one day set up; it makes the future seem pleasant. But what if another year goes by, and then another five and then another ten and you still haven't gone for it? Just do it, Dina! Seize the day and do it!' He broke off, suddenly self-conscious. 'Sorry. I hope I haven't pissed you off . . .'

But Dina nodded.

'God, no, Steve, you're right. You're absolutely right.' She grabbed the phone and punched in Archie's number with shaking fingers. Steve, exhilarated, sat down beside her, listening in.

'Hi, Archie?' she said breathlessly.

'Dina? Um, this isn't a great time right now, darling – my chef has flipped. He's got madly drunk and is now in the kitchen, wielding carving knives and sticking cocaine in the chicken breasts and olive and onion stuffing up his nose. Is it important?'

Steve nodded his head fiercely at Dina.

'Well – it is, yes it is,' Dina said. 'Look – I saw the job ad in the newspaper for a restaurant manager at exquisite and I thought perhaps I could do it. I know I don't have any experience, but I've learnt so much from watching you and hearing about stuff from you, and if you just gave me a bit of training, I know I could do it. I could help you expand the restaurant chain – there's a great place on the Uxbridge Road we could develop . . .' She trailed off, wincing, waiting for Archie to howl with laughter.

But he didn't. He just paused. Then he said, 'Uh-huh.' He paused again. Then he said, in a very reasonable voice, 'So what's the *real* reason for this? Come on, Dina. It's chocolate-related, isn't it? You're hoping you might get hired as restaurant manager and then get promoted to official desserts taster, huh?'

In her nerves, Dina found herself bursting into laughter and Archie joined in, their laughter swirling together.

'So, any other great ideas?' Archie teased her. 'Why not call up Madonna and ask if you can be her new stylist while you're at it – after all, the sky's the limit! Seriously, Dina, we've had over twenty applicants for the job and we really do need someone with experience. Anyway, darling, I've gotta go. Big kiss. Oh – and I'm taking you to The Ivy tonight so go splash out, get yourself a dress, I want to see you looking your most gorgeous.'

Dina put down the phone.

'Well – that was the dumbest idea I've ever had. Archie was so right. Still.' She let out a sheepish little laugh, but Steve saw the hurt flickering in her eyes.

Steve pressed his lips together, resisting the urge to shout: *Call Archie again and tell him that you are so much more, so much more than a bloody silly little chocolate taster. Call him up and tell him that you deserve to be encouraged, not patronised; nurtured, not crushed.*

Dina made a breezy remark about it being time for tea. But just as she was about to get up, she slumped back down, then leaned in towards him. As Steve hugged her, he could feel her disappointment flowing from her heart into his. He held her tightly, closing his eyes, squeezing his lips and holding back the furious flurry of emotions building in his chest.

As Steve approached Jether's place, he realised, rather sheepishly, that the last time he'd come to visit him, he'd intended to return within a week. And how long ago was that? Several weeks, if not more. He feared that Jether might not have a clue who he was and was certain that Jether would have completely forgotten all his problems. But to Steve's surprise, the moment he entered, Jether smiled at him as though they'd only been chatting the other day.

'So how is Dina?' he asked.

Steve started, and then sat down, catching his breath. He breathed in the flowery smell of incense, the scents tingling in his lungs. He felt an overwhelming sense of relief just to be sitting in Jether's presence, and realised his soul had been yearning for this for some time.

'Well – it's just incredible – she can *hear* me. We can talk. She can even see me! I mean, we've been out to the zoo and everything. And the weird thing is, Dina can't actually see any other ghosts, she can only see me, which makes me think we have a special bond—' Steve broke off, checking himself.

Last week he'd made the fatal mistake of telling Harrison about his outings with Dina. Harrison was rather bored and bitter at the moment; he'd broken up with Nancy and had gone from having his head in the clouds to his heart in the gutter. He'd started to take it out on Steve a bit, teasing and riling him and saying, 'So – you and Dina, right – what a great couple! I mean, I'm sure she won't mind that your cock is made out of thin air, oh no!'

Steve had quickly and vigorously denied that he had any feelings for Dina whatsoever.

Harrison wasn't fooled.

Nor was Jether. Steve looked into his eyes and saw two bright tunnels of understanding.

'OK,' Steve admitted, 'I'm still in love with her. It's awful, really. I thought that my feelings were under control. But the moment I started talking to her again, it all flooded back. But I just don't know what she thinks of me . . . sometimes I get all hopeful and then the next minute I'm convinced it's hopeless . . . well, obviously it is hopeless with her being alive and me being . . . but . . .'

Jether was silent for a while and then he said:

'"The Sun and Moon should ever doubt, they'd both go out."'

'Is that Buddhist?' Steve asked suspiciously.

'No, it's William Blake.'

Steve blinked, and then a smile twitched at Jether's lips and suddenly they both burst into laughter.

'I'm telling you to have more faith in yourself. I have told you time and time again to transcend your desires, but you never listen. If you must chase after them – as foolishly as chasing after a butterfly – then remember that you are not enlightened, so you'll have to progress down the path from innocence to experience. On the path to fulfilling your dreams, you'll make mistakes. But the biggest mistake is to get cynical. You expect life to be perfect and to achieve instant fulfilment. When that doesn't happen, your innocence is lost and you decide that life isn't fair. But there'll always be a gap between having a wish and fulfilling a wish, and in that gap you learn lessons. That's the experience part.'

'You sound like those self-help books I used to read,' Steve said gloomily. He looked at Jether carefully, not wanting to offend him. 'I mean – there are these aphorisms, like *I am handsome, I am wealthy, women love me,* and you're supposed to repeat them before you go to bed. I'd be really virtuous for a few days, and then by the end of the week I'd have completely forgotten them. Mind you, while I did do them, I did feel . . . it did make me realise that thoughts are powerful things.'

'Your life is a reflection of your thoughts. The people in your life are a reflection of you. If you have an enemy, it's because your anger needs an expression. If someone loves you, it's because you love yourself. That's why your life as a ghost isn't any different from life on earth.'

'But how can we really change inside?' Steve asked, adding a postscript: *so that I can make Dina fall in love with me.*

'If you go into a relationship looking for happiness from someone else, wanting to draw it out of them like water from a well, you'll never find love. Sooner or later, you'll end up resenting them for not solving your problems, for not filling up that empty void inside you. All happiness comes from within and you can only share happiness with someone, not take it from them.'

Steve pondered for some time.

'The thing is, she's asked me to go with her next week. She's going all the way up to Scotland to visit Archie's mother for the first time, and she's terrified. She said it would just make her feel better if I was there to – you know – fill her in, help her out.'

As Jether started to speak about Buddhism, about the Four Noble Truths, Steve found himself drifting away. He realised that he felt ashamed in Jether's presence: Jether seemed to live and think at such a high level of purity, while Steve just wanted to drag his philosophies down into the earthy, the mundane, the trivial. *Because, let's face it,* Steve thought rather sheepishly, *I really don't get all this stuff he's telling me about nirvana, and nor do I really care. I just want to get my girl.*

Much later, Steve walked out into the cold night air. Two drunken girls were staggering down the street, singing. He smiled, surprised to feel a flow of affection rather than distaste for them. Then he realised that this was how he had felt after the last time he'd spoken to Jether; a profound but subtle shift had taken place inside his heart.

As he walked home to Harrison's place, he pondered Jether's words. Maybe Jether was right. He thought of the children's story he'd loved as a kid, a peeling Ladybird book about the hare and the tortoise that he'd begged his father to read again and again. Archie might be the hare, he might have swept Dina off her feet, but Steve was going to take the long-term, plodding tortoise approach that won in the end. He was going to get to know Dina – really know her. So many relationships in life, Steve mused, were just false impressions, mirages and smokescreens of identity. Different people brought out different flavours of your character, limited by their own perceptions and views of you. Steve had seen plenty of couples who thought they were in love, but as far as he was concerned, they were in love with ideals in their minds.

True love, he felt passionately, was about really knowing someone, knowing every thought in their mind, every drop of feeling in their heart, every shade of their soul. That was why Archie was, slowly but surely, failing Dina: failing to see the depth of her ambitions, failing to see how her intelligence and talent were veiled by her doubts and her dyslexia. And Jether was right: Steve couldn't do this overnight. He was going to make numerous mistakes; he was going to misinterpret her; he was going to suffer confusion. But one day, he'd get there. He'd know her, and love her for her; and she'd know him and love him for him.

Steve looked up at the stars. The moon was full, gleaming in the reflections of windows like coins. *I'll win her in the end,* Steve told the moon. *However long it takes, I'll win her.*

22
Dina

Archie swung the car sharply round the corner, causing spurts of gravel to fly up from his tyres. Dina, who had been sleeping hazily in the passenger seat, suddenly woke up. She blinked as the car eased up a wide gravel drive bordered by two thick avenues of brooding pine trees. The castle stood out as a jagged silhouette against the twilight sky, the bobbing half-moon impaled on the spiky edges of a turret. They stopped beneath a curved stone arch which had the motto SERVE GOD. WORK HARD. BE PIOUS inscribed on it.

Well, thought Dina, with a flutter of nerves, *we're here.*

Archie's mother was celebrating her first wedding anniversary to Archie's stepfather, Sir Ian McMillan, with a large banquet for close friends and family, not to mention the odd photographer from *Hello!* magazine. Unfortunately, Archie and Dina's journey up from London hadn't been terribly pleasant.

All week long, Dina had been fretting over the prospect of meeting Archie's mother.

'Whenever she's called up and I've spoken to her, she sounds very scary. You have to give me advice about her. I mean, I know you said the marriage thing was hard on her—'

'She's not scary,' Archie cut in, and Dina sensed the marriage subject was something he felt too touchy about to bring up again. 'Yep, she's had some hard times, but she's always been quite tough. I mean' – he laughed affectionately – 'once a burglar attempted to break in and she tacked him to the floor with one of her golf clubs, phoned the police on her mobile and sat on him until they turned up.'

'Shit!'

'She hates swearing.'

'I mean, sugar.'

'She also hates bad manners. Remember your pleases and thank-yous.'

'Right, and does she—'

'What is this, Twenty Questions?' Archie began to get impatient. 'Dina, just relax. She'll love you.'

'But have you ever taken any other girl to see her?'

'I took Heidi,' said Archie lightly.

'Did she like Heidi?' Dina tried not to show her jealousy.

'She loved her! See, there's no Oedipus problem going on. She'll be really happy to meet you. Don't bite—' Archie, seeing her start on a nail, slapped her hand.

Dina had devoted nearly a whole day to packing. Every so often, Archie poked his head round the bedroom door, eyed up the array of clothes on the bed, and rolled his eyes. She knew that he thought she was making a mountain out of a molehill, but Dina felt an awful lot was riding on the meeting. Their relationship had been bumpy recently, with more rows than discussions, more taking than giving. Archie seemed to love and respect his mother highly; Dina was desperate to make a good impression.

She was aching to talk to Steve but he wasn't around. *Oh God,* she panicked, *he promised he'd come with me and be by my side. Steve, where are you?*

As a result of her prolonged packing, they'd missed their flight.

'Another thing you might like to know about my mother,' said Archie tersely, 'is that she *hates* people being late. She's *obsessively* punctual.'

Catching the later flight, Archie had spent the whole time reading *The Da Vinci Code* and exchanging flirty looks with the blonde air hostess. *Don't let him hurt you,* Dina told herself, feigning sleep. When he did this to her, she always felt that she needed to construct a wall around her heart, but despite her best efforts, the wall felt as though it was made of paper.

They'd picked up a car at the other end, and despite Archie's insane ninety-mile-an-hour driving round winding Scottish roads that had once or twice nearly sent them flying into a loch, they were still late.

'I'm sorry,' Dina repeated quietly, giving Archie a sheepish glance.

'Don't worry.' He reached over and touched her cheek; his bad mood seemed to have lifted. 'Come on, sweetheart, let's go in.'

The moment they entered the castle, a handsome boy in his early twenties appeared, ready to take their cases.

'Hi, Scott,' Archie greeted him. 'How's it going?'

'Dinner is being served in three minutes,' Scott said, looking worried.

'Shit!' said Archie. He grabbed Dina's hand, hurrying her up the stairs with him.

In their bedroom, they got ready hurriedly, unzipping their cases, spilling out clothes, pulling on their outfits, yanking up zips, combing their hair quickly. Archie's mobile rang and he answered it, frowning. Dina, unpacking her make-up kit, watched Archie out of the corner of her eye as he went over to the window, saying in a quiet, intimate voice, 'Look, this isn't really a great time right now . . .'

Dina frowned. She thought of the person who kept calling their house and then hanging up, and unease flickered through her. But as soon as the fear rose, she dismissed it. Archie couldn't be . . . no, he couldn't . . . he had, after all, brought her up to see his mother, hadn't he?

'You must be Dina.' A Scottish voice tickled Dina's ear. 'How lovely to see you. You are a pretty thing, aren't you?'

'I'm sorry?' Dina whirled round, shocked. But there was nobody there. Archie was still chatting quietly.

Then there was a second voice, creaky and old and cobwebbed: 'You're right, she is lovely. Better than a lot of the trollops we get here.'

Dina's heart was pounding violently. She quickly turned to the mirror, unscrewing her lipstick, trying to pretend this wasn't happening. Archie switched off his mobile and came up behind her, tweaking his bow tie. In the background, the wind whined down the corridors and groaned and hissed into the bedroom, swirling about in chilly blasts.

'Sounds as if it's the ghost,' said Archie.

'I'm sorry?' Dina stopped applying lipstick in mid-pinkness, eyes wide.

'It's just a silly myth,' Archie laughed. 'An old wives' tale about this place being haunted. It's all bollocks, of course.'

'Really?' Dina asked.

'Mum says that she keeps getting pestered by calls from that *Most Haunted* programme. They want to come up and do a feature on it.'

Dina rolled her eyes.

'Still,' Archie went on, 'Mum won't have any of it. Mind you, Dina, you're into all that ghost rubbish, aren't you?'

'Oh well . . . not really . . . you know . . .' Dina mumbled, trailing off. Her heart was thumping uneasily. *Oh great,* she thought, *just great. I am trying to impress my future mother-in-law and I have to spend the weekend listening to ghostly voices. Oh Steve, please hurry up and get here. I need your help.*

Steve and Harrison had arrived at the castle about an hour before Dina. They had looked around the grand, chilly rooms and were now out in the grounds, standing by a circular stone pond and staring into its dark, murky depths, watching large grey carp with whiskers and tired faces ripple beneath the surface. Then, quite suddenly, a voice came out of nowhere, shouting: 'WHAT THE HELL ARE YOU YOUNG BRATS DOING IN MY GROUNDS!'

Steve and Harrison started, swinging round. A volley of birds exploded from a nearby tree and soared across the sky, cawing. There was an eerie silence.

Then the owner of the voice revealed himself. A large man sporting a long grey beard and a kilt, looking like a cross between Father Christmas and Alexander the Great, came storming up. He was brandishing a pair of bagpipes as though they were a weapon rather than an instrument.

He was accompanied by a guy wearing a full suit of tarnished silver, who squeaked with every step he took.

'What the hell d'you think you're doing here!' the man in the kilt cried. He had a thick Scottish accent and a voice as rough as gravel. 'This is private property and you're trespassing.'

'Shit!' Harrison cried excitedly. 'More ghosts!'

'NOT ANY OLD GHOSTS!' the man bellowed. 'We're not common folk, you know. My name is Sir William McAvoy and my ancestors lived in this castle; I can trace my line back over five hundred years.'

The suit of armour raised an arm, brandishing a heavy sword. Harrison and Steve found themselves stepping backwards in alarm.

'Look,' said Steve, holding up his hands, 'we really don't mean any harm, OK? We just want to stay for one night—'

'Look,' Harrison interrupted, 'Steve here's in love, OK? We've travelled all the way up from London. We've hitchhiked, we've jumped from cars to vans, we've been on the road for fifteen hours and we've done it all for the sake of Steve's love for Dina. Dina is a human; Steve is a ghost: like *Romeo and Juliet,* their love is impossible, doomed, tragic. Surely you must feel pity for the dear fellow? Surely you can let us stay here one night? God, maybe you can even help us woo the fair Dina!'

The expression on Sir William's face didn't suggest he was particularly moved. Then a tear trickled down the visor of his armoured friend.

'Ewan, you big baby,' Sir William said scornfully. 'Honestly, your armour will rust like it did last time and then you won't be able to get it off.' He turned back to Harrison and Steve. 'All right,' he barked. 'We'll help. But first you have to come and meet the gang. We're throwing a wee party tonight. We've got a TV crew from *Most Haunted* coming down to film us.'

'Really?' Harrison asked excitedly, keen to grab his fifteen minutes of fame.

Sir William led them into the castle and down a damp, musty-smelling winding staircase, chatting all the way: 'I'm afraid the stupid woman who owns this place doesn't believe in ghosts. So we called up *Most Haunted* ourselves and we've asked every damn ghost in the fucking country to turn up. All the celebs are here – even the Headless Lady of Lyndham Manor!'

Sir William pushed open a heavy oak door. Instantly, a blast of noise and heat hit them. Steve blinked. He'd never seen so many ghosts in one room before – nor so many drunk ghosts. The place was overflowing with alcohol and one headless chap was on the floor, the ruff around his neck soaked with beer, whilst his friends stared at him.

'He's off his head!' one cried and the other burst into roars of laughter.

Steve became uncomfortably aware of a tuneless warbling noise coming from the back of the room. He blinked and did a double-take. If he wasn't much mistaken, that was Anne Boleyn standing on a wooden stage. She was clutching a mike and staring at a blue screen, singing along to a Kylie Minogue song.

'See!' Sir William put a plump arm around Steve. 'Isn't it a riot? You can join in later. Now don't be shy, we're all crap but it's just a good old laugh!'

'Well, actually,' Steve spluttered, 'I kind of feel I should check on Dina. I mean, she doesn't even know I'm here yet.'

'Don't you worry, she probably wants some peace right now. Relax, have a drink,' said Sir William, thrusting a wooden beaker of foaming beer into his hand.

'OK,' Steve muttered uneasily, taking a sip as Harrison downed his enthusiastically.

Sir William walked away with a leer on his face, muttering, 'Oh, don't you worry, we'll take very good care of Dina, we so *love* taking care of humans . . .'

OK, Dina, she told herself. *You can do this. Just get through this dinner and you'll be fine. Just think – this time tomorrow you and Archie will be back home. You'll have impressed his mother and he'll love you for it and everything will be wonderful again.*

'Shit, we really are late,' Archie muttered, checking his watch as they clattered down the spirals of stone staircase, tapestries flapping gently as they rushed past.

Archie led her through the Great Hall, down a dark passage and then into the dining hall. It was terribly grand. There were three long oak tables filled with guests dripping diamonds and refined accents. Waiters were scurrying about, transferring delicious-looking things from silver platters on to delicate china. An enormous chandelier trembled delicately as Celtic music warbled from two large Sony speakers discreetly concealed behind a large tapestry depicting scenes of Sir William Wallace fighting to liberate Scotland.

Dina noticed that the moment Archie entered the hall, all the women reacted as though someone had tweaked their antennae, breaking off from their conversations and flicking hungry glances at him. Dina looped her arm through his and pecked him on the cheek. Archie smiled, but in a rather distant sort of way.

'Where are we sitting?' Dina asked, checking the seating plan. But Archie laughed and pulled her away.

'We're with Mum, silly.'

'Great,' said Dina nervously, as Archie led her to the top table. As they approached, Archie's mother stood up, a frown knifing her forehead.

'Hi, Mum.' Archie gave her a warm hug and a kiss on the cheek.

Dina concealed her surprise. Archie's mother didn't look as she'd expected – but then people never did, did they? Her vision of a plump woman in a floral dress with a bossy Hyacinth Bucket manner vanished, replaced with the reality: a tall, dark-haired woman with a European tan, dressed in an elegant powder-blue suit. Dina could see now where Archie got his good looks from. Though she was in her fifties, her skin was barely lined, and her dark beauty was accentuated by her rather commanding air of self-assurance.

All of which made her choice of partner somewhat surprising. Ian was a dapper Scottish man; he looked at least a foot shorter than her, with a jolly, whisky-soaked face and a curly grey moustache.

'And you must be Dina.' Archie's mother shook her hand: a cool, ringed handshake. 'You're late,' she added, in a tone that scared Dina. But Archie merely grinned a charming, boyish grin.

'Sorry – traffic was manic.'

'We're already on the starter. Your stepbrother is here. He managed to turn up on time.'

Archie shrugged and then started nattering away, boasting about his latest business successes, enjoying the flash of pride in his mother's eyes.

Dina sat down and turned to Ian, who smiled at her kindly. She couldn't understand why Archie was lukewarm about him; he seemed utterly benign. Still, she'd never had a stepfather and she guessed she had no real idea how it would feel.

'So have you been—' she started, then broke off. Was it her imagination, or had a cold, clammy hand clamped itself over hers? Steve? She looked behind her, but she couldn't see anyone.

'Yes, dear, what were you saying?' Ian asked.

'Er – I was saying . . .' Dina began. And then, all of a sudden, the hand gripped hers tightly, so tightly its very fingers seemed to slice through her skin, and then – *wham!* She'd just picked up a sliver of salmon on the end of her fork and it went flying on to Ian's kilted lap.

'Don't worry, my dear,' he said kindly, as Dina stuttered apologies. 'Happens to me all the time – well, after a few wee whiskies.'

'Honestly, Dina, I can't take you anywhere,' Archie tutted.

'I – I—' Dina spluttered. What the hell was going on?

'I can see why she gave up being a waitress,' said Archie's mother drily. 'And you, Ian, ought to be cutting back on the salmon. You know you're on a diet.'

Ian shrank down into his seat like a naughty schoolboy, looking rather sulky.

Dina smiled and ducked her head. She tried to push down the rising panic in her chest. *OK*, she kept telling herself, *just keep calm. There's a ghost about; don't try to make it angry, don't try to engage it. Just sit still and pray that you can get through the next hour.*

To Dina's relief, Archie's mother was distracted by the head waiter, who came up and whispered something in her ear. She burst out angrily, 'No, I most certainly do not want them here. For goodness' sake, *Most Haunted* can't just turn up at my wedding anniversary with a camera crew. Tell them to get out.'

'Oh, because this is *your* castle, isn't it?' a loud, beery Scottish voice suddenly cried from behind Dina's ear. 'Well, as it happens, I'm the one who called up Yvette Fielding, and I damn well want her to stay.'

Dina, who'd just taken a mouthful of wine, choked violently. Archie patted her on the back.

'Are you OK?' He looked at her closely. Then suspicion crept into his eyes. 'This hasn't got anything to do with you, Dina, has it? I mean – you're the one who's into this sort of stuff—'

'Absolutely not!' Dina cried. 'And Archie, I'm *not* into this sort of stuff, I've decided that ghosts are a load of rubbish,' she said loudly.

For the first time that evening, Archie's mother turned and actually *smiled* at her.

'I'm glad to hear how sensible you are.'

Archie turned and flashed Dina a quiet grin.

'See?' he whispered in her ear. 'Told you you'd be all right.'

And for the rest of the meal, it *was* all right. The voice disappeared. The hand disappeared back into the ether. Dina felt herself relax into the flow of good food, wine and conversation. As they finished the last of the delicious cranberry pie for dessert, Archie's mother chinked her glass and stood up. Immediately the guests hushed and heads swivelled to face her.

'I'm delighted to be here tonight,' she said in her grand voice, 'celebrating my first wedding anniversary with Ian . . .'

'So you don't believe in ghosts, then?' Suddenly the beery voice was back. 'Steve told me you were special, but you seem just the same as all the rest.'

Dina felt her heart start to pound. 'Go away,' she whispered, staring intently at Archie's mother and trying hard not to move her lips. '*Please*,' she begged.

'I don't think so.'

Suddenly the invisible hand had curled around her wrist like a snake. She tried to wriggle away and succeeded in knocking a fork off the table. It hit the stone floor with a clang that seemed to echo in every nook and cranny of the dining hall. Archie's mother broke off from her speech and raised a thin eyebrow. Archie rolled his eyes and picked the fork up.

Archie's mother continued telling the room what a wonderful year she'd spent with her second husband, how much they cherished and adored each other et cetera, et cetera. The pressure around Dina's wrist became more intense. She felt as helpless as a puppet as the ghost bent her fingers back and then, ignoring her silent hiss of pain, curled them around her wine glass, clamping his clammy hand over hers.

Suddenly Dina guessed what he was playing at.

'Oh no!' she cried out loud.

'Oh *yes*!' cried Sir William.

'*Steve!*' Dina cried in panic. 'Steve, help!' But Steve wasn't there to help her, couldn't stop the hand that gripped hers and flicked the wine glass. It seemed to happen in slow motion – the wine leaving the flute in a flurry of gold liquid and then – *splash!* – hitting Archie's mother right across her pale blue bosom. Dina stared in horror, wishing the floor could swallow her up. Archie's jaw dropped. Ian piped up in a slurred voice: 'Good on you – I've been wanting to do that for the last year!'

Steve felt as though his brain had been extracted and his head stuffed with wads of cotton wool. He slowly came to, realising that he was slumped in a dark booth, over a table littered with empty beer bottles and mugs. For a moment he wondered where he was and where all the noise was coming from. Then he remembered the unfortunate chain of events. Sir William forcing extra drinks on him. The alcohol rushing straight to his head and turning his clear, precise thoughts into a blurry slur. And, oh God, Harrison and Sir William had forced him to go up on the karaoke stage and do a duet with Anne Boleyn, only Jane Seymour had got jealous, crashed on to the stage and provoked a cat fight. They'd been tearing each other's hair out and crying, 'Henry loved me more!' and 'I'm not the one who got sent to have my head chopped off – is that how much he loved you?' This all happened just before Steve passed out – God knows what Sir William had put in those beers.

He let out a groan, burying his face in his hands. He had a sneaky feeling that he was about to experience his first hangover as a ghost.

Then the thought flashed through him: *Dina.* Dina. Oh God. As he leapt to his feet, he became uncomfortably aware of Harrison, slumped on the floor by his feet. He jumped over him, pushing through the crowds, through the heavy door, up, up, up the staircase, into the Great Hall. Then he heard Dina's voice crying, 'Look, it really wasn't my fault, I swear . . .' Steve stopped short and hid behind a pillar, looking on.

Dina was crying. The sight of her made his heart ache. *Oh God,* he wondered hazily, *what happened?* What was so bad that Archie and Dina were dragging their cases through the hall, leaving the house at *midnight* when they should have been enjoying intimate liqueurs with Archie's mother? He listened to the crunch of their feet on gravel, the slam of the car door, the growl of the engine starting and then dying away. He turned away, fraught with shame. Whatever had happened to Dina was his fault; he should have been there for her.

23
Dina

Dina woke the following morning to find a KitKat lying on the bedside table of the hotel they'd booked themselves into after leaving the castle. She got out of bed, picked it up, flung it into the bin and returned to bed.

The next day, back in London, she went into the toilet and sat down on the spotless cream seat. She was about to tug the roll when she saw that on the first sheet of paper someone had written: *I'm sorry.*

Dina bit back a smile. Then she tore the sheets off – they weren't even worth wiping her arse with – and flushed them down the toilet with a cold face.

Two days later, she was in the kitchen, baking. Not from her *COOKING FOR FUN!* book, which had been relegated to the shelves along with Archie's stash of *GQ* back copies, but from Nigella Lawson's latest treasure, which Archie had recommended to her.

She picked up a bag of self-raising flour. The heat of the oven had filled the kitchen with steam and flushed the cool windows. Up on the glass, letters began to appear:

WILL YOU EVER FORGIVE ME?

Dina put down her flour, picked up a tea towel and furiously wiped the window clear.

Then, mouth as thin as a pencil, she went back to her recipe.

A voice behind her asked:

'Dina, please can we just talk about this?'

Dina weighed out the flour, forming a dusty white pyramid in the silver measuring dish. She stared down at the recipe with a frown. Then she heard sounds coming from the living room: clicks and rustling, followed by the jazzy beat of a CD on Archie's stereo. She found herself swaying and doing an automatic little jig despite herself. Then she grabbed her tea towel and stormed into the living room. Steve was standing by the stereo.

'You've got a nerve, turning up here,' said Dina.

'You're pissed off with me about the castle?'

'You're damn right I'm pissed off with you. I mean, what the hell did you think you were doing!' Dina burst out. Suddenly she felt tears burning in her throat and she stared down at the tea towel bunched in her hands. 'I just don't get why you'd do that to me, Steve. I thought you came up to Scotland to *help* me. Look, you just have to accept that Archie is the man I want to be with and trying to sabotage things and get in the way isn't going to help. I love him, OK? I mean, he's only just about forgiven me for causing a scene and he's still being cool with me.'

Steve concealed a wince.

'Dina, you have to hear me out, OK? Firstly, it wasn't my fault that things went wrong. You were tormented by another ghost.'

'Well, they were your friends – you must have known!'

'As a matter of fact, no, I didn't. I was as shocked as you to find them at the castle. I asked them to help you out, only that son-of-a-bitch McAvoy thought it would be funny to take the piss and mess things up. And look, ghosts aren't some special breed that all stick together and are responsible for each other. Ghosts are, essentially, people – remember? And ghosts, like real people, are individuals, with their own quirks and perversities. Ghosts can be completely unpredictable too.'

Dina let the towel fall slack in her hands, though she still looked vexed.

'Well, until you turned up, Steve, I'd never met a bloody ghost in my life. I was in peaceful ignorance, just like everyone else,' she burst out, slumping on to the sofa.

There was a terse silence. Then Steve said:

'And another thing. I really have no intention of breaking you and Archie up.' Steve felt as though his nose might grow half an inch. 'I'm really happy for you to be together.' God, he'd go to the hell for liars for this. 'As you know, I have my own girlfriend, Beth, who I was meant to spend the weekend with, only I chose to drag myself up to Scotland at your request. And don't tell me I don't want to help you and I don't have your best interests at heart. I mean, every day I go and visit Roger and check up on him, just to keep you happy, so you know he's safe. And didn't I try and help you get a job? I mean, God, I'm not trying to rack up points – I'm just saying that I do all these things because I – because I care about you.'

'Oh God, yes, you did help me with that job, even though I didn't have a hope of getting it,' Dina sighed, sounding tearful again. Steve ached to hug her, but, given her accusations, felt it was better to play it cool. 'I don't know. Sometimes life smiles down on you and gives you everything, and at other times it just rains like shit all over you. And I'm having one of those weeks; I'm in the middle of a thunderstorm.' She managed a smile. 'I'm sorry – I didn't mean to have a go at you.' She sat up, looking at him with soft eyes. 'I *do* appreciate your help, Steve, really I do.'

She has such a good heart, thought Steve lovingly, smiling back fondly.

'Will you forgive me if I give you some cake?' he asked her innocently.

'Steve!' She thwacked him with the tea towel. 'I'm the one who made that bloody cake! How about I'll forgive you if you eat a slice?'

'Sounds good.'

Dina brought in some sticky slabs of walnut, coffee and cherry cake, which Steve declared was her best yet. Then, feeling deliciously lazy and self-indulgent, they flicked on the TV. That was the nice thing about Steve, Dina reflected. You could just sit back and put the telly on and he wouldn't be offended, he'd just go with the flow. With Archie, she always felt as though she was on her guard, anxiously checking those tell-tale changes in his expression to see if she'd displeased him.

She took another mouthful of cake. It was delicious; thank God. Since Archie had knocked her back for the position of restaurant manager, she had found herself wanting to do more and more cooking. Unfortunately, last night she'd made a rather overly ambitious attempt at risotto. The result had been a burnt disaster. Archie had thought the whole thing was hysterical and repeated his *Masterchef* comment, and though Dina had laughed too, inwardly she had been smarting. This evening she had a whole three-course meal planned and she was determined that by the end he would be both romanced and impressed.

And maybe, she thought, *maybe he'll even start thinking to himself, 'God, perhaps I should have given Dina that job after all . . .'*

No. That's silly. Archie was right. I'm not up to the job.

Still – it would be nice for him to see I'm good at something.

They channel-hopped for a bit, having a playful argument over the remote control, flicking from a trivia gameshow to one of those awful Australian hospital dramas where an arrogant, debonair consultant was having an affair with a buxom blonde nurse.

Then the phone shrilled. Dina picked it up.

'Archie! Hi,' she giggled. 'What? Oh, we're just – I mean, I'm just watching TV, it made me crack up . . . Uh-huh . . . no, I'm just on my own . . . but tonight I – oh. Right. OK. Sure. Well, I was going to cook for you, you know . . . OK. Right. Bye.' Dina put down the phone. 'Archie's working late tonight, so I guess . . . I guess that's that.'

Suddenly she became quiet and restless. She took a few mouthfuls of cake, then jumped to her feet. 'Fancy a walk?' she asked.

As they waited for the lift, Dina thought of the safest and most private place for them to go.

'Steve, would you mind if we went to the canal?' she asked cautiously. 'I know it's a bad place for you, but we'll be able to talk there . . .'

'Sure, it's fine,' said Steve hastily, grinning. 'Don't worry about it at all.'

They travelled to Wormwood Scrubs and took a leisurely walk along the Grand Union Canal. The summer was fading and autumn had begun to bite into the leaves, which were turning brilliant yellow and crimson. Blue dragonflies darted across the water, boats eased gently through the water, and in the distance there was the happy sound of children playing, yelling catcalls to each other.

'Steve,' Dina broke their comfortable silence, 'you know, it struck me the other day that here I am, moaning all the time about me and my career and – well, you never talk much about yours, about what you want to do.'

'Well, it's a bit late for that now,' Steve said, nudging her.

'OK,' said Dina, grinning awkwardly. 'But you always said you worked in The Greasy Spoon because you wanted to get out of the rat race and do something else. But you never seemed to know what the something else should be . . .'

'You know, Dina,' said Steve, 'I guess it's that old cliché where people say you never worry on your deathbed about how many hours you worked in the office; all you think about is the people you loved—' He broke off, suddenly realising that he was skirting dangerous territory, that his feelings might begin to spill out, and he quickly said, 'Anyway, what about you? Why did you end up in a greasy spoon in London? You always said it was your ex, Jason, who drove you here. Was that really true?'

'It was true,' Dina said defensively. She let out a sharp breath. 'I've never actually told anyone what really happened with him – not even Archie. I don't know why, because it's hardly an original story. I'd known Jason since high school. We acted in the school play together – we both took the leads in a horrendous reworking of *Romeo and Juliet* which made people laugh more than cry. But from then on we were boyfriend and girlfriend; I shared my first cigarette with him; my first taste of beer; I lost my virginity to him. After high school, I skipped college as my grades were so crap, and he went out and got a job in banking. He started off quite low down the ladder but within a few years he was getting promotion after promotion. Even though he was my first real boyfriend, I felt he was the one. I didn't want to try out other guys or play the field – I was all ready to be with him. When he proposed to me, it was the most amazing night of my life.

'We got an apartment together. And then one night I came

home – Jason thought I was going to visit my parents, but my mother was sick and they cancelled – and found him in bed with a mutual friend. So. That was that.'

'The bastard,' Steve said, struggling to keep the fury out of his voice. 'Jesus, Dina, you really deserve better. First Jason, now . . .' He trailed off quickly, realising how close to the bone he was. 'Sorry . . . I didn't mean . . . I mean . . . Oh God, you know what I mean. Archie's great, he's really great.'

'But you don't really believe that, do you?' Dina asked, her stare piercing. 'Come on, Steve, tell me the truth.'

'OK, I don't think he is the greatest,' said Steve carefully, feeling as though he was walking along a linguistic tightrope; one ill-chosen word could send him flying to the ground and snap their friendship for good. 'I just think that he tends to take you for granted a bit. He expects you to mould yourself around his life. And whenever you argue he manipulates you. Every time you row, you're the one who ends up apologising. Have you noticed that?'

Dina shook her head.

Oh God, thought Steve, *I've gone too far.*

'But so long as you're happy, then that's fine,' he said hastily.

'But . . .' Dina said, her voice laced with bewilderment. 'I'm not sure if I am . . .'

'Go on,' Steve pressed her.

Dina sat down on a bench, grabbing a grass stalk and tearing it into nervous fragments with her fingernails.

'I don't know. It's just a feeling I've got – that Archie's cheating on me too.' It was shocking to say it out loud, the fear that had been burning inside her over the last few weeks. 'I mean – lately he's been weird. Really moody. And he's been working late, and I've had dropped calls at home. But then maybe it's my paranoia after what happened with Jason. I mean, when we start a new relationship, we should be able to scrub out our past and start again with a completely fresh outlook, a new heart. But it's not that easy, is it? We bring all our old baggage along and it distorts our vision so we can only see the next person we love with cracked, smeared glasses; it takes longer to see them clearly because we're too busy regarding them as a collection of parts, snippets of the other people we've dated all sewn together. I worry that it's going to pile up inside me and I'm just going to end up a bitter, wizened old spinster. But hey . . .' She blew out a sharp breath.

Steve sat down beside her.

'Give it time,' he said softly. 'Take it as it comes. And if you keep getting suspicious, then gently confront him.'

'Confront him? That means at least three hours of shouting.'

'Explain about Jason. Tell him what you've told me. He'll understand.'

Dina nodded, then bit her lip and lowered her head, knowing there wasn't much else she could do. Steve chewed his lip too, wondering if now was the time to mention his news.

He decided to take the plunge.

'You know that next week is my' – Steve coughed – 'my thirty-first birthday.'

'Oh my God!' Dina cried, glancing round the canal uneasily. 'But you're not really – I mean—' She caught herself quickly, realising she'd been about to say something rather offensive.

'Yes, I know I'm not really ageing as such.' Steve picked up her thoughts. 'But, hey, maybe I can celebrate being thirty again!'

'God – I wish I could stay twenty-eight for ever.' Dina nudged him quickly, relieved to be joking again.

'So, so . . .' Steve paused. Suddenly he felt himself losing his nerve. *This is a crazy idea,* he told himself. Then he remembered Harrison's pep talk, the maxims he'd drummed into him just before he'd left tonight. *Just go for it, Steve. Stop faffing about. Find out once and for all if you have a chance with her.*

'So I was wondering if you'd like to go out for dinner with me?'

Dina stopped short and burst into laughter.

'Sorry,' said Steve hurriedly. 'Stupid idea. Completely crap idea. Though I didn't mean anything other than friends, so you don't need to start on a "let's just be friends" lecture—'

'Steve.' Dina touched his arm. He noticed with a flash of misery that she still felt uncomfortable touching him. It was as though she feared her fingers might pass through him, or inadvertently snap his arm off. 'Look, it would be lovely, really lovely. But we can hardly go to Pizza Express, can we?'

'I know that,' said Steve abruptly. 'I wasn't about to suggest it.'

'Sorry,' said Dina, feeling meek.

'I was going to suggest we go to a private place. It'll just be you and me. And some nice music. And a surprise.'

'A surprise? Can I ask what sort of surprise?'

'No. Just a surprise.'

'And what about Beth?' Dina asked. 'Don't you want to spend your birthday with her?'

'We – ah . . . well, things have been winding down between us,' Steve confessed, wincing as he realised he was directly contradicting his earlier assertions. But to his surprise and relief, Dina put a hand on his arm and said:

'God, I'm so sorry – I'm sure it was half my fault, dragging you off to Scotland when she wanted to be with you—'

'Oh, it's fine,' said Steve hastily. 'I didn't really feel we were going anywhere. And I'm not really . . . not really in the mood for a relationship now anyway. So. Would you like to come?'

They walked in silence for a few minutes. Dina bent her head, chewing her lip uncertainly. With every step, Steve became more and more convinced that she was going to say no. Oh God, being turned down by her beside this very canal *once* had been bad enough; to go through it a second time was pure torture. *Why am I doing this?* he asked himself. *Why do we put ourselves through this agony, all in the name of love?*

As they walked, Dina wondered why she was hesitating. Of course she wanted to go; it sounded like the perfect recipe for a lovely evening. So why did she feel so uneasy? A delicious sort of uneasy. The last few times she'd seen Steve, she'd been aware of something building between them; it felt just as it had when they'd worked in The Greasy Spoon together and their friendship had blossomed and blossomed until it felt it might flower into . . .

But that was ridiculous. Steve was a ghost. Besides, he had just said, quite blatantly, that he wasn't in the mood for a relationship.

Then she looked up at him and saw the hurt in his eyes.

'Of course I'd love to come,' she cried, slipping her arm through his. And then she saw two stars sparkle in his eyes and she smiled too, a big beaming smile. 'After all, you're my best friend, and if you can't celebrate your birthday with your best friend, then who can you celebrate it with?'

'Quite right,' Steve agreed, beaming too. 'Absolutely. Couldn't agree more.'

Steve waited until Dina had said goodbye, walked down the canal and disappeared under the bridge before punching the air.

'WHOOPEEEE!' he yelled, jumping up.

He went to see Jether again and they had a long talk about the nature of love that left Steve excited and bewildered. Back home, he lay on the warm roof and gazed up at the stars pinpricking the sky, feeling breathless with their sense of infinity. He kept pondering Jether's words over and over like a mantra: *If you want Dina to love you, you have to love yourself, Steve . . . you have to accept yourself . . .* He kept telling himself that it was all self-help bollocks again, and yet on some deep level he felt as though the words were resonating, rippling through his subconscious . . .

Suddenly the sky distracted him. A few stars up from the Big Dipper, he found a pattern that was just like the turned-up curve of Dina's nose. Steve felt his heart sing and decided that it deserved to go into all the stargazing books, that between the constellations Delphinus and Dorado there ought to be an entry saying:

> DINA: a collection of stars based on an ancient myth about a girl called Dina who was good at cooking, wanted to open a café and whom the gods decreed to have the most delightful nose in the universe.

He smiled dreamily, letting the air carry and caress him, as the hours slid by, the stars faded and the sun rose, each hour an hour closer to their date, their dinner, and his surprise.

24
Dina

Thirty minutes to go.

Where was it, where was it? She scrabbled about on her dressing table, pushing aside tubs and lipsticks and brushes, only to discover it had been sitting right in front of her all along. She unscrewed it, pulled out the delicately fringed brush and then nearly poked her eye out. She slammed the mascara back down on the table, gazing at her reflection. Her pupils were dilated, her cheeks flushed. Just what on earth was the matter with her?

She was going to dinner with Steve. So why did she feel like a fifteen-year-old preparing for her first date?

Twenty-five minutes to go.

She was about to attempt her mascara again when she heard the front door slam. Oh. Archie. Her stomach did another fluttery little flip.

'Hi,' she said, as he came in. 'I thought you were working late.'

After all, he had worked late for the last five nights. It was so bloody typical that tonight of all nights he was home early.

'Yeah, but we're going to Home House for drinks. Remember?' Archie broke off, suddenly looking her up and down, drinking in her new dress. It was a coppery shade of honey, with slender straps, made of two layers: a silky, slinky under-dress covered with a patterned veil of gold roses and leaves, and a frilly hem. Gold earrings sparkled through her newly washed, freshly curled hair. 'You're looking great. I wasn't expecting you to be ready.'

'Well, I'm, er, just about to go out for a drink with Anita, for her birthday.'

'But it's the Home House do, in honour of *Heidi's* birthday. Remember? Dina, don't tell me you forgot.'

'Oh shit.' Dina felt her stomach contract. She looked into the mirror, her eyes meeting Archie's angry ones. 'When does it start?'

'Nine.'

'Well, I can meet you there! St— Anita's do is at seven. I can go to that and then come on later.'

'Oh sure. You know what Anita's thing is going to be like. You'll probably have to end up untangling yourself from a male stripper or something.' Archie let out a long sigh. 'OK. I'll see you there.'

Dina waited for Archie to go into the kitchen. Then she hurriedly went to the wardrobe and pulled out the W.H. Smith bag containing the silvery wrapping paper and ribbon, and then the Waterstone's bag containing Steve's present. Now, where were the scissors? She'd planned this all out so carefully so that she wouldn't be late; Archie's unexpected arrival had left her flustered, thrown off kilter.

Hearing Archie's footsteps, she panicked and hastily tore off a piece of Sellotape with her teeth.

'So what did you get her?' he asked, standing in the doorway, a can of Coke in his hand.

'Uh – a necklace,' said Dina quickly.

'Is that why you're wrapping up a book, then?' Archie asked casually.

Dina looked down.

'Yep – I got her a book. And a necklace too,' she said hastily.

'Two presents?' he drawled. 'Well, lucky Anita. I don't suppose you got anything for Heidi.'

Dina didn't answer that one. For God's sake, why the hell should she buy a present for a girl who'd done her best to break her and Archie up? Archie was lucky she was going to Heidi's party *at all.* Sullenly she shoved the wrapped-up present into the bag and gathered up her things. Archie came towards her, and for one paranoid, insane moment she thought he was going to tear the bag off her and demand to see what the presents really were.

Instead, he gently tore a sliver of Sellotape off her lip.

'Oh – whoops,' Dina laughed a high, curious laugh, lowering her eyes. Then, to her surprise, Archie pulled her into a tight hug. Archie wasn't much of a hugger – kisses he favoured, yes, but not hugs. But he held her so tightly she could barely breathe. She wrapped her arms around him too, suddenly pricked with guilt at her deceit.

Archie pulled back, gently rubbing his nose against hers.

'Well,' he said, 'have fun.'

Just as she was leaving the flat, it started to rain. She didn't have an umbrella, so she held her handbag over her hand and ran down the road, heels clicking, hair flying. Halfway down, she stopped for breath and looked back up at the flat. There was a yellow square of light shining from their bedroom window. Archie was standing there, watching her. She couldn't see his expression. She gave him a nervous little wave and hurried on, skipping with fear and excitement. She had to admit that underneath her guilt, the forbiddenness of it all, the deceit, made it all the more exciting. It was almost like having an affair. Not that she'd ever in a million years cheat on a guy, and especially not Archie . . .

She took the tube and got out at Kensington Olympia. Steve wasn't there yet, so she waited near the entrance, watching commuters. Autumn had definitely overtaken summer now; the air was cool and smoggy, the wind whipping up crispy leaves. She fretted that she hadn't cleaned her teeth before leaving, so she went to the little newsagent's and bought a packet of mint imperials, sucking nervously.

Then, suddenly, deliciously, she felt a gush of air and his presence, the coldness of his lips brushing against her cheek. She felt a shiver run up her spine and catch in her throat.

'Hi,' he whispered. 'Sorry I'm late. I wasn't prepared for all the rain.'

'Happy birthday,' Dina cried. Then she saw the newsagent, no doubt convinced that she was talking to herself, give her a weird look and she quickly shut up.

Steve led her out through the commuters and then took her hand. Now she could see him properly. He was wearing – bless him – a proper dinner suit with a little black bow tie. His fringe was slightly wavy from the rain and she had a sudden urge to reach out and stroke it. But then he said:

'Follow me. It's not far now.'

Dina tried not to be too disappointed when he led her into the Olympia multistorey car park. She'd kind of been expecting a balcony table with roses and violins, but, well, a car park could be romantic. If you tried really hard.

They took the lift up to the top floor. Dina was slightly bemused to see that there were no cars there, for someone had blocked off the entrances with large red signs screaming 'ENGINEERING WORK IN PROGRESS'.

'Don't worry – we put those up to keep people out. Now close your eyes,' Steve whispered.

Dina felt a shiver breeze up her spine. Steve pushed open a door and led her through. She felt the wind on her face, heard traffic from below. In the distance was the sound of a dog barking. Steve muttered something about the rain and she heard him click open an umbrella. She could sense his excitement, in the pressure of his hand against hers, as he led her forward. Then she heard music. A guitar. Not a CD – a live guitar. And then a voice, rather out of tune:

'*I'm singing in the rain . . .*'

'Hey,' Steve objected. 'I thought we'd agreed to drop the guitar bit, Harrison.'

'But I thought it was a nice touch,' Harrison objected.

Silence. Steve fumed. *I knew I shouldn't have got Harrison involved,* he thought.

'I'm, er, opening my eyes now, if that's OK,' said Dina.

'OK,' said Steve.

Dina opened her eyes. She let out a cry.

There before her, on the empty top storey of the multistorey car park, was a table set for two. A white cloth was draped over it, with a single candle in the centre, the flame fluttering in the breeze as though uncertain whether to cling to its wick or disappear off into the night. There were two plastic garden chairs and the whole thing was sheltered by an elaborate canopy of umbrellas. Golf umbrellas, black umbrellas, striped umbrellas, small girly umbrellas with cats and mermaids squiggling over the sides, all precariously propped up in a rainbow of spokes and sheets.

It was so much more fun than a balcony and roses.

'Oh my God, this is great!' Dina cried. 'It's just – totally wacky – and totally wonderful!'

Then she turned and let out a small cry.

'Harrison is scary,' Steve agreed, following her gaze.

'Harrison? There's another ghost here?' Dina gasped.

'Yes, don't worry, it's just my friend Harrison. He's perfectly harmless. Well, most of the time. So you definitely can't see him then?'

'I can see the guitar he's playing, but not him.'

Harrison's playing faltered. Steve tried not to smirk when he saw the indignant expression on his face. Then Harrison, remembering that it was, after all, Steve's night, put down the guitar and grinned.

'Well, Steve, I think it's very romantic that Dina can only see you,' he said. 'I think it surely means you're destined to marry, have kids and live happily ever—' he broke off as Steve shot him a threatening look.

'Ignore him,' said Steve, drawing Dina towards the table. He tried to suppress the smile tickling his lips, not wanting to spoil the surprise.

Dina sat down and then yelped as something warm and wet burrowed into her thigh.

'*Roger!*' she cried in shock. 'Oh my God! What's he doing here?'

'I borrowed him for the night,' Steve said, with a wry grin.

Roger broke into a tantivy of wild barking and licked her face so joyously it became soaking wet. Dina buried her nose in his warm fur, breathing in his wonderful doggie smell.

'Seriously – this is all so wonderful, it feels as though it's *my* birthday, not yours. I feel so spoilt—' Dina broke off as a few spots of rain escaped through the eye-shaped gaps between the umbrellas.

'Oops,' said Steve.

'Don't worry,' said Dina. 'I love it! So does Roger!'

Roger barked in enthusiastic agreement.

'The thing is,' said Dina, looking down, 'I, er, can't really stay too long tonight. Just an hour or so and then I'll have to be off . . .

I'm really sorry – it's just that Archie's got an important do on, so . . .'

She flicked her eyes up nervously. She waited for Steve to look pained. She waited for the familiar flash of guilt Steve always seemed to give her. That guilt-twist in her stomach seemed to encapsulate the essence of their relationship: that she could never quite give Steve what he wanted.

To Dina's surprise, Steve just shrugged and said, 'No worries. Hey, *garçon*!' He clicked his fingers and Harrison appeared, brandishing flimsy menus.

'I mean – I might be able to call Archie and stay a little bit longer,' said Dina quickly, feeling even more guilty now that Steve *hadn't* made her feel guilty.

'No, it's fine,' said Steve, shrugging. 'Now, choose from the amazing selection on our menu.'

Dina laughed, relieved that Steve genuinely seemed cool. She perused the menu.

Starter
No such luck

Main course
Roast chicken with vegetables

Dessert
Chocolate cake

Coffee
If you're lucky

'Don't spend all night deciding,' said Harrison, irritably tapping his pencil on the pad, as though keen to get back to his guitar.

'Er – well, I guess I'll have the roast chicken followed by the chocolate cake,' said Dina.

'Same for me,' said Steve.

Roger whined as though to say: *Don't forget me!* and Dina patted him lovingly.

Steve turned back to Dina. God, she was looking so lovely, the rain beading her hair like dewdrops, quivering on the tips of her long lashes.

'I got you a present,' said Dina. 'Two, in fact. Though I, er, didn't quite have time to wrap the first one.'

'Huh,' said Steve. 'I don't know if I can be bothered if you haven't even wrapped it. Just kidding,' he added, grinning, when Dina's eyes widened.

'Oh. OK. Well . . .' Dina passed over a little box. She recalled how, this time last year, she'd given Steve a gorilla. She'd been so confident that he'd like it. Now she felt the tips of his fingers brush hers as he took the box, and nerves, like a spurt of lightning, trembled up her arm. *He's not going to like it,* she panicked, *it's too old, too strange.*

Dina couldn't see Harrison, who had forgotten their dinner in his curiosity, creeping up behind Steve. Steve opened the box and pulled out a fine layer of tissue. Beneath it was a chain with a cross. The silver was slightly dirty; the cross chunky, with an elaborate pattern spiralling on its arms.

'Well, that's a bit crap, isn't it?' said Harrison, forgetting himself. 'It looks like the sort of thing old women bring on *Antiques Roadshow* that turn out to be worth nothing, surprise, surprise.'

'Well, sorry, I mean – it's not worth a million, obviously,' Dina began, 'but—'

'Harrison,' said Steve, 'just fuck off.'

Dina was taken aback. There was Steve, surprising her again. She'd never once heard him swear in her company. Let alone tell someone off. His authoritative tone reminded her a little of Archie, only Archie's orders were propelled by ego and sometimes a scorpion-sting of spite, whereas Steve's bolshiness was benign and playful, rude but not nasty.

'So you're saying fuck off and don't come back and eat all the food myself?' Harrison retorted.

'No, just fuck off for five minutes and then bring the food.'

'Yes, sir.'

Steve began to wonder if their agreement for Harrison to be a waiter for the night was really worth him having to creep into Blockbuster and steal twenty DVDs for him.

But Harrison did disappear and Steve had a chance to examine the cross.

'It was my grandfather's,' said Dina.

As Steve held it, her story seemed to infuse into the gift, making the chain gleam, the crucifix glow with beauty. He slid it over his neck and tucked it into his shirt, enjoying the cold feel of the silver against his skin. Dina noticed that the metal, once connected with his ephemeral presence, seemed to become fainter, as though the chain was fusing with his flesh. A warm, intimate sensation tingled over her and she knew then that her intuition had been right; after a fraught day of rejecting socks and ties and other stupid things that blokes never really wanted, let alone ghosts, the cross had been the perfect present.

'Oh, I got you this too,' said Dina. 'One last thing . . .'

Steve tore off the silvery paper and howled with laughter when he saw it: *How To Find Out If Your House Is Haunted: A Beginner's Guide To Dealing With Ghosts*.

'Oh, you must look at page twenty-five,' Dina giggled. 'There's this bit where it gives advice on contacting ghosts.'

'"It is a good idea to wear white so that your aura will attract ghosts to you",' Steve read aloud, shaking his head in disbelief, '"and speak softly when you try to contact them or else you might scare them off." What is this bollocks!' He carried on reading and soon they were giggling so hard they were nearly crying.

'You're different,' Dina suddenly blurted, as their laughter faded away.

'I'm sorry?'

'You're different. I'm not sure what it is . . . it's as though . . . look – don't take this the wrong way, but before you always looked a bit . . . as though you were apologising to life for existing . . . and now you seem . . . well, confident.'

Steve smiled, wishing that Jether was here so that he could shake him by the hand and thank him.

'I guess,' said Steve, 'I guess you're right. I've finally learned to like myself. Someone just helped me to see it. I realised recently that I've spent my whole life worrying about what other people think of me. You know – trying to impress the hard guys at school, only no matter what I did I was never going to be cool enough.

Then going to university and trying to please my parents by getting a first when I wasn't really sure if I even wanted a degree. Worrying whether girls liked me – and then wondering why guys who were much more ugly than me managed to pull, not realising that I was putting them off with my insecurity. And now – now, I've just stopped worrying, y'know? I just figure that this is me, this is who I am, this is Steve MacFadden, and I may as well learn to like him.'

'Hear hear!' Dina laughed and raised her glass, secretly rather touched by his honesty.

They were interrupted by Harrison, who was carrying a tray of dishes concealed beneath silver domes. Roger barked hopefully and put a paw on the table.

Steve felt a bit guilty for swearing at Harrison earlier and he smiled apologetically; Harrison had done a good job.

Harrison removed the lids with a flourish. Steve tried not to gape. He looked up with a questioning glare. Harrison grinned quickly.

'I know you were planning on a *takeaway* but I thought it would be more romantic if I cooked myself, to show how much I care,' he said, enjoying Dina's admiring, touched glance.

'Very smooth, Harrison,' Steve muttered under his breath. Still, the food looked OK: a roast dinner, with chicken, vegetables and gravy.

'*Bon appetit*,' said Harrison, returning to his guitar.

Unfortunately, the meal didn't taste quite as good as it looked.

'Well, this is lovely,' said Dina, trying to ignore Harrison's throaty rendition of 'The Power of Love' as she sawed on a potato as hard as a pebble.

At the start of the meal, Steve had felt buoyant. He'd known Dina would love the wacky romance of umbrellas on the top of a multistorey; the pleasure on her face had confirmed this. But now his self-confidence, which had felt so tightly sealed at the edges of his soul, began to peel away, letting doubts leak in. The food was the key bit. How many sumptuous dinners had Archie used to woo Dina? And now Steve was offering her *this*. Stringy roast chicken. Peas like liquid bogey. Gravy like cement.

This wasn't what Steve and Harrison had agreed at all. Harrison was supposed to have snuck into their local restaurant in

Hammersmith, stolen the dishes from the kitchens and brought them over.

Harrison, sensing that his well-intended meal hadn't gone down quite as well as he'd hoped, quickly walked up to the table and decided to employ a distraction tactic. He drew a pack of cards from his pocket, directing the sprayed fan at Dina. From Dina's perspective all she could see were cards hovering in the air.

'Pick a card. Any card.'

Steve buried his face in his hands. Dina giggled and took one, shaking her head.

'Look at it. Remember it. Now put it back in the pack. Ignore Steve, this is fun – part of the free Harrison Entertainment Service. Now, I'm just going to shuffle the cards like so. Is this your card?' He held up the ace of spades.

'No.'

'This one?' The king of diamonds.

'Er, no.'

'This one?' The three of hearts. 'Right. Well.' Harrison pocketed the pack.

'Great card trick,' said Dina.

'Yeah, I kind of feel it's an existential trick – it encapsulates the pointlessness of life. I'll go get dessert,' said Harrison quickly.

'*No!*' Steve yelped, raising his head. 'Harrison, really, we've had enough of your cooking.'

'OK,' said Harrison, 'I'll play the guitar and then you guys can dance, right?'

'D'you want to dance?' Steve asked Dina tentatively. His heart skipped; when he had planned this evening he had felt determined that whatever happened, it should finish on a high, leave an impression of wonder and beauty stamped in her memory. 'I mean, you probably have to go, but, hey, it might help us work off the indigestion from eating this shit.'

'It's raining.' Dina laughed uncertainly.

Steve took an umbrella and swirled it above her head, holding out his arm like an eighteenth-century gent inviting her to a ball.

Laughing and shaking her head, Dina got up. Harrison grinned and launched into Wet Wet Wet's 'Love Is All Around Us'.

Dina was surprised again. When Steve was alive, she could

remember once taking him to a nightclub – just for a laugh. She had tried to get him to boogie on the dance floor but he had flushed bright red and said no, he couldn't possibly. When Dina had finally yanked him on, Steve had suddenly grown two extra feet and arms twice as long as his body. It hadn't helped either that Dina was a good dancer and only showed him up.

But tonight, Steve was *volunteering.* And though he wasn't doing much except moving from one foot to the other, he carried it off with an air of classy confidence. He held the umbrella over them, looking deep into her eyes, clicking his fingers, humming along tunelessly, all in a spirit of *I don't care if I look like a prat, I'm just having fun.*

Dina found his *joie de vivre* utterly infectious. She jived and spun and kicked up her knees. Soon her feet were completely soaked, but she didn't give a toss. Harrison, realising he was on to a winner, kept singing the same song over and over, and even Roger joined in, yapping and diving between their legs, nearly sending Dina toppling over.

Steve saved her, catching her arm.

'Are you OK?' he chuckled. Suddenly they became acutely aware of how close they were. Steve saw Dina's pupils dilate and a flush seep across her cheeks.

'Shall we dance?' he whispered, and slid one arm around her waist, holding the umbrella over them.

Dina moved in close. It felt strange, for she was used to the smooth muscle of a man's chest and Steve's torso felt light as a feather. Steve too was slightly awkward, struggling to keep the umbrella upright. But then Dina leaned in very gently and Steve softly brushed his hand up and down her spine and they seemed to seep into each other, as though the edges of their souls were overlapping.

Steve felt as though he'd been waiting for this moment his whole life. The past and all its disappointments slid away; the future didn't matter. The present was simply perfect, standing here now, with her. Slowly, the umbrella drooped in his hand and then slid to the ground. The wind picked it up and tossed it over the edge of the building. Neither of them cared as the rain washed over them; they were barely conscious of the lightning playing tag across the sky, hiding behind the clouds laughingly and then sprinting across the clear expanse in blue streaks. Dina rubbed her cheek against Steve's chest and then lifted her face to his. Their mouths were inches apart. Her breath, so much stronger than his, warmed his skin and seemed to infuse it with life, spreading a glow up over his lips and cheeks so that his face no longer looked pallid but luminous, almost human.

'Steve,' she whispered dreamily, 'there's something I need to say.'

'Go on,' he whispered.

'Something about the night you – you passed away. Something I didn't get to tell you—'

And then her mobile rang. They both blinked, the spell broken. Dina went over to the table and reluctantly picked up her handbag, drawing her mobile out.

'OK – sure, yes – I'm sorry, I'm coming, I'm coming . . . OK.' She switched it off and said lamely, 'I have to go.'

A minute ago, she had been in his arms; now she had never seemed more distant.

'Dina,' Steve grabbed her. 'Please just stay five minutes. Tell me what you were going to say.'

'I – I—' Dina looked up at him for some time, and then snapped her mouth shut, pulling up her handbag strap. She turned to Roger and gave him another huge hug and a kiss. 'I – I have to go. You will look after Roger for me and take him back?'

'Of course.'

Steve and Harrison stood on the top storey and watched the ant-like figure of Dina walking below.

'Your cooking was shit and I'm going to kill you,' said Steve tersely. Then he added nervously, 'D'you think I did OK? D'you think she likes me?'

'Hard to tell. She seemed to be getting horny during your dance. But then again, she didn't even bother to wrap your present.'

'Well, Harrison, you didn't even *get* me a fucking present.'

Steve watched Dina turn the corner and disappear into the night. Her words were echoing in his mind: *Steve, there's something I need to say . . . Something about the night you passed away . . .*

'Harrison,' he said suddenly, 'I have to speak to her. Stay and look after Roger for me. I've got to go after her.'

'But—' Harrison began, but Steve was already dashing off. Harrison turned back to Roger and shrugged. He strummed his guitar and Roger barked enthusiastically. 'Oh well – what else is there to do but make beautiful music. OK, Roger, you're the backing vocals. Let's sing "Bohemian Rhapsody" . . . try to keep up . . .'

25
Dina

Dina felt as though her stomach was filled with a bucket of ice. She took a sip of champagne, feeling it tickle its bubbly path down her throat. It didn't make her feel better. She kept telling herself, *Don't look at them, don't look at them.* But she couldn't help it. After all, he was her bloody boyfriend, wasn't he?

She knew Archie had good reason to be annoyed with her. She had promised him that she'd be there by nine and she hadn't made it until ten. She had crept into Home House feeling sheepish and strangely disorientated and out of place. She climbed up the rather grand staircase to the second floor, where guests were lounging on the blue-striped sofas or clustered in tight-knit, gossipy groups. After the intimacy and honesty of her evening with Steve, Archie's friends seemed shockingly superficial. She'd pushed through the crowds, occasionally spotting someone she knew vaguely from one of Archie's previous parties, air-kissing them distractedly. Finally she had been relieved to bump into Ralph, who was deep in discussion with the literary editor of *The Times*.

'Ralph.' She touched his arm gently.

'Dina! Darling, lovely to see you.' He kissed each cheek.

'I've been looking for Archie everywhere – have you seen him?'

'Yes, he's over there—' Ralph broke off and moved quickly in front of her. But Dina had already seen what he was gallantly trying to hide.

Archie was sitting on the other side of the room, behind a piano. He was smoking a cigar, and as Dina looked over, a furl of grey smoke uncurled from his laughing mouth. A red feather boa was draped around his neck. Dina presumed that it had been put there by the rather ravishing brunette balanced on his knees. Or perhaps by the equally ravishing blonde by his side, who was leaning over him and showing off a voluptuous, velvet-clad cleavage.

'He's just flirting,' Ralph said with desperate gentleness. 'You were late . . . and . . . you know what Archie's like. He got a bit upset. He doesn't like it when people are late.'

'Just like his mother,' Dina observed bitterly.

She stared across the room at Archie. He stared back. His eyes were bloodshot and fiery and simply begging for a fight. *OK, fine,* Dina cried inside, *we can fight. Two can play at your game.*

She threaded her arm through Ralph's and turned her back on Archie, knowing full well that the quickest way to get him over was to ignore him completely. She found herself coming face to face with a balding man in a tweed jacket. He had shrewd eyes and a smirk on his face.

'So are you and Archie off then?'

'I'm sorry?' As far as she knew, this man was a total stranger.

'She has nothing to say to you,' said Ralph, forgetting his gallant manners in a sudden fit of temper. 'Just leave her alone.'

The balding man left, but his smile lingered like the Cheshire cat's.

'Was he a reporter?' Dina asked in horror, and Ralph nodded tersely. She chewed her lip, realising that media attention could have its down side. Suddenly she felt hot with paranoia that every girl in the room was whispering and laughing at her and gossiping: *Oh, haven't you heard? Yes, Archie's got tired of her, well I'm not surprised, she must have been naïve to think she could hold him . . .*

Ralph, who had been trying to distract her with an anecdote about Lord Byron, trailed off. He glanced up and cleared his throat, looking mildly embarrassed. Dina turned to see that Archie was standing behind her, his arm curled tightly around the birthday girl herself.

Heidi.

She was looking sickeningly beautiful in some sort of pale blue diaphanous floaty thing that was more like a nightie than a dress.

She flicked back a sheaf of blonde hair and smiled up at Archie, and he tightened his arm around her. For one surreal moment, Dina felt as though the last nine months had rewound like something out of a sci-fi movie, so she'd never dated Archie and was just a stranger meeting him and his girlfriend for the first time.

'Hi,' she said, trying to ignore the sing-song smile teasing Heidi's lips.

Archie raised his glass and then downed his wine.

'Nice of you to turn up, Dina,' he said.

'Well,' said Dina shakily, glaring back at him, 'I wasn't sure if you really wanted me to come. I mean, you seem to be having plenty of fun with everyone else.'

'And did you have fun at Anita's?' he asked, in a patronising tone.

'It was fun, yes. I took Roger along. We had a good time.'

'Glad to hear you took Roger. Did he taste good? In some countries, you know, dog is a delicacy, though I should imagine Roger's only fit for dodgy curries.'

Heidi stifled a giggle. Ralph, who was sensing a rather odd criss-cross of tensions between the trio, looked uncomfortable and began to edge away.

'Roger is – is—' Dina broke off shakily, unable to think up a suitable put-down. Oh God, why did he always have to win every fight, why did he always make her feel so small? 'Roger is a lovely dog,' she said furiously.

'I'm finding all this talk of hairy beasts rather boring,' said Archie languidly. 'Now – don't you think you should be polite and say happy birthday to Heidi?' He turned to Heidi and trailed a line of kisses along her creamy cheek, his hands fluttering across her hip bone and then skirting the frilly hem of her dress.

Dina watched them. *Don't cry,* she kept telling herself, *don't let Heidi have that satisfaction.* She folded her arms, refusing to even acknowledge Heidi with a glance.

'You know what?' she said in a trembling voice. 'I think this party's fucking boring. I think I'd prefer to watch TV. I'm going home.'

'Fine,' said Archie. As she walked away, she heard him saying to Heidi drunkenly, 'Ignore her – she's no fun anyway,' and Heidi's frightful, piercing giggle floated across the air. As she left, she was horribly aware of the balding man watching her intently.

Back home, Dina sat in the bath for an hour until the water was cold. She was too numb even to cry; her heart felt like a lump of dead wood. She leaned out of the bath, dried her hand, picked up the suede curl of her watch strap. 11.30. Only three hours ago she'd been dancing on a rooftop in the rain, enjoying the happiest night of her life. Now it felt as though her dinner with Steve had happened weeks ago.

She realised that she wanted Archie to come home. She knew that the tensions that had been simmering beneath the surface for the last few months had finally come to the boil. The thought made her feel sick with nerves.

Dina sat on the stool before her dressing table. She stared at her smiling reflection and realised that she was holding her face rigid. She let it slacken and saw the fear in her eyes, the downturn of her lips.

She combed out her hair until it fuzzed into a static halo. Her roots were starting to show, a dark inch before the blonde began. She remembered how Archie hated short hair on girls. Suddenly a fiery, miserable urge gripped her. Flinging open a drawer, she pulled out a pair of scissors and held a sheaf of hair between them.

Dina, a voice whispered behind her. Steve gently took the scissors and put them down on the dressing table.

Dina was so touched by his gentleness that tears welled up in her eyes. She felt him take a handful of her hair. And then another. He began to plait it, revelling in the different shades that wove and melded together. Dina closed her eyes, sighing softly, feeling soothed by his touch. Every so often, his ghostly fingers flicked against the soft delta of skin at the back of her neck and she felt a shiver tickle down her spine.

'Dina,' Steve said softly. She flicked open her eyes. His fingers went limp and the plait fell to her back, a few strands coming loose. 'I don't know . . . I . . . I don't want you to be mad at me . . . I didn't know how to tell you this . . . but I followed you to the party . . . I just wanted to make sure you were OK and—'

'Steve—'

'No, let me finish. I have to tell you this. After you'd gone, I stuck around for a bit. I saw Archie taking – taking a girl outside for a walk, and . . . you know . . .'

Dina sat still for a few minutes. *So,* she thought. *So.* Despite the icy feeling of shock, part of her was relieved to finally discover the truth.

'Who was she?' she suddenly asked.

Steve's eyes met hers in the mirror and he gently brushed his fingers over her plait.

'I think you need to talk to Archie,' he said.

Dina let out a deep, tear-laced breath. Steve gripped her shoulder.

'Don't worry,' he said. 'It'll be OK. I'll be with you all the time, OK?'

Dina nodded quickly. They remained in silence for a few minutes; then Steve said tentatively:

'Dina, I know this isn't really the time or the place, and you might not want to talk about this right now . . . but . . . just before you left tonight, you said there was something you wanted to tell me.'

Dina looked up sharply. For a moment Steve feared that she was offended, but then she swallowed and said:

'Yes, there was something . . . it's quite a long story, really. It's just – on the night you died, something quite special happened to me.' She broke off, letting out a deep breath.

Then, suddenly, they heard the grate of a key in the lock. The bang of a door.

'He's home,' Dina hissed.

'OK, talk to him right away,' said Steve. 'Don't put it off, just confront him, OK? Look, Dina, you have the biggest heart and you're so loving, you always see the best in people. But Archie's taking advantage of that. Just don't let him get away with anything, you deserve better, OK?'

Dina nodded and Steve slipped away into the shadows. She went into the living room with a furiously beating heart. Archie was standing in the doorway, his hair mussed up, lipstick on his cheek, his eyes wild and bloodshot.

'Good night?' said Dina.

'Great.' Archie went over to the drinks cabinet and began pouring himself a whisky.

'You're having an affair, aren't you?'

Archie turned, slopping a glug of whisky on to the cabinet. Dina saw the shock on his face and felt relief wash through her. Because deep down, she hadn't really believed that Steve had seen Archie with another girl. Archie might be a flirt, yes, but he wouldn't cheat on her. Steve must have been seeing things. Maybe he had even been lying.

But why, asked a quiet voice at the back of her mind, *would Steve lie to you?*

'Yes,' said Archie. 'I'm having an affair.'

'I'm sorry?' Dina thought she was going to be sick.

'I'm having an affair.' His tone was light. He looked her straight in the eye. 'Well, more like a series of one-night stands, actually.'

'Who with?' she whispered.

'Guess.'

'Guess – you want me to guess? God—' Dina broke off in disgust. She looked at his eyes again. This felt like another of Archie's games, only it wasn't sexy and teasing and playful like his usual ones. There was fury flashing in his pupils.

Suddenly he stormed forward. For one terrified moment, she thought he was going to hit her. Then he picked up her handbag, emptying the contents all over the sofa.

'Archie, what the hell are you—'

'Here.' Archie picked through the chaos of lipsticks and tampons and keys and tissues, pulling out Dina's little Nokia mobile. 'I bought this for you, remember? Remember?' He pressed the MENU button, the square of blue light reflecting on his angry face. 'And oh – let's see what text messages you have on this phone. A message from Steve. And what's this? Another message from Steve. Oh, another one – "I think you should tell Archie just where to go." Guess who that's from? Steve.'

'How did you know – how—' Dina stammered.

'D'you think I'm stupid? D'you think I haven't noticed that

you've been completely different over the last few weeks? You've been getting KitKats. You've been getting silly notes – which, by the way, you ought to have flushed down the loo, instead of screwing them up and then chucking them into my study bin for me to notice.' Archie swallowed. Dina kept trying to interrupt him but he ploughed on furiously. 'And aside from all that, you're clearly in love. You're giggly, your head's in the clouds. And I thought, why shouldn't I fuck around? Why shouldn't I go and get laid? I mean – you've been seeing this guy since way back, before I even took you to my mother's, right? I saw a text on your mobile then. And I kept thinking it was a little flirtation, but no, it appears to have been going on for quite a while, right?'

'No – Archie, no, you've got it all wrong. Steve is just a friend. He's not even real . . .'

'Right. And when I went to bed with Heidi last week we were just *friends* and she didn't really exist, she was just a product of my imagination.'

'Heidi.' Dina felt bile in the back of her mouth. Her throat felt hoarse, her lungs raw, as though she'd been running for miles. 'You slept with Heidi again?'

'What did you fucking expect—'

'Why didn't you just say something to me, why didn't you just ask—'

'Why should I have to ask? Why? I mean, God, Dina, you're the first girl I've really trusted. You knew how I felt about relationships after all that mess with my father – and you're the first girl I've ever lived with. And then you go screwing around. I mean, what am I? Clearly, I'm the Bank of Archie Hamilton. The guy who pays your bills and buys you dresses whilst you have fun with *Steve*.'

'I'm sorry,' said Dina in a small voice. 'I'm sorry you got the wrong impression, but honestly, Archie, I'm not after you for your money. When I moved in, I really did love you.'

'I like the way you use the past tense.'

'I'm sorry, I—' Dina broke off. Suddenly she felt a flare of anger. She remembered Steve's words: *Every time you row, you're the one who ends up apologising.*

'Archie,' she injected fresh confidence into her voice, 'I'm not going to say sorry, I'm not. Why should I? I'm not having an affair, and you have no right to have a go at me. I mean, you should have told me you felt suspicious and trusted me enough to talk to me about it, instead of going off behind my back with . . . with . . .' Dina felt too ill to say her name.

'Well, why don't you just move out?' said Archie. 'Go on – go.'

Dina felt herself grow cold.

'Look,' she tried desperately, 'can't we just talk about this, like grown-ups? Instead of you just freezing me out like you always do? I mean, OK, I admit I've been spending a lot of time with Steve – though he is just a friend – but I've been bored.' Suddenly it all came pouring out, all the emotions and frustrations that had been simmering inside her over the last few weeks. 'I've been stuck in this flat all day. And you expect me to just wait here like some princess in her tower so you can gallop in from work whenever it suits you. All you seem to want from me is just to look pretty. You don't want me to get a job, or open a café—'

'Because you opening a café is obviously the most fucking stupid idea,' Archie yelled.

Dina yelled back, 'No – you know what it is? It's as though you're scared of me changing, or meeting other people, or anything where you might lose your hold over me. You don't want me to change, ever, or grow up, or evolve. And look, Archie, I know you said all that stuff about your father, and I know how hard it must have been, but that doesn't give you a licence to go around flirting and having affairs! You're not your father, you have to learn from what happened, you have to move on.'

She broke off, drawing in deep breaths, trembling violently.

There was a long silence. She saw the hurt on his face; oh God, had she been cruel to bring up his father? Then he said quietly:

'Dina, I'm sick of fighting. Just go. Please.'

Dina looked into Archie's eyes and saw a door close in his mind. She'd seen him do this to people before. Whether he was getting rid of a friend or firing a member of staff who wasn't doing what he wanted them to do. He was black and white; he loved people, or he hated them. And they'd gone past a point; he was ready to cut her clean away and forget her. Despair welled up inside her.

'I'm going for a drive,' he said. 'I'll be gone an hour, that should be long enough. OK?'

He walked out and slammed the door. The flat shook. Einstein's bowl trembled, the water rippling into a storm. He swam to the front of his bowl and stared at Dina with big, worried eyes.

Dina sat down on the sofa and burst into tears. Steve came out of the shadows, his face white with anger.

'Jesus – what a complete *bastard*,' he said. 'You know, I had to clench my fists to stop myself from picking up a vase and smashing it over his head. But I figured you might not appreciate my ghostly interference.'

'No, maybe not.' She was trying to sound tough, but her voice was as thin as tissue paper and the tears broke through. At some deep, intuitive level, underneath the torrents of pain and confusion, she knew that this was for the best; she realised that she had always known their relationship was unreal and unhealthy. And yet still she found herself having to fight the urge to run out of the flat and chase after Archie and beg him to come back.

Steve ached to touch her, but he held back. He watched the tears pour down her cheeks and a fury tightened in his chest, for all the times Archie had made her cry, for the way he had reduced Dina – sweet, happy, wonderful Dina – to this, to an insecure, unhappy, pathetic wreck.

Dina was glad that Steve held back. She could not bear to be touched, to be loved. This final guillotine blow to her relationship with Archie made her feel utterly cold, as though she would never love again. She wanted to hide that part of her which was soft and vulnerable and tender as a child, and seal it away so that nobody could ever hurt her like this again.

Steve helped her to pack. She called Anita, terrified that Anita would just tell her where to go after the recent lapse in their friendship. But Anita was incredibly warm and kind, and all she had to say was, 'Dina, just get out of that place and back over here now!'

Back at the flat, Anita understood that Dina didn't want to talk. She dumped her suitcases on the floor and got into bed, shivering. She lay in the grey darkness, her eyes shut, and Steve gazed down at her and thought with a chill that she looked more dead than alive.

He left her and went to St Simon's church, to light a candle for her in the way he had so often seen Dina do for him. He looked up at the statue of the Virgin Mary and felt something unexpected stir in his chest, a sensation that was not quite faith, but close to belief. In that moment of openness, the prayers fell swiftly from his lips: *Let me heal her, God. Let me help her. I'm frightened, God; I don't want Dina to be like this ever again. Let me heal her and help her to be whole again.*

PART THREE

26
Dina

What hobbies do you enjoy taking part in?

I like reeding.

Dina reached for the Tippex and slashed a savage white stroke through the sentence. She picked up her biro and chewed the end. *Reeding.* She closed her eyes and tried to tug the letters into their right places, but they swirled into illogical patterns: *readding, reding, rieding.* She felt as though she was seven years old again, unaware that she had dyslexia, sitting in a school spelling test. The heat burned behind her eyes from the effort of concentration, until her pen felt as huge and clumsy as an axe in her hand and she ended up handing in a blank piece of paper.

Whenever she was stressed or upset, her dyslexia reared its ugly head. In despair, she threw down her pen, close to tears. The job application had to be posted by noon. But how the hell was she going to get a job if she couldn't even spell?

Life hadn't been easy for the last three months. Anita had been a total saviour. The morning after Dina returned to the flat, Anita laid on a gorgeous breakfast to cheer her up. She had flung her arms around her and cried: 'It's so good to have the old Dina back!'

Dina sobbed, slightly confused by Anita's words.

'Well, come on, Dina, Archie was so crap. I mean, yes, I know he was good-looking and all that, but anyone could see he was just an arrogant prick who was trying to control you all the time. I didn't like to say before you moved out, 'cos I had a feeling you weren't in the mindset to really hear me . . .'

Dina wiped away her tears. Anita's words had shocked her. Was Archie really that bad? Had she really been that naïve? She felt as though she was still too emotionally blurred to understand their relationship; it was like those Impressionist paintings that are a confusing collection of dots when you stand too close, that you need to step back from to make sense of and see the true picture.

That night, they ordered a takeaway and watched *EastEnders.* Dina barely took in a word. She felt gripped by a wild exhilaration. She kept thinking: *I don't have to check my make-up is fine so I look as good for Archie as possible. I don't have to worry about leaving a dirty mug on the table or a hair in the sink for fear of him going mad. I don't have to go to a party and feel terrified that I might not get on with Archie's friends, or fear that they'll think I'm not good enough for him.*

I'm me again.

She went to bed early, had a brief chat with Steve and gave him a hug good night, then switched off the light.

This is easy, she thought, staring up into the darkness. I'm not sad. I feel OK. Maybe I never loved him.

And then, at 3 a.m., she woke up feeling as though someone had stuck a knife into her heart. She ached for Archie's body. She longed to reach out and feel his hair, the curve of his shoulders, feel him giving her a sleepy kiss. *Remember Anita's words*, she kept telling herself. *He's an arrogant prick.* But her heart wailed back in protest, *I don't care. I love him. Love doesn't make any sense. I want him.* She switched on the light and reached out blindly for the phone, about to key in his number. Then she felt a ghostly hand gently take it away.

Dina cried for an hour whilst Steve held her in his arms, and then went back to sleep again. 'You need time to heal, Dina,' he whispered.

But though Dina's heart did finally begin to heal, she felt listless. She found herself going into newsagents and masochistically flicking through the gossip columns in society magazines and finding, inevitably, pictures of Archie with his arm around Heidi, or some other blonde. It was horrible how quickly she was forgotten, how easily she was replaced as 'Archie's latest love interest', how dispensable the columns made her feel. Christmas came, then New Year. Anita invited a few guys over for a festive gathering; they snapped crackers, shared jokes, sipped wine and watched the same old repeats on TV whilst working their way through about six boxes of Quality Street. But Dina felt as though she was just going through the motions. She had arranged to pay back Archie's loan by borrowing from her parents, and though her mother kept telling her she needn't return the money, Dina was determined.

After New Year, she managed to get some temping work. She sat in an office, answering the phone, watching the minute hand inch round the clock. She didn't have lunch with the other temps; she felt too raw, too antisocial. *What was I doing this time last year?* she asked herself. *I was stuck in The Greasy Spoon, going nowhere.* It was as though she'd come full circle. She realised that her relationship with Archie had been like wearing an amazing designer dress when you were fat. It might sparkle and shimmer, but the moment you took it off, you realised your figure was still in a right old state. Archie had made her forget, for a while, that she had no purpose in life.

Not that a job waitressing at Pizza Express was really a purpose in life, thought Dina, as she glared down at her application again. But she felt it would be more fun than just being stuck in an office. At least she'd be dealing with people and food, two things she enjoyed. And at least it was more permanent.

Suddenly rage and frustration swallowed her up. She picked up the application, ready to tear it into tiny pieces, when suddenly a cool hand shot out and pulled it away from her.

'*Steve!*' she cried. 'Stop creeping up on me like that.'

'Sorry,' said Steve, smiling, 'but I thought you could use a hand. Want me to write it for you?'

'I'm not a baby, you know,' said Dina sulkily. 'I mean – I do know what to put – I just can't spell it.' She knew she was being churlish when Steve was offering his help, but that was just her mood. The mood she'd been in ever since breaking up with Archie, in fact.

'I know, I know,' said Steve, as patient as ever. 'You tell me what you want to put, and I'll do the spelling. You're the real brains, my dear. Now – what about extracurricular activities? I guess you'll want to put down about your caring job at the local old folk's home, your love of bungee jumping and other dangerous sports.'

Dina giggled and flicked her rubber at him.

'You are crazy, Steve. OK. Put down that I enjoy contacting ghosts in my spare time; that'll make them sit up. No? Maybe not. OK . . .'

Twenty-five minutes later the application was done and dusted and being slid into a crisp brown envelope.

'I'll go and post it,' said Dina.

'I have to go and see Harrison,' said Steve. 'See you around.' He gave her a brief, chilly hug and then he was gone.

Thank God for Steve, Dina thought as she left the flat and took a walk to the postbox. *If it hadn't been for him, I just couldn't have survived these last few months.*

Dina had been aware that something tender had been blossoming between them, but her break-up with Archie had withered it instantly. Their roles had changed: Steve had had to become her counsellor and confidant. Sometimes Dina felt guilty when she thought of how many hours she spent talking to him, pulling apart her relationship with Archie like a patchwork quilt and examining every detail endlessly. But Steve was wonderful. He listened. He made her laugh. At night when she lay awake crying, he sang silly songs to her to get her giggling, and then softer songs to help her drop off. She woke every morning to find a mug of tea and a KitKat by her bed. He visited her when she was bored in the office and made silly models out of paperclips or helped her to survive her irritating boss by doing spot-on impressions of his terse Yorkshire-accented commands ('Dina, I asked for milk in my coffee – have you heard of the liquid that comes from cows?'). He made her feel as though she wasn't alone, that she had one person in the world whom she could always turn to, always rely on.

Dina posted the job application, then crossed the road, rubbing her hands, which were pink and sore with cold. She was dying for a cup of tea and the thought suddenly struck her: *Why not go to The Greasy Spoon?* After all, she'd been meaning to pop in for ages and have a laugh.

All the same, she felt butterflies in her stomach when she pushed open the door and stepped inside. How would Luigi react? She was half afraid he would shout at her, still smarting from the wig incident. But to her surprise and delight, when Luigi spotted her, he put down his jug of frothy milk and flung his arms around her. For all his faults, he had a big heart.

'Dina!' he cried. 'This is so wonderful! You have been away for so long! Why did you not come back to visit your old Luigi?'

Dina smiled as he pinched her cheek and then shouted to Fatima to get her a cappuccino.

'You're serving *cappuccinos* now?' Dina cried. 'Wow, Luigi, I'm very impressed.'

Luigi failed to notice her slightly tongue-in-cheek tone. Instead, he muttered something that sounded like, 'They won't last long,' then made a fuss of finding her a nice, non-creaky seat by the window, clearing aside the tatty remnants of yesterday's copy of *The Sun.* Fatima brought her drink over with a broad grin. Dina tried not to laugh – or, more importantly, spit out – when she took a mouthful of the cappuccino. She wasn't convinced there was much coffee in it. Maybe a lot of sewage water. Possibly even some milk past its sell-by-date. But not much coffee. Still, it was the thought that counted and all that.

'So how is your band going, Fatima?' Dina asked.

'I think I might sing full-time,' said Fatima, 'now that this place is closing down.'

'You're closing down?' Dina asked in shock.

Poor Luigi, tears trembling on his black lashes, brought over a newspaper article and placed it in front of Dina.

GREASY SPOON FORCED TO CLOSE

The owners of The Greasy Spoon on Uxbridge Road have announced that the café will have to close after twenty years of cheering locals with their infamous hot dogs and Mars bars in batter.

The announcement came soon after restaurateur Archie

Hamilton bought the empty sandwich bar down the road. 'Though we have many devoted customers, we feel that the competition will be too strong for us to continue running,' said Luigi, founder and manager of the Spoon.

Eyebrows were raised at news that Hamilton planned to open a branch of his 'exquisite' chain of restaurants, which are renowned for their expensive cuisine and celebrity clientele. Hamilton said, 'I feel that with the recent increase in local house prices, the area is on the up. My goal is to bring a bit of glamour to Shepherd's Bush.'

'This Archie Hamilton! He's the one who wrote that evil review!' Luigi cried, obviously feeling persecuted. 'And now he closes me down!'

'But hang on,' said Dina, her voice shaking, realising that it was her suggestion that Archie was taking advantage of, 'you don't have to close down. You can fight! You can have two cafés in one road.'

Luigi shook his head sadly.

'We can't survive. Business has been bad as it is – this is the last straw. I thought the cappuccinos would save the day. I said to Fatima, I said to my wife, if we serve these amazing cappuccinos, our spoon will be full! But though our cappuccinos are the best in London, it is not enough! That Archie has money and he has—'

'Er, Luigi,' Fatima interjected, 'I think Dina might actually know Archie—'

'No, it's OK,' said Dina quickly, blushing and frowning at the article, frankly rather relieved that Luigi had forgotten about her connection with Archie.

A crowd of customers came in and Luigi and Fatima had to excuse themselves to take more orders – mostly for tea, despite Luigi's vigorous speech upholding the merits of his new espresso machine.

Dina looked down at the article, anger churning in her chest. OK, so Luigi was bonkers and didn't know the first thing about food, but he'd owned this place for twenty years and was genuinely dedicated to it. And, above all, Archie had quite clearly stolen her brilliant idea. It had been Dina who had spotted the empty shop. Life was too unfair.

She wished that she could interpret Archie's actions as pure revenge. Then she could have got even madder. But she knew that he wouldn't have thrown away thousands trying to wind her up. She wasn't that special. Archie was simply a good businessman. He'd probably forgotten the idea was even hers. He had seen an opening and taken it, without giving her a second thought.

Her anger came and went in waves. She longed for Steve to turn up so that she could vent it at him, but he was nowhere to be seen. Then she felt a flash of guilt. Perhaps she'd been venting a bit too much on Steve lately. Perhaps she'd been taking him for granted. She must do something to make him realise just how much she valued their friendship, how much his support meant to her.

An hour passed; they snatched a little more gossip; Fatima brought over a cup of espresso, which Dina discovered was a cupful of black sludge and appeared to have been shovelled from the tar on the road outside. She sat and sipped politely and glanced around The Greasy Spoon, watching people. There was a mother with her baby boy in her lap, laughing and tutting at him as he tried to grab the salt and pepper pots with his pudgy fingers and sprinkle them into her tea. There was a group of paint-splattered builders who were laughing raucously at a rude joke.

It struck Dina that even though The Greasy Spoon was universally awful, and greasy, and the drinks had, unbelievably, got even worse, the reason people did keep coming back was because it was comfy. Everyone was completely relaxed. Everyone was just being themselves.

She made a mental comparison with Archie's restaurants. They might have been a hundred times more beautiful than The Greasy Spoon, but everyone in them had been as stiff as cardboard cut-outs. Everyone had been on their guard, watching everyone else, worried that they might say the wrong thing, that they might be wearing an outfit which was last season, that the person on the next table had more money than them or a girlfriend with bigger tits. Archie was wrong: nobody cared about his chefs' amazing cooking. They just went to measure their place in the hierarchy of their small world. Nobody was truly happy; sure, they had all climbed a precipice of success, but they were teetering nervously at the top, terrified of the drop they might slide back down.

She watched the mother plant a kiss on the top of her son's head.

The little boy waved at Dina, and Dina smiled and waved back. And a glow of wisdom and happiness flowed through her. She felt shaky with her epiphany. She jumped up and went over to Luigi and asked him there and then if she could take over The Greasy Spoon.

OK. Don't panic. Heads you do it. Tails you don't.

Dina tossed the pound coin, watching sunlight fracture off it in arrows of gold. It tumbled . . . tumbled . . . and then suddenly a hand shot out and caught it. Steve.

'Oh God! Steve! I was wondering where you were. I've just done something crazy. *Really* crazy.'

'You told the Pizza Express guys that you'll only work for fifty quid an hour?'

'Worse. I'm going to run The Greasy Spoon.'

'*What!*'

'Luigi wants to retire and I'm going to run The Greasy Spoon for him. I mean, obviously it's not going to stay a greasy spoon – it's going be a café. But . . . *but* . . .'

'But, Dina, that's fantastic news!'

'Is it?' Dina sat on her bed and tried to put into words what had happened to her. When she'd been sitting in The Greasy Spoon, when she'd decided to go for it, she'd been overwhelmed by an uncharacteristically clear sense of decision and purpose. It was the dream she'd been nurturing; life was offering it to her on a plate, telling her to take this golden opportunity. As she walked home, listening to birds in the trees singing as though hoping to egg spring on, she felt a glorious optimism in her soul. She felt like whirling around and yelling: *See, Archie! See that I can have a life without you? I'm going to run a café, so ha! Fucking waitress indeed – I'm going to have my own place!*

But, over the last few hours, doubts had begun to rush in. Her old indecision gripped her.

'I mean,' she gabbled to Steve, 'I mean – it's crazy, isn't it? I've never run a café before. I don't know anything about health and safety, nothing.'

'You're a brilliant cook. We'll just phone up the right people and find it all out. We'll learn as we go along.'

'But what if it's not meant to be? I mean, earlier today I thought it was all a big coincidence that I happened to be in The Greasy Spoon just when Luigi was talking of selling up, right? I thought, this must be meant to be. But what if I'm fooling myself? I thought Archie was meant to be, and look what happened there.'

'Don't worry about meant to be,' said Steve forcefully. 'Dina, make your own luck, your own decision. Just go for it.'

Dina suddenly burned with fury, tears in her eyes.

'I hate you!' she burst out. 'You're going to make me take over The Greasy Spoon and it's going to be a huge failure!'

'No,' said Steve, 'you're going to run The Greasy Spoon and it's going to be called Dina's and everyone in London will know your name, it'll be so big.'

Steve smiled as she sobbed, and stroked her hair. 'That's it, let it all out.'

'You're right, it *will* be great,' she said, with a flash of fierceness that made Steve's heart sing – a flash of the old Dina. She stood up, wiping away her tears. 'Why am I being so down on myself? We'll repaint the place. We'll have real sandwiches – ciabatta, not those crappy pathetic excuses for bread that Luigi has. We'll have muffins! And cakes! And proper espressos! We're going to make this happen!'

Steve grinned and spread open his arms. Dina flew into them, hugging him breathlessly.

'So, are you going to be my partner?' Dina whispered into his ear.

'I don't think you can really put a dead person's name down on the application, Dina,' Steve whispered back, blushing at her proximity.

'But we'll be D&S,' said Dina. 'That's what I'll call the café. Not Dina's. But D&S. Nobody will know what it stands for, just us. It'll be our secret.'

'Dina, I – I—'

'After all you've done for me, how could it be anything else?' said Dina. Steve wrapped his arms around her tightly and they held each other for some time, their souls sparkling with expectation.

27
Dina

Dina let out a deep breath and wrote three names at the top of her pad, her forehead wrinkling with indecision:

Paul Henry Amanda

She chewed the tip of her pen, then got up and decided to make herself a cup of tea. As the water in the kettle bubbled to boiling point, she felt a smile stretching across her lips. And it struck her as she stood there, doing something as mundane as making a cup of PG Tips, that despite the fact that she was dog-tired, that she'd been working twelve hours a day for the last week, that her knees ached and her back was buggered, she was happy. She grinned again. Life, she thought, had finally come good.

Well, almost.

The last three months had been the busiest, craziest and most exciting that she'd ever experienced in her whole life. She and Luigi had gone into joint ownership together. Dina would be the café manager; Fatima would retain her position as a waitress; Luigi would pop in from time to time to give them inspiration. Dina agreed, rather dubiously, insisting that she should have full creative control over the menu. Luigi pointed out that he had just introduced a wonderful new range of cappuccinos and they ought to stick to his famous Italian recipes because food was in his blood. Dina pointed out that the whole reason she was taking over the café was because Luigi's cappuccinos, as wonderful as they were, were mysteriously failing to bring in the crowds.

After several heated discussions and much cajoling from his rather more discerning wife, Luigi sulkily conceded that he wanted to retire anyway and Dina could be the boss. It transpired that Luigi had been rather careful with money over the years, and was willing to redecorate the whole café. That night, they opened a bottle of champagne and had a drunken celebration on those sticky old Formica tables. Their elation was dampened slightly when, on their way home, they saw that a gleaming scarlet sign had been newly erected on their competition's site. Luigi had given Dina six months to turn the business around. If she failed, he'd have to sell up.

Dina set to work on revamping The Greasy Spoon with so much gusto that even Steve was surprised. Overnight, she went from having the most indolent lifestyle imaginable to being a complete workaholic. She amazed Anita by going to bed at midnight and getting up at 5 a.m., raring to go. Only Steve realised that it was Dina's way of expunging her grief. By channelling every drop, every thought into the café, she finally managed to forget Archie.

They got in a team of builders to redo the place, and in the mean time, Dina and Steve spent their days in the kitchen in Anita's flat, trying out recipes and creating a menu that customers would find both healthy and indulgent. They had the time of their lives. They experimented with all sorts of sandwiches and ciabattas, ranging from the conventional to the downright bizarre (though Dina insisted that Steve's raspberry jam and mustard on brown bread was simply not going to make the final cut, and he was equally scathing about her carrot and jello cake).

Then came the day that they all gathered in the café to see the final transformation. For about five minutes, nobody said anything. They just stood there, gaping. The disgusting yellow lino had been replaced by sparkling diamond-shaped tiles that lay in zig-zags of yellow and blue. The walls were now sky blue. The counter was cream and complete with a shiny black cappuccino machine and a long line of mugs with the D&S logo swirling across the side in blue letters. The windows, which had previously been more smear than glass, were now glitteringly opaque. Outside it began to rain, and the drops slithered down the glass like liquid crystal, highlighting its new-found cleanliness. Dina was so overwhelmed that she let out a huge whoop. Then Luigi's wife burst into tears and Fatima burst into song. Only Luigi, Dina noticed, was rather quiet.

'Well?' she asked him gently. 'D'you like it?'

'I kind of liked it the old way,' he sighed, 'but yes – it is not bad. Not bad at all.'

Now Dina was sitting in D&S, sipping her tea. She yawned and stretched irritably, and looked at her watch. 4.30 p.m. She had to make a decision about who to hire.

As well as Fatima, they needed more staff to fill the afternoon and Saturday shifts. Dina had been conducting interviews all day. At first she'd found it a wonderful novelty to actually be giving an interview rather than going to one. Then, after her initial high, she'd realised that the applicants were more than a little disappointing. The first had been painfully shy, the second completely uninterested in food. The third might not have been so bad if Steve hadn't appeared and kept making Dina laugh by making expressive faces and saying, 'God, you can't hire her, Dina, she makes Queen Victoria look uptight!' She'd spent the whole interview suppressing explosive giggles and the interviewee had clearly thought she was mad.

'Right, Steve,' she'd giggled crossly, pointing at the door. 'Out! I can't carry on like this! Go off with Harrison and have fun messing about with people's keys and pulling their flies down.'

Steve had given her a sheepish, apologetic kiss on the cheek and exited meekly.

Now Dina was feeling in a more sober mood as she pondered the problem. She knew that she was in a Catch-22 situation. It was going to be hard finding someone good. A job working in a café was hardly going to bring a big salary and company car and benefits. But Dina couldn't help it: she wanted perfection; she wanted this café to be the best café in the world, and she wanted the best assistant to help her.

Someone who understood the simple importance of saying 'please' and 'thank you'.

Someone with such a beaming smile that customers would leave the café floating in a rosy glow of good cheer.

Someone who could turn up on time and understand that an appointment at 2.30 p.m. didn't mean you could arrive at three, as the last candidate had.

Still, she'd arranged another set of interviews for tomorrow – maybe they would yield the perfect employee. Now it was time for an afternoon break. Dina decided to go to the Coffee Parlour down the road and get a cinnamon bun. That was one of the very cool things about opening your own café. It gave you the perfect excuse to eat in other cafés and pretend it was research. And cinnamon buns, Dina felt, were a *very* important way of checking out the competition.

She had just pulled on her coat when a figure blurred behind the glass and the shop door tinkled.

'Um, hi,' said Dina.

A girl was standing in front of her. She looked about twenty-one, twenty-two. She had dyed shoulder-length hair, bright and gleaming as a red setter's coat. Her eyeliner was so heavy it could have been worn by an Egyptian princess. She was wearing a long, tasselled tie-dye skirt covered with swirls of green, purple and ochre, and a sleeveless black T-shirt advertising some punk band. A tattoo of a dolphin adorned her arm and a stud gleamed in her nose.

Despite her rather intimidating appearance, there was something familiar about her face that Dina warmed to instantly.

'Hi – I was just wondering if I could, ah, look around,' she said.

'Well – it's not exactly the Tate,' Dina said, grinning uneasily.

The girl put down her little khaki rucksack on a table and glanced around.

'I was just walking past and I noticed that the place looked different,' she said in a slightly shaky voice.

'Yep, I've taken it over,' Dina said proudly. Then, to her amazement, tears welled in the girl's eyes, threatening to turn her eyeliner into black rivulets. And Dina clicked. 'Rachel? God – I'm sorry – you must think I'm so rude, acting like you're a complete stranger.'

Rachel nodded, smiling through her tears and fingering her hair self-consciously.

'Yeah, I know I look a bit different.'

She certainly did. Dina had met Steve's younger sister, Rachel, a few times in the past. Back then, she had had dark hair tied back in a ponytail and a fresh, shiny face. Now, she seemed to have grown up overnight; it wasn't just the copious make-up, but the slightly cynical, guarded air.

'I saw you at the funeral,' said Rachel, biting her lip. She was fighting very hard to keep her tears inside her and was clearly ashamed of them, prompting Dina to hold back the urge to give her a hug. 'Sorry I didn't come up, but I was just a bit . . . y'know . . . I hate funerals, everyone saying *I'm sorry* a hundred times and . . . and . . . but anyway. I loved the reading you did. 'Dirge Without Music'. It was the most beautiful thing I'd ever heard and so, so true.'

I am not resigned to the shutting away of loving hearts in the hard ground.
So it is, and so it will be, for so it has been, time out of mind:
Into the darkness they go, the wise and the lovely.
Crowned with lilies and with laurel they go: but I am not resigned

Dina recited softly. She broke off, realising she had lost herself.

'So,' she went on, keen to change the subject, 'what are you up to these days? Sorry – d'you want a cup of tea and a muffin? Sit down, I'll bring them over.'

After Dina had brought the tea, Rachel explained, 'Well, I was mostly, y'know, bumming around, helping out at the animal rescue centre down the road. I'm still living at home, but now I'm just planning to go to college and start an art and media course, two days a week, and combine it with a part-time job so I have some "pocket money", as my parents put it.' Rachel rolled her eyes. 'I think most of the time they forget I'm twenty-three and imagine I'm still twelve.'

'That's why parents are so wonderful and so annoying,' said Dina, grinning. She opened her mouth and then closed it. As Rachel had been talking, an exciting idea had ignited in her mind. Inwardly, she tossed the idea like a coin: *Shall I, shan't I, shall I?* Then she burst out, 'Look, I know this is out of the blue, but why don't you work here? I've got a part-time post and I just can't find anyone decent to fill it.'

'Here?' Rachel stopped in mid-chew.

Suddenly Dina feared she'd been walking on eggshells and crudely smashed them. Maybe this place held too many memories; maybe she'd just made a terrible faux pas.

But then Rachel suddenly smiled – a big, beaming, chuffed smile, and said, 'Why not?'

When she smiles like that, Dina mused, *she stops looking scary and suddenly looks quite sweet.*

'But,' said Rachel, looking troubled, 'to be honest, I was kind of avoiding waitressing stuff because – well, look, to be frank, I'm a strict vegetarian and I just can't handle meat.'

'Oh, that's fine, Fatima can do that,' said Dina. 'There'll still be plenty for you to handle – you can do the drinks stuff.' She paused. 'So I take it you've no experience at all in catering?'

'Nope,' said Rachel, looking a bit sheepish. 'So I'm not really sure if—'

'It's fine,' said Dina hastily. 'We'll train you, we can all work together. Don't worry – it's going to be great. We'll be a great team!' She broke off, seeing the doubt on Rachel's face. She suddenly realised Rachel was looking for obstacles, making excuses. 'Sorry – maybe it's a bad idea—'

'No,' said Rachel quickly. 'I mean – I'm flattered that you've asked me. I mean, is it OK if I think about it and call you?'

'Of course,' said Dina. 'Of course.'

After Rachel had gone, Dina cleared away their plates, suddenly suffering indecision again. Had she been insensitive to offer Rachel the job, knowing Rachel would have to return to the very place Steve had worked? And if Rachel did accept it . . . well, was Dina being crazy, hiring Rachel when she really wasn't all that well qualified? Even some of the more dubious candidates today had had more experience compared to Rachel's stint in her animal sanctuary. *Great, Dina,* she told herself, *so the next time a wounded hedgehog comes into the café and orders a cappuccino, Rachel will know just what to do with it. And oh, as for her not being able to handle meat – what a bonus.*

She argued back fiercely that it was better she worked with

people she knew and liked, in order to have a good team to support her. But deep down, she knew why she was so keen on Rachel.

She was hiring her because she had seen Steve in Rachel's face, a familiarity in the curve of her eyebrow, the shape of her cheek, the way she laughed, her tone of voice. An echo of genes. And Dina knew that that was the attraction; having Rachel around her made her feel closer to Steve, to the real Steve she'd once known.

And as for Steve – what was he going to say when he found out Dina was hoping to hire his kid sister?

28
Rachel

Rachel left the café in a strange, churned-up mood. She couldn't face the walk home and, seeing a bus a few feet away about to depart from its stop, she ran down to it, banging on the doors and forcing the irate driver to open them and let her in.

She climbed upstairs and sat at the front, her bag strap wrapped tight around her hand. *Why did you do that?* she kept asking herself. *Why didn't you just say yes to Dina? God, how many crappy job interviews have you failed in the last week?*

Quite a few. There had been that interview at the art shop she'd screwed up by turning up half an hour late. And the part-time one at the library post, though, God, the elderly woman there had just looked her up and down with pinched lips and Rachel had known then that she hadn't got the job. And she'd felt so hurt and incensed that she reacted as she always did when she felt miffed: her hackles had stiffened and she'd gone on the defensive and made cheeky remarks about the library being full of geriatric staff and perhaps they ought to lend zimmer frames as well as books. Back home, her mother had given her a lecture: *Don't go looking for a fight, Rachel, like you always do. Don't get a chip on your shoulder. Remember, they actually want to give someone a job.* Rachel winced at the thought. She knew she could come across as aggressive and moody at times, but it seemed to her that people never bothered to look beneath the surface. And here was Dina, who hadn't batted an eyelid at her tattoos and had been warm and generous and welcoming and—

Rachel felt a tear creep out of the corner of her eye and run down her nose. She brushed it away fiercely, sniffing.

It just felt so strange, being in that place, she whispered to herself. *Even though it's all freshly painted and spanking new now, it's still the place he walked into every day. It's as though his laughter and conversation are still there, simmering in the walls. I can see a coat hook which must have once held his anorak. And I wonder: what would Steve think? I mean, I don't believe in ghosts or any of that shit, but am I somehow being disloyal to him, taking a job he should have had?*

Feeling vexed, she got off the bus and dragged herself down the road to home. In the kitchen her mum was cooking up a huge dinner.

'Rachel!' She rubbed her hands on a tea towel, fluffing up her perm excitedly. 'How did it go, love?'

'I got a job at a café,' said Rachel sullenly, picking an almond off the trifle on the sideboard.

'Well, that's great.'

'Yeah,' Rachel said. 'But I don't know I'm going to take it yet.'

'Why on earth not?' Her mother sighed in exasperation as Rachel walked out. Then there was the stomp of her feet on the stairs and the slam of her bedroom door. Her mother sighed and stirred the sauce she was making.

Upstairs in her room, Rachel put on Radiohead and slumped on her bed. She picked up her diary, which also served as a sketchbook and doodling pad, and drew a picture of Dina with soft strokes, capturing her curly-haired beauty. There. She always felt better when she drew, as though all her emotions, her anger and hate and fear and confusion and general paranoia, slid out through her pencil and fizzled out on the page. The sense of release was better than any drink or drugs; the only time she ever felt at peace with herself was just after she had finished a picture, when she sat staring at her creation and marvelling that she had this one gift, this one thing in life that she was truly good at.

The CD player made a whirring noise as Radiohead came to a halt. Rachel put down her pencil, scowling. She figured she ought to go down and apologise to her mum. She let out a sigh. She didn't much like living at home. She knew that it wasn't unusual for a twenty-three-year-old to be living with her parents. Rachel tended to gravitate towards older people and most of her friends at college were mature students; hell, she knew some guys who were *thirty* and still living at home. It was the inevitable result of top-up fees, rising house prices and an explosion in personal debt. Personally, she would have liked to move out and get her own place, even if it meant doing a second job in a bar at weekends. For Rachel was fiercely independent and had such a strong sense of privacy that her friends teased her about being secretive, a girl who liked to keep her cards close to her chest.

But the real reason that Rachel was still living at home was because of Steve.

It had been over a year since her older brother had died and Rachel had just about come to terms with his death. She was an atheist and accepted that life was unpredictable and often harsh. Yet the paradox of their relationship never failed to puzzle her: *Here is a guy,* she would muse, *who I've shared bunk beds with, who I've sat up until midnight telling ghost stories to, who I've climbed trees with.* And yet, when he'd died, he'd virtually been a stranger. She had no idea if he'd had a girlfriend, what his hopes were, what his fears were.

The other major thing that had changed since Steve's death was that Rachel had been forced to grow up overnight. Suddenly her parents were no longer invincible gods who fed and clothed and loved her unconditionally; they became human, fragile, damaged, needing support and love as much as she did. And so Rachel stayed home because she privately felt that they needed looking after, because she saw how much comfort her presence gave them. The trouble was, now that Steve had gone, she felt such a weight of responsibility on her. When they were teenagers, Steve and Rachel had joked that, unlike other siblings who competed to be the apple of their parents' eyes, they took it in turn to disappoint theirs. Steve getting beaten up by bullies; Rachel getting expelled from St Catherine's Girls' for smoking pot; Steve ditching his brilliant law job; Rachel declaring she wanted to be a drop-out and join the gypsies.

She had been serious about the gypsy idea. She wasn't ambitious and loathed the idea of the rat race, of having to keep up with the Joneses, of spending your life sweating just so that you could go to a cocktail party and boast about how much you'd achieved. When

Steve had left his city firm to work in The Greasy Spoon, she'd been filled with admiration for him. But now that he was gone, she was the only one holding the MacFadden baton. Her parents kept dropping hints about accountancy courses or management training, for crying out loud. So Rachel had compromised and signed up for the art and media course at her college.

Maybe Steve would be happy for me, she mused. *I'm sure he'd want me to get on with my life; I'm sure he'd be proud of me for finding something I love to do.* She reached for her mobile and let out a deep breath. *OK, Steve, here goes.* And as she keyed in the number, suddenly it all felt so right. *Maybe life is smiling on me after all. Maybe this is the start of something good . . .*

29
Steve

Juniper House, Steve copied neatly from the Yellow Pages. He checked the address in his trusty A–Z. Not too far from The Greasy Spoon – good.

He clicked his biro on and off for one uncertain moment. *Can I really do this?* a small voice asked uncertainly. *Can I really go through with it?*

Then he stood up, full of resolve. He had to do it. There was no other choice. Not if he wanted to keep Dina.

Steve hadn't wanted Harrison to come along. But, typically, he bumped into him halfway there.

'Hey, man, how are you? Where are you off to?'

'Oh, just walking.' Steve shrugged.

As they strolled towards Juniper House, Harrison chatted breezily and Steve silently tried to think up ways to get rid of him and failed miserably.

'What the hell are we doing here?' Harrison asked, as they slipped through the black railings.

Steve ignored him and marched into the building via the double doors, following a woman wearing a white lab coat. Her auburn hair was tied in a coil of plait and her frosted fingernails were curled around a clipboard. Steve flicked a look at the plastic signposts on the wall and noticed she was heading towards AUTOPSIES. Well, that sounded promising.

They followed her down the corridor, through another set of double doors, and into a small room. There was an elderly man laid out on a table, withered as a dead bird. A man with a goatee beard was just pulling on a pair of blue rubber gloves and rattling a tray of scary, tortuous-looking metal implements. Harrison grimaced. Steve felt rather queasy.

'Where are the bodies?' Steve muttered.

'Steve, what the hell is this all about?' Harrison asked.

Steve didn't reply. The auburn-haired woman was again proving useful. She went into an adjoining room which seemed to be filled with lockers, each with a neatly labelled lozenge detailing name and date of death. Harrison started, but Steve silenced him. He watched the woman take out a set of keys from her pocket and open one of the lockers. A black body bag slid out on a metal tray. She unzipped the top. Out popped a head, shocking: a man with gingery hair and a drooping moustache. She checked his file, then made a note on her clipboard.

Then she zipped up the bag and slid him back into darkness.

As she walked past them, Steve stood close to her and flicked his hand into her lab coat, pulling out her keys. He quickly slipped them into his own pocket. Hearing the jingle, she stopped, frowning, looking round, frowning some more. Steve and Harrison stood very still. She shrugged and went on, heels clicking like gun shots. They stayed still, listening to her chatting in the next room with the man with the blue rubber gloves.

'God, it's a long day.' A yawn, the click of her neck as she stretched. 'I'm going to make some coffee, want a cup?'

'That'd be lovely. Three sugars, thanks, and no milk.'

'Sure thing.'

Harrison looked straight at Steve.

Steve could tell from the look on his face that he'd twigged.

'Steve, I think I know what you're about to do and I think it's very sick.'

'Oh come on, Harrison. Don't tell me the idea hasn't crossed your mind at some point.'

'Yeah, sure. Every ghost thinks that thought. But you have to face the fact that your body is now just a skeleton lying in a coffin. And that's final.'

'But Dina,' Steve said. His voice caught and he gulped. 'I've got to do something. Look, Harrison, tomorrow is the opening day for D&S. I want it to be really special. It's just . . .' Steve swallowed; he wasn't very good at expressing his emotions and he had to squeeze them out, his heart contracting with every word. 'It's just . . .'

'I thought you and Dina were really hitting it off, man,' said Harrison. 'You've given her all that help and support with the café thing. Come on, it's obvious how grateful she is.'

'Is she?' Steve demanded. 'I don't know, Harrison. I just feel that she doesn't fancy me. It's like the old days. Yeah, I'm giving her a lot of support, but I'm not sure she's even really noticing, she's so wrapped up in the café opening. I don't blame her for that – God, I want it to be a big success, and that's the point. I've worked bloody hard on this café too and tomorrow I'm just going to have to stand around in the background, keeping quiet, not being able to talk to Dina, not being able to congratulate her until everyone else has gone. And for once, I just want to be able to *talk.* To be there. In person, in human form, to be able to enjoy it like everyone else.'

'OK, OK, Steve, but I still think she does fancy you. I can tell by the way she looks at you. I really think she likes you as you are—'

'But it can never be real, can it! How the fuck can it ever be real? How can someone really love a person they can't even see properly?'

Harrison didn't have an answer to that one.

'D'you remember,' said Steve in a brittle voice, 'that conversation we had, about reality and fantasy, about how much easier it is to live in fantasy land? Well, this is it, Harrison. It's a fantasy to ever imagine Dina and I can be together. How can we be? I'm just living an illusion, I'm telling myself this lie every day that something's building between us, that something *might* just happen. But it's bullshit. The only way Dina can ever love me is if I have a body.'

They had to wait another hour or so, until the woman and the man had gone home and clicked off the lights, until the building quietened and there was just the occasional sound of footsteps, a cleaner humming, doors swinging.

Steve, who had been sitting on the floor, head slumped against the metal locker of a *Mrs J. Sullivan, death by drowning*, got up. He spread out the keys in a fan on his palm. They were soon damp with sweat. His heart was hammering.

'Are you really sure about this?' Harrison asked. He was sitting cross-legged on the floor. 'I mean – maybe you should try the body of a woman. Hey, you can be a celestial transvestite!'

'Shut up, Harrison,' said Steve in a trembling voice. 'I'm absolutely one hundred per cent sure, OK?'

He slotted the keys into a lock and slid out a metal tray. The zip snagged and caught when he tried to slide it open. He cursed and tugged it free.

The man stared up at him from his shroud of plastic. Steve gazed down. There was a slackness in the man's face, as though he was truly resting in peace. Steve felt jealousy in his stomach, sharp as bile. How had this man got to go to heaven? Why wasn't Steve lolling about in beautiful fields listening to harps instead of spending his days wandering about Shepherd's Bush? Death simply wasn't fair.

Suddenly all his doubts dissolved and he was filled with resolve. *I'm going to do this,* he thought. *Right now.*

Last night, he'd gone to see Jether. He'd expected him to be angry, or shocked, or repulsed by the idea, but he had just sat calmly and nodded. Surely it must be OK; if it was the wrong idea, Jether would have told him. Indeed, he'd given Steve precise instructions and his only caveat was *Take care. Choose your body carefully.*

Steve slid into the bag, into the body. He felt his soul pass through the layers of skin and muscle and bone. He lay still inside the body.

It felt strange. As though he'd been walking about naked and suddenly he'd put on clothes. Or he'd been out in the snow for a long time and entered a warm house. He gazed up at the closed eyelids, at the roots of the man's eyelashes: ginger flecked with gold. Suddenly he felt a spurt of happiness. Steve hated lots of things about his body, but most of all he'd always hated his eyelashes, which were too long and girlie for his liking. This man's eyelashes were short and stubby and manly. Steve closed his eyes and wriggled about, feeling his soul spread out, seep into arms and legs, connect with cells. He sensed the man was a bit shorter than him – the legs were a tight fit, but once he got used to that, he felt fine.

Jether had said: *Remember, bodies are just houses for souls to live in. Believe that you own your new body and you will.*

But suddenly he felt afraid. What if when he tried to get up he just slid out of the ginger man's body and found himself a ghost still?

Then again, he couldn't lie here for ever either.

He opened his eyes. The man's eyes opened too. He looked up and saw Harrison's face staring down at him with a deeply troubled expression.

'It worked!' Steve cried joyfully. He moved his jaw – he had a jaw, a proper, solid one, shot through with bone, and a wonderfully wet tongue, and hey, teeth, proper hard teeth, and – and—

It had worked. It had worked. He had a body.

'Eeek!' Harrison stepped back swiftly. 'Jesus, your breath totally stinks.'

'Well, what d'you expect? He's been lying here a few days.' Steve made to get up and banged his head on the metal edge of the locker with a loud 'Ouch!' He was used to a shadowy existence, to being able to slither through any substance. Suddenly his world had become sharp and full of dangerous edges. 'Can you unzip me? I'm actually stuck in this bag thing.' He wriggled his feet, feeling the edges of the plastic.

'Jeez, Steve, I don't know. I mean, I think you're going to have to suck a whole packet of Extra Strong Mints. Dina is hardly going to be impressed. She'll run a mile.'

'Come on, all I need is a dash of toothpaste and I'll be fine.'

'Nah,' said Harrison, on reflection, 'I think it's better that you stay put. As a service to mankind, because you smell so bad I think you count as a new kind of pollution.' He giggled as Steve growled. 'OK, OK. So I'm exaggerating. Let's unzip you.'

He pulled the metal tray out as far as it would go, unzipping the body bag.

'We're going to have to get you some clothes,' he added, wincing as he revealed a naked body covered in little gingery hairs. 'Oh my God.'

'What?' Steve demanded. '*What?*'

But Harrison was laughing much too hard to reply.

Steve rolled his eyes at Harrison – how good it was to feel them moving in their sockets – and clambered down. The lino felt wonderfully solid beneath his feet. He felt a breeze tickle over the hairs on his chest, moving them lightly. Bliss.

'What's so funny?' he demanded. Suddenly panic rippled through him. Had he chosen a naff body?

'It just gets better and better,' Harrison spluttered, rolling about on the floor. 'You have ginger pubes . . . *ginger pubes* . . .' He lost his voice again in a spiral of laughter.

Ginger pubes? Steve glanced down. Oh. So they were. Still – he was well hung, he noted with a flush. Much bigger than he'd ever been.

'There's nothing wrong with ginger,' Steve spluttered. 'Don't be a gingerist.' He spun around, saw a thin oblong of mirror pinned to the wall at the end of the lockers. He leapt in front of it, surveying himself.

'Hey, I'm OK!' he cried in triumphant delight. 'Well, I think so anyway.'

He *was* OK. Staring back at him was a tall man with closely cropped ginger hair. He was quite handsome, with a freckled face and a crooked, rather sexy grin.

'Steve!' He felt Harrison's clammy hand on his shoulder. 'Can you hear that?'

Steve paused. A sound of footsteps. Clicky footsteps. High heels. They sounded as though they belonged to the woman who had been here earlier . . .

'She can't see me!' Steve said automatically, and then he realised. 'She *can* see me! Help, Harrison!'

'Get back into the tray!' Harrison hissed.

'But I'll suffocate!'

'It'll just be for a few minutes. Now get in!'

Steve clambered back into the tray, pulling the body bag up around him.

The footsteps grew louder.

Steve lay down and Harrison pulled up the zipper, leaving an inch open at the end to allow air in. He was about to shove the metal tray back in, but it was too late. The auburn-haired woman was here.

'There they are!' she cried, spotting her keys hanging from the lock. Then her face darkened. 'What the . . .' She frowned at the body bag. 'Did I forget . . .' She swallowed, looked around. She went back into the adjoining room. 'George?'

'George?' Harrison mimicked her voice wickedly.

Steve, his breath warm in the body bag, smothered a hot giggle, praying she'd hurry up and go away.

But she came back in, tut-tutting. She eyed up Steve's bag, noticing it wasn't zipped up, and was about to close it, then stopped. Slowly she unzipped the bag, exposing his head.

'Nigel Matthew Simmons,' she murmured, reading aloud from the label. 'OK. Well. I must have forgotten to lock you in. God, it's been a long day.'

'Nigel Simmons!' said Harrison. 'Ooh, Steve, that can be your new name!'

Steve felt a bubble of laughter pulsing up his throat. He struggled to keep his lips straight. He could feel the warmth of the woman's breath on his face, sense her leaning down over him. *Don't laugh, don't laugh,* he shouted at himself. He was biting his lip so hard now he could taste blood. But it was no good, no good, the bubble exploded and his eyes flicked open and he burst into a shriek of laughter.

The woman stared down at him, white-faced, glassy-eyed.

A second later, she had gone. There was the sound of her footsteps in the corridor, the echo of her screams.

Harrison swallowed back another giggle.

'Shit, Steve, you had better get out of here fast. If they come back and find you're alive . . .'

Steve got out of the bag.

'I mean – get out of that body, you moron! Come on, you're naked! Just turn back into a ghost, we can find another body another day. This is an emergency, Steve, get out!'

'I can't—'

'STEVE, YOU HAVE TO!'

'No – I can't! *I can't get out of the body! I'm stuck!*'

'In that case, we've got no other choice. We're going to have to make a run for it!'

30
Dina

Dina woke up suddenly, staring at the fluorescent green digits on her clock: 4.15 a.m. She reached for the plastic Volvic bottle by her bed, glugging the water down. Then, feeling the chill of the night air around her shoulders, she snuggled back under the covers in a foetal ball. At the bottom of her bed, Roger thumped his tail and went back to sleep.

She'd been woken by a horrible nightmare. Her third that night. In the first, she'd gone to the café and no customers had turned up all day. In the second, she'd checked all the muffins to discover that the chocolate chips had turned into green flecks of mould. In the third – and this was the craziest – Nancy Weiz, the bitch who'd given her a hard time at elementary school, had turned up and started taunting her with childish, sing-song insults, 'So you think you can run a café, do you?' Jesus – she hadn't thought about Nancy Weiz for years. Which showed how stressed she was.

She shut her eyes. *Go to sleep,* she ordered her brain, *and settle down. Otherwise you'll be even more exhausted and you won't be able to cope.* But within five minutes she found her rebellious eyelids springing open again. In approximately five hours' time, she'd be opening the door to her café, letting the sun sparkle over the brand-new chequered floor and greeting her very first customer.

Dina felt a plague of butterflies dance around her stomach.

The last two weeks had been incredibly demanding. Fatima and Rachel were a fun team to work with, thank God, and they'd come up with all kinds of wonderful ideas for the menus. Dina had privately nurtured doubts about Rachel, but she was rapidly turning into a close friend. Rachel, Dina had discovered, wasn't what she seemed. She was fierce on the outside but very gentle when you got to know her, and despite her whole sulky-teenager act, she was surprisingly mature and level-headed for her age. As she hadn't started her college course yet, she had been able to help Dina every day. They had gone out for several drinks together and Dina had rather drunkenly poured out the story of Archie. Rachel had listened to her with huge sympathy and given her wonderful pep talks. The only pinch Dina felt was not being able to tell her about Steve, especially when Rachel talked about him so much.

Steve had been completely freaked out at first when he'd discovered that Dina had hired Rachel as a waitress. He'd made Dina laugh by confessing, 'Every time I see her ponytail, I want to give it a tug.' But over time, he'd secretly become quite pleased to see his sister blossoming in her new job and actually enjoying something for once.

At 4.30, Dina finally gave up on sleep and got out of bed. In the living room she found a bouquet of flowers and a little card from Anita. *Good luck and try not to poison anyone on your first day,* her flatmate had scrawled cheekily. *Don't joke,* Dina thought palely, adding another worry to her list of nightmare possibilities.

She felt slightly more reassured when she called her mother for a quick chat. Then she took Roger for a long early morning walk before going to the café and opening it up. She made herself a cup of coffee and watched the sun rise. Then she checked that everything was working (twice), picked a few imaginary specks of dust from the floor and made a head-start on the sandwiches.

Steve hadn't turned up, and she felt a little hurt. She hadn't seen him last night, either.

Still, she mused, cutting some olive and rosemary bread, maybe it was her own fault. She had been neglecting him lately. Steve had been funny for the last few days. She'd sensed something building up in him, sensed he'd like a talk. But she'd just been too wrapped up in the café, too burnt out and fraught and frazzled to make time. *I must, must make time to see him alone tonight,* she told herself. *I don't want him to think in any way that I'm taking him for granted.*

At 8.30, Rachel and Fatima turned up. Feeling tense at Steve's absence, Dina gave them a rather terse lecture on customer relations. As she turned away, she saw, in the reflection of the window, Rachel making an is-Dina-being-a-moody-cow-or-what? face at her back.

'Rachel!' Dina spun back.

'Sorry sorry sorry sorry times a million,' said Rachel, putting her hand on Dina's arm. 'I just think you should relax, that's all. I mean, look' – she pointed at the huge, colourful signs in the windows screaming, 'OPENING DAY, FREE DRINKS FROM 10 a.m. to midday' – 'nobody can resist a freebie. Don't worry, they'll turn up in floods.'

Dina let out a deep breath.

Twenty minutes passed. It was now 9.15. Fifteen minutes after the café was officially open. Rachel started doodling cats on her pad. Fatima kept eyeing up the muffins like a starving dog faced with a plate of juicy sausages. Dina stood in the doorway. She so longed for Steve to be with her, just standing by her shoulder, holding her hand in his pale, cold one, making her feel, as he always did, that everything would be all right.

People strolled past. She felt like grabbing them and yanking them in. And then – Dina nearly had a heart attack – a couple came and looked at the windows *with interest.* She tried not to cry, *Please, please come in, we'll pay you to come in.* They eyed up the menu tacked to the door and had a brief, intense, whispered discussion. *What?* Dina wanted to yell. *Are the pecan and toffee twists really so controversial?* Then, to her outrage, they gave her a look that was both sheepish and bemused, smiled and walked off. *Bastards*, she felt like shouting after them, and then stopped herself.

Oh God, she wailed inside, *nobody's going to come. My café is going to be a horrible flop. This is a bad omen; I know it.*

She checked the menu. The first thing she noticed was a typo: the cranberry and maple syrup muffins were priced at £25, not £2.50. No wonder they'd walked off. Fatima had been in charge of typing the menu and putting it up. Now Dina was about to kill her.

And then she scanned the menu in full and a deep sense of

horror swept over her. She wanted to vomit. She tore it off the door and ran back into the café. Rachel dropped her pen. Fatima, who had been about to pick up a muffin, hastily dropped her hand.

'Look!' Dina screamed, holding it out.

The menu now said:

Mushroom and feta cheese panini: £35
Prawn and lettuce sandwich with lemon mayonnaise: £29
Roasted vegetable and humus panini: £450

'Oh my God!' Fatima cried. 'Dina, I swear I didn't type up those prices incorrectly.'

Rachel burst into confused giggles.

'This has nothing to do with me!' Dina howled. 'It's Archie. It's bloody Archie. It's sabotage.'

'But – that's so childish,' said Rachel. 'I mean, I thought he was meant to be a high-powered businessman or something.' She broke off, shocked. She'd always secretly felt that Dina's claims of Archie's villainousness were exaggerated. Now she saw what she was driving at.

'Yeah, well – did you see the restaurant reviews he used to write? They were childish, they were nasty, just dressed up in fancy language and given credibility by being printed in a newspaper. This is just typical, so typical of him,' Dina said, ripping the menu into shreds. 'I HATE HIM, I HATE HIM, I HATE HIM!'

'Er – Dina—' Rachel began.

'Dina!' Fatima hissed.

Dina turned to see two Chinese guys in the doorway. They looked about nervously, uncertain whether free drinks were really worth the trauma of having to cope with a hysterical proprietress.

Dina hastily composed herself. She, Rachel and Fatima all leapt forward to serve them.

'Please just sit down and relax,' said Dina. 'What can I get you? Anything you like.'

They picked up the menu cards on the table. A second later, they looked extremely bemused as Dina whipped them out of their hands.

'Ah,' she said, finding to her relief that the menus hadn't been defaced too. Thank God – even Archie wouldn't go that far. 'OK, these are fine. Right.' She passed them back. The two men exchanged raised-eyebrow what-the-hell-is-this-place glances. 'There we go. Have these.'

'They don't look very different from the ones we saw five seconds ago,' said one sarcastically.

Dina wore her smile like a label on a bottle and took their order.

The Chinese guys seemed to enjoy their food and drink, thank God. Dina found herself calming down and feeling quite sheepish about her rant about Archie. Steve had been right: time had healed her wounds and she no longer felt raw, but from time to time her anger did seem to resurface. Perhaps it wasn't so much anger at Archie as anger at herself for being foolish enough ever to have been taken in by him. When she looked back on their time together, she felt as though she was witnessing the behaviour of a stranger. Why had she been so attracted to him when he'd given her such a runaround? Why had she put up with all those dreadful rows? Why hadn't she seen the Heidi thing coming – God, there had been enough signs? How could she have been so naïve? It seemed as though her love for Archie had been a curse, making her blind to his faults. Thank God she was cured; thank God she was sane again.

She'd known that she would have to face him eventually – with his new restaurant down the road, it was inevitable. And whilst she didn't ever feel they could be friends, she'd hoped they might at least be civil to each other, like grown-ups. But no: Archie had defaced her menus and declared war.

Watching the Chinese pair leave, Dina felt alarmed again. Another hour passed and nobody came. Dina got her hopes up when a thin blonde wearing a belly-button ring came in, but it turned out she was Rachel's friend, and all she wanted was a mineral water.

Then, at around eleven thirty, three more people walked in. Five minutes later they were followed by another couple. Dina felt hope flicker in her stomach. It was going to be all right; oh thank God, it was going to be all right.

Then, at midday, the café door swung open and two people walked in.

One was a tall and rather handsome man with ginger hair who was wearing jeans and a grey jacket that was slightly too big for him.

The other was Archie Hamilton.

Dina was so shocked by the entrance of the latter that she barely registered the former. She'd been holding a pair of long silver tongs and removing three honey and chocolate muffins from the rack. At the sight of Archie, she lost her grip and one thudded to the floor in a brown splat. Beside her, Rachel's face tightened.

'Shit, he's got a nerve, coming in here,' she said. 'Shall I go and tell him to piss off?'

'No, no, don't!' Dina hissed. 'We have to act professional. That will wind him up much more.' She let out a deep shaky breath and bent down, sweeping up the muffin crumbs and stray chocolate chips, shoving them into the bin. When she stood up, she flicked her eyes in Archie's direction. He was staring at the menu as though in deep concentration. There was a smug little smile flickering on the corners of his lips. Suddenly anger erupted inside her. How dare he do this? He was hugely successful, he had millions in the bank, he had a chain of acclaimed restaurants – why turn up on the very first morning of her café's opening and do this to her? It was bad enough that he'd ruined her menus.

Suddenly she felt tired, almost defeated. She'd put so many hours, so many weeks of work into this place. It was her baby chick, and now Archie felt like some cuckoo who'd swooped in, ready to wreak havoc, to crush her darling. She felt like giving up. Flinging off her apron and walking out, and then turning to Archie and crying, 'Well – are you satisfied? Yes, my café's likely to be a failure. Yes, I feel as though I'm totally out of my depth.'

Or, better still, she'd like to take one of her large-size cappuccino mugs, fill it up to the brim with frothy milk and pour the whole lot over his head. She pictured it soaking into the seams of his Jermyn Street suit, and smiled.

Then she shook herself. This wasn't a movie and she couldn't go around behaving like that. Nor could she walk out. Everyone was depending on her. She had to be strong and handle this. This was her first test, her first trial, her first challenge. Suddenly it felt very important that she pull herself together and get through it.

Oh Steve, she begged him silently. *Why aren't you here to help me through this?*

'I'll serve him,' she said aloud. 'Fatima – can you take these muffins to Table Three? Thanks. Right. I'll go.'

She picked up her pad. She was about to walk towards him when he turned and looked at her. Suddenly he was in her soul, in her body, making love to her, kissing her. Then he was screaming, his face up close to hers, telling her it was all over. She began to shake.

'Rachel,' she said in a small voice, 'can you do it?'

'Sure,' said Rachel, her eyes gleaming. 'I tell you what, I have an idea.'

Dina had confided every detail of her relationship with Archie to Rachel. Including the first night that he'd taken her out to his restaurant. Now she frowned as Rachel tore a sheet off her notepad, scrabbled around for a biro and wrote: *As Oscar Wilde once noted in* Dorian Gray, *brains and beauty are frequently incompatible, and we feel you are much too handsome to eat in our café.* Then she folded it up and put it on a saucer.

'Let's give him a taste of his own medicine.'

'Rachel, we can't,' Dina whispered, all panicky. 'It's too much. It'll seem childish and petty.'

Then Archie turned and called, 'Isn't anyone around here going to serve me?'

Dina experienced another volcanic spurt of anger. Childish and petty it might be, but it was also deeply satisfying. Archie was asking for it.

Rachel picked up the saucer, singing lightly under her breath, and took it over. She noticed that he flicked his eyes over her and thought, *Sleazeball!* But for a moment, she had to admit that she felt pleased. In a flash, she saw a glimpse of Archie's charisma. There was something about him that made you want to please him, to be admired by him; she saw then how Dina had been reeled in, manipulated by him. Slightly off guard, she put the saucer down without the rebellious panache she'd been meaning to pull off, and walked back to the counter.

'Dina,' Fatima came hurrying up, 'there's a man sitting over there in the corner who wants to speak to you. I asked for his name but he didn't give it . . .'

But Dina and Rachel were oblivious, surreptitiously watching Archie through the muffin counter. They were as giggly as schoolgirls as he folded open the note. Dina felt disappointed, for his face was expressionless.

'He's pissed off,' Rachel whispered authoritatively. 'I can tell.'

But not pissed off enough to leave, Dina noted, as Archie stayed put, drumming his fingers on the table. She felt deflated, as though he had somehow won.

'*Dina!*' Fatima tugged her sleeve again. 'He wants to speak to you. He won't take no for an answer.'

'I'm not speaking to Archie—'

'I'm not talking about Archie, I'm talking about the man with the ginger hair sitting in the corner of the café who's been staring at you for the last fifteen minutes only you've been too busy winding Archie up to notice,' Fatima burst out, all in one breath.

'Oh.' Dina looked over at the man curiously. Immediately, he dropped his eyes shyly. 'But I don't have a clue who he is.'

'Well, he seems completely obsessed with you,' Fatima hissed.

Dina felt a flutter of panic in her belly. Jesus, what a morning! They'd only been open three hours. First Archie; now her first weirdo.

Her confidence wasn't aided when Archie called out with a sneer, 'I've only been waiting for, oh, twenty minutes, but perhaps one of your members of staff could serve me before the day's out?'

'I'll take care of him,' said Rachel quickly, gently pushing Dina forward. 'You deal with the weirdo.'

Dina walked up to him and said in a bright voice, 'Excuse me, can I help you?'

And then he turned and looked at her, and Dina jumped. *I know you,* she thought, her heart pounding. And then: *Who? How?* She looked into his pale blue eyes and saw a familiar spark that made her stomach turn. She shivered. She didn't normally go for ginger guys, but this man was really rather handsome, and there was . . . just something, some charisma, something special about him that made her feel all fluttery and girlish.

But she still didn't have a clue who he was.

'Could you sit down, please?'

There it was again. His voice: deep, but familiar.

She sat down opposite him. She couldn't help noticing that he smelt faintly odd. There was a strong aura of deodorant around him, but beneath it just a hint of something dark and putrid; a scent that reminded her oddly of graveyards.

'Dina, it's me,' he said.

'I'm sorry?' Dina blinked.

'It's me. Steve.'

Dina stared at him. Her jaw dropped.

'Please, just listen to me. I got a body. I did it for us. The thing is, Dina . . . the thing is . . . OK, let me get the difficult bit over with first. I'm really, *really* sorry about your menu. It was Harrison.'

'*What?* Steve, this is insane – what are you doing? You have ginger hair and . . . and . . .' Suddenly the penny dropped. 'Do you mean it was Harrison who sabotaged the menu?'

'It was just meant to be a joke. Really, Dina, I didn't know he was going to do it or I would have stopped him. The thing is, he has this crazy sense of humour and he doesn't know when to stop. I only found out just now, and I just came to say sorry and then to say . . . to say . . . Anyway, he says he's really sorry and it was just meant to be a laugh.'

Dina felt hot with confusion. Just what the hell was Steve doing, turning up like this in a new body? Was it meant to be some sort of joke? Well, she wasn't amused. All the anger that Archie had provoked, that she'd had to push down and suppress for the sake of her customers, suddenly erupted and vented itself at Steve.

'Steve, how could you do this to me?' she cried in a low voice. 'It's my first day at the café and you freak us all out by doing this. I mean – are you totally insane? How long is it going to be before this – this body you're wearing starts to go off? You look ridiculous. You – you're just – you're not *you.* Is this your idea of support? Just get out, OK, just get out.'

Steve stared at her, his eyes bright with pain. Dina looked away, overwhelmed with guilt and confusion. She realised then that this clearly wasn't a stunt, that there was a warped logic to whatever it was about, but she just didn't have the emotional energy to deal with it right now.

'OK, I'm going,' he said angrily. 'But d'you want to know why I did this?'

'No,' she said quietly. 'Please just go.'

Steve made to stand up and then sat down again. He grabbed her hands. She pulled back in horror.

'Dina . . .' His voice was very cool, at complete odds with the words flowing out of his mouth. 'I don't know how to – OK, I'm going to say it. The thing is, I really love you. I've always loved you, ever since you started work in The Greasy Spoon, and to be honest, I've been lying to you ever since. I mean, all that stuff about Beth being my girlfriend – it was bullshit. I just said it because I didn't want to scare you off. And I thought that if I had a body, if I was human, then maybe you might . . . we might have . . . a chance together . . . I did this because I love you. I really love you, and though you deserve it more than anyone, I don't think that you really have been loved by a guy before. And – and you know something else? That night that you were lying in bed with Archie, when you went to bed together for the first time and you *thought* he said "I love you"? Well, that was me. Archie didn't say it, I did. You didn't realise. Archie never once told you he loved you.'

Dina felt tears rising up her throat. She closed her eyes, burning with love for him. But when she opened them, she saw this strange shell of a body, and shook her head in bewilderment.

She winced as Steve's chair scraped backwards and he got up and left the café.

'Well, Dina's taste in boyfriends seems to have gone downhill,' said Archie wryly.

Rachel tried to glare at him, but despite herself she couldn't help emitting a giggle. Then, seeing Dina's face, she quickly shut up.

'Dina, are you OK? Was that guy bothering you. Was—'

Dina shook her off and stormed into the back room, taking off her apron.

A minute later she came out again.

'Rachel, can you look after things for just half an hour? I need to deal with something, OK?'

She ran out, leaving Archie and Rachel both open-mouthed.

'Well, it's all go around here,' said Archie archly. 'What an eventful morning.'

'D'you want me to tip this all over your lap?' Rachel asked him sweetly, holding up his drink.

Archie didn't seem worried; if anything, he was amused. He looked up at her and their eyes locked. Despite herself, Rachel found herself sucked into his game. A smile quivered on her lips. For a second they stared at each other, intently, like kids having a staring match. Fatima, who was serving an elderly gentleman, looked up and saw them with a frown. Then Rachel dropped her eyes and both she and Archie burst into laughter.

'Here's your drink,' said Rachel, putting it down with a blush on her face.

'Thank you, ma'am,' said Archie, picking it up with equally flushed cheeks.

31
Dina

Dina ran out of the café, pausing on the pavement. In the distance she saw Steve at the bottom of the road. She watched him pushing through crowds; he didn't seem very comfortable in his new body, walking with a sort of funny waddle, as though he was used to having longer legs, and his arms swinging all over the place. He looked simultaneously so ludicrously comic and poignant that she found tears in her eyes and laughter bubbling in her throat. She shook her head, then ran after him.

She pounded down the pavement, pushing through crowds, through commuters, puffing apologies. At the end of the road she stopped, her head swivelling, shielding her eyes from the glare of the sun.

Then she saw him. He was walking towards the park, making for the path that led to the fountain. She picked up pace, but just as she was about to cross the main road, the lights changed to green and she nearly walked out in front of three lanes of traffic. She cursed and stepped backwards, watching Steve's figure disappear into a cluster of trees.

The lights changed and she ran into the park. Despite the sunshine, there was still a chill in the air and it was relatively empty except for the odd mother pushing a pram. She looked around, panting, for Steve, his words still whirling in her head. And then she saw him. He'd slipped out of the stranger's body, left it discarded in the bushes like a snakeskin, and was now cleaning his soul in the fountain. She watched him raise his head and let the water sluice over it, the sun glinting and dappling through the water and fracturing in sparkles and shadow on his ghostly figure. He turned towards her, then looked away, burying his face back under the water as though hoping it would wash away his embarrassment.

Fuck it, Steve thought. *I'm glad I said it. The old Steve would have been tying himself in knots right now, fretting that he'd confessed his real feelings. But Jether has made me realise that you can't lie or let things build up. You have to be honest, you have to be true to yourself.* He turned and looked at Dina, sitting on the bench, biting her nails, the sun sparkling in her hair, and his heart contracted. For all his new-found confidence, the pain of his love hadn't diminished in the slightest.

Finally he left the fountain and came and sat beside her. She gave him a wobbly smile. His eyes were sad but he was the real Steve again, and his blue eyes and snub nose and freckles looked all the more beautiful for the contrast.

'I'm sorry,' he groaned, sitting down next to her. 'I've been a total idiot. I don't know what I was thinking of. If I was going to choose a body, I could at least have chosen Humphrey Bogart, hey? But I just got overexcited. It was so amazing to be – to be real again. Human.'

Dina laughed and then said, 'Don't worry about it. Really. I understand. Though I don't think ginger hair really suits you . . .'

Steve laughed, his eyes crinkling, and gave her a gentle punch. And then Dina knew she had to say it. She had to finally tell him what she'd been holding back for so long.

She smiled distractedly, her heartbeat jangling, her stomach churning with nerves. 'Steve,' she blurted out, 'I have to tell you something. I've been meaning to tell you . . .'

'Right.' Steve swallowed. *Keep calm,* he told himself, *she isn't about to tell you to fuck off and never see her again. She wouldn't do that to you. You've been a good friend to her. You don't deserve that.*

'Steve, you remember the night you died? I mean – that's stupid, of course you do . . .'

Sensing that she was struggling, Steve reached out and held her hand.

'D'you remember – we were walking by the canal, and you said that you cared about me?'

Steve remained silent. There was something in her expression that gave him a sense of premonition that she was going to say something important. He felt his chest tighten.

Dina threaded her fingers together and gently scuffed up the grass with her trainer.

'You know – you know I said to you that I wasn't ready for a relationship, that I just wanted us to be friends? Well, I know it sounded really clichéd, but actually it was the truth. After Jason, I was nervous of any relationships. And I knew that we were already close, and it wasn't as though we could just have a one-night stand and then come into work the next day and forget it. I knew that if something happened between us, it was going to be special.'

She paused, as though waiting for him to say something.

He didn't know what to say. He just nodded urgently, not wanting her to stop.

'You know, don't you, that I was the one who found your body?'

'I – I didn't know that. No.'

'Yes. I walked away from the canal and left you there. I walked all the way down the street and I got to the tube station. I bought my ticket and put it in the machine and went down to the platform. And then I turned around and came back. I remember, afterwards, going to the police station and having to make a statement . . .'

Dina went into a reverie as she recalled the evening.

She was back in the police station. Cold tea in front of her, harsh white lights stinging her eyes. Her teeth chattering, an old coat that the policewoman had given her wrapped around her shoulders, smelling of chlorine and dead people. A policeman scrawling out a statement and staring at her suspiciously, demanding to know why she'd gone back for Steve. 'What, d'you think I murdered him or something?' Dina nearly burst in disgust.

'Look, I got all the way to the tube station, but I just felt so uneasy, so scared that something might happen to him. It was an *intuition.* And, and he was very drunk. So I turned and went back to the canal . . . and I saw . . .' This was the worst bit. The moment she felt she'd always remember for the rest of her life: the canal glittering like a black snake, the wind shrieking in the trees, and, just as she was turning away, the thing that caught her eye.

A dark shoe, floating in the water, its laces trailing like seaweed . . .

'I saw his body,' Dina said. The words sounded so cold, so conclusive. 'And I pulled him out – he was so heavy, but I was angry, so shocked, it gave me the strength to drag him out. I tried to give him the kiss of life, but – I think he was already dead. I just – I just don't know what happened to him.'

The policeman gave a grunt and carried on scribbling, absent-mindedly picking his nose.

She was hoping they'd finished but he kept asking more questions: Had she been trained in first aid? How did his pulse feel when she took it? How did she administer mouth-to-mouth? Dina felt heavy with tiredness and goose-bumps were starting to prick her body, so she took another sip of tea, but it was cold and the milk had congealed into white spots. Finally, the policeman read her statement back to her, took a signature and then drove her home in the pale dawn to her flat.

She didn't even have the energy to undress; she cuddled under the covers in her damp clothes, hugging Roger and burying her face in his comforting fur, the sweet sadness of blackbirds singing for the new day in her ears as she fell into a deep slumber . . .

'I'm sorry,' said Steve. 'I'm sorry.'

'It's not your fault,' said Dina gruffly, 'and anyway, the point was, I lied to the policeman.'

'What d'you mean?'

Dina looked up at him, her eyes filled with tears. She'd ached to tell him this for so long, for the whole of that long, desert stretch of months after he'd gone. She'd ached to tell him when she'd broken up with Archie, too, but she'd been too scared of taking the plunge.

She took a deep breath.

'It had nothing to do with *intuition.* I was walking home after our kiss and thinking of you. How much fun we'd had together over the past months. All the laughs. The things we'd done for each other. The way I'd helped you to become a little more confident, the way you'd helped me to be more focused. I went down into the grey tube station and I thought of my bed, cold and empty. And I imagined – with a shocked thrill of surprise – lying wrapped in the sheets, you hard on top of me, kissing feverishly. I thought of holding each other afterwards, and what a crazy, kooky post-coital chat we'd have.

'I know you thought that you didn't deserve me. But I don't deserve you. Maybe I was just afraid, when you kissed me. Afraid that I might actually have a successful relationship with a man who cared. Maybe the reason I've been attracted to men like Archie is just a perverse masochism, knowing it would never work out . . .

'The tube came into the station. I watched the door slide shut. A few drunken lads waved their beer cans at me. And I found myself turning and running up the escalators, pushing past people, excitement shooting up inside me. I kept praying: Please God, please can he still be there, please let me get there in time. I think he is the man for me, I think I've made a terrible mistake . . .

'I thought I might be too late. And I was. I was too late.' Dina started to cry. 'I could have saved you.'

'Oh Dina.' Steve held her. He was on the verge of tears himself, but he felt it would be too girlie. He forced his emotions back down and said in a trembling voice: 'It's *not* your fault, Dina, it absolutely isn't. Look, some time ago I heard Rachel saying it was *her* fault because she didn't bother to get me a present or turn up to the pub, and if she had turned up, she could have walked home with me. I heard my mum saying it was *her* fault because she ought to have made me have swimming lessons when I was a kid. I mean, it's nobody's fault, least of all yours.'

'You're being kind. But I was the one there that night, nobody else was. It's my fault . . .'

'OK, you're right. It's your fault.'

Dina started and then looked up and saw the taut, teasing smile on his face. She managed a smile too. Then she started crying again.

'Why didn't you tell me this before?' Steve asked; his tone was wondrous, not chiding, but Dina tensed with guilt.

'I've been wanting and wanting to tell you,' she said in a choked voice. 'When I was with Archie and you suddenly turned up again, I felt so mixed up. And then, after Archie dumped me, I didn't want to get into another relationship again. I felt so betrayed, so cynical. I'd been through it all once with Jason and then with Archie . . . I just wanted to hide away and never go out with anyone again. So I threw myself into the café and tried to shut out all my feelings for you. I tried to persuade myself that you were like a brother to me, that you were my bosom buddy, my pal, even though I knew underneath that there was more than that. I'm sorry I pushed you away, I really am, but I mean, it's not as though we can ever . . . I mean, what good is it now, anyway, Steve? I screwed up. I lost my chance. I didn't tell you how I felt that night and now it's too late.'

'But it isn't too late. We've got here and now.' He hadn't been quite able to digest her words at first. Every time they sang in his head, it was like dropping a stone into his consciousness, sending ripples of tingling bliss through his mind. A warm euphoria pounded in his heart and pumped through his bloodstream. After all these months of his wintry experience as a ghost, he had never felt more gloriously alive, more human.

Or more happy. To discover that he wasn't Steve the loser, Steve the sad old git who spent his hours mooching after a woman who didn't love him. He'd always felt that he and Dina had something so tender, so special, and now, to find out she felt the same, that the fantasy in his mind was actually reality . . .

He stared down at her. A shaft of sunlight suddenly broke through the clouds, dancing in sparkles in her eyelashes, wriggling into her hair and playing hide and seek in flashes. She looked up, smiling, embarrassed and relieved and frightened by her confession, and he felt she'd never looked more beautiful: a beauty that knocked him breathless.

He found himself reaching out and slowly tracing back her hair from her face. Dina twitched uneasily. He realised, just as she did, that without thinking he was mimicking a gesture he'd seen Archie make time and time again. But he didn't need to be like Archie. He was Steve, and she loved him for being Steve.

Do what feels natural, he told himself. He grabbed her shoulders. She smiled. He leaned in. She tilted up her chin. He felt like whooping with anticipation, giggling like a schoolboy, but he managed to gulp back his overwhelming elation, and gently press his lips to hers . . .

A second later he drew back, his face sad. The kiss had been brief, beautiful and utterly frustrating: his ghostly lips weren't formed to meet human ones.

'Jesus – I can't even kiss properly,' he burst out. 'I can't – I can't . . .'

'It was a lovely kiss,' said Dina, taking his hand. Then she drew away, burying her face in her hands and letting out a strange sort of snorty giggle and then a sigh.

'Dina, are you OK?' Steve stroked her hair, but she just carried on making ambiguous noises that were so Dinaesque he had to grin with affection despite his pain and confusion. 'Dina, tell me what you feel.'

'I don't know what I feel,' she said, looking up. 'I'm feeling all these conflicting things – it's just all going round in my head . . . I—'

'OK,' said Steve, grabbing her hands tightly, 'start with the good stuff. Tell me why we should be together.'

'OK,' said Dina, smiling up at him, relieved by his guidance, 'that's easy. Look, Steve, I adore you.' Seeing the smile on his face, her eyes became soft and liquid with love. 'And what you said just now – about the kiss – well, fuck it! I mean, really, Steve, I've had all these so-called amazing nights of passion with Archie and Jason' – she blushed a little, and so did he – 'but they don't add up to much when you wake up in the morning with a sick feeling in your stomach, convinced you're with the wrong person. I don't know why it feels so right with you, but it does. When I'm with you, I stop worrying. I feel calm. I feel so serene. Life seems to make sense. You make me feel strong . . .'

'And the bad stuff?' Steve's voice quivered.

'Well – look at us,' said Dina. 'We're from different worlds. I hate having to spend all day with other people. Every conversation I have with someone else seems so superficial, so shallow – it's as if I'm just on autopilot, I'm not really engaging with them, because in my heart I'm always talking to you. I hate all the lies and the secrecy, I hate having to stop myself from talking out loud to you for fear of people thinking I'm crazy . . .' Seeing Steve's face, she leant her head against his shoulder. 'But it doesn't mean I don't want to be with you . . . it's just . . . Oh, I don't know, Steve . . . what are we going to do with ourselves . . . what are we going to do?'

'I don't know,' said Steve, wondering if he had ever been so sad or so happy in his life before. 'I don't know.'

32
Steve

'Steve,' Harrison announced grandly, 'I've got some really cool news. Good news. Well, bad news too, kind of. I'm finally going back. Back to nirvana, all that shit.'

'Really? Mmmmm.'

'Jether helped me out. I told him about my uncle and he got some guys to contact my family and let them know about it. So they've dug up my body – it's in a bit of a fucking awful state, mind, but they can still take it into the Buddhist temple and perform the last rites so that I can move on to my next life.'

'Hmmmm.'

'Hey, if I get to meet God, I'll put in a good word for you, right? Ha ha. Then maybe I'll have a say in my next life. Jether told me that the last thoughts you have when you die determine where you go next, so I'm definitely going to be really focusing on fast cars, loads of beer, a huge bank balance, and plenty of hot blondes.'

'Mmmmm.'

Harrison and Steve walked down the busy street for a further five minutes, Steve in a blissed-out daze, Harrison boiling. They were on their way to see Jether, and just as they reached the entrance to his building, Harrison's exasperation exploded and he grabbed Steve by the shoulders.

'Have you been listening to a single word I've been saying?' Steve, who was still in the park with Dina in his arms, suddenly stumbled back into reality. 'I'm leaving you,' said Harrison softly. 'I'm going home. In a few weeks' time it's going to be goodbye time,

Steve. I mean – I've really valued our friendship, and it's the one thing I'm sad about . . .' He trailed off as Steve digested the news, his face flickering with conflicting emotions.

'Well, I'm really happy,' said Steve, fighting a momentary sadness. 'I'm really pleased for you, Harrison. Well done. You deserve it.'

They paused awkwardly before slipping into Jether's room. Jether was sitting cross-legged as usual, serene as the Buddha. Harrison quickly started to jabber on and on about his chance at a new life. Steve watched impatiently. He was burning to tell Jether all about Dina. He felt triumphant. For the first time, he wasn't coming to see Jether to whinge or moan or beg advice and then disagree with it. He was coming to tell the master that his disciple had finally sussed something out.

As he watched and waited, however, Steve felt as though, in some silent way, that Jether already knew all that he had to tell him. It was as though his Dina-tainted bliss was flowing out from him in waves that Jether's exquisitely sensitive antennae picked up. And as Harrison finally paused for breath, Jether turned and flicked Steve a private smile.

He knows, Steve smiled inside, *he knows.*

'And how about Steve?' Jether asked pleasantly. 'Have you had a good week?'

'Not so bad,' said Steve, and they both grinned. Steve was suddenly assailed with a wave of love for Jether, for his compassion and patience, for all that he had taught him.

'Well,' said Jether, 'since my two disciples have done so well, I think it might be a good day to fly, don't you?'

They stood on the rooftop above Jether's rooms. It was a good twenty feet from the ground. Steve gazed down at the flat, grey expanse of pavement. Then he looked up at the sunset, blazing fireballs of pink and orange across the horizon, slivers of golden light winking in between the clouds.

'Jump,' said Jether.

'Steve's tried that one before when he was a bit depressed,' said Harrison, grinning wickedly as Steve punched him.

'The idea is not to fall, but to fly.'

Steve eyed up Jether with nervous amazement, Harrison with deep cynicism.

'He tried to get me to do this exercise, Steve,' Harrison said. 'And did it work? Could I do it? No. It just did my kneecaps in the end, all that hitting the pavement at top speed.'

'I want to try it,' said Steve, feeling an excited flicker in his heart. 'How?' he asked Jether.

'You fly with the wind. Become one with it. Let it carry you. It's about surrender.'

Steve pondered his words.

'Don't think too much about what I've said,' said Jether. 'Just feel it. Be innocent, be spontaneous.'

Steve walked to the edge of the roof and jumped.

A few seconds later, he found himself crumpled in the road. He looked up at the two faces staring down at him. Harrison was laughing his head off. Steve sighed, and slowly climbed the long flight of stairs back up to the roof.

'The one good thing about this test,' Harrison mused, stretching like a cat, 'is that you do shed a few pounds.' He lay back with his hands behind his head.

'Shut up,' said Steve. 'I want to try again.'

Harrison rolled his eyes. Jether waited, his gaze bright.

Steve walked to the edge of the roof. He looked down at the tiny dots of people and cars below. He told himself: *I'm not going to fall, I'm going to fly.* He closed his eyes. *I'm not going to fall, I'm going to fly.* Fall, fly, fall, fly. What had Jether said? Feel the words, don't think about them. What did flying feel like? He thought about Dina, and falling in love. It struck him then what an unfortunate expression it was. Falling, he thought, was the wrong word. The expression 'falling in love' was really about the pain of love. About losing yourself and landing with a sudden, sharp bang. Flying in love was better; it summed up the high of it all, the dizzy sense of letting yourself go, letting someone else sweep you along.

Then he thought about the wind and how to be one with it. What was the wind like? Infinite. It could do anything it liked, flow in any direction, assume any mood. It could be angry and growl through the trees, or whisper softly, gently washing over your face like tears; it could tug or caress, croon or sigh or sing. He thought of how he had felt when he died, that dizzy rush of freedom, the words of the poem he adored:

I have been a stag of seven tines, running . . .

And the last lines of the poem:

I am the womb of every holt,
I am the blaze of every hill,
I am the queen of every hive,
I am the shield of every head,
I am the tomb of every hope.
Who, but I, gives birth to all that was, is, and shall be?

And he stepped off the building and it happened.

He felt himself fall a few feet, and then a sigh spread through his body and he wasn't falling any more.

The wind caught him. It curled around him like divine hands. It caressed him for a moment, as though pondering whether he deserved to be carried by it, and he felt his heart silently beg to be worthy. And then it cupped him, and Steve felt as though his soul was safe. He opened his eyes. The outside world blurred past: buildings, trees, clouds. A bird, as though playfully competing, momentarily joined him, then whirled off into the clouds, squawking. He closed his eyes again. He felt as though he was surfing waves on an ocean. He didn't need to do anything, or control anything; just let it carry him on his current, dipping and diving and flowing. His soul sang and he let out a whoop, and the wind laughed with him.

Then it was as though he and the wind were like playmates. He sensed that it had now passed some power to him, that he could push the current the way he liked. He veered left, then right. They passed through a tree, the leaves fluttering over them. They darted side by side, seeing who could go faster. He felt his soul zinging with an ecstasy that grew and grew until it reached a quivering point. And then Steve surrendered completely, and it was as though he melted into his friend and the wind crashed over him into a wave and he was lost in an ocean of bliss.

Some time later, Steve found himself gently deposited back on the rooftop. His face was flushed and his eyes were sparkling. The wind gently licked the back of his neck, patted him on the head and then whirled off to look for more fun elsewhere.

Harrison was completely aghast. Steve looked over at Jether, who was smiling proudly, and he smiled back, feeling as though his heart might burst open in gratitude.

Later that evening, Steve and Harrison sat on the rooftop, staring up at the stars. Harrison was happy to be quiet for once; a dreamy, contented smile lingered on his lips. It was as though his previous lack of purpose had led him to pursue as much booze, women and debauchery as possible in order to distract him from his despair. But now that he knew his purgatory was up, he was content to sit and contemplate the night sky in all its splendour.

Steve searched through the chains of stars for his favourite constellation, Lacerta, that cluster of stars shaped in a zig-zag like a lizard's tail. Every so often he was tickled by a memory of flying with the wind, and a shiver of bliss went through him. *It was strange,* he pondered, *for there were moments, while I was in the wind, when my soul felt so thin. As though I was disappearing, fading into smoke, becoming essence. As though I was on the trembling brink of some other realm and I was pulsing on its edge, as though I could have slipped into it if I'd wanted to, and been lost for ever.*

And the funny thing is, I felt exactly the same way with Dina this morning. When she told me she loved me, I sensed all the agony seep out of my soul and I felt at peace. And then I began to lose myself . . .

Steve wished he had thought to discuss it with Jether, but in truth, he already knew what the moments signified. And with the relief came a wave of panic that crashed over him and destroyed his state of serenity.

Why now? he silently asked the stars that winked down on him. *Why, after all this time, after all this pain and this desperate search for answers, for release? Why now, just when I finally have a reason to stay on earth, do I find a way to move on?*

Then he recalled how, when he had been holding Dina, he had felt his soul losing definition and had consciously torn himself away from the sensation, clung on to Dina with all his might, forced himself to stay.

And I'm going to keep on staying, he told the stars grimly. *I'm not going to leave Dina now, just when I've finally found her. I'm going to stick around for as long as I can. It's up to me. I don't believe in destiny and people all being little cogs in some wheel of life and everyone and everything having a place and a purpose and all that shit. It's my life,* he cried angrily, *and I have a choice.*

At least, I hope I do.

33
Rachel

28 February 2004

Dina's been incredibly scatty over the last few weeks. It's kind of weird – when we first opened, she was ridiculously tense, obsessed with making this the best café in the whole bloody world. Now she seems to be walking about in a dreamy swoon. Yesterday she forgot to put flour in our order, creating a muffin disaster and an emergency ASDA trip. And I keep catching her talking to herself. God knows what's up with her. Maybe it's all the stress getting on top of her. Great – I finally get a job I like and a boss I like and then she has a breakdown.

Haven't seen X at all. Got a text from him, which I ignored. I had a dream about him last night. We were swimming in an ocean together, playing with dolphins, and then he swam through the waves and kissed me.

God, I've just reread that last line. I sound like a fucking Mills & Boon. How sad am I?

Rachel chewed the end of her biro, reading over her diary. She was taking a well-earned fifteen-minute break whilst Dina and Fatima held the fort out front. She put the diary back into her satchel and then carefully rearranged her denim jacket over the top of it. Though she mostly used code for the most important names, she definitely didn't want anyone finding it.

She was just retying her ponytail and adjusting her apron when Dina came storming into the kitchen. For once, she didn't look dreamy. In fact, she looked very red-faced. She was clutching a sky-blue sheet of paper in her hand.

'Look what that fucking son-of-a-bitch-of-a-total-bastard has done now!'

'Eh?' Rachel took the piece of paper from her hand and read:

SPECIAL THEME NIGHT
at exquisite
SALSA MUSIC * FREE FOOD * DANCING

'So what? That's cool.' Then, as Dina jabbed the paper sharply, Rachel's eyes flicked to the date. 'Oh. I see. He's having *his* special night the same night we've having our spring celebration. Well, I guess it could be a coincidence.'

'Oh yeah, right!' Dina snarled. 'I mean, how long have we spent organising our bloody theme night – the menus, the food, the extra catering. I can't go back and cancel it now, it's too close – and it puts people off, it make *us* look crap and disorganised. I mean, I just can't believe Archie's doing this.'

Seeing Dina's unhappiness, Rachel said, 'I can think of a way to help. Archie suggested that I have lunch with him the last time he was here. I could go and act as a spy, sound him out.'

'What?' Dina cried. 'How come he's asking you to lunch?'

'Well, I think – I think he felt guilty over his behaviour last time. I think he realised it was all a bit cheeky. Hey, I might even be able to bring him round and get him to have his theme night on another date.'

'Well, I guess it could work,' said Dina doubtfully. She turned to go, then swung back, frowning. 'I hope Archie isn't about to hit on you. I mean, I could just imagine him using you to get at me.'

'Well, if he is,' said Rachel flippantly, 'he hasn't a hope in hell. I think he's a total loser.'

'Good,' said Dina, feeling relieved; she searched Rachel's face for telltale blushes, but there were none. 'Anyone else on the scene, anything else going on in your love life?'

'Oh, there is someone special . . .' Rachel dipped her head, biting back a smile. 'But I'm keeping quiet about it for now. He's my mystery man – well, *if* something happens between us.' She narrowed her eyes at Dina. 'How about you?'

'Me?' Dina jumped, then shrugged coolly. 'You know me – I'm

young, free and single. I'm much too busy with the café to get into relationships.'

Yeah, right, thought Rachel, watching Dina leave. *You, my dear, are quite clearly in love. You're just not telling who.*

Normally, whenever Archie made a lunch date with a woman, he liked to turn up at least ten minutes late, just to keep her on her toes. Then he could enjoy the pleasure of approaching her and seeing from a distance the fraught look in her eyes, that anguish of oh-my-God-is-he-really-going-to-stand-me-up, which, of course, intensified the relief and pleasure when she saw that he had finally arrived.

Today, however, Archie was early. He sat at the back of exquisite at a small table, shielded from the other diners by a large screen. It was just before midday and his restaurant was fairly full. He sat and watched the minute hand ticking around his watch.

Five minutes went by, and Archie distracted himself by calling Ralph for a quick gossip. Another five minutes, and his mobile rang; seeing Heidi's number flare up on the screen, he ignored it. He drummed his fingers on the table. He examined his nails. He tried to squash down the knots of irritation tying up in his stomach. Could it be possible?

Was Archie Hamilton – for the first time in his life – about to be stood up?

Finally, at 12.15, she walked in.

The last time Archie had seen Rachel, she had hair like a skunk, and was wearing jeans with more rips than material and a sort of lacy gothic top that showed off a profusion of body piercings. Today she was wearing a long dress. It was tie-dye, a swirl of pink and red and mauve blotches – normally the sort of thing Archie hated and would have sneered at as 'hippie'. But it lapped around her body in elegant waves and fell to her knees in little spirals, showing off slender calves that tapered into surprisingly delicate ankles. Her hair was loose and flowed around her shoulders like a fox's coat. She looked lovely.

'Hi,' she said abruptly, pulling back the chair with a grating squeak. She was chewing gum again. 'So what are we having? I'm starving.'

Archie felt his jaw tighten. He was about to point out that an apology for her tardiness might be in order, when a waiter glided up, brandishing menus.

'It's fine, we'll have the avocado salad followed by the salmon with new potatoes,' said Archie, with a touch of pride.

'Hang on,' Rachel interrupted, hanging on to her menu. 'Don't I get to choose my own food?'

'But the salmon here is amazing,' said Archie, reaching over and touching her arm. Rachel jumped visibly and he smiled. 'I guarantee that you'll love it.'

Rachel shook her head obstinately. She scanned the menu, enjoying the feel of Archie's glare on her, picturing herself telling the story to Dina and co. back at the café. Finally she handed the menu back to the waiter, requesting the melon, followed by spinach and onion tart. She saw amusement in the waiter's eyes and wondered how many of Archie's girlfriends he had had to serve at this very table.

Then she saw the look on Archie's face.

'What?' she asked. 'So you find it hard to have lunch with a woman who can think for herself?'

'No,' said Archie, narrowing his eyes, trying hard not to show how riled he was. 'But I'd like to point out that I wasn't trying to boss you about. I own this restaurant, after all, and I spent a good while sitting here and really thinking about a meal that you'd enjoy. That's all.'

'Oh, sure,' said Rachel, taking the bottle of mineral water before Archie could and pouring herself a glass.

'What d'you mean, "sure"?'

'Nothing.' Rachel took a sip of water and smiled sweetly. Then she glanced around the restaurant as though it was full of people a million times more fascinating than Archie.

'Nothing? It's something! Come on, tell me.'

Rachel paused, feeling anger flare up inside her. *Calm down,* she told herself, *you're meant to be winding him up, not the other way round. This is just a game, remember? To please Dina. To find out what his theme night is about.*

'Look,' she said, 'I've come to this lunch and I'd just appreciate it if you didn't feed me any bullshit, OK? For one thing, I'm a vegetarian. And secondly, I'm sure you've got this set seduction menu that you've tried and tested on several thousand women over the years, so don't try and pretend that I'm *special* and you've got this once-in-a-lifetime meal planned out, because I know what you're like. I mean, even if you did wine and dine me and work your charm on me and—' Rachel broke off, blushing. 'And . . . well, I wouldn't fall for it, OK?'

'And what?' Archie demanded, pinning her with his eyes and making her squirm. 'From my side, I have no desire to get you into bed. I just asked you to come over for a friendly lunch, that's all. It's not a date; I can't help it if you've got the wrong idea.'

Rachel dropped her eyes to the table, furious. The waiter brought their starters and Rachel managed to devour hers without looking at Archie once.

'You are really giving that melon a hard time,' said Archie, watching her wielding her spoon as though it was a knife.

Despite herself, Rachel burst into laughter.

'So,' said Archie, 'if you really think I am such an incorrigible womaniser, why did you agree to have lunch with me in the first place?'

'Because Dina asked me to,' said Rachel. She saw Archie's face fall and felt a flash of guilt, but ploughed on all the same. 'She was hoping I could talk some sense into you. We have noticed that, by amazing coincidence, you happen to have scheduled your freebie salsa night to clash with our spring celebration. And we thought it was a tad – cheeky.'

'It's a free country,' said Archie. Suddenly his intimate tone was gone, his caressing gaze withheld; he became brisk and businesslike.

'But can't you just change your night? I mean, we're a new café, struggling to get customers, and you're already a big restaurant chain with an established reputation. Would it really hurt you to have it another night?'

'But this is business, Rachel. We're a free market economy. Business is about competition. But I know your type. Don't tell me – you don't eat meat and you go on peace marches and you won't buy a single item of clothing from a mainstream store because you're worried about sweatshops and that would be bad karma . . .'

Rachel let out an insulted gasp. She sensed that Archie liked winding her up. And in truth, a part of her liked it too, but another part of her hated it.

Then the main courses arrived and she concentrated on trying to think up a seething put-down while she ate.

'So how is Dina?' Archie asked.

'She's great,' said Rachel sharply. 'Practically every man who comes into the café chats her up. And she's seeing a guy at the moment – she won't tell us who, but she seems very much in love. So that's Dina. How about you?'

'There hasn't been anyone since Dina.'

'Uh-huh?' Rachel raised a very cynical eyebrow.

'There hasn't been anyone since Dina,' Archie repeated, in such an injured tone that Rachel very nearly said sorry. But she was the sort of person who found apologising extremely hard, so she made do with pouring some more wine for him with a conciliatory smile.

'So you're feeling pretty rough, huh?'

'Pretty rough,' Archie mimicked her. Then, suddenly, he changed tack. He swallowed and said in a wobbly voice, 'To be honest, I – I think that since Dina and I broke up, I've been having some sort of crisis.'

'A crisis?' Rachel was amazed.

'I – I didn't realise until after she'd gone how much I cared for her. And then I sat down and really thought about how I'd treated her, how selfish and difficult I was to live with, and you know what – I didn't blame her. I think the problem is that I need someone who can stand up to me, and Dina couldn't do that. And – and the other thing is . . . you see, my father wasn't completely loyal to my mother, and I guess I was scared of getting married and finding everything went wrong . . . but Dina also made me realise that I had to move on from that. And I felt . . . I know this sounds stupid . . . but I felt like a failure. I felt I was just repeating my father's mistakes. All of a sudden all my success, all my restaurants, didn't mean anything. I tried one-night stands, a few flings, but it wasn't the same; now I'd had a taste of intimacy, I was thirsty for it. And even now, I've still got this lurking feeling that I've failed myself.'

'You're not a failure,' said Rachel quickly. 'It's not your fault. I mean, these things happen. It's part of life. It's something I realised recently, that life isn't hunky-dory all the time, it's full of ups and downs, and if you just relax and accept that's the case – well, you stop worrying so much when you get the downs.' She was aware that she was gabbling and she trailed off, gazing across the table at him. A dizzy rush swept over her and she thought: *Oh, he's so sweet.* Archie stared back at her. Then he leaned across and kissed her gently.

The feel of his lips was as light as the brush of a feather.

Archie sat back in his seat, swallowing, awaiting her reaction. Rachel hastily picked up her fork and carried on eating as though nothing had happened, trying to ignore the frantic pulse of her heart, the rush of blood to her lips.

'How's your love life?' Archie suddenly asked.

'Nonexistent.' Rachel let out a light laugh. Suddenly she found she had lost control. She was all girlie and self-conscious and she hated it. She took another hasty bite of her tart, collecting herself. 'The last guy I went out with was from my college. He was also my tutor.'

'Ah,' said Archie.

'I know. He started messing about with another girl and so I dumped him. I won't stand for any crap from men. You know what he used to say to me? "Treat 'em mean and keep 'em keen." Well, as far as I'm concerned, that's bull. I want to be treated like a princess and I won't put up with anything else.'

'I wouldn't treat you badly.' Archie shocked her for a second time by going straight to the point. 'I think you're incredible. The moment I saw you in the café, I just felt completely blown away by how beautiful you are.'

'I'm not your type.'

'Why d'you say that?'

'I'm not interested in your celebrity status, like the girls I see you with in magazines. I don't have a low IQ or a big bust. I'm just a sodding waitress who's doing a media degree on the side. And when I finish my media degree, I plan to have a career – a proper one, directing films – and I'm not ready to put it on hold for any guy.' Rachel ran out of breath.

'I love movies,' said Archie. 'And travelling. We'll travel together. You can make movies; I'll set up businesses.'

Rachel swallowed, concealing her shock.

'I'm not the type who's a doormat. I won't just roll over and do whatever you want me to do.'

'But I think that's just what I need,' Archie said earnestly. 'I need someone who's feisty. I think that was the problem with Dina – she was feisty, but not feisty enough. I need someone to come up against and keep my – let's face it – fucking enormous ego in line.' He smiled, so endearingly that Rachel found herself gazing at his lips with longing.

Then the waiter came to take away their plates, and Rachel sighed and said she had better go.

Archie looked disappointed. He stood up and gently guided her through the restaurant. *Well, you could at least ask me on a date,* Rachel cried with inward indignation. Suddenly she felt panicky that she wasn't ever going to see him again. As they walked past the tables, heads turned and people waved, wanting to talk to Archie, but he ignored them all, focusing his attention on Rachel. Outside, in the sun, she turned to him, squinting sulkily.

'Well,' said Archie, 'I'm doing my hardest not to harass you – but d'you think we could stay in touch? I mean, I was thinking, y'know . . . we could meet . . . now and again, just for a friendly coffee . . . maybe it could be a monthly thing, or a weekly thing, even . . .'

Rachel shrugged and said that would be OK. Archie leaned in and gently kissed her cheek, close to the corner of her mouth. Rachel walked away, and spent the next twenty minutes in such a daze that it was only when she was back in the café, chopping feta cheese, that she realised, with great embarrassment, that she had completely forgotten the point of her mission: to get Archie to agree to move his theme night.

Rachel fretted about this for much of the afternoon, composing stories in her head about how Archie had been like a clam and refused to give anything away. When, at 3 p.m., Dina burst into the kitchen, whooping, Rachel tensed, ready for interrogation.

'Listen,' said Dina, 'Archie called.'

For one terrified moment Rachel feared he had told her everything. Maybe Dina was right; maybe the seduction was all a joke, and she'd fallen for it and now he was laughing behind her back. *I hate him*, she thought savagely, gripping her knife, *I hate him hate him hate him—*

'He said he felt it was unfair to hold his theme night at the same time as ours. So he's cancelling his and he's going to hold it next month. Isn't that totally cool? It's so gentlemanly of him, I was almost suspicious . . . but he seemed sincere.'

Rachel agreed that it was wonderful. Dina went out to serve customers and Rachel went back to filling the dishwasher. A slow smile crept across her face and stayed there for the rest of the day.

34
Dina

Dina swept up the last bit of dust from the café floor, deposited the dustpan and brush in its place by the bin and then collapsed on to a chair. She rubbed the knobble of spine at the base of her neck that ached with tiredness. She closed her eyes, picturing how tonight Steve would visit her and gently run his fingers over that bump, his massage as light as feathers, and she smiled dreamily . . .

When she was a teenager, Dina had got into the habit of marking her days out of ten. Most of the time they'd barely hit six. But today, she thought, was a ten. In fact, the whole week had been a damn fine ten. They'd had their spring celebration night and Archie hadn't interfered at all – in fact, he'd turned up and been surprisingly polite. Ever since then, things had rocketed and the word-of-mouth effect had suddenly kicked in. The café was now a happy, swirling cauldron of commuters and students and builders and nannies, all pouring in from dawn until dusk, to the extent that Dina was going to have to order in several more chairs and tables and apply for a licence to put extras on the pavement outside. *Ha – if bloody old Nancy Weiz could see me now,* Dina thought with a flash of triumph and satisfaction. But perhaps her biggest fulfilment had been phoning up her parents and proudly telling them how well things were going, and hearing the relief in their voices that their daughter's crazy move to England had finally come good.

She went into the kitchen. She still suffered jittery nightmares about Health & Safety inspectors turning up out of the blue and catching them out over one crucial, tiny detail they were too amateur to remember. But yup – it looked fine: knives, gleaming in a crescendo of cruelty, hanging up on the board; surfaces scrubbed; floor spotless; dishwasher chockablock with cutlery. She had just flicked off the light when she noticed something lying by the aprons and switched it back on again.

It was Rachel's satchel – she must have forgotten it. Dina picked it up, and was wondering if Rachel was without her purse and mobile and going frantic when something large and hard slipped out and hit the floor.

It was a chunky notebook, which fell open in the middle, and as Dina leaned down to pick it up, the words leapt out as though magnified:

Dina doesn't know anything, though I keep thinking I should tell her

Dina picked the book up slowly, her eyes wide. Keeping her thumb on the page, she checked the front. DIARY, it said, in small gold letters.

OK, Dina, she told herself sternly, *put it back. You can't read someone's private thoughts. Rachel is your friend, remember?*

But another voice shouted back: *Hang on a minute – what am I not supposed to know. What if it's important? What if Rachel's pregnant? Having a crisis? What if she left this here because she wants me to find it and see it? Come on, just read a teeny bit . . .*

Tonight we had the spring celebration at the café and X came. He asked if I wanted to talk and we ended up going into the kitchen for a bit of privacy. He shut the door and said he had a little present for me. It was a set of artist's pencils. I was so touched I couldn't even thank him, and some weird part of me just kept being really off-hand and rude to him.

'So you don't like them then?' he said, looking hurt.

I shrugged. Then all of a sudden I felt his arms slipping around my waist. I was terrified Dina was going to come in, but I couldn't resist him. He leaned down and kissed me softly . . .

Suddenly Dina suffered a strange sensation in her stomach. How had Rachel managed to get away with that right under their noses?

Mind you, Dina had been in such a flap that night she wouldn't have noticed if Rachel had been having an orgy back in the kitchen.

And more importantly – who was X?

This is none of your business, Dina told herself, flipping on a few pages and skimming over the entries . . . *X and I exchanged twenty texts today . . . X waited at the end of the road today and offered me a lift home . . . X sent me a bunch of flowers this morning and I'm hopeless with flowers, I got Mum to arrange them, but I have to admit, they looked fabulous . . .* As well as scribbled entries, there were also rather wickedly drawn caricatures of several customers, not to mention Fatima. Utterly gripped by curiosity now, Dina flipped to the final entry.

There was no writing. Just a picture. This one wasn't a cartoon; the face had been drawn softly, as though each pencil stroke was a caress. There was no doubt who X was; every line sang with love.

Stunned, Dina sank on to a stool and flipped back to the entry before last.

13 March 2004

Things aren't going so well with X. He's been very funny with me for the last few days. Last night he took me out to dinner and spent practically the whole meal in silence. So I stood up, flung down my napkin and walked out. X looked really upset and rushed outside after me. I had a massive go at him, shouting at him in the street (you know what I'm like when I lose my temper), saying I'd told him I wouldn't put up with any crap. And he got really upset and funny again. Oh God, I hope he's not losing interest. What if he is? What if everything he's said is lies and I'm just another notch on his bedpost?

15 March 2004

You will not believe what happened today. X came in and asked for an almond croissant. As he passed me the money for it, he asked if I could see him on my next break.

'It's not for another half-hour,' I said coldly. Then, with terrible timing, Dina came out and she bloody well overheard us. She took one look at X and told him to stop pestering me or 'I'll call the health inspectors and tell them I have a large, ugly rat in my café and I want him removed.'

X slunk out. He gave me a sorrowful look and I gave him a look back that said: Wait for my break. *At least, I meant it to. In books people are always giving other people looks that mean things, but most of the time it's pretty hard working them out.*

The next thirty minutes seemed like thirty years.

I kept serving people and giving them the wrong change and burning paninis and the whole time praying, Oh please, God, please can he still be waiting for me outside. *Finally, Dina let me go five minutes after my break was due. I ran out of the shop and looked everywhere for him, but – nobody. I started walking down the street and I could feel my eyes watering – it must have been my hay fever. And then I heard a voice behind me say: 'Hi.'*

I turned and there he was. All through my break, I'd imagined myself flinging my arms around him at this point. But now he was here, I went back to feeling like I wanted to punch him.

'Can we talk?'

'My break is nearly over,' I said, trying to walk away. 'I really have to go. But it was nice to see you—'

'I really have to speak to you.'

I've never heard anyone say the word really *with so much tension.*

The nearest place was McDonald's. X bought me a vanilla milkshake and himself a coffee. We sat down at a yellow plastic table.

I drank my milkshake and folded my arms and glared at him.

'You're looking really rough,' I said.

He was. He had stubble all over his chin, and his suit was creased and crumpled.

'Couldn't you get one of your many maids to iron your suit?'

'I—' He looked down as though only just noticing his suit was in a state. 'I'm tired. I haven't slept much over the last week. It's because [mumble mumble mumble].'

'WHAT?' But no, he couldn't have said that. *It had to be my imagination.*

'Nothing.'

I slurped my drink even though there was really nothing left and the straw kept hitting chunks of ice.

Maybe he'd said, 'I've got a glove for you.'

Or, 'I want to buy a dove with you.'

He put his hand over mine.

'I think I'm in love with you,' he said. I had to hand it to him. He looked as if he totally meant it.

I laughed. He looked crucified.

'What do you want?' I said.

'Look – and I know you're probably too young and I don't deserve you, but I do really, really, really love you. Really.'

This really *was even stronger than the last one.*

'I've never said that to anyone before in my entire life.'

And I said: 'I love you too. And I've never said that to anyone in my entire life.'

Only I didn't. I said: 'But we haven't even slept together yet.'

Why did I say that? It was so, well, crass. X looked startled and then he said, 'Well, let's make love. Right now.'

'But my break finishes in five minutes.'

'Fuck your break.'

So I fucked my break. I called Dina on my mobile and made up some lame excuse about being sick. I was too dazed to even tell if she bought it or not.

Then he leaned over the table and kissed me, and I couldn't stop kissing him back, and he didn't even care when I overturned his coffee by mistake and a bit splashed on his trousers. I started covering it with a hundred soggy napkins but he just grabbed my hand and left a girl to clear it up and we laughed and ran out into the street, weaving through crowds, treading on people's feet and crying, 'Sorry . . . sorry . . . sorry . . .' and dashing across roads and nearly getting run over until we came to his block and we got into the lift and kissed all the way up and ran panting into his flat.

It was a total mess, but I hardly noticed, or cared. We lay down on the bed and he closed the curtains.

Up until now, it had all been so fast, and now it was all so slow. It was like being in a dream, being underwater. He kissed me and stroked me for hours. He was all nervous and kept asking me if I liked it, if I was turned on, and I kept kissing him and saying yes, yes, yes. And we made love and looked into each other's eyes the whole time and then afterwards I found my eyes watering again and then I saw his eyes were watering. 'Hay fever,' I said, wiping them on the sheet. 'Me too,' he said, wiping his, and then we laughed, and he said, 'I just want to hold you,' and he pulled me into his arms and we lay there for ages, just lying there together whilst the world went by outside and the sun pulled away and the room darkened. And then we started all over again.

Dina snapped the diary shut. Anger boiled through her; anger and disbelief that Rachel could possibly be *this* naïve, *this* stupid. She picked up the satchel and swept out of the café, slamming the door and swiftly locking up. Then she hurried down the road, heading towards his flat, ready to give him a piece of her mind . . .

Dina hadn't ever imagined that she'd find reason to visit this flat again. Just standing outside the door brought back a flood of painful memories. But this had to be dealt with. She rang the doorbell sharply.

No answer.

She pressed her ear to the door, heard faint riffs of music. So he *was* in. Right. She was damn well going to ring on the bell until he came and then she was damn well going to—

The door opened. Archie. He was in mid-laughter at some joke. Dina looked him up and down and her stomach fluttered. He was looking amazing, despite wearing a very un-Archie-like sweater, which was brown and frayed and had holes in. And then she saw Rachel. She was wearing a red dress and looked much older than usual. She walked up to Archie's side and circled her arms around his waist and leant her head against his shoulder, eyeing Dina coldly.

'Look,' said Archie, 'I think we all need to have a talk.'

'No, we bloody don't!' Rachel cried indignantly. 'We can do whatever we like. Dina's not our mother, we don't have to get her permission for anything. Oh, and by the way, Dina, I'm resigning.'

'Don't do that!' Archie cried. 'Rachel, that's nuts.'

'I can do whatever I like.'

'Yes, you can do whatever you like, but is it really what you want to do? Look, let's all go out and get something to eat,' said Archie.

'Come on, Rachel, it'll be really nice, I promise.'

Dina blinked. If this was a Mr Nice Guy act Archie was putting on, he was doing a very good job of it.

The restaurant was very quiet.

Dina was feeling strange. She'd expected Archie to start being a bad boy. She'd been waiting for him to start flirting with the waitress, or get up and work the room or dictate what Rachel ought to eat. In fact, she almost wanted him to, so that she could let rip and have a massive go at him and then grab Rachel's hand and yank her out.

But Archie truly was on his best behaviour. He was polite and sweet. He congratulated Dina on the success of her café, and she was so surprised, she forgot to even say thank you. He told an anecdote about the recent histrionics of his new chef and Dina found herself laughing. And suddenly she found herself remembering all the good things about Archie, his wit and charisma and cheekiness, all those qualities she'd forgotten in her mental demonisation of him.

By the time they reached dessert, Dina felt an unexpected flash of nostalgia. This was the place Archie had taken her on their very first date together. God, to think it was only a year ago. She might have been sitting in this very seat. She remembered the way he had sat across the table and pinned his eyes on her, and she flicked her gaze up at him, but he was looking at Rachel, watching her dip a nail-bitten finger into her tiramisu and lick it off with deliciously rude manners. His eyes blazed with fondness. He leaned across and gently placed a kiss on her temple, and Rachel smiled up at him: a secret, intimate, lover's smile, as though they were thinking about their time alone together after this tedious dinner had ended.

Archie turned back to Dina, starting slightly, as though he'd forgotten she was there.

'Shall we get the bill?' His eyes were bright, his whole face aglow.

Dina nodded numbly. She thought in shock: *They're in love.*

And then: *What the hell am I going to tell Steve?*

*

They left the restaurant at around ten. Outside, they stood about awkwardly.

'So?' said Archie. 'D'you approve of me as a suitable chap for Rachel? Or do you still hate me? Not that I can blame you – I mean, I was lousy, wasn't I . . .' He trailed off.

Dina jumped; she'd forgotten how direct Archie could be. But then she saw Rachel smiling at him proudly, and the anxiety in Archie's eyes. She realised that he really did want to make amends. Perhaps not for her sake, but certainly for Rachel's. She was Rachel's boss and friend and Archie wanted to be a part of that.

'Of course I don't hate you.' She laughed awkwardly. 'Look, I'm happy for you, OK? Really happy—' She broke off as Rachel suddenly enveloped her in an ecstatic hug.

She politely rejected Archie's offer of a drink or a lift home. She managed to shake hands with him, and then gave Rachel another tight hug and whispered 'See you at work tomorrow – don't you dare dream of not turning up!' Rachel laughed and gave her a thumbs-up, then whirled away and disappeared into Archie's car, clutching his hand tightly.

Dina paused, waiting by the road for the lights to change. She knew that Steve would be waiting for her back at her flat. They'd agreed to meet there tonight. He would be in her bedroom, humming gently, probably tidying up her mess, watering her little cactus plants and teasing Roger, Dina thought with an affectionate smile.

Knowing that he would be there, she slowed her pace. Steve was terribly protective of Rachel. She knew that he was going to completely freak out – there was no getting round it. And the last thing Dina wanted to do was hurt him, row with him, burst the delicate bubble of love that enclosed them.

The last few weeks had been so tender. It was amazing – if anyone had told Dina a year ago that she would have a platonic love affair that would also be the most intimate thing she'd ever experienced in her life, she would have laughed in their face.

Steve kept asking if she was happy, and Dina always said, *Of course, I'm the happiest I've ever been.*

Which was the truth, and also a lie.

She felt every day as though a tide of peace and love flowed into her life, and then receded again, leaving a spiky landscape of uncertainty and fear. Sometimes at night she lay beside him and thought, *How can this last? And how long will it last? I mean, we can't go on like this for ever. I'm twenty-nine. What if I want to have a proper relationship, meet a guy, settle down, do the whole marriage and kids thing?* But therein lay the problem – she couldn't imagine ever settling down with any guy except Steve.

Like this morning, for example. She had been taking an order from a handsome blond student when he'd suddenly looked into her eyes and asked her on a date. She'd found herself saying yes. She hadn't even thought about it. And then he'd asked for her number. And she'd seen the arrogant smile creeping across his lips, his delight that he'd won her, and she had thought: *How could I have possibly imagined I could prefer this guy to Steve?* She'd given him a fake number and then spent the rest of the day feeling fraught that she would never find anyone as wonderful as Steve, that she would be stuck in the trap of this utterly impractical and impossible relationship for life.

Seeing Rachel and Archie together had accentuated her confusion. She felt touched by their happiness. She had looked at them and thought: *That's how I feel about Steve, that's how we should be.* It seemed upside down that Rachel and Archie, two of the most dysfunctional people she had ever met, could have found love in real life when she hadn't.

As she turned the corner, her heart suddenly flipped. For Steve was waiting for her, standing at the end of the road on the opposite side, hands in his pockets. She made to cross the road but found herself pausing on the edge of the kerb, staring at him. He stared back, their intimacy occasionally interrupted by the flow of taxis and cars and people milling down the street.

Dina suddenly felt an old, familiar fear grip her. *I can't do this,* she thought, *I can't. His love for me is so pure, so absolute, so unconditional, that I can't bear it. I feel I don't deserve him.* She felt her body quiver with a desperate urge to simply turn and run.

Steve, watching from across the road, felt such delight at simply seeing her that something quivered in his heart, a sensation that was the closest he'd yet felt to a heartbeat. And he noticed the shadow over her face and knew then that something was wrong.

He watched her press the button and wait for the lights to change. But, as they moved from green to red, she stayed standing, looking at him with hooded, worried eyes. He smiled at her, a reassuring smile that said: *Don't worry, everything will be fine.*

And then he saw her expression change. His smile seemed to wriggle into her heart and soothe whatever was bothering her. And suddenly the tension eased from her face and she smiled too: a bright, beaming smile, her eyes singing with love for him. She stepped out into the road without looking, all her attention fixed on him.

Steve didn't see the taxi until it was too late. The driver was rounding the corner fast, looking forward to getting home and eating the meal his wife had cooked for him; the lights were flashing amber and he figured he might as well take the risk and whiz through.

Steve yelled: '*DINA!*'

Though her scream was short and shrill, barely lasting a second, a silence swept like an ocean through the street. Heads turned. People cried out. The taxi screeched to a halt, the driver ashen. Crowds gathered. Steve ran the length of the street, pushing, tearing himself through souls. He knelt down beside Dina, clutching her face in his hands. He saw her eyelids flicker briefly and heard a groan hiss from her lips. Blood ran stickily through her hair, splashing on to his fingers and dissolving into nothingness. Steve was aware of the taxi driver coming up behind him, nervously looking down over him, and Steve turned and screamed at him: 'I'm going to kill you – get away from her, just fucking get away from her!' He turned back to Dina breathlessly, his tears splashing on to her face. She shivered as they hit her cheeks and, as though summoning every drop of energy in her body, she opened her eyes and smiled weakly at him. Then her lids dropped and her head fell to one side and she was lost to the world.

35
Dina

Dina opened her eyes.

A nurse was staring down at her. She was wearing a gown and a green mask. Her brown eyes were stern, hardened after having to experience death after death, feel people slipping away from her no matter how hard she tried to hold on to them. Yet something flickered across her pupils – sympathy? Regret? Dina suddenly felt afraid. She could hear the woman speaking to a cluster of doctors. They were all shaking their heads and looking serious.

'Erm – excuse me?' she said weakly. 'I'm OK . . . really . . . I feel OK . . .'

They just ignored her.

She sat up. She was on a white-sheeted trolley, in some sort of operating theatre. The lights were low and luminous and she was surrounded by machines, connected by a rainbow web of wires.

'I'm . . . feeling OK.' She slipped off the trolley and walked up to the nurse, her feet curling on the cold floor. God, this was all so embarrassing, they really didn't need to worry about her.

But even when she tapped the nurse on the shoulder, she didn't take any notice.

Now I know why people say the NHS is such a load of crap, Dina thought, with a surge of indignation.

Then she saw the nurse turn and go to her body. *Her* body. *Her body lying on the table.* Her body lying there with a patch of hair shorn away, leaving a semicircle of spiky little brown bristles. Her face, pale and tinged with a greenish hue. Her forehead with a deep red scar cut into it, sealed up with a zig-zag of silvery stitches.

She stood very still for some time. She could hear her breathing: very fast, wheezing out of her lungs in shocked gasps. She couldn't process what had happened, just stare. Stare and listen to the doctors discussing the possibility that she might come round; she would have to go into intensive care. Machines beeped. Someone said they needed some tea. Someone was crying—

Wait. Someone was sobbing. Suddenly she felt very alert. The sobbing became a point of focus, something to arrow her mind away from the horror building in her chest. It was coming from the corner of the operating theatre. Someone was sitting there with hunched shoulders. As though in a trance, she walked over to him.

Then she realised.

'Steve?' she cried.

He looked up. He blinked. In a moment, his expression metamorphosed from one of infinite sadness to a kind of insane joy. Then he shouted, so loudly he nearly deafened her: 'DINA – YOU'RE ALIVE!'

He stood up and grabbed her into a huge hug and Dina held him back just as tightly. Then she felt his arms stiffen. And slacken. He pulled back.

'Dina. You're . . .' He swallowed, watching the doctors wheel her body out of the theatre.

'I know,' she said in a small voice. 'I'm like you.'

All Steve could do was gape. Dina stood and chewed her fingernails. Finally he said: 'I'm sorry.'

His words were so ridiculously ineffectual that they triggered a torrent of emotion in Dina, bursting open the floodgates of her anger. She raised her fists to flail them at him, to shout at him how could he, how could he have distracted her on the road, how could he have let her walk out in front of a car, how dare the doctors fail to save her, how dare everyone fail her like this, let her life just slip away. And then Steve giggled. A nervous little peep of a giggle.

'You're laughing.' Dina was astounded. 'I can't believe this. I'm dead – well, not dead, I'm in a coma, but still – and you're laughing. It's just all so—'

And then Steve saw something change in her face. He laughed

again and he saw her anger transmute into wonder, and suddenly she was laughing too. And it was infectious – they were both having a terrible laughing fit, as bad as the ones they used to have when they'd worked for Luigi.

The sound echoed eerily around the empty operating theatre.

As Dina's laughter died away, Steve saw her stand still again. And in a rush he remembered just how he had felt, back when he had discovered his fate: that sense of fragility, of extreme vulnerability, his body so slight and subtle it felt as though it might shatter or dissolve at any minute. He went to her and put his arms around her and made her feel solid. He shushed and soothed her as she cried into his chest, and then she laughed, and then cried some more.

Steve took her by the hand and they strolled outside into the fresh spring air. Dina stopped short. She put her hands over her ears and looked around painfully.

'It's – it's—'

'I'd forgotten what it was like,' said Steve. 'You feel so raw, don't you, like all your senses are a million times more powerful.'

'It's like being on drugs or something,' Dina muttered, trying to pull herself together.

'I think we should go and see Jether,' Steve said. He could see Dina fighting her panic and he was beginning to feel lost himself, unsure what to say or do.

'Who's Jether?' Dina asked.

'He's this guy . . . and he kind of knows everything . . . Come on.'

Before they left, Dina took one last look back at the dirty white walls of the hospital. She wondered if the nurses were going through her bag, finding her diary, calling her parents. She pictured her mother receiving the call, her face crumpling in shock. She swallowed. Then Steve tugged her sharply and they were out on to the crazy chaos on the streets. Dina could barely take it all in – the intensity of noise and smell, the painful proximity of people walking past her or even *through* her, grating and smashing against her soul, and she kept her eyes tightly shut, trying to curl in on herself, clutching Steve's hand as he led the way.

*

Thank God, thought Steve. *I knew it was right to bring her here.*

They were sitting in Jether's place, and though Dina was still freaked, a little of her previous bounce and strength had returned. Steve also sensed that Jether liked Dina, that he had taken to her at once, and he felt a flash of beaming pride that he had brought her.

'This is all so weird,' Dina kept bursting out. She glanced at Steve. 'I mean – you're still you, and I'm still me. I don't feel any different, really, now I'm getting used to it.'

'It's the soul that holds the grains of personality,' said Jether pleasantly. 'The body is just a shell that the soul lives in. The body slowly deteriorates and dies, but the soul lives on for ever.'

Steve glanced at Dina, worried that she would be rather affronted by this challenge to her beliefs, but she looked quite open, ready to listen to Jether and hear what he had to say.

'When I died,' she said, her face brightening and her voice shaking slightly, 'you know – it was beautiful. I mean – when the car hit me, there was all this pain, so much pain I felt as though every cell in my body was screaming. I was aware of my heart beating so hard against my chest I thought it was going to explode, and tasting blood in my mouth, because I was biting my tongue with the agony. And then the darkness came and it took away the pain. I floated in it for a while and there were voices and then the voices faded and the darkness became much thicker. I was aware of memories. It wasn't like that thing you read in books about your life flashing before you. It was slow and dreamy and it seemed to go on for hours, though I guess it could only have been minutes. I remembered things I thought I'd completely forgotten – being in the back yard, and my mom in the kitchen making lemonade, riding round on my bicycle and smelling the freshly cut grass. I remembered my dad taking me fishing, I remembered the feel of my grandmother's gnarled hands on my hair. And then I was drifting, drifting through all these memories and I became aware of some sort of warmth, like hidden sunlight on my face, and I became aware that this wasn't a memory any more, it was here and now. I was lying in a garden, and it was beautiful. There was sunlight, though I couldn't see the sun, and the grass was warm and sweet. And I could hear the wind, and it was the most exquisite thing I'd ever heard. I heard it flowing through the grass and the trees and it had a sort of celestial sound, like a bell ringing, or birdsong speeded up. It's hard to explain. And behind the sound, I could hear people talking, just this babble of conversation, and I knew that all the people I loved and had lost were very, very close, just beyond the trees, and it was so soothing. I felt as though I wanted to stay there for ever . . . and then, just like that, it was gone.' She turned to Steve and said, 'Did you have anything like that?'

'No, I just died and that was it,' said Steve, in such a forlorn voice that Dina laughed gently, and then Steve smiled too.

'But – but—' Dina looked to Jether for guidance. 'What next? What do I do now?'

'Your body's in a coma,' said Jether. 'You can still go back. You can return to your body and lie still inside it, let your soul mesh back into your body. You'll feel as though you've passed out again and then you'll be lost in the darkness of your coma. When the time comes, you'll wake up again.'

'But hang on,' said Steve nervously. 'Some people never wake up from comas. I mean – what if Dina doesn't come round again?'

Jether looked at him and shrugged. Clearly it was a risk they were going to have to take.

They were silent for a while. Dina frowned and chewed her lip and Steve held her hand tightly. Then she said:

'Can I . . . kind of . . .' She laughed. 'Oh God – this does sound crazy, but can I kind of . . . you know . . . delay going back to my body?'

'The longer you spend away from your body, the harder it will be. You'll gradually break your soul's association with your body, break all the fine threads of recognition that connect them.'

'Well, that's it then,' said Steve bravely. 'We'll go back right away, we'll go now—'

'No,' Dina interrupted. 'It's OK. I – I – don't want to go back.'

'*What?*' Steve felt as though his heart was a cocoon and a butterfly had just danced out and was fluttering about wildly.

Dina reached out and put her hand on top of his.

'The thing is, I want to stay with you.'

'What . . . what do you mean by that?' Steve asked slowly.

'I mean – I want to stay with you.'

'But you heard what Jether said. If you take time out—'

'No – you're not getting me, Steve.' Dina let out a slightly scared laugh. 'I want to stay with you. I don't want to go back. I want to be with you, like this.'

'Are you sure?' Steve was amazed. He kept looking from Dina to Jether as though convinced it was all some big joke they'd cooked up between them.

Dina paused. She looked up at Steve and then grinned and said a great big definite 'Yes.'

Steve burst into laughter and Dina began to giggle too, and suddenly they found themselves laughing with the wildness of the idea. Then they saw Jether raising his eyebrows and quietened down sheepishly, feeling like kids before a teacher.

'It's a big decision,' said Jether. 'You'd have to make a clean cut.'

'What d'you mean?' Dina asked jumpily.

'Whilst your body lies in the hospital, all of your family and friends will cling on in hope. If you truly decide that you choose death, that you choose life with Steve, then Steve ought to pull the plug. Make it final. It's only fair.'

Steve gulped. He'd always agreed with the idea of euthanasia; after all, why waste life in suffering? But Dina wasn't suffering. She was only twenty-nine, and . . . He turned and looked at her, and saw that she'd turned very pale. He pictured himself pulling the plug, stamping out Dina's life just like that, like a snap of his fingers, and shuddered.

'Think about it,' said Jether.

Steve felt like hitting him for bursting their fantasy bubble and being such a smug bastard. And then he reminded himself that it wasn't Jether's fault they found themselves in this horrendous situation.

'Well, we'd better go,' said Steve heavily.

Steve led Dina back to the house he shared with Harrison. Harrison, to his relief, was out on the town and they had the place to themselves.

'Wow, this place – it's amazing,' said Dina, gaping at the living room, the high ceiling, the winking chandelier and the enormous marble fireplace.

'I know,' said Steve, 'and we've got plenty of spare rooms, so you can stay . . . if you want . . .'

'Sure.'

Steve led her up to a large bedroom with a double bed.

'Is this OK?'

'Yes – it's great,' she said. 'Lovely . . . though I'm going to miss Roger snuggling up to me. Not to mention Einstein too – sometimes I wake up in the night and see him flipping about . . .'

Steve nodded sadly.

'Well . . . maybe . . . I don't know . . .' He trailed off. 'Anyway, well. I guess you must be pretty knackered and all that. Good night.'

He was just at the door when Dina's voice stopped him.

'Steve?' She patted the bed self-consciously. 'Sit down with me. I just want to chat about what Jether said . . . and also a few other things.'

Steve sat down next to her.

'I—' he began.

'I—' she began, and they both laughed.

'First of all,' she said, letting out a deep breath, 'there's something I think you should know about, er, Rachel. I was going to tell you about it that day when – well, anyway. Look, I don't want you to be upset or throw a fit or—'

'Dina,' Steve interrupted her gently, 'I know what you're going to tell me.'

'You do?'

'I do. And yes, I was upset at first. I was furious, in fact. I happened to see them together –we must have found out at the same time because I think you were coming to tell me and I was coming to tell you!'

'Archie *is* a bastard but I think she's making a good man out of him.'

'I know. I could see how happy she was, and more importantly, I could see he was happy too. He wasn't faking, he wasn't using her or trying to manipulate her. I'm just really happy for her.' Steve smiled, shaking his head. 'It's a funny thing, seeing your kid sister in love. I remember the days when she used to kick me under the dining table and I used to pull her ponytail – when you have a sister, you never stop thinking of her that way . . .'

Dina smiled too, then their grins faded and their faces became sober and there was a brief, uncomfortable silence.

'And about Jether . . .' Dina began rather nervously. 'Look, I just wanted to say – well – look, I know it seems like I'm being totally crazy, but – I meant what I said.' She took a deep breath. 'I want you to pull the plug. I want to be with you.'

'Dina, you really don't have to—' Steve said nervously.

'No – no – just let me finish. Look, I want to explain. All my – I – God, I don't know where to begin. OK.' She breathed out shakily and so did Steve, and they both laughed, feeling the tension ease a little.

'Go on,' said Steve.

'The thing is – I know I've always been very cynical about love. I mean, I'm probably not that much different from a lot of people heading towards thirty. I look at my parents' marriage and I see them limping along, not really in love, just companions sharing a house together, and I've always thought I'd rather not bother with marriage, just live with someone, or spend my life having flings, having fun – feeling I'd rather be free and a little lonely sometimes than suffocated in some awful marriage.

'But really, deep down – I am a romantic, Steve. You're right. I've always been a bit embarrassed about admitting it, but . . . I do believe in love. I certainly did when I was a teenager, when I read *Wuthering Heights,* and got all soppy over Heathcliff. I really wanted to care for someone with that much passion. And then, you know, I grew up, I met Jason, I met Archie, I got sucked in, I got hurt, I got cynical . . . I turned into a commitment-phobe, I stopped believing love could really happen, I started to think it was just something that happened in the movies. And then I came back to you.'

Silence. Steve hardly dared to breathe.

'You are just the guy I've been looking for. I didn't realise it at first because you're not like some white knight on a horse – don't get me wrong, Steve, don't look like that. When I first met you I judged you purely on appearances, and you know, you read *Nexus,* and had a goldfish called Einstein, and seemed a bit nuts . . . but I've got to know you, and I love you. I really love you for who you are, and—'

'I love you too.'

'I know you do, and I know with you it's real. I know you mean it, and that you're not going to do what Archie did and walk out on me.'

'No, no, I'd never do that!'

'Exactly, Steve. This is it, I just feel we have something so precious, so rare. So many people out there don't have this kind of love even once in a lifetime. And I just don't want to throw it away. I mean, what's the most important thing? Being happy. Being with you. It might be just about the most unconventional relationship that ever existed, but that's what I want.'

Steve was so moved he couldn't speak, just squeezed her hand.

'But,' he said, hating himself for voicing doubts, yet knowing he had to bring them up; he felt as though Jether was watching over him, prodding him, 'what about your friends . . . your mum and dad . . .'

'I know.' Dina was tearful. 'I keep thinking about that, and when I do, I can't bear it . . . But I don't know . . . I just feel I want to be with you. I don't want to go back to my old life. I don't want to be in my stupid café, serving customers, pretending I'm OK, when all I want is to be with you. I don't want my crappy old life with debts and worries and taxes and all that stuff.'

'But Dina – the café – it was going so well, you'd achieved so much . . .'

'I know.' Dina lifted her chin: that familiar, petulant gesture he loved, signifying that she wasn't going to be persuaded. 'But life is full of choices. You can't always have everything, and my career isn't really all that important. It's like that cliché that when you're lying on your deathbed you won't treasure all those hours you put in at the office – well, now I'm lying on my deathbed, I know it's true, and I feel so lucky to have been given this insight – to know that love is all that really matters, that nothing else is worth it.'

A huge smile stretched across Steve's face. He kept trying to subdue it and bite it in, but he couldn't.

'So what do you think?' Dina asked anxiously, suddenly full of fear. Was she mistaken? Maybe Steve didn't want to be with her for ever; maybe he—

'I . . .'

'Yes?'

'I think . . .' Steve suddenly hugged her, and his hug said it all, 'I think I'm just about the luckiest guy on earth.'

The evening ought to have finished with lovemaking. They lay in bed together, arms around each other, staring into each other's eyes. Every so often a smile would start to tremble across Steve's lips, and then Dina would find the same happening to her, and then his smile would stretch across his face, and her smile across hers, and they'd find themselves exploding into laughter and hugging each other.

'Are you sure?' Steve kept asking breathlessly. 'Are you sure, are you sure?'

'Of course I'm sure!' Dina caressed his face. He could sense a change in the air, a heightening of mood, and he feigned an achy yawn, drooped his eyelids.

'God, I'm tired,' he mumbled, letting his head sink into the pillow. He could feel Dina's disappointment flowing from her in waves. But then she gave a little shrug, curled in close with her head against his cheek, and sank into sleep too.

Steve didn't dare open his eyes. His chest was burning, his head felt hot. He was silently lashing himself inside. He felt like a total idiot. It was obvious what she'd wanted. What they'd both been waiting for for so long. Yet some prickling fear had held him back. He was convinced he'd suddenly forget how to kiss, that his whole body would conspire to screw up and put her off him. He was simply overwhelmed by Dina's decision. Nobody had ever given him anything like this before. He tried to think about the most amazing thing he'd ever been given, and he came to the conclusion it was the huge Meccano set he'd got for Christmas at the age of eight. He suppressed a smile.

No girls had certainly ever offered him anything of value. Nor his friends. If he thought about it, today's me-me society wasn't that big on giving, for fear it was naïve and wouldn't really be appreciated. Romance was dead, there were no dragons to slay or damsels to save, and nobody really made these kind of huge gestures these days.

And here was a girl who was offering him her *life*.

It was like being handed a beautiful jewel. It was wonderful at first, and then horrible, because there was the fear that you'd drop it and it would smash into a thousand pieces. He was already obsessed with making sure they did it tomorrow. Before she changed her mind. But then what if she changed her mind afterwards and ended up hating him for ever? What had he done to deserve this? Surely the universe, fate, the gods had made a mistake? They were probably sitting up now with the angels, going through their filing, and were about to frown and say, 'Hang on – this isn't right. This is plain old Steve MacFadden. He's here for a crap life. We can't be doing with Steve getting something like this . . . Quick, undo it! Whip up some stormclouds and put a few turds on the road for him to step in.'

And then he shook himself. Where were all these silly doubts coming from? They belonged to the old Steve. He didn't want to think like this any more. Why shouldn't something great happen to him? He wasn't jinxed; he was just an average guy. Everyone deserved love at some point in their lives, and now his moment had come.

He had to keep hold of this jewel and polish it, but also enjoy its rays and sparkles. He pressed his chin down on the top of Dina's head, breathing in the smell of her hair, delightfully conscious of it all night as he slept.

36
Dina

Dina couldn't bear the waiting. She was sitting by the canal. A boat moved sleepily through the water; a couple frolicked under a tree; kids ran past, playing with a red ball. She tried to watch them but all she could think about was how it was going to feel when Steve pulled the plug. Would it be like something out of a movie? Would there be lightning forking out of the sky, shaking her violently and leaving her lying on the grass? Or, more likely, she thought wryly, I won't feel anything at all. It'll be like going to the dentist when you have an injection and suddenly see your tooth in their palm and you didn't feel a thing. I won't even know it's happened until Steve comes back here and tells me . . .

She plucked another daisy, shredding the petals in turn, adding to the white pile by her feet. She plucked another, then stopped herself. She stared at the flower and thought how beautiful it was. She would never have noticed when she was alive; it would just have been a plain old daisy. But now she was struck by the beauty of its simplicity. She dipped her finger in its furry yellow centre and traced the petals, soft as skin. She lifted it to her nose and breathed in its scent. She thought: *When he pulls the plug, will I lose my sense of smell? Will the world become dull?*

Suddenly all her doubts poured out in a rush. She didn't want to die. She'd been rash and insane to suggest it. Now, when it came to the crunch, she realised how much she loved life.

The things she loved danced around her head like a merry-go-round of joy, all those simple everyday delights. Chatting to her mom on the phone. Waking up in the morning and hearing birdsong. Flashes of sunlight breaking through a stormy sky. Snuggling up on the sofa watching TV when it was dark outside. Lying in a warm bath reading a book. Going out to dinner with a friend and gossiping and talking about nothing much. Cooking in the café: the feel of the soft, firm dough beneath her fingers, slowly taking shape and form. And what about all the things she wanted to do in the future?

Like travelling and seeing the world?

And getting married?

And having children: she'd always umed and ahed and worried that she couldn't handle them, but right now she realised that yes, she did have a maternal urge, that her life would feel hollow without children. She wanted to be able to proudly show her parents their grandson or granddaughter. And she wanted her child in turn to grow up and turn her into a grandmother.

She jumped to her feet and clenched her fists. In the distance she could see the white outline of the hospital. She felt like screaming at the top of her lungs, 'STEVE, STOOOOOOOOOOOP!'

And then she reminded herself of how much she loved him, how much she'd wanted them to be together, and she sat down again, dizzy with confusion, tears springing to her eyes.

A few minutes ticked by, and she didn't move. She just sat, staring at the daisy. Then she jumped up and started to walk. Not to the hospital, just out on to the street, walking, walking so fast that she wouldn't have time to think, to face the horrible regret burning in her chest, this urge to grab hold of her life and cling on to it. She walked and walked and walked and realised she had, without thinking, through some sort of habit, arrived at Archie's flat. Then she thought grimly: *Well, if there's one way to remind myself that life wasn't all that great, it ought to be Archie's flat.* It would be teeming with unhappy memories. She slid through the doors and up the stairs.

Some sense of stubbornness made her resist doing the simple thing and just walking straight through the door to his flat. Instead, she found herself pressing the doorbell, hard, several times. As any normal person would do.

Eventually the door opened. Archie was wearing his blue

dressing gown and looking very dishevelled. He looked about irritably, swore a few times, then slammed the door shut again.

Dina followed Archie down the hallway and into the bedroom. She started when she saw Rachel lying in the bed, curled up under the covers. Dina stood about awkwardly. Was this how Steve had felt when he'd watched her? Suddenly she felt a flash of pain for him.

Archie slid into bed next to Rachel. He cupped his hands around her face, wiping away her tears with his thumbs.

'Sssh,' he whispered. 'It's all right, honey, I'm here now.'

'But I'm frightened,' Rachel said, sniffing and wiping her nose on one of Archie's old hankies, blowing hard and prompting an exasperated, affectionate smile from Archie. 'I'm frightened of losing you.'

Though Dina knew that Archie had changed, she was still astounded by his response. The Archie Dina had known would, at this point, have got very freaked out, made an excuse about having to tackle a work crisis and jumped out of bed.

But the Archie she saw now held Rachel tightly, rubbing her back.

'You mustn't be silly,' he said in a low voice. 'I'm never going to leave you, you know I love you.'

'I know, but I just – I must be jinxed. First my brother and now Dina. Everyone I love dies. I swear that it's all my fault . . .'

'Ssh, ssh.' Archie kissed her gently. 'You're talking nonsense.'

'And I miss her. I miss her so much. Dina was the only real friend I ever had. She was the only person who really knew me. Except for you,' she added unhappily, tracing her finger over his jaw. 'You're all I've got now.'

'And you're all I've got,' said Archie.

'Oh come on,' Rachel protested, her temper flaring up, 'you with your Archie Hamilton fan club—'

'None of them really know me, I've never been out with any girl who understood me, or really liked me for me. You're the first one, and there's never going to be anyone else. How many times do I have to fucking say it?' he said gently. And then she smiled and he whispered, 'Close your eyes,' and showered her face with languid, healing kisses, the start of a slow and tender lovemaking. Rachel opened her eyes and whispered, 'I love you. I won't lose you. I won't.'

Dina turned and ran, passing straight through the door this time.

She stood in the hallway, heaving in deep breaths. She recalled how she had felt when Steve had died. How she'd had to call her parents every night for fear that she would lose them, how she was perpetually frightened in just the same way Rachel was suffering now. She realised with a flood of emotion that no matter how much she loved Steve, no matter how deeply she wanted to be with him, she was being utterly crazy, wildly, stupidly irresponsible to let him throw away her life. And it wasn't even just *her* life. People lived in their own little worlds, but life itself was not something that truly belonged to any individual. It was a web of consciousness, an interlinking of friendships and family and love affairs, and here she was, about to snap and tear all those fine threads that bound her to the people who loved her and depended on her.

She started to run. As she tore through the streets she kept mistaking faces in the crowds for those of the people she had known throughout her life: Lisette, her first friend from elementary school . . . Anita's round, smiling face . . . Luigi's proud one . . . And most of all her parents: her mother's lined face, fraught with worry; her father's round, jolly one . . . And she kept praying, over and over, like a mantra: *Please God, please don't let me be too late. Please let me get to the hospital in time.*

37
Steve

Steve walked through the maze of corridors in Hammersmith Hospital until he found himself standing outside Dina's room.

He stared in through the circular window. There she was. Holding on to life by a thread, held up by machines.

He turned away. He let out a deep breath. A doctor walked past, pushing an old lady in a wheelchair; she was telling him how much he looked like her son, and he was smiling.

Steve turned back to the door.

He was about to enter when a voice floated down the hall.

'Hiya, Stevie – boy, am I in a good mood. Today's my last day as a ghost! Anyway, buddy, what are you doing here?'

'Harrison.' Steve went pale. *Great, just what I need right now.* 'Look, this really isn't a great time. I want to be alone with Dina for a bit.'

Harrison frowned. 'But Dina's a vegetable. What d'you want with her body?' He pulled a face. 'Steve, I hope you're not thinking what I think you are. That's *so* gross—'

'Of course I'm bloody not, you sicko!' Steve shot back, nerves making him angry. 'I just – just want to check up on her, that's all. See how she's doing.'

'OK, OK. Keep your skin on.'

Steve stormed through the door. He turned, fearing Harrison might have followed him, but no face, no hands were seeping through after him. He was alone.

He went up to Dina's body. Today it seemed even more fragile than her soul. Her breathing was slight and its hissing, regular rhythm seemed mechanical, as though the machines were forcing air in and out of her lungs but her heart wasn't really in it. Her fingers were limp and her closed eyes looked hollow, as though they were sinking into her skull. If she'd been encased in purple velvet, Steve wouldn't have had any trouble believing she had gone. *See, she can't last,* he told himself fiercely. *She's going to go anyway.*

He went over to the chaos of machines and computers and traced his fingers along the wires, down to where they were plugged into the socket in the wall. Somehow, the thought of raking his soul right through all that metal didn't appeal to him. He'd do it the human way: he'd kneel down, crawl through them and then – with one quick yank – it would be done.

He stood up and went back to her bedside, looking down on her. He picked up her hand and stroked it gently – then dropped it in shock.

He could have sworn he felt it *quiver.* He picked it up again, scanning her face frantically, searching for a flicker in her eyelashes, a tremor in her lips, but – nothing.

He swallowed. *Well, here goes . . .* He bent down and reached out, curling his fingers around the plug. His palm sweated across the plastic. He looked up an inch, convinced he could see Harrison out of the corner of his eye.

There was no Harrison, but he did catch sight of Dina's head. And he saw something that made his fingers go slack.

The triangular patch that had been shorn away on the night of her accident . . . Steve peered closer. The last time he'd seen it, it had been nothing but naked skin with a few flecks of seedling hair. Now it was peppered with bristles, all sprouting joyously. They looked like the spines on the cactus plants he'd given Dina for her sill. Steve was speechless. Despite the fact that Dina's mind had closed down, her body was still acting in its own way, growing, evolving. In a few weeks those bristles would be real, silky hair; they'd flow over her ear and kiss her neck and curl over her shoulder.

Tears blossomed in his chest. He leaned over and brushed his hands over the patch, feeling the spikes tickle his fingers. He clasped his hands around her skull and kissed her gently. One of his tears fell on to her pallid face, trickled down her cheek and then down her chin and into her nightgown. He kissed her again, and was about to crawl back out from among the machines when—

Suddenly he felt two hands grip his shoulders and yank him back roughly, banging his head against a machine with a blow that made his brain sing. Steve gasped and found himself toppled on to the floor, the air knocked out of his chest. Harrison leaned down. He was so close Steve could see the anger pulsing behind his eyes.

'Harrison – what the hell are you doing?' Steve tried to stagger to his feet, but Harrison pushed him back down, knocking him against the bed, briefly crushing Dina's fingers between his shoulder and the mattress.

Steve flipped. He got up and put both his palms up, and when Harrison came at him again, he shoved him right back. Harrison stumbled, catching the bedpost to keep himself upright.

'What the hell's wrong with you?' Steve cried.

'What's wrong with me?' Harrison shouted. 'Me? You're the sicko round here, Steve, trying to kill off your own girlfriend! I was watching you through the door, you – you—' And before Steve had a chance to reply, Harrison came at him again like a raging bull. Steve tried to dodge him but Harrison flung himself at him, catching him in a snaky hold and locking his arm around his neck. Steve struggled wildly but Harrison's grip was iron.

'You might be some sad old ghost who's stuck on earth and can't move on because he's too afraid to believe in anything, but Dina has her whole life ahead of her,' Harrison ranted.

'Harrison . . . I didn't . . . I . . .' Steve tried to speak, but the words were pushed back into his chest. He could feel Harrison increasing the pressure, his fingers sliding through his skin and squeezing his windpipe. Steve felt tears automatically stinging his eyes. Pain screamed through his body and tingled in the ends of his fingers. His heart choked. The past rushed into the present; it was like being back in the canal, back in that moment when the water had swirled into his lungs and filled them like balloons. *This isn't the canal,* a calm voice said over the top of the panic. *You're dead and he can't kill you again; it's just pain, this isn't death.* But with that realisation came another wave of fear: *If I can't die, how long can this go on for?*

The life instinct kicked through him. With a spurt of adrenalin, he thrashed about wildly, kicking the trolley by Dina's bed and sending it shooting across the room. It hit the wall; the monitor overturned and crashed to the floor, smashing into glittering shards; the cables burst away from the wall in a crushed tangle.

Harrison let him go.

Steve collapsed to the floor, rubbing his wounded neck.

'You don't understand. I didn't want her to die,' he wheezed tearfully.

'What?' Harrison asked, stunned, breathing in gasps.

'I changed my mind. I want her to live.'

'Steve!' Harrison's voice was suddenly shot through with fear. 'Oh my God. Look.'

Steve sat up. Harrison was pointing at a cable which lay on the floor like a fat red worm. *The cable which had linked Dina to her life support machine. Now torn away from the wall.*

'Oh my God!'

Steve ran to her side. Her face was pale, her breathing barely a whisper. 'Oh shit oh my God Harrison get a nurse quick QUICK!'

Steve turned back to Dina. He leant down over her beautiful face, clutching her hands tightly. Her fingers felt as fragile as a baby's. Her breath was still there, thank God, pulsing against his cheek in faint circles of warmth. He was dimly aware of Harrison outside, yelling uselessly at nurses, and he leant so close he could hear her breath, magnified in his ear like the sound of the sea in a shell. And then he felt it; it was like that change in the air when summer dies into autumn; it become brittle, colder, ephemeral.

'Dina, no, hold on,' he begged her.

He let go of her and turned away desperately.

He ran across the room and gathered up the shards from the monitor in his hands, then burst out through the door. A couple of nurses were walking down the corridor, laughing over a handsome doctor.

'They can't hear me,' Harrison panted, dizzy.

'They'll hear this.' Steve flung the shards at their feet; they jumped violently. He swung the door to Dina's room open, forcing them to look in.

'Oh my God!'

They ran into the room.

'What on earth happened in here!'

'Get Dr Raj, quick!'

Steve and Harrison stood by, trembling violently. Within minutes, the double doors swung open and Dr Raj hurried in, a nurse behind him wheeling a trolley with a machine on it. Steve saw the doctor pick up two pads and for one bewildered, hazy moment wondered what on earth he was doing. Then he pressed them tight against Dina's heart, counting down from three, and *snap!* – her body writhed and bucked against the sheets.

Steve couldn't bear to watch. He turned away. Harrison put a gentle arm around his shoulders, twisting his head back to watch Dr Raj. The doctor picked up the pads again and there was a crackling noise that made Steve hunch his shoulders and bite against his teeth in pain. He kept his eyes shut, bracing himself for the next sound. For the first time in his life, he found himself praying desperately: *Oh dear God, I know this is much too late in the day from my side because I've spent all my adult life swearing you don't exist . . . but please let her live, please let her live. I didn't even pray to you when I faced death myself, I didn't even believe you then when I felt the air hissing out of my lungs. But I have to believe in you now, God, because I can't handle this. If I've killed her, if I'm responsible for her death, I'll never be able to live with myself . . .*

There was a long silence and Steve felt his heart cave in. *It's too late*, he wailed, *it's too late . . .*

Dina ran into the hospital. She found herself in a maze of white corridors and stopped short, panting. The irony of the situation struck her: *Here I am,* she thought, *in a hospital, looking for the room that contains my own body. And I'm lost. I don't have a clue where it is. Oh God, Steve, please don't let me be too late, please don't do it . . .*

She retraced her footsteps back to the reception, running so fast that she found herself sliding through an elderly black woman carrying a large bunch of flowers. Then she overheard the woman speaking to the receptionist, asking where intensive care was. Level four . . . of course, level four! Seeing the metal doors of the lift closing, Dina flew across the tiled floor and made it just in time.

The lift stopped at level two to release two nurses, and then at level three to pick up a young boy and his mother. *Hurry up, hurry up, hurry up,* Dina screamed. Finally, the bell pinged at level four. The boy's mother frowned, looking about, as nobody appeared to either leave or enter the lift. Then she shrugged, pressed the button and continued upwards . . .

Dina ran down the corridor, her trainers skidding on the polished floor. She recognised where she was now; she just had to turn left and she'd be in her corridor.

And then she saw Steve. He was standing outside her room, leaning against the wall, hands hunched in his pockets. He looked terrible. Suddenly fear overwhelmed her.

'What? What happened?'

Steve held her tightly so that she couldn't see his face.

'I couldn't do it,' he said. 'I'm sorry, but I couldn't do it . . . and it's fine. You're fine. They had to shock you back to life. God, Dina, it was so close, and I was so scared, but the third time they applied the pads, you came round. I saw your chest rising and falling and you were alive and I just felt—' He broke off, sobbing quietly.

Dina was silent for a moment, shocked that she had been so close.

'Oh, thank God!' she breathed out, and then felt him stiffen. 'I'm sorry,' she said, drawing back and touching his face. 'It's just – I didn't feel . . .'

'It's all right,' said Steve. 'I understand.'

They walked out on to the street. Dina paused on the kerb, crossing her arms. Steve waited as people flowed past. He still felt raw and poisoned by the ugliness of what he'd done. He reached out and touched Dina's shoulder, but this time she flinched.

'I need time to think,' she said abruptly, taking a step back. 'It's just . . . it was . . . I need a bit of time to be alone.'

'Sure,' said Steve, gulping. As she backed off, he suddenly suffered a terrible premonition that this was going to be the last time he saw her, and as she turned away he called, 'Dina!'

'Yes?' She turned back. She was biting her nails to shreds.

'Please don't . . . go back to . . . go back without saying goodbye.'

'Of course not,' said Dina. 'I just – just need to be alone.'

She walked away and then the crowds swirled around and swallowed her up.

Steve found Harrison outside the Buddhist temple, hands in his pockets, chewing gum and wearing dark glasses.

'You were right,' said Steve glumly. 'The whole thing was a lame idea. The lamest idea in the world. I just . . . just don't know what to do.'

'You'll work it out,' said Harrison. Then he reminded him gently, 'Steve, I'm going now.'

'I'm sorry?' Steve suddenly became aware that people were filing into the temple, many of them crying.

'It's time. For me to go. My relatives are holding the ceremony today.'

'Oh God. I mean – that's great . . . that's great . . .' Steve said, with as much sincerity as he could muster. Because deep down – and he knew this was terribly selfish of him, but he couldn't help it – he wanted to cling on to Harrison and beg him to stay. Suddenly it seemed to Steve that everyone he loved was deciding to leave him, all at once.

'Well, goodbye,' said Harrison awkwardly.

'Bye,' said Steve.

They paused and looked at each other. Steve opened his mouth. And then closed it. He'd always had trouble conducting serious and sincere conversations with Harrison, and now it seemed harder than ever. He wanted to say something about how much their friendship meant to him, without sounding all schmaltzy and sentimental. He wanted to tell Harrison how he didn't think that he would have survived being a ghost if Harrison hadn't gatecrashed his seance, or kept him from falling into despair with his wonderfully crude pep talks, ghost matchmaking and general appetite for wild living.

He wanted to say all these things, and no doubt Harrison wanted to say them too. But neither managed to do much except shuffle their feet and look away.

'Well, bye,' Steve said again.

'See you around.' Harrison grinned and spat out his gum.

'Sure.'

Steve shuffled forward as though to hug Harrison at the same time as Harrison held out his hand, and they both ended up in a mess: Harrison's fist balled in Steve's stomach, Steve's shoulder bumping his arm. They jumped apart awkwardly, said goodbye again and parted without looking at each other.

Steve walked away, passing through bins and lampposts and people in a blur. He got to the traffic lights at the junction. Over on the other side of the road, a girl ran out just as the lights changed to green; her mother whisked her back just in the nick of time as the cars poured forth, crying out angrily, 'You stupid girl!' and then engulfing her in a tight hug. Steve swivelled round, retraced his footsteps and slipped into the back of the temple.

The smell of incense was thick and musky. Harrison's family and friends sat in two rows. It was all quite different from a Christian funeral, where everyone wore black and cried and was embarrassed to look at each other. They held hands and smiled and their chatter sounded high and excited.

At the front of the temple a huge sculpture of the Buddha's face smiled down on them. A fire flickered around Harrison's coffin. Monks sat in front of it in a circle, chanting. A blue ribbon ran from the coffin to the monks, and Steve remembered that Harrison had told him it was called the *bhusa yong,* linking the deceased with the divine.

Then he caught sight of Harrison. He was standing by the fire, his ghostly figure ephemeral with smoke. He looked boyish, afraid. Steve felt embarrassed, as though he was witnessing something deeply intimate, and he quickly hid behind a carved pillar, watching surreptitiously.

The sound of the monks' chanting rose and fell like waves.

'*Phra Arahant*,' they chanted, one of the names of Buddha.

'*Phra Arahant*,' Steve echoed in a whisper. He watched the flames devour Harrison's coffin. Smoke drifted across the Buddha's face, blurring his features. Harrison walked slowly into the flames, watching his friends and family with liquid eyes. He was saying something to them but Steve couldn't make out what it was. The chanting grew stronger; Steve felt it drumming in his head and swelling in his chest and a wave of dizziness passed over him and he clutched the pillar. He thought of all the things he loved about Harrison, all the good times they'd shared, savouring every memory. When he opened his eyes, Harrison was fading: a ghost, an outline, a smile hanging, and then nothing but air and flames. Steve felt tears running down his cheeks as he whispered, 'Goodbye, Harrison, goodbye.'

38
Steve

For a while Steve wandered around Shepherd's Bush, walking the streets, watching the people around him. When he stood still, for one moment he perceived a sense of order in the cosmos, that the people walking by wrapped up in their worlds were all intricately bound, cogs shifting together to create a world order. *But what's my place in all this?* he thought. *If I can't be with her, then what is the point of my existence?*

He went back to Dina's flat, but she wasn't home yet. He played with Einstein, dropping yellow feed into his bowl, one flake at a time. He looked at the clock. Where was she, where was she? He ran his hands over the knobbly heads of the cacti on her windowsill, fondly remembering that trip they had taken to the market together. He lay down on her bed. Her pillow felt bumpy and he reached underneath, pulling out a brown envelope, cautiously peering inside. To his surprise, he discovered pictures of himself as a boy, and his *yellow notebook!* He'd been wondering where that had got to. He flipped through it, past his physics and astronomical notes, and then at the back he suddenly noticed Dina's handwriting. The intimate thought of her writing in his notebook filled him with warm pleasure. She had written, no doubt inspired by Steve and their conversations: *THINGS TO DO BEFORE I DIE.*

Steve spent some time reading through the list. Then he closed the notebook. Where was she?

*

Dina finally came back in the early afternoon. To Steve's relief, her anger seemed to have faded and she hugged him tightly.

'Thank God you're back.' He clutched her. 'I thought I wasn't going to see you again.'

'Steve, let's go for a walk,' she said gently. 'Let's get out of Shepherd's Bush. We'll go to the canal, to our favourite place, then we can talk properly.'

They spent the long walk to Wormwood Scrubs in silence, both lost in thought. As they approached the grassy banks of the Grand Union Canal, Dina came out of herself, noticing a sense of change in the air. Spring was in full flourish; white crocuses had sprouted here and there in the grass, shivering tenderly in the breeze. Blossom was shy on the trees and there was a feeling of warmth and new life in the air that blew on their faces.

They sat down on the springy grass. Steve stared at the water, rippling in circles; Dina pulled a daisy apart.

'Steve, I think I have to go back,' she said at last.

'I agree,' said Steve. He heard the doubt in his voice and pushed it away, trying to ignore the tiny, horrible, selfish part of him that wanted her to say, *Actually, Steve, I love you so much, I want to stay here with you for ever.* 'I mean, really – I knew all along deep down that that was the best thing.'

Or perhaps she didn't really love him. Perhaps she was searching for polite ways to say, *Steve, I feel it would be better if we could just be friends. I don't really fancy you anyway so why I don't leave you to your funny old ghost existence whilst I get on with having a proper life?*

'But I will stay for one last weekend with you,' Dina said. She was looking at him, but he continued staring at the water. 'We can do all kinds of things, celebrate our last forty-eight hours together. What d'you think we should do? What would you like to do?'

Steve didn't reply. The tightness in his chest made it too painful to talk. He looked up at the sky, at the ragged tendrils of cloud, and a profound sense of loneliness swept over him. Yet again, he was to be alone. Harrison was gone; now Dina.

Dina put a hand on his cheek and he jumped.

'I don't know,' said Steve tonelessly. 'Maybe we should say goodbye now.'

'You want me to go?' She frowned incredulously.

Of course I don't want you to go, he shouted inside, *but I don't know if I can stand another minute like this.*

He shrugged. 'Well, there might be all kinds of things you want to do with your forty-eight hours,' he said miserably. 'All those touristy things you didn't get round to doing while you were alive. You know, go on the London Eye for free and all that.'

Dina dropped her daisy chain and took both his hands in hers. She stared deep into his eyes and saw and understood his sorrow. She couldn't think of anything to say; the easiest thing to do was to lean forward and kiss him gently.

When she drew back, Steve didn't look just sad any more. He looked sad and happy, the emotions mixed all over his face like watercolours.

'I know how I'd like to spent our time,' said Dina in a low voice, and Steve smiled. 'And now we're both ghosts, we don't have to worry about—'

'Falling into each other,' Steve finished wryly, blushing at the memory of his failed attempt at kissing her.

'Close your eyes,' she said.

He closed his eyes, and the kiss on his lips, all the sweeter from expectation rather than surprise, was the loveliest he'd ever had.

'Oh, Dina,' he said, kissing her face. 'I know you have to go, I do understand . . .'

He wrapped her in his arms and they clung together, apologising silently. And then they made up with another kiss.

They sank down on to the grass and lay amongst the bluebells and dandelions. Small insects twiddled their antennae and burrowed deep into the grass, alarmed by this intrusion. A large oak spread its green-laden arms over them, and they were shielded by a thick holly bush; Dina knew it was silly, for nobody could see them anyway, but still she felt glad to be hidden in their own private glade, their own little paradise.

Traffic zoomed in the distance. Boats creaked past. Passers-by strolled along nearby. Birds sang.

They didn't hear a thing, lost in each other.

Steve felt his desire recede with a moment of self-consciousness. He began to undo the buttons on Dina's blouse. They were little white ones, awkward, and his hands were suddenly all buttery and clumsy. Dina reached down to help and he blushed, feeling like some sort of inept schoolboy. Then he looked up at her face and remembered that this was Dina, the girl he loved and trusted most in the world, and he didn't need to feel a shred of nerves or fear. He pushed her hand away and undressed her himself.

She smiled and arched back her neck. He lay and drank it all in, wanting to memorise every part of her body, every scar and freckle and ridge. Then he ran a trail of kisses down it. Her skin was so soft! he thought, bliss shivering up his spine. He ran a faint trail of whispering kisses across her breasts, over her ribcage, down over the flat of her stomach. Then, examining with childish curiosity the whorl of her belly-button, he flickered his tongue into it like a snake. She giggled and shook and they looked at each other and smiled again, dizzy, delirious smiles. And Steve stopped worrying and let go. He kissed her thighs and pressed his cheek against the skin, rubbing against it, feeling the softness of the down, her sighs like music to his ears.

Dina felt him explore her, examine and kiss and caress every part of her body. Her ghostly skin was so fine, and every touch sent ripples of love-lust shivering all over her body in a way she could never have experienced as a human. Sometimes when he touched her it felt as though his fingers dipped through her skin and teased her very soul.

As he entered her, Steve felt himself become thin and light with ecstasy. *This is heaven,* he thought joyously, covering her face with rapturous kisses. He closed his eyes, feeling their bodies move together, and it felt then as though the layers of his personality, those skins of childhood and experience and upbringing, fell away and all that was left was a flavoured essence, that purest part of himself, like the very heart of a candle flame that is not yellow or purple or orange or even white, just pure, invisible heat. All his problems seemed to melt away and he felt simple, at peace, as though he had returned to some dark, primeval place where his life had begun and ended.

Afterwards, they held each other tight, trembling and rubbing noses tenderly.

'I don't want you to go,' whispered Steve.

'I don't want to go either,' said Dina, 'but I can't leave my life behind. I can't.'

'Everything I love always gets taken away from me,' Steve said.

'Don't say that,' said Dina, but she couldn't think of a way to comfort him.

'So what time will you go tomorrow?' Steve asked. All he could think was: *Saturday, Sunday, Saturday, Sunday.* As though the world would end after that.

'Oh, I'll go first thing on Monday morning,' said Dina. 'I'll slip away. I'll go to the hospital and lie down and . . . then . . .'

They fell silent for a while. Steve threaded flowers in her hair and they made up stories about the stars. Then they made love again, for it seemed that no matter how much they touched each other, they just wanted to feel more, as though there was another nook or cranny that they might discover; and no matter how many times they said *I love you* they had to say it again, just in case. They slept in fits, waking to kiss and caress and laugh and kiss, and slowly they sank into an intoxicated state where the rest of the world seemed distant, in another realm, as though they had created their own private heaven.

Then it was morning again, and the birds were singing, and once again time seemed to race away; it seemed that every time Steve looked at his watch the hands were spinning round and inside he was counting, like a death-knell, *Twelve hours to go . . . Nine hours to go . . . Eight hours to go . . .*

They talked idly and vaguely about things they ought to do with their last day, but in the end, they barely moved from the grassy bank.

The clouds parted and the afternoon was blue. Then the clouds gathered again, their undersides lit up by a blazing red dusk. The birds started singing good night to each other. Steve and Dina made love one last time, a little desperately, and as Steve came inside her, he pressed his hot lips against hers and said *I love you* and the words danced around her mouth and down her throat and into her heart, and Dina felt tears in her eyes.

One last post-coital chat:

'I won't go to sleep,' Dina promised him. 'I'll stay awake all night.'

'Please sleep.' Steve stroked her face. 'I don't want you to be tired.'

'No. Not for one minute.'

Silence. In the distance, a tramp shouted and sang his way down the road, and then the world was quiet again.

'Maybe it would never have worked anyway,' said Steve suddenly. 'Maybe we would have ended up in some shitty apartment like the Slobs, with a screaming kid, yelling at each other.'

Or we would have ended up in a lovely little place, maybe somewhere in the country, and had a baby together, or maybe two, and grown old together being happy.

'Yeah,' said Dina, laughing, 'you would have got sick of my American accent after a while.'

'And your snoring.'

'I don't snore.'

'You do so. Look, I'm the ghost, I used to hear you at night when I lay watching you. Sorry, I didn't mean . . .'

'No, no, I want you to keep watching me.'

'But maybe my time is going to come too.'

'What d'you mean by that?' She knew she was being selfish, wanting Steve to be around for her, but she couldn't help it.

'Well, Jether said that I was still on earth because I needed to find fulfilment. And maybe this is why I waited. To find out if you loved me, and to let you know I loved you. Maybe this is it.'

Another long silence. Dina made a daisy chain.

'If we'd had kids, what would we have called them?'

'If we'd had a girl, I would have liked the name Lacerta – there's a cluster of stars called Lacerta. D'you like that?'

'Not really,' Dina giggled. 'I like posh British names. Like Hugo and Harry.'

'*Hugo!* Would you have wanted our kid to grow up smoking a pipe?'

'You see, it would never have worked,' she laughed, and they looked at each other and Steve thought: *It would have worked, it would have worked so well. We wouldn't have been like other couples.*

'I'd have liked to have grown old with you,' he blurted out, stroking her hair and kissing the ends.

Silence.

'I – I hope you don't mind,' he said suddenly, 'but I read what you wrote. In my notebook. About all those things you want to do before you die. I thought it was a great list – except the bungee jumping. We don't want you to die too! Not after surviving this . . .'

Dina laughed.

'But promise me this,' Steve said strongly, 'promise me you'll go and do all those things. Promise me you won't forget; don't sink into boredom again, don't let one single day of the rest of your life be unhappy or boring.'

'I promise,' said Dina. 'I'll do everything on my list – I'll do it all for you.'

They lay still for some time, listening to the birds calling goodnight to each other.

'When we say goodbye,' said Steve, 'I don't want it to be a big thing. I don't want a hug and a kiss and all that. Just a quick goodbye and that's it.'

'Sure,' said Dina in a high voice.

Steve took her face in his hands.

'Don't think it's because I don't love you,' he said. 'It's because I love you, because I love you so much. If I hold you and kiss you one last time just before you go, I know I won't be able to let you go. When the moment comes, I just want to say goodbye quietly. Just to pretend we're friends. Just to wave and walk away.'

'Of course,' said Dina, kissing him softly. She rubbed her nose against his in an Eskimo kiss. 'Of course I understand.'

Steve lay watching Dina sleeping. He was glad she'd broken her promise to stay awake all night. It felt so deliciously intimate to lie and watch her. To have the licence to do it. He remembered the day at The Greasy Spoon when he had fallen in love with her at first sight, and yearned to just stare and stare at her, until by the end of the day he was so worn out with having to stop himself that the muscles at the back of his eyes ached. Now he could watch her in total peace. The freckles on her cheeks. Her upturned nose. The perpetual smile tucked into the corner of her lip.

Any minute now, she'd wake, and it would all be over.

He searched inside himself for sadness, but he couldn't find it.

It was strange; he had been dreading this moment so much, fearing it would tear his soul in two. But as he lay there the dawn rising softly, as though gently warning them that time was short, the sensation in his heart was quite unexpected. It was as though all the clouds of torment, all the whys and what ifs, his fears for the future, his regrets over the past, had cleared away. He felt simple. Pure. Unworried. Nothing seemed to matter. *Over the last thirty years,* he told Dina silently, *all I've done is get a pointless degree and work in a greasy spoon. I'm not going to be rich and famous. I'm not going to win the lottery or open a restaurant or be a star. My dreams and ambitions are over, fading like smoke. But I've found you; I've loved and been loved. And that was the most precious thing in my life, even if I'm about to lose that too. In the end, we lose everything, and all we can do is surrender.*

He gazed out at the celestial dawn breaking across the sky. The round undersides of the clouds were caressed with gold and edged with soft pink tendrils. The sight, so tender, seemed to paint in a way that words never could, the feeling of his last night with Dina, and he felt such a sudden and deep sense of connection with the sky and earth that the vision before him seemed almost divine.

He thought of what Jether had said about the word *shantih* – 'that peace which passeth all understanding' – and smiled. He would take this feeling, wrap her love around him like a shroud and keep it with him always.

A leaf curled down and drifted on to her cheek. She opened her eyes, starting, and then drank in his loving gaze and smiled softly.

'Well,' said Dina, 'I guess it's well and truly goodbye time.'

The silhouette of the hospital where Dina's body lay waiting for her loomed in the distance. Birds chattered and swooped across the canal; butterflies danced in the grass.

Steve was struggling. The peace was still there in his heart, but waves of panic and pain were rippling over the top.

'What's the first thing you're going to do when you're back?' he said, managing to keep his voice normal.

'Eat some decent food,' said Dina impulsively. 'I really fancy something to sink my teeth into. Something to remind me what life is really about.'

They both laughed.

'Well.' Dina bit her lip. *I mustn't cry,* she kept telling herself, over and over, like a mantra. She felt as though she was holding her hands around her heart, squeezing it tight, but tears were still leaking out through her fingers, trammelling up her throat, burning behind her eyes. She drew in a deep, shaky breath and swallowed. 'Look,' she said, staring into the canal, 'I know we've agreed to part, but – well – look me up again maybe. Just once more?'

'Dina, you know I can't,' he said in a flat voice. 'We agreed not to.'

'Yes.' Her chin was wobbling like mad. 'I know. Well. Bye.'

No reply.

She flashed him a quick glance. He was staring into the water, his eyes blank. *This isn't as hard for him as it for me,* she thought in shock. *He doesn't care about me, or how could he just sit there like that?*

'It was nice knowing you.' She punched his shoulder.

She had meant the punch to be light, a 'goodbye buddy' sort of punch. But instead it bristled with anger and indignation, and he flinched violently. He looked up and she saw the pain flashing in his eyes, just as acute as her own.

'Sorry . . . I . . . bye,' she whispered, and turned and walked away.

She was crying so hard she could hardly see where she was going; the footpath and bridge were a black blur. When she thought of herself waking up in the hospital, of being in the world again, it still seemed unreal, impossible, years away. And yet in half an hour it would be her new world; and then she'd be home again. *And I can assure you, Steve, that whatever I said, I won't be eating. I'm just going to sit and look at your things. Read your notebook. Brush my face against your clothes. Find photos to keep and treasure for ever.*

She was halfway there when she heard the sound of his feet behind her. She turned and heard him say, 'Oh Dina,' and they flung their arms around each other and held each other so tight they could hardly breathe. Then they searched and found each other's lips and kissed deeply.

'Goodbye,' Steve croaked, pulling back.

'Goodbye.'

They kissed again, and he ran his hands through her hair, their wet cheeks sliding against each other.

Dina stepped back and grabbed hold of his lapels tightly.

'Well, this really is goodbye,' she said.

'Yes.'

She looked up and he swooped down and kissed her again, tasting the salt of her tears.

'Goodbye, Dina,' he said.

She curled her arms around his waist and showered his face with kisses, before finally kissing him on the lips again, a true ghost's kiss: so tender it was just a whisper.

Steve buried his face in the silk of her hair and clasped her to him again.

Finally, she pulled back an inch.

'I guess I'd better go,' she sniffed, rubbing her eyes.

She turned away, but Steve caught her and held her again. Just one last time. He breathed her in, desperate to hold it all in his heart. He had burned her face on his memory as he watched her this morning. But remembering a scent, the essence of a person, clearly enough to bottle it in your heart was another thing altogether.

He wanted to go on holding her, but he could feel her resolve weakening. Any longer and she'd never make it. He untangled himself, pushed her away. The cold air came up between them.

As he watched her go, he had to bunch up his fists and press his feet to the ground to stop himself from chasing her. He felt as though his heart was a wild creature in a cage, clawing after her, screaming and sobbing and whimpering.

Dina managed not to look back at him until she reached the end of the canal path. But before she passed over the bridge and he was gone for ever, she took one last look back and knew she would never forget the look on his face. There were tears running down his cheeks and his mouth was twisted into a terrible smile; but underneath the agony, in his eyes there glowed a soft satisfaction, a kind of infinite wisdom, a sense of peace.

39
Dina

She heard the noises as though they were at the end of a distant tunnel: birdsong, a radio playing, a doctor calling down the corridor. Slowly, as though drawn upwards from an ocean, she came to the surface and opened her eyes. The world converged on her in its rawness, its shocking vitality: the smell of flowers in a vase fighting against a lurid stench of disinfectant; a clock banging like a bomb; the violent pounding of her heart, relentlessly pumping blood around her body. She was aware of a figure sleeping in a chair by her bed but she was still too blurry to register who it was.

She closed her eyes again and remembered Steve's caress, his voice. The temptation came to just sink down and let the darkness take her back; she ached to give in and let it do so.

It took great effort to yank herself back out, to open her eyes. She wriggled her fingers and splayed them across the cotton of the bed, curled her feet over the bedstead, made herself feel flesh again. She saw the door swing open and a nurse walked in. She was humming, and when she saw Dina she broke off and dropped her clipboard. Beside the bed, Dina's mother woke up and put her hand over her mouth, stifling a cry. Dina looked up at her and saw how much she had aged from the shock of nearly losing her daughter, the new lines and crevices wrinkling her face. Her father, a desolate figure hunched over by the window, turned and gaped. Dina licked her lips and smiled weakly and managed a 'Hi.' The nurse ran off to find a doctor.

Voices clashed around her. For a moment she felt as though she was surrounded by strangers, and her heart ached for Steve to take her away from it all. But then her mother held her and her touch triggered something, some connection with the outside world, with all the things, all the people she loved.

Her mother lay with her head on Dina's chest, crying, and Dina held her like a baby. Tears stung her eyes and she felt every cell singing with a gladness to be alive.

Epilogue

Dina Hardman, Dina signed on the dotted line with a flourish and a swirl.

She looked up into Archie's warm eyes, smiling nervously. Rachel, sitting at the back of the café next to Archie, bit her lip and then touched her swollen stomach. Archie grinned and smoothed his palms over her bump, hoping for a kick, his face glowing with paternal pride.

Dina stood up.

'Well – good luck,' she said. 'I just know you two will do an amazing job running D&S. But don't let me come back in six months' time and find it's become R&A,' she added, laughing. 'I *will* be back in six months, you know,' she added firmly, seeing Rachel's rather sad expression. 'And it'll just fly by.'

'Have you decided yet where you're going?' Archie asked.

'Kind of. I'm going to try living in Italy for a few months. Roger's coming with me – can you believe it, I had to get him a pet passport! And then I'd like to maybe live in Amsterdam for a while. Oh God, I want to go everywhere.' She sounded more confident than she felt.

They exchanged hugs and kisses and Dina gave Rachel a fierce 'you have to call me the moment he's born' lecture. Then she said one last goodbye and left the café.

Outside, she stopped at the traffic lights, waiting carefully for them to change to red and double-checking before stepping out into the road. She kept waiting to feel a rush of excitement. She was finally, finally embarking on the first of her 'Things To Do Before I Die'. She was going to see the world. She was going to learn Italian and float down canals on gondolas and eat delicious ice cream. But her stomach was strangely devoid of fizz; not even one lame, lone butterfly could summon enough wings to flap about. Instead, she just felt strangely numb. As she reached the other side of the road, she was vaguely aware that her mobile was shrilling. She drew it out of her bag – damn, she'd missed the call. She listened to her voicemail: it was her mother, checking that she was OK. *Funny*, thought Dina sadly, *before the accident I was always calling her to see that she was OK. Now she's the one calling me every night.*

On the way home, it suddenly hit her again. She had gone into the newsagent's to buy a bottle of water and she caught sight of the trays of chocolate bars – Mars, Twix, Snickers, KitKat, the red wrapper leaping out at her. Why was it that when she tried to cry out the pain in her heart at home, her eyes remained obstinately dry, but whenever she was in a public place, she turned into a human waterfall? As she paid for the water, she made a shaky remark about having terrible hay fever, then hurried home to her flat.

In her bedroom, she lay on the bed, listening to 'Something Stupid'. Einstein flicked around his bowl as though dancing to the music, making her smile through her tears.

These were the worst moments. The pause after her tears drying up and before the peace that came from release: a feeling of blankness. Her eyes wandered round her room, over the paraphernalia of life: clothes, books, CDs. It all seemed so material, so meaningless.

Then she caught sight of the crumpled edge of a piece of paper. The list she had been reading last night: all the things she wanted to do before she died.

She unfolded it and got up, went to the window. Her cactus plants were growing, glowing under the caress of sunlight. Her eyes wandered over the paper. She looked out again. She realised that she was watching, but not watching, that every moment she experienced was pregnant with anticipation. For the last few days she had been waiting. Waiting for that breath tickling the back of her neck, a caress on the back of her hand. But there was nothing, just the spring breeze running playful fingers through her ponytail. Last night she had eaten half a KitKat and left the other half, nestling in its silvery wrapper, by the side of her bed, almost knowing it would still be there the next morning. And despite the disappointment, in a funny way she felt relieved.

I think you're happy now, Steve, wherever you are. I think you're at peace. She gazed down at the people walking in the street below. *I still miss you, so very much. I can't help it. But I'm getting on. Tonight I'm going to go out with Anita and Fatima for a drink. Maybe I'll meet another guy, and maybe when I kiss him I'll find myself pretending he's you. Maybe we'll have a relationship, maybe we'll marry and in ten years' time, or twenty years' time, I'll be kissing my kids good night and coming downstairs to do the washing-up and I'm going to think of your smile. With affection.* She thought of that smile, of walking away from him at the canal. *But at least I'm not afraid of death any more. I have a feeling I'm going to be around here for quite a while, and when it's my time to go, I'll go, and I'll find you again. I remember you telling me that the last thoughts you have determine where you go in your next life, and when I'm slipping away, I'll think of you, and maybe next time we'll be together again.*

And in the mean time I'm going to enjoy life. I'm going to do everything on this list. I'm going to go bungee jumping and scuba-diving and have all kinds of crazy adventures. I'm going to have fun, I'm going to be happy, I'm going to make the most of this wonderful gift that life is.

She stood by the window for some time, aware of the bright, anticipatory thump of her heartbeat. She watched pink blossom, caught on the wind, swirl from the trees and touch the pavement. She looked up and saw birds circling on the wind, cawing and soaring with happiness. She watched the sunlight glittering gold on window panes, pouring on to the pavement like an oblation. She breathed in the air and smiled, for under the smog there was the unmistakable sweet taste of a wonderful summer on its way.

THE REBEL FAIRY

Deborah Wright

SOMETIMES, FALLING IN LOVE CAN BE MAGICAL . . .

Meet JACK: he's funny, good-looking, a bit of a loser . . . a lot of a loser, in fact, having lost his flat and car in a game of snooker. He's just fallen inexplicably in love with his exceedingly ex Ex LEILA, who can't stand the sight of him and is more than happy with her handsome boyfriend HENRY. Henry, though, has suddenly found he's got the hots for KATIE, Leila's best friend and flatmate, who's been carrying a torch for Jack for so long, the Duracell batteries are beginning to run out . . .

What's going on? Can't Cupid shoot straight anymore? It's not his fault for once, but Charlie and Puck's, a couple of badly behaved fairies who have been acting more stupid than cupid. And unless they work out how to fix things pronto, theirs is going to end up one seriously grim fairytale . . .

UNDER MY SPELL

Deborah Wright

Cara is twenty-five years old and beautiful, intelligent and kind. She's also a witch. Unsure of her feelings towards magic and desperate to escape the clutches of her overbearing mother, she takes a 'proper' job as a nanny for the Wilkins family. But things don't go quite as she has planned.

Cara moves in to the Wilkins' home and before long the whole family come to rely on her as a source of fun and excitement in their lives. But Nick and Andie Wilkins' marriage is falling apart so Cara sets about trying to reconcile them. When her benign attempts to fix things result in Nick flirting with her and Andie contemplating an affair, Cara can't resist any longer. She resorts to the magic she's been trying so hard to give up and soon the whole house is in uproar . . .

Other bestselling Time Warner Books titles available by mail:

☐ The Rebel Fairy	Deborah Wright	£6.99
☐ Under My Spell	Deborah Wright	£5.99
☐ Something Borrowed	Tina Reilly	£5.99
☐ Wedded Blitz	Tina Reilly	£5.99
☐ Lazy Ways to Make a Living	Abigail Bosanko	£5.99
☐ A Nice Girl Like Me	Abigail Bosanko	£6.99
☐ Playing James	Sarah Mason	£6.99
☐ The Party Season	Sarah Mason	£5.99
☐ High Society	Sarah Mason	£5.99

The prices shown above are correct at time of going to press. However, the publishers reserve the right to increase prices on covers from those previously advertised without further notice.

TIME WARNER
BOOKS

TIME WARNER BOOKS
PO Box 121, Kettering, Northants NN14 4ZQ
Tel: 01832 737525, Fax: 01832 733076
Email: aspenhouse@FSBDial.co.uk

POST AND PACKING:
Payments can be made as follows: cheque, postal order (payable to Time Warner Books), credit card or Switch Card. Do not send cash or currency.

All UK Orders	**FREE OF CHARGE**
EC & Overseas	25% of order value

Name (BLOCK LETTERS) ....

Address ....

....

Post/zip code: ....

☐ Please keep me in touch with future Time Warner publications

☐ I enclose my remittance £ ....

☐ I wish to pay by Visa/Access/Mastercard/Eurocard/Switch Card

Card Expiry Date

Switch Issue No.